ELTON

For my mother and father,
Mabel and Harold Buckley,
with much love

ELTON
THE BIOGRAPHY

DAVID BUCKLEY

André Deutsch

First published in Great Britain in 2006 by

André Deutsch
an imprint of the
Carlton Publishing Group
20 Mortimer Street
London W1T 3JW

HB ISBN: 978-0-233-00183-8
PB ISBN: 978-0-233-00221-7

Discography compiled by David Bodoh. David would like to thank
Peter Dobbins and Elizabeth Wilcox for their assistance.

The publishers would like to thank the following sources for their kind permission
to reproduce the pictures in this book.

Section 1:

Page 1: (top) Mirrorpix; (bottom) Michael Ochs Archives/Redferns; Page 2: (top) TopFoto.
co.uk; (bottom) TopFoto.co.uk; Page 3: (top left) © Mick Rock; (top right) Terry O'Neill/
Getty Images; (bottom) Public Record Office/HIP/TopFoto.co.uk; Page 4: (top) Anwar
Hussein/Hulton Archive/Getty Images; (bottom left) © Monitor Picture Library/Retna
UK; (bottom right) Richard E. Aaron/Redferns; Page 5: (top) Terry O'Neill/Getty Images;
(bottom) Terry O'Neill/Getty Images; Page 6: (top) Columbia Pictures/Photofest/Retna
UK; (bottom) Steve Morley/Rex Features; Page 7: Terry O'Neill/Getty Images; Page 8: (top)
Richard Young/Rex Features; (bottom) Ebet Roberts/Redferns.

Section 2:

Page 1: Harry Goodwin/Rex Features; Page 2: (top) Retna UK; (bottom) Globe Photos/
Rex Features; Page 3: Hinze/DPA/Corbis; Page 4: Bettmann/Corbis; Page 5: Tim Graham/
Corbis SYGMA; Page 6: (top) Evening Standard/Getty Images; (bottom) Private Collection;
Page 7: (top) Frank Tapper/Corbis; (bottom) Stephane Cardinale/People Avenue/Corbis;
Page 8: Charles Green/PA/Empics.

Every effort has been made to acknowledge correctly and contact the source and/or copyright
holder of each picture and Carlton Books Limited apologises for any unintentional errors or
omissions which will be corrected in future editions of this book.

Typeset by E-Type, Liverpool
Printed and bound in Great Britain by Mackays

CONTENTS

'It is ironic that since we recorded this album, our lives have become the title. Bernie has become the Brown Dirt Cowboy living on a ranch in California raising cutting horses and prize-winning bulls, and I have become Captain Fantastic travelling from the edge of the world to your town collecting photography and art and living a life beyond my wildest dreams.'

Elton John, speaking in 2005 on the occasion of the 30th anniversary reissue of *Captain Fantastic and the Brown Dirt Cowboy*

ACKNOWLEDGMENTS

During the writing of this book I have been very fortunate to be able to talk to and correspond with a number of people who have known Elton John as a friend or colleague. In Liverpool, the writer and broadcaster Spencer Leigh was an enormous help in the early stages of the project, giving me advice, ideas and numerous contacts, one of whom was Elton's former collaborator, Gary Osborne, who, in turn, was extremely helpful. Chris Charlesworth, commissioning editor at Omnibus Press, and in the 1970s a journalist on *Melody Maker*, also gave generous, above-and-beyond-the-call-of duty help with the text.

Stephan Heimbecher, the curator of the Hercules Elton John web site, also offered many helpful suggestions and corrections, while my wife, Ann Henrickson, has made invaluable comments on the manuscript. I am grateful also to the endless support of the Buckley family: my two daughters, Louise and Elsa, my parents, Harold and Mabel, and Harold, Gill, John and Beth. In Munich I would like to thank David Blackshaw, Bob Adkins, Graham Johnstone, Ang: Andrews and Klaus Federa, and in Liverpool, Richard Freeman and Ron Moy.

I would also like to thank all of my interviewees, especially Clive Franks, who has been part of the Elton John team since 1972 and who spoke and corresponded with me at great length, and Ray Cooper, who wined and dined me in Munich while reliving his career with Elton. My thanks, therefore, to:

Mike Appleton, Rex Bishop, Jet Black, David Bodoh, Paul Buckmaster, Brian Catlin, Kevin Cann, Chris Charlesworth, BJ Cole, Ray Cooper, David Costa, Geoffrey Davis, Kiki Dee, Peter Dobbins, Bobby Elliot, Stuart Epps, Gary Farrow, Clive Franks, Paul Gambaccini, Roger

Greenaway, Bob Harris, Stephan Heimbecher, David Hentschel, Tony Hiller, Patrick Humphries, Mick Inkpen, Dylan Jones, John Jorgenson, Spencer Leigh, Simon Lewis, Charlie Morgan, Trudie Myerscough-Harris, Gary Osborne, David Paton, Mark Paytress, Helen Piena, Mal Pope, Sir Tim Rice, Mick Rock, Ken Scott, Phil Sutcliffe, John Taylor, Paul Trynka, Judie Tzuke and Elizabeth Wilcox.

I also had the pleasure of interviewing producer Gus Dudgeon for my 1998 book on David Bowie, *Strange Fascination*. A few of the quotes from Gus in this book have been taken from this interview.

Finally, I wish to thank my editors at Carlton Books, Lorna Russell and Ian Gittins (whose idea it was), and also my agent, Ros Edwards, for guiding the book from idea to reality.

AUTHOR'S NOTE

Elton is one of the most famous people in the world. He has packed more into his 60 years than any other living musician: more triumphs, more disasters, more fun and, of course, more songs. It's been a life lived to the fullest, both in its fellow-feeling and also in its almost endless enthusiasm for the world and everything in it.

As a child, I used to think he was American and was surprised to discover that he was actually English. His Americanised vocal put me off. I loved *Goodbye Yellow Brick Road*, though, and I was allowed to stay up on Christmas Eve 1974 to see his wonderful Hammersmith Odeon Show on BBC 2. In the Seventies and Eighties I bought some of his singles and albums, but was never a real fan. The closest I ever got to him – both musically and physically – was at Live Aid, when a limo carrying Elton and Renate pulled up feet away from where my brother and I were queuing to get in. To me he belonged to the light entertainment side of the music business; I did not see him as part of rock culture.

Researching this book has therefore been a revelation. Like many others, I suspect, I have in the past been guilty of sniffily dismissing his mawkish ballads, not realising that they were only one aspect of his musical story. In fact, Elton has recorded more great songs than you might think and boasts a catalogue of brilliant moments. So my book attempts to tell his astonishing life story, while at the same time reminding the reader of why he is such a huge star in the first place, namely, by talking again about the songs, the albums and the stage performances. While this book is unauthorised and has been written without the cooperation of Elton or his management, I have spoken to many important people in his story.

Elton John has been a blues singer, a singer-songwriter, a glam rock icon, a drug addict, a married man, a moaner and whiner, a tireless fundraiser and humanitarian, a married man (again), a controversialist and, ultimately, a living legend. This is his story.

David Buckley, Munich

FOREWORD BY GARY OSBORNE

Elton was kneeling on the floor in the corner of my room. 'Osborne!!!' he shouted as I looked up from the backgammon board. 'I've been going through your record collection for nearly an hour and I've just noticed that you haven't got any of my bloody albums!' 'What do you want me to do,' I asked, 'sit here listening to your old records? I told you I wasn't a fan of yours. Anyway, I'm sure I've got something of yours over there, haven't I ?' 'Only *Yellow Brick Road*,' he replied. 'Well, it's your best one, isn't it?' I said, backpedalling. 'I really love it.' 'Too little too late,' said Elton.

The following afternoon a courier delivered a copy of every album, compilation, soundtrack and bootleg Elton John had ever released. I still look forward to listening to many of them.

First of all we were mates. Kiki and Davey lived in LA and usually stayed with me and my partner, Jenny, when they were in England, while Elton lived in Windsor and often dropped in when he was in town. So for a couple of years we all just hung out, playing games, listening to music, watching TV, going to shows in the West End, concerts at Wembley and football matches at Watford. Laughing, playing and partying just like ordinary people. Well, almost.

Elton knew my work; he had heard *The War Of The Worlds*, although it hadn't yet been released. I'd also written lyrics for three songs he had produced for Kiki (including 'Amoureuse'). So when he suddenly played me the tune of 'Shine On Through' and asked me to write a lyric, it didn't seem strange at all, but it changed my life forever. Over the next five years, Elton would become my closest collaborator and one of my dearest friends.

As a lyricist I choose my words very carefully, so you can believe me when I say that Elton is the most talented, charismatic, generous and funny person I have ever known and I am fiercely proud of him. I'm proud of him for his beautiful music, for his ability to move an audience, for his honesty in 'coming out' when he did and for the incredible work he's done in raising funds for, and awareness of, people afflicted by AIDS. I'm proud of him because more than any person I've ever met Elton John has made a difference.

If this sounds like a love letter, in many ways it is, because Elton is the only man who has ever broken my heart. Now, before you start feeling sorry for me, please remember that an occasional broken heart is one of the most useful things a lyricist can have. So even there, Elton did me a favour. Anyway, hearts tend to mend and, apart from a little scar tissue, I've been left with great songs, fantastic memories, continuing royalties and the house that 'Blue Eyes' bought. How bad is that?

Elton has always given his friends far more than he's ever taken, but if he has a fault, and everybody does, it is that he's not very good at 'ending things'. These unhappy endings are a recurring theme in this book and in many ways I got off lighter than some.

I was close enough for long enough to see it happening to people who I knew he really adored, people like Dee, Nigel, Ray, Gus, even Davey. So I was pretty well prepared for the fact that eventually one of these 'unhappy endings' was bound to come my way. Even so, I was crushed to learn from a newspaper that, in spite of the recent worldwide success of 'Blue Eyes', I would no longer be working with Elton. I tried not to take it too personally, but even now, over 20 years later, I often have dreams about Elton and on some level there is an ache which never quite goes away.

It is a tribute to Elton that he inspires ferocious loyalty. To my knowledge, nobody who has been really close to him has ever gone to the papers with the kind of tittle-tattle which might have made them a lot of money. I for one would have happily gone to my grave swearing I'd never seen Elton taking drugs. Fortunately, he spared us all from having to live that lie by coming clean and turning his life around. Another reason to be proud of him.

Elton has been Elton John for far longer than he was ever Reg Dwight, so he's become rather good at it. And since he has the constitution of an ox and the energy of a small nation, I expect him to spring a few more surprises before he's done. To me, the biggest surprise so far is that he's managed to withstand decades of power, pressure and pampering without going quite insane. I'm damn sure that I would have gone completely bonkers by now.

Like me, David Buckley came to Elton John as an admirer rather than as a fan and he has approached this book with no agenda other than to chronicle as accurately as possible the extraordinary life of one of the greatest composers and performers of all time. As a force in the history of British entertainment Elton can only be compared to The Beatles and Noël Coward, and capturing him in a book is no mean feat. I suspect that, like me, along the way David Buckley has wound up becoming a fan in spite of himself. One of the most respected books previously written about Elton covered my five years of living and working alongside him in a couple of pages, without the author ever attempting to interview me. Buckley has spent the best part of a year talking to every single colleague of Elton's he could possibly find, and it shows. This is not the first book I've read about Elton… but it is the best.

PART 1

THE MAKING OF A SUPERSTAR 1947–1974

CHAPTER 1

INANIMATE OBJECTS AS MY FRIENDS

'When you're 40, you'll either be some sort of glorified office boy or you'll be a millionaire.'

Bill Johnson, Reginald Dwight's history teacher

'I had a quit-me father, had a love-me mother,
I had Little Richard and that black piano.'

'Made In England'; lyrics: Bernie Taupin; music: Elton John

Sitting in a pub, in front of a battered and plonked-out piano, is a teenage lad riffling through a wad of sheet music. It's ten o'clock on a Sunday evening and Reg Dwight is singing, if not for his supper, then for a future. In the days before easy credit, youngsters saved up hard for life's 'essential' purchases. Reg's essential purchase is an electric piano and amplifier. A musician at the mercy of the house piano could find himself out of tune all night, and good equipment meant at least partial control over the quality of the musical fare.

As a local lad and member of the band Bluesology, providing pub cabaret is an obvious way of raising funds, and Reg has a 'residency' at a local pub, the Northwood Hills Hotel, on Fridays, Saturdays and Sundays, the nights when Bluesology are not gigging. Unlike most of the other local musicians enamoured of rock, pop and soul, Reg can read music and can play more than competently. In fact, according to friends, he is 'bloody good'. He can lay the Yankee rock 'n' roll drawl on with a trowel, bashing his rather stumpy fingers into the keyboard in a percussive fashion to beat out the tune. He can also sing the mawkish Irish ballads, the current Jim Reeves hits and the standard pub sing-a-longs. He can also make a passable attempt at lighter pop and soul material. In fact, he can give the punters more or less what they want. And, at 17, that's not bad.

Occasionally there is a bit of bother, such as a disaffected drinker expressing his unhappiness with the evening's repertoire by threatening to 'spill' a half of bitter down the back of Reg's piano (which, given the quality of the noxious keg beer, is possibly the best place for it). But on the whole, there is no real trouble, especially since the arrival in the pub of the gypsies who act as his unofficial bodyguard. In addition, a red-haired Romany girl has taken quite a shine to Reg.

To the mild annoyance and disappointment of his parents, but much to his own relief, Reg – who is in fact a bright lad – has just left school, a term before he is due to sit A Levels in English and Music. He has already decided where his future lies. The lure of a job as an office junior at Mills Music, a music publisher with offices on Denmark Street, London, is irresistible to someone for whom music is his life. Earning a princely £5 per week for making tea and running errands, Reg spends his free time scrutinising the charts, buying records, going to gigs and listening to the radio and consuming music with a desire that makes him an aficionado. In his small bedroom, rows of records are neatly arranged in alphabetical order. He knows who wrote the B-side to this, he knows who published that and he knows who covered the other. Seldom has anyone been so submerged in popular music as the young Reg Dwight.

But the main problem for the aspiring musician is sex, or rather sex appeal, and, in his case, his conspicuous lack of it. He is a chubby boy who makes everything he wears look wrong. At school, even though there was nothing wrong with his eyesight, he wore dark, wide-rimmed spectacles as a tribute to one of his musical heroes, Buddy Holly. His eyes damaged from wearing them, the glasses he wears now are for real. Overweight and already showing the first signs of a receding hairline, he looks more like Piggy out of *Lord Of The Flies* or Billy Bunter than any of the pretty boys of the r 'n' b and Merseybeat boom currently dominating the UK charts. He's by no means ugly but, in the age of the Beatles, the Stones, and the Kinks, he looks very plain indeed.

Nobody would have thought that, in less than ten years time, affable Reg Dwight, with his love of spoonerisms and silly names for everyone he met, would be responsible for more than three per cent of all records sold in one calendar year in the United States. But the rock 'n' roll gene pool has a contrary way of throwing up the oddest mutations. As the months progressed, it would become apparent that Reg Dwight was more than just an ordinary pub entertainer. This shy, self-conscious, lower-middle-class boy would eventually become the biggest recording star of his generation and one of the biggest media figures in the history of popular culture. Adopting his alter ego of Elton Hercules John, Reg would morph out of the podgy body that nobody loved to become a preening, glitzy, bespangled popular music behemoth. This is the story of that almost unbelievable transformation.

*   *   *

Elton John was born Reginald Kenneth Dwight on March 25, 1947. His father, Stanley Dwight, a squadron leader with the Royal Air Force, had married Reg's mum, Sheila Harris, in January 1945 and, like so many newly-wed couples of the day, set up home with Sheila's parents, Fred and Ivy Harris, at 55 Pinner Hill Road, Pinner, a semi-detached council house. The couple had met in 1942 when Stanley was serving in the Royal Air Force and Sheila, just 16, was working for United Dairies delivering milk. Stanley rose through the ranks of the RAF, becoming a flight lieutenant in 1947. Frequent postings meant that he would often be away from home.

There was music in the bones of the Dwight family. Edwin Dwight, Stanley's father, had been a cornet player for the company brass band at Callander's cable-making firm in Belvedere, Kent. Stanley, born in 1925, and one of six children, was himself a trumpeter with Bob Miller and the Millermen. At little more than toddler age, Reginald Dwight could already play a tune on the upright piano with astonishing ease. But it was Reg's mother, rather than his father, who seemed most keen on encouraging the fast-emerging natural talents of the youngster, along with Reg's grandmother, Ivy, and his piano-playing Aunty Win. Both Ivy and Win used to sit little Reg on their knees in front of the piano and offer encouragement.

It was clear that Reg Dwight had found the area in which he could excel. His school reports over the years described a slightly above-average student, with a modest intellect in most subjects, doing just enough to get by. Sit the lad behind the upright piano at home, however, and it was a different story altogether. Reg could pick up a tune at a very early age. When he was three, his parents heard him play a rudimentary version of 'The Skater's Waltz' by the late-nineteenth century French composer Emile Waldteufel – a romantic, memorable piece that was a popular hit of its day. Although only able to play in the key of C at this stage, Reg was clearly, if not a musical prodigy, then an extremely gifted pianist with a fantastic ear. He would only have to hear a melody once and he could immediately replicate it, virtually note-for-note.

'When he was four, we used to put him to bed in the day and get him up to play at night for parties,' Sheila has admitted. Even before Reg started school, there was already a certain amount of pressure on him to perform. Yet the ability to play in front of an audience, whether a dozen family members and friends, or tens of thousands of paying customers, was to be the key to the fledgling pianist's future success. Some musicians have had their careers blighted by stage fright, but Reg Dwight was confident almost from the beginning.

By the age of five, Reg was taking his first lessons on the piano under the tutelage of a local teacher called Mrs Jones. At six, when asked what he wanted to be when he grew up, he confidently announced that he intended to be a concert pianist. A photograph of Reg dating from 1952 shows him in blazer and short trousers, his hair neatly parted, sitting dutifully at the piano, his hands resting neatly on the white keys.

Smiling, somewhat charismatically, in semi-profile, he makes it look for all the world like his first publicity shot.

Music was the overriding passion in the Dwight household. Back in the day when radio was still the predominant means of entertainment for the average family, the wireless held centre stage. It was always on, Elton has explained. 'I grew up with Frank Sinatra, Rosemary Clooney, Nat King Cole. I looked forward to Sundays so much, when there'd be *Family Favourites*, *Round The Horne* and *Educating Archie*. I listened to plays, which got the brain cells working. I'm glad I was born then and had the privilege of listening to great radio programmes.'

Young Reg's mother and father were keen record buyers. 'I was three or four when I first started listening to records,' he has said. 'The first records I ever heard were by Kay Starr and Billy May and Tennessee Ernie Ford and Les Paul and Mary Ford and Guy Mitchell. I grew up in that era.' Johnny Ray was also a firm favourite. In the immediate pre-rock 'n' roll era, his father seemed intent on filling his young son's head with a more adult musical repertoire. 'He did influence me,' Elton later said. 'He used to play me [jazz pianist] George Shearing records. A four-year-old listening to George Shearing is a bit off.' When Reg was seven, his father presented him with a copy of Frank Sinatra's *Songs For Swinging Lovers*. 'It isn't the ideal present for a seven-year-old,' Elton was to reflect. 'I really wanted a bicycle.'

In the UK, the music that Reg found the most inspiring was skiffle: 'I went through the skiffle thing with Lonnie Donegan,' he told the BBC in 2002. 'He was the first person I ever saw on British television who played something different. It was fantastic to see someone change music that much.' However, Reg's first real love was American rock 'n' roll. 'I picked up a copy of *Life* magazine,' he has explained. 'There was a picture of Elvis Presley in there. I'd never seen anything like it.' The same week, his mother came home with two early classic rock 'n' roll singles and Reg was hooked.

'My mother introduced me to rock 'n' roll,' Elton claimed in 1971. 'One day she came home with "ABC Boogie" by Bill Haley and "Heartbreak Hotel" by Elvis Presley. She has always been well up on what's going on.' In no time, he was equally smitten by the Dionysian charms of monster piano man Jerry Lee Lewis. The first records that Reg Dwight ever bought were Little Richard's 'She's Got It' and 'The Girl Can't Help It'. 'But the first 45s I ever owned were "Reet Petite" by Jackie Wilson and "At The Hop" by Danny And The Juniors,' he told *Billboard*'s Timothy White in 1997.

As with so many children of his age, (and, come to think of it, like so many future musicians), it was Little Richard who would make the biggest impact. There was something dangerous about the music, something otherworldly about the combination of sounds that seemed to make sense even in their nonsense: 'A-Wop-bop-a-loo-lop a-lop-bam-boo'. There was something altogether radically different about the man himself, stylish in a suit yet with a bouffant hairdo and in make-up, which made him exotically alluring and transgressional. Other rockers such as Elvis may have been prettier, while others like Jerry Lee Lewis might have seemed more authentically possessed by the new spirit of danger and rebellion, but Little Richard presented something even more startling: a version of a man that appeared to poke fun at masculinity.

'Well, we were ready for it in England,' Elton would later say. 'Up until that point, the songs we heard were very prim and proper. Then we got things like "All Shook Up", which lyrically were far and away different from Guy Mitchell doing "Singing The Blues". All of a sudden you had Bill Haley singing "Rock Around The Clock", Little Richard screaming on "Tutti Frutti" – lyrically, it was a whole new ball game. Something just exploded.'

Elton was to reflect on these twin inspirations on his emergent talent: 'Jerry Lee Lewis was always a big influence on me. He's the best rock 'n' roll pianist ever. I couldn't play like him because he's too fast. I've got terrible hands for a pianist – they're midget's fingers. I play more like Little Richard. I used to go and see Little Richard at Harrod's Granada and he used to jump up on the piano and I'd think, I wish that was me.'

The adolescent Reginald Dwight also admired another pianist of a very different vintage: Winifred Atwell. Born in 1914, Atwell studied classical music in New York and then moved to London and Decca Records, where her honky-tonk piano motored through several UK hits, including 'Poor People Of Paris', a Number 1 when Reg was nine years old. Reg would later develop a distinctive, percussive way of playing. But the musical shadings and nuances he would bring to his playing, from classical to country and from rock 'n' roll to ballads, were the direct product of his astonishingly catholic musical tastes.

For a lonely child, records, as artefacts, assumed an incredible importance. His love of music stretched far beyond a mere love for the sounds of the music. The look and feel of the records themselves mattered equally. As the boy became a man, and a very wealthy one at that, record collecting became an obsession. By the age of 25, Elton John would be a walking one-man record shop and art collectors' fair rolled into one. Looking back on his younger self, he was to reflect in melancholy mode: 'I would buy records and file them. I could tell you who published what and then I would just stack them in a pile and look at the labels. I like my possessions. I grew up with inanimate objects as my friends, and I still believe they have feelings. That's why I keep hold of all my possessions, because I'll remember when they gave me a bit of happiness – which is more than human beings have given me.'

As a child, Reg Dwight was keen on sports – cricket, tennis and football. Unfortunately, his secondary school – Pinner County Grammar, which he attended from 1958 to 1965 – specialised in rugby, and no football was played. Despite this, the young Reggie fell in love with Watford FC and this was to prove a lifelong commitment. In adult life, he would become an aficionado not only of football but also of tennis, as well as being well informed on sporting matters in general.

Reg's cousin, Roy Dwight, played for Nottingham Forest in the 1959 Cup Final, his goal contributing to the team's defeat of Luton Town by two goals to one. Having scored after just nine minutes, Roy sustained a broken tibia in a tackle after 33 minutes and ended up watching the second half in hospital, refusing to be X-rayed until the match was over. In those pre-substitute days, Forest had to hang on for the rest of the game with ten men.

In interviews throughout the 1970s and beyond, Elton's bitterness towards his father was a recurring theme. In a 1976 *Playboy* interview he reinvented history by claiming: 'My dad never saw me for two years. I was two years old when he came home from the Air Force. He'd never seen me. And it got off to a really bad start, because Mother said, "Do you want to go upstairs and see him?" Father said, "No, I'll wait till morning."'

However, as Elton biographer Philip Norman has pointed out, this was not what happened. 'Stanley Dwight was then on home posting, with the RAF's Number 4 maintenance unit at nearby Ruislip,' Norman wrote in *Sir Elton: The Definitive Biography*. 'He was in the house when Reggie was born, and registered the son's birth on the following day. For almost the first year and a half of Reggie's life Stanley was stationed at Ruislip, but living off-base: he would return home to his wife and baby each evening just like any normal Metroland commuter.'

In 1949, Stanley Dwight was posted to Basra, Iraq and was heart-broken to be away from his young son. 'For their first Christmas apart, he arranged with Hamleys, the West End toy shop, for an expensive pedal car – the first of many future flash motors – to be delivered to Reggie,' noted Norman. However, the reality of the situation was that Reg Dwight and his dad were never close and Reg would not even attend his father's funeral in 1992. A disintegrating marriage, and the inevitable rows and silences, had created an atmosphere of tension in which the young boy had felt uncomfortable.

'My parents used to argue a lot when I was young,' Elton told the *Sunday Telegraph* in 1997. 'I would lock myself in my bedroom. My father would come home and there would be a row. I expected it. And lived in fear of it.' He also ascribed his journey from loner child to extroverted superstar to his need for attention: 'I don't think I had a dysfunctional background, but when your parents aren't getting on you tend to go into your own world. Mine was music, and that became my life. Every performer starts with a cry for attention: "I love doing this, but I want applause and verification that I'm good."' Indeed, cries for attention were to become a recurrent theme in the life of Elton John.

As a child, Reggie was hardly a tearaway. Rather, like so many future musicians and popular entertainers, his childhood and adolescence were marked by feelings of deep insecurity and loneliness. As he would later reminisce, he was 'too shy to say boo to a goose'. Astonishingly, even to this day, Elton displays an off-stage awkwardness and natural shyness to all but his very closest of friends. Loath to make eye contact, he will shuffle his feet and talk distractedly with his head down.

'As a kid I was always on the fringe of everything,' he told Tony Parsons in 1995. 'I wasn't part of the gang. Going to the cinema with mates, I was always the last one to be asked. I think being raised by women shaped my personality because I spent a lot of time on my own, in my room, playing records. It made me a loner. It made me shy with other kids. I created my own world. I was immersed in music and records even at that young age.' His father was a disciplinarian who thought it necessary to counter the wholly feminine upbringing of little Reggie with a raft of rules and regulations. Reg grew up to be not a little spoilt and Stanley saw the need to correct this. But it obviously made him an unpopular figure in his son's eyes.

Stanley was also to disapprove of his son's career choice. His mother Sheila recalled in *Time* magazine in 1975 a letter Stanley sent from overseas warning that Reg, then 16, must 'get all this pop nonsense out of his head, otherwise he's going to turn into a wild boy. He should get a sensible job with either BEA or Barclays Bank'.

Meanwhile, Stanley's RAF career was in the ascendant and in 1953 he was made squadron leader. After a second posting to Iraq, he was offered a long-term posting at RAF Medmenham in Marlow, Buckinghamshire. The family moved out of Pinner Hill Road and into a modest detached house at 11 Potter Street, Northwood, two miles from Pinner. Yet life here was not happy. Philip Norman later noted that 'so uncomfortable were to be the associations of this modest villa that later, when Reggie's past life became of interest to journalists, he would always omit it from the chronology'. Reg's mum and dad were by then staying together 'for the sake of the child'. And in 1960 Stanley was on the move again, this time to a posting in Harrogate, Yorkshire.

The atmosphere in the Dwight household was both tense and rather buttoned-up. Reginald's friends were mostly girls: his unfailing courteousness and personal charm made him a popular, if unthreatening, escort. Sex was, of course, never mentioned. 'At school I used to have crushes on people, but not really any sex at all, male or female, until about 23,' Elton said when interviewed by Pet Shop Boys' Neil Tennant in 1998. 'And then it was like a volcano. Out it came; it was such a relief. I never had any sex education when I was at school. Sex was never discussed.

'The first time I masturbated I was in pain. I was so horrified. And my parents found out because I'd used up all my pyjamas. And then I got ripped apart for doing it. Sex was completely frightening. At school everyone boasted about sex. Meanwhile, I was dying to be molested by someone. When I went into therapy, my therapist said, "I have to ask you if you were molested." And I said, "No, actually." But I was dying to be molested by someone – just to teach me, just to find out, you know?'

The same strict approach was applied to that other great teen obsession – clothes. Any attempt to buy even remotely trendy clothes was frowned upon or barred by his father. Hush Puppies were deemed beyond the pale. Photographs of the teenage Reggie show a formally dressed boy, with no trace of the Teddy Boy stylings that were then so popular.

Reggie's upbringing was to influence the later life of Elton John in two important ways. His status as an only child gave him a slightly spoilt and stubborn nature and a self-regarding demeanour that would erupt into numerous infamous hissy fits over the years. The relative lack of closeness to his father led, perhaps inevitably, to the adult Reg feeling insecure in others' affections and unable to accept love or praise readily. Yet from his early teens onwards, he was ambitious and driven, highly, perhaps overly competitive, and totally focused on the music business. 'I feel as though I'm living my life at double speed now, as if I'm now the child that I should have been when I was eight,' he confessed in 1975.

As Reg grew into a talented pianist, his father made it clear that he was dead set against any fanciful, bohemian notions that he should take his calling seriously. 'I had an uneasy relationship with my father because I was scared of him, but now I see his point,' Elton reflected in 2000. 'He wanted me to have a stable job. I needed something else.' His dad wanted Reg to take up a more conventional career, such as banking. 'He didn't want me to go into music and I can never understand that, because he was a trumpeter in a band,' Elton told *Playboy* in 1976.

Reg Dwight's relationship with his father was, according to Elton, at best distant, and at worst almost non-existent. 'I suppose the only regret I have about my life is that I had a bad childhood,' he said in 1973. 'I mean, I wasn't hit on the head every three minutes with a saucepan. But my father and mother didn't get on too well, so I didn't have too many friends or anything like that, and I was very, very clammed up. I suppose I'm rebelling against that now. That's why I do all those things, because I was never allowed to go out or do anything.'

Developing the theme a few years later, he added: 'I had an awful inferiority complex as a kid. My father wasn't the slightest bit inter-ested in me and he was a snob, which I hated. I couldn't play in the garden in case I knocked the rose bushes over – you know, one of those efforts. I was petrified of him, too. I'd dread it when he came home.' Even more damningly, Elton proclaimed in 1976: 'My father was so stupid with me that it was ridiculous. I couldn't eat celery without making a noise.'

His parents' marriage finally ended in divorce in 1962 on the grounds of Sheila's admission of adultery. During Stanley's RAF posting in Harrogate, Sheila had taken up with the affable Fred Farebrother, a local builder and decorator. Stanley would within months have a new wife, Edna, a 33-year-old lab technician whom he met in Harrogate. Together they would go on to have four children in four years, a fact which the teenage Reg found himself unable to cope with.

'When my parents got divorced, there was a point when I did feel bitter because of the way my mum was treated,' he later reflected. 'When they got divorced, she had to bear all the costs. She more or less gave up everything and had to admit to adultery, while he was doing the same thing behind her back and making her pay for it. He was such a sneak. Then he went away and five months later got married to this woman and had four kids in four years. My pride was really snipped, 'cause he was supposed to hate kids. I guess I was a mistake in the first place.'

Elton would also admit to being 'terribly upset I was an only child', which must have made his father's alacrity in starting a new family all the more hurtful. 'That completely destroyed me. To be honest, I think my childhood had a terrible influence on what I am, on what I do and what I'm trying to fight my way out of.' However, as Philip Norman and others have pointed out, in fact Stanley paid all the costs of the divorce and continued supporting Reggie financially throughout his schooling. In February 1963, he even bought him a second-hand piano for the not-inconsiderable sum of £68.

Stanley Dwight gave up his RAF career and moved with Edna to Chadwell Heath in Essex to run a stationery shop. He continued to provide for Reg and correspondence between father and son hints at a rather more cordial relationship, at least initially, than Elton would admit to. Quite why Elton has been so eager to criticise his biological father in the media is not altogether clear and may be a curious manifestation of some deep insecurity about his adolescent self-image. By using his dad as a scapegoat, however, he seems to have attributed much that was wrong about his personality to this breakdown in communication.

Elton admitted that as a young boy he craved his parents' attention and that he wanted to be accepted by both parties. 'Divorce is a traumatic thing for kids,' he told US interviewer Barbara Walters in 1994. 'I actually wanted my parents to get divorced because I couldn't stand all the rows going on. But their rows affected me and the atmosphere in the house affected me. I thought that I had a lot of resentment against my father. I was frightened of my father as a kid. All that fear and intimidation.'

In yet another similarity to so many of the British pop stars of his generation, Elton John was a product of suburbia and, specifically, the suburbia that surrounds the metropolis. It can surely be no coincidence that Mick Jagger (Dartford), David Bowie (Brixton, then

Bromley), Siouxsie Sioux and Billy Idol (both Bromley), The Stranglers (Guildford), Paul Weller (Woking), Damon Albarn (Leytonstone, then Colchester) and Brett Anderson (Hayward's Heath) all lived on the outskirts of the Big Smoke. In 2000, Anderson spoke for many when he told *Q*: 'Being born on the outskirts of London, able to peer in, but not quite see what's going on, is a tantalising thing – it makes you hungry, it gives you ambition.'

The conformity of semi-detached orderliness and attendant social-climbing and hypocrisy that was part and parcel of the lower-middle-class mindset of post-war suburbia proved suffocating for musicians and artists who felt semi-detached themselves: so close to the excitement of London, yet tantalisingly apart from it. Yet perhaps it's this very position, of being outside of the scene geographically and emotionally, which provided such a unique viewpoint. At a distance, these people became brilliant commentators on the scene without being destroyed by it. They were sufficiently separate from London to be relatively immune to its showiness and self-confidence.

The suburb of Pinner is situated just over 12 miles from Charing Cross train station. Every Saturday morning from the age of 11 to 16, Reg Dwight made the journey to study at London's Royal Academy of Music, where he had won a place as a junior exhibitioner starting in the autumn of 1958. Situated on Marylebone Road opposite Regent's Park, the Academy was one of the world's most prestigious musical institutions. Notable alumni include the composer Harrison Birtwistle, the jazz composer John Dankworth, the classical and film composer Michael Nyman, the conductor Sir Simon Rattle and, from the pop world, Annie Lennox and Joe Jackson. Junior exhibitioners got a scholarship from the London County Council. The programme was set up exclusively for children in state schools and ran every Saturday from 9am until 2pm, with no breaks. Traditionally, children took lessons on their musical instrument of choice and were part of the choir and, if appropriate, the orchestra.

Reg studied piano under Miss Helen Piena. 'I always called him Reginald. He was about 11 when I first met him, and he was charming,' she recalls with fondness today. 'When he went away on holiday he always used to bring me a present back. He used to send me postcards with kisses on them. It was a very nice togetherness really. He was plump, but not overweight. He wore ordinary teenagers' clothes. I mean, teenagers weren't teenagers then, they were just children growing up and that's what he was – a nice boy. We got on well together. I'm very fond of him.'

Reginald's particular musical gift soon revealed itself to Piena. 'I started him off with some Handel,' she says. 'I remember playing him one piece four pages long and he played it back to me like a gramophone record. He had an absolutely extraordinary, wonderful ear. And I never played to him again, ever, because he had to learn to do it himself. He had this wonderful ear but he could not read a note of music. That's the first thing I had to teach him. When he started he couldn't, but when he finished with me he could. He always did what he was told and he was always perfect by the following lesson – not five or six lessons on, but by the following lesson.'

However, Piena immediately sensed that the rarefied atmosphere of the Academy was a little stifling for the boy. 'At the beginning, I think he was ashamed of being in the Academy,' she reflects. 'It was the wrong type of upbringing. It was too highfaluting.'

At this stage in his musical development, Reg was performing a classical repertoire. He took part in school concerts at Pinner County Grammar School and, at age 12, played the piano at the Northwood Music Festival in Ruislip, Middlesex, where his performance included Grovlez's 'Les Petites Litanies de Jésus'. But as Reg hit his teens it was obvious that his real musical passion lay elsewhere.

During the period of his classical music instruction, Reg had begun playing piano at the Northwood Hills Hotel in Pinner. 'I used to sing Jim Reeves songs, Cliff Richard songs, anything that was popular,' Elton has explained. 'And also play things like "Roll Out The Barrel", Cockney songs and "When Irish Eyes Are Smiling". You had to play "When Irish Eyes Are Smiling" or you'd get a pint of beer slung over you. Al Jolson songs were also very popular. I used to have a box that got passed around at the end of the evening. When I first started my residency nobody used to go to the public bar, but eventually people started to come in and, after a while, it was packed out every weekend. With the money people used to put in my box I was earning £25 a week, which was great.'

Although he was living a pretty busy life and had a certain number of mates at school, Reg remained an insecure teenager. 'Monday to Friday I went to school,' he recalled in 1975. 'Saturday was the Royal Academy of Music. Sunday I had to sit at home and practise and do my homework. I was introverted and had a terrible inferiority complex. That's why I started wearing glasses – to hide behind. I didn't really need them, but when Buddy Holly came along, God, I wanted a pair like his! I began to wear them all the time, so my eyes got worse.'

Elton would later comment that he studied classical music 'half-heartedly'. By the time he was 14, Piena could also see that Reginald's interest was waning. 'He got on very well until he was about 14, which is a crucial age,' she says. 'About that time he began to realise what it was he wanted to do. He told me afterwards that he had formed a jazz [sic] band of his own and that's what he was doing. He wasn't doing very much for me. I gave him one of the most wonderful things I could think of, some Mozart. I just wanted to cajole him and make him do some practice. I knew there was a lot of music in him that I couldn't bring out. That was one of the things I pride myself on, being able to bring out the gift that was in them. And I couldn't, because I was doing the wrong type of music.'

Decades later, as a mature artist, Elton spoke of the advantages his classical training gave him. 'I'm very glad to have had the experience of having a classical background, because it makes you appreciate all sorts of music,' he mused. 'It also helps you as a writer because, as a keyboard player, you tend to write with more chords than a guitar, and I think that has a lot to do with my piano playing and my love of Chopin, Bach and Mozart and my love of singing in a choir. I think my songs have more of a classic leaning to them than other artists who haven't had that classical background, and I am grateful for that.'

Two of Elton's future collaborators, the arranger Paul Buckmaster and the producer Chris Thomas, also studied at the Royal Academy as full-time students. But the teenage Reg was simply not cut out for a career in classical music and certainly harboured no aspirations to further his academic career after school. 'I used to look at him on the stool next to me,' recalls Helen Piena. 'I remember sitting there for three-quarters of an hour trying to persuade him to go to university. And he said, "No, none of my family has ever been to university, I'm not going to university." And I couldn't make him change his mind.' At 16, Reg obtained grade six piano. 'That's very low for a talented child,' concludes Piena. 'I think he got a merit but he certainly didn't get a distinction. The examiner said he didn't know his scales.'

Despite the fact that Piena played a crucial role in developing the talent of the future Elton John, she looks back on her time with the future world superstar with a certain regret. 'He isn't my best pupil technically. The playing was not of solo pianist calibre,' she admits. 'I think his gift is to be able to stand up in front of a crowd and talk to them. I think that's a wonderful gift to have. His musical gifts, I don't want to sound nasty, but they are not very great. If you come to the Royal Academy of Music, you expect to learn classical music and to be able to perform and play these wonderful things that famous people play and he didn't do any of this. So, from that point of view, I failed.'

Yet the sweeping European romanticism of so much of Elton's later music is surely testimony to the fact that his five years studying 'proper' music was not in vain. 'He couldn't have written music without doing our course, it wouldn't have been possible,' says Piena. But the fact that Reg would later become one of the world's most famous popular musicians was something she never dreamt could happen. Piena herself simply doesn't like popular music: 'People gave me a tape of his many years ago. I didn't play it. I couldn't face it.'

The 'jazz band' referred to by Helen Piena may well have been an early incarnation of the better-known Bluesology, who released three singles and who, in a later incarnation, became Long John Baldry's live cabaret band. However, there was a band that pre-dated Bluesology, called the Corvettes, in which Reg played electric piano along with the singer and lead guitarist Stewart Brown and the bassist Geoff Dyson. Elton was then in his fourth year at secondary school, so was just 15 when a member of this short-lived band. Dyson went on to play for the Mockingbirds, a group which did enough business to be awarded a support slot for the Yardbirds.

In 1961, Reg began his residency at the Northwood Hills Hotel. Live music was played at this Benskin's hostelry in the saloon bar on Fridays and Saturdays. When a vacancy came up for the gig, Reg's step-dad Fred persuaded the pub landlord George Hill to give Reginald a go. 'His hair was cut very short,' George's wife, Ann, told Philip Norman of the young Reggie. 'He wore a collar and tie, grey flannel trousers and this Harris tweed sports jacket that was a kind of gingery colour. He was very shy. But he did tell us he'd written a song that was called "Come Back Baby".'

Today, the pub, which is situated at 66 Joel Street in Northwood Hills, has become something of a Mecca for Elton John fans, though the original piano he played on was removed some years ago. 'I started to play semi-professionally when I was 14,' Elton later reminisced. 'Little Richard and things like that. And then we used to try to find the most obscure blues when everybody else was playing rock 'n' roll. I was paid a pound a night and my father would come round and collect with a box. Then I would sing some Top Ten songs and I started to know the American songs.'

The initial response to the new weekend entertainment was pretty hostile and included barracking, turning the PA off and hurling objects in the direction of the teenager dressed like a middle-aged librarian. But Reggie battled through and, although it could be a boisterous gig, he remained a feature of the pub's entertainment until the mid-1960s.

Reg's first serious attempt to break into the music business came with the formation of Bluesology in late 1962 when he was 15. He played piano and sang, together with Stewart Brown, a journeyman lead guitarist with a more-than-capable soul voice, Rex Bishop on bass and Mick Inkpen on drums. Originally a member of the band, Geoff Dyson from the Corvettes, who had more experience of the London music scene, graduated to become the band's booker.

Reg left Pinner County Grammar School on March 5, 1965, six weeks before he was due to take his A levels in Music and English and three weeks short of his eighteenth birthday. He had secured just four O Levels (English Language, English Literature, Music and French), a result which he would later call 'disgraceful' for someone of his ability. But the lure of a job in the big bad music business, albeit on the bottom rung, proved too tempting.

Reg's football player cousin Roy, well connected to the entertainment scene of the mid-1960s, had arranged through a friend of a friend for Reg to be interviewed for the West End publishing company Mills Music. Reg's father was reportedly angry with Roy for going behind his back and, in a move which must have looked to the outside world as if he was washing his hands of the whole business, he relocated to the Wirral with his new family. In March 1965, Reg Dwight started work as a messenger at Mills Music. The initial salary was £5 a week. He had begun his apprenticeship in pop music.

CHAPTER 2

HARDLY A HERO

'They were always two months behind the latest trend.'

Elton John on Bluesology

'Captain Fantastic, raised and regimented
Hardly a hero
Just someone his mother might know.'

'Captain Fantastic And The Brown Dirt Cowboy';
lyrics: Bernie Taupin; music: Elton John

Reg Dwight has been sent out to get a cup of coffee for Terry Venables. The young Chelsea midfielder is visiting Mills Music, a publishing house in Denmark Street, after training. Chelsea is the most fashionable football club in Britain. Manchester United, Everton, Liverpool and Leeds United are more successful on the pitch, but none can boast the celebrity following of the Kings Road set: Terence Stamp, Raquel Welch, Michael Caine and Richard Attenborough are just some of their current high-profile admirers.

Terry has always had a love of the show business world. At the age of four he tap-danced with the Happy Tappers and later learned a mime act that he used to perform at local disabled peoples' homes. At 17, he was entering talent contests and in later years he was to sing several times with the Joe Loss Orchestra. Today though, he has popped into Mills Music to meet the songwriter Tony Hiller, who is going to offer him advice on writing songs. As an aspiring songwriter hoping to develop some off-pitch income, this is a potentially lucrative meeting.

Venables regards Reg as the office loon, a chubby teenager regaling the customers with his Kenneth Williams impersonations. Clad in brown overalls, for his part Reg looks forward to his mundane existence in the packing department in Denmark Street being enlivened by the odd celebrity visit. His colleagues at Mills Music find Reg unfailingly polite. He addresses all the older men as 'Sir'. Working with Reg is the teenager Eric Hall. They spend their days running errands, making tea for their superiors and any celebrity guests and packing parcels of sheet music. For both of them, it's their first full-time job. Caleb Quaye calls in every day, too. Caleb, a year younger than Reg, works in nearby Old Compton Street as a gopher for Paxton's wholesale music delivery firm. His father, Cab Quaye, was a pre-war bandleader and Caleb is already a proficient guitarist.

Just a mundane day in 1965, then, at Mills Music: a future England football team manager, a future Eurovision Song Contest-winning song-writer ('Save Your Kisses For Me'), a future pop impresario and football agent and a future singing superstar and his guitarist all together under one roof.

Denmark Street, named after Prince George of Denmark, the husband of Queen Anne, is, by the mid-1960s, better known as London's Tin Pan Alley. Close to the bars, clubs and theatres of Soho, and three minutes' walk away from Tottenham Court Road tube, it has been popular with music publishers since the 1890s. Today, the Giaconda Café Bar is the locale of choice for the hundreds of would-be musicians and entrepreneurs, making Denmark Street a hive of activity for planners, plotters, dreamers and schemers, including many of the future superstars of the late 1960s and early 1970s.

The advent of recording studios in Denmark Street is a relatively recent development. In 1963, the Rolling Stones recorded their first album at Number 4, Regents Sound Studio. In a basement studio at Southern Music at Number 8, Donovan has just recorded 'Catch The Wind'. In 1965, Number 11 houses Rose Morris and six floors of instrumentation and sheet music. In Central Sound Studios at Number 12, David Bowie and his new band, the Lower Third, have just been recording. Lawrence Wright, 'The Duke Of Denmark Street', who died just a year ago, founded *Melody Maker* in 1926 and its offices are at Number 19.

Mills Music, where Reg Dwight and Eric Hall work, is at Number 20. A little-known songwriter by the name of Paul Simon has recently been into the office to ask if they would like to publish two of his songs, 'Homeward Bound' and 'The Sound of Silence', but he's been turned down. Number 21 houses Peter Maurice Music, publisher of 'Hang Out The Washing On The Siegfried Line' and Lionel Bart, and, in Number 22, the Small Faces and Manfred Mann have just been recording in the basement studios. Above it is Rhodes Music, where future stars Jeff Beck, Eric Clapton and Pete Townshend bought their guitars. At Number 25, Denmark Productions, the Kinks – who will later pen a tribute to Denmark Street – have been cutting new material. Denmark Street is teeming with stars waiting to happen.

Reg spends his working hours at Mills Music as a general dogsbody, but is close enough to Berwick Street to indulge his all-too-consuming passion for riffling through the latest vinyl releases at Music Land record store. What he doesn't know about the new pop, soul, and rock 'n' roll isn't worth knowing. This information will stand him in good stead for his next musical incarnation.

*   *   *

Today, Mick Inkpen is a fifty-something jewellery valuer and craftsman, making and repairing jewellery out of his studio in Torquay, Devon. But back in the day, Mick, like thousands of other teenagers up and down the UK in the early 1960s, was a would-be professional musician, a drummer learning his trade on the live circuit. For over two years, he played with Reg Dwight in the band Bluesology.

Mick, then 15, had been practising in a back room at Father Aymes' Youth Club at St Edmund's Church, halfway between Pinner and Northwood Hills. 'This is where I got to hear about Reg, or at least first met him,' he says today. 'I knew there was a kid who used to bash away at the piano who was pretty good; a lot better than any other pianist I had seen of his age.' Mick was into the blues and would frequent the New Fender Club in Kenton to check out the likes of John Mayall's Bluesbreakers and The Graham Bond Organisation. Also appearing would be veteran rhythm and blues stars from the US such as Muddy Waters, Lightnin' Hopkins, Howlin' Wolf and Memphis Slim. Blues music was making a huge impact on youth culture in the early 1960s.

'There were lots and lots of people forming bands,' Inkpen says. 'You could fetch up at a pub and say, "We're a band, we play," and they'd say, "Right, fine, Tuesday nights are free, you can play then." Or they'd say, "You can play during the interval of another band." There were so many groups about, so much music being done. We were all at it.'

Indeed, back in the early 1960s, many teenagers didn't go to see specific groups in the manner of today. Rather, with so many clubs and pubs offering live entertainment with several acts on the bill, if you were lucky someone like the Rolling Stones, the Beatles, Rhode Island Red and The Roosters (featuring the talents of a young Eric Clapton) or the High Numbers (on the verge of morphing into the Who) would simply be part of the night's entertainment. Bluesology were just another of these new bands to hit the road and, although they didn't make the big time, their story plays an important role in the creation of Elton John.

The original Bluesology bassist, Rex Bishop, now a lawyer with a practice near Toronto, remembers that the band evolved partly out of his own school band, fronted by Ian Krause, a man whose nickname at school was, rather improbably, 'Aunty' ('I think it may have been the way he carried his schoolbag,' says Bishop). 'We put an ad in a local paper and Mick Inkpen answered it. So we started up a band, and it hadn't been going long when Mick said he couldn't play with Krause because he didn't think he was a very good singer.'

Mick Inkpen had heard of a great local piano player called Reg Dwight and he took Rex round to speak to him at home. By now the Dwight family had moved into a maisonette in Frome Court, Pinner. Reg was working with another local musician, Stewart Brown, a singer and lead guitarist, and on the lookout for a drummer and a bassist.

'So our bands eventually merged into Bluesology,' says Rex Bishop. 'Bluesology was, in effect, the remnants of my school band, plus Mick Inkpen, and whoever Mick put us in touch with. It pretty soon got the name Bluesology, which came from Stewart Brown.' The name was a tribute to guitarist Jean Baptiste 'Django' Reinhardt, a Belgian Roma musician who formed the Quintette du Hot Club de France with violinist Stéphane Grappelli and three others. *Djangology*, recorded in 1948, was one of his famous works. Stewart Brown himself had a rather different stage presence to that of Reg Dwight.

'Stewart was a great guy,' says Mick Inkpen, of his former bandmate who died in 2001. 'I don't suppose he would have said he was the world's greatest guitarist, but he had the most amazing blues voice. He was only a teenager when I first met him, but he could sing like a real blues wailer, he was terrific.' 'He was good-looking, a really nice, easy-going fellow,' concurs Rex Bishop. 'I thought he had a great voice.' For most of Bluesology's live set, it would be Stewart Brown, and not the future Elton John, who would be the main vocalist.

Nobody is quite sure exactly when the band started playing. In an interview in 1973 with the BBC DJ Paul Gambaccini, Elton said that the band 'got together when I was about 14, playing in scout huts and youth club dances. Just one ten-watt amplifier with the piano un-amplified.' However, Bluesology were rather idealistic in their musical mission. 'Although we all seemed to have similar musical tastes, it was nothing like the pop music of the day,' says Mick Inkpen. 'In fact, I think we were a bit snobbish about the hit parade and refused to play anything remotely popular. As a result, gigs were a bit thin on the ground.' 'Bluesology were always two months too late, or three years too early. We were never playing the right thing at the right time,' was Elton's later, more damning verdict.

It was obvious, though, that the real musical talent in Bluesology was Reg Dwight. When the band first started, Reg was still travelling in to the Royal Academy in London on Saturday mornings. 'He was pretty exhausted from travelling into town and coming back again, so we had to make sure that we didn't press him too much for time on a Saturday,' remembers Inkpen. 'He had an enormous personality even then. He had an encyclopaedic memory; he remembered lots and lots of detail. He was funny and had a very peculiar and witty sense of humour. He loved making up names for people and he loved spoonerisms. He wasn't one of those people who tried to be funny and would make you wince. He was just so funny you ended up in tears. He looked terrible and he wasn't built like a pop star – he still isn't! But he was an amusing bloke and he could play the piano like nobody's business.'

Fred, Reg's genial step-dad, had his name inverted to 'Derf' by Reg. 'Derf was marvellous, a gentle man,' Inkpen says. 'We took advantage of him something rotten. We had no way of getting to gigs so it was a question of begging him for lifts. I called him Derf because I thought it was his real name! It didn't occur to me for ages that it was Reg was having a joke. I thought Reg's mother, Sheila, was great too. They were obviously very keen on Reg doing well in music.'

The band's first, unofficial manager, the former Corvettes bassist Geoff Dyson, secured them gigs at a small chain of dance halls that ran talent contests for unsigned bands. 'We entered one of these competitions and we were doing quite well,' remembers Inkpen, 'We got through a few heats. But it was a complete con, because you'd perform free and then, if you won, you were supposed to get a recording contract, which wasn't worth the paper it was printed on. Anyone could get a recording contract; it didn't mean you were going to get your name in lights or anything. But that helped us along; we played in front of more people than we'd ever done before.'

Dyson's role would eventually be taken over by Arnold Tendler, the band's first proper manager. 'Geoff Dyson was well-meaning and he worked hard, but he was just a lad, the same age as us basically,' says Inkpen. 'I'd left art school and got a job working for Arnold Tendler, a jeweller who had a repair business in Berwick Street, right in the middle of Soho, across the road from a knocking shop.' For the teenage Bluesologists, Arnold, by then well into his thirties, must have seemed like a relic from a bygone era. 'He was very dapper, dark hair, plenty of Brylcreem,' says Inkpen. 'He always wore a very nice, thick dark-blue woollen coat and a three-piece suit with polished shoes; he was every inch the businessman. I think he came along to hear us play at some club. He knew nothing about the music business at all, only what he'd read.' 'Arnold could talk the hind legs off a donkey,' adds Rex Bishop.

Tendler became their manager at a time when Bluesology were still a fairly impoverished outfit. 'My mum used to type addresses for *Reader's Digest*, she was endlessly typing them on bits of card,' says Inkpen. 'That paid for a couple of tom-toms at £70 each. Reg was in the same fix as us: he needed money to buy kit. As a keyboard player, you couldn't rely on pianos everywhere you went, because pianos were always out of tune, or somebody had poured beer in them, or the keys were missing. We tried using *in situ* pianos, but it was just hopeless. So we thought the thing to do was to buy one of these new electric pianos that were coming onto the market.

'Reg did that by playing at the Northwood Hills Hotel on a Friday and Saturday night, whenever we weren't doing anything. He had a huge stack of music from Winifred Atwell to sing-a-long pub music. I went along there once or twice to see him play and it was good fun. To stop any unpleasantness, he had four or five sturdy gypsies to look after him. One red-haired girl was Reg's first girlfriend, I suppose. That's interesting, in view of what we all know now.'

Bluesology used to practise at the pub and Reg had unsuccessfully asked the Northwood Hills Hotel publican George Hill for a £200 loan so he could buy an electric piano. In the end he managed to save up enough money to buy the fabled Hohner 'Planet' electric piano, giving Bluesology a consistent, if hardly sonorous, sound from their most talented musician.

However, Arnold Tendler put up money for equipment, a van and even stage uniforms. He was genuinely impressed by the band and also used to watch Reggie perform at the Northwood Hills. 'Even then he used to kick away the piano stool and play sitting on the floor,' Tendler told Philip Norman. The Ford Thames van in particular was a major boost for the band, who were now beginning to find gigs on the local circuit. 'Before that, we had to borrow a friend's Dormobile,' says Inkpen. 'Stephen Hutchins was our first roadie. He was two years older than me. We used to pay him petrol money and a couple of quid.' With his Mills Music salary and his live work, Reg Dwight was making around £35 a week, 'a fortune' for a lad of his age.

A further move towards a greater degree of professionalism came when Tendler suggested that they wore matching outfits on stage. 'When we were in Bluesology, we were supposed to be earning a living out of music, and our appearance became a bit more significant,' says Inkpen. 'Arnold thought it would be a good idea if we all looked the same. In those days, wearing uniform was what you did if you were in a band. We had these striped jackets and black trousers and they looked pretty terrible. Reg looked awful, although I don't think any of us looked particularly wonderful. We didn't really want to be that kind of band. I mean, I thought we were going to be a rhythm and blues band along the lines of John Mayall's Bluesbreakers or the Yardbirds.'

The 18-year-old Reg Dwight was definitely still suffering from self-image problems. 'He wasn't bald or anything, but it was obvious that he was going to lose his hair as time went on,' says Inkpen. 'He wasn't obese either, but we were all skinny as rakes and he was well-covered, so that made him look a bit heavier than us. I don't think there's an awful lot he can do about his weight. If you met him, though, you'd be charmed. As far as I was concerned, he made the band worthwhile, because he knew what he was doing. He was a good musician and he made it fun.'

Things were a tad different for the eye candy that was Stewart Brown. 'With Stewart it was ridiculous,' continues Inkpen. 'He had girls all over the place. He was blessed with dark good looks so it wasn't surprising. Reg wasn't, so the fact that he didn't have a girlfriend didn't signify anything. He was just an awkward-looking kid, not the sort you would expect to have girlfriends on both arms. I wouldn't have said there was a big sex drive in evidence. He certainly wasn't effeminate, though. He liked rugby and football, and he played tennis.' The image of Elton we have grown used to today – witty, hard working, professional, with some decidedly bloke-ish interests – was obviously already in evidence in the teenage Reg Dwight.

Alongside the talent contests at venues such as Rory Blackwell's Club, the band had begun gigging regularly to often-unappreciative audiences. 'We did a horrible community hall in South Harrow,' says Inkpen. 'It had got a reputation for being a bit rough – I don't know why, because South Harrow was a perfectly respectable area. What they wanted was rock 'n' roll, something lively, and a decent show. What we went on and played was not what they had in mind. So they stayed at the back, arms folded, staring at the band. Later on they decided to liven up proceedings a bit by driving a motorcycle through the hall. Or rather, they were about to, but somebody intervened. But we just bashed on. We didn't care, we were playing, which was the main thing.'

The next step was to announce the band's existence to the world by releasing a single. The song chosen was Reg Dwight's ballad 'Come Back Baby'. Now, 1965 was the year of 'Satisfaction', 'I Got You Babe', 'I Feel Fine' and 'Mr Tambourine Man' but not, unsurprisingly, the year of 'Come Back Baby'. Reg's trite lyrics were pure cod romance, and an early indication that, whatever talents he might have, they weren't as a lyricist: 'Come back baby/ Come back to me yeah/ And you will see yeah/ How I've changed/ 'Cause you're the only love that I ever had.' The music, on the other hand, was acceptable: a period piece, to be sure, but no disgrace for a first effort. A medium-paced pop ballad, it lay somewhere between Motown and the poppy blues which were in favour at the time. The voice of the future Elton John is perfectly recognisable, though without the Americanisms of his later style. To his credit, the singer hasn't tried to sweep this piece of juvenilia under the carpet, and it was officially released on CD in 1990 as part of the *To Be Continued...* box set.

'Reg always used to say, "I can't do words",' says Inkpen. 'He never had a facility with words, but the tune's all right, and I thought we played it quite well. If you saw where it was recorded, you wouldn't believe it. The only way to get a song recorded, if you were an unsigned band, was to pay for it yourself. The idea was to record a demo version and then to punt it round record companies.'

The nearest studio any of the band knew was Jackson's Recording

Studio in Rickmansworth. Jack Jackson was a veteran former Radio Luxembourg DJ who had also appeared on the BBC. His sons were recording engineers and they owned a small four-track studio. 'It was really a glorified shed, and the interior looked a bit like the outside,' says Inkpen. 'It was manky in the extreme – there were rotten old bits of carpet strewn all over the floor and chicken wire and padding on the walls for sound-proofing. But for some reason they managed to get a decent sound there. We only got a couple of shots at it doing it, so what you hear on there is really the product of one day in the recording studio.' A second track, the Jimmy Witherspoon cover 'Times Getting Tougher Than Tough', featuring Stewart Brown's earthier vocals, was also cut and was more typical of the band's live repertoire than the poppy Dwight original.

Armed with a demo, Tendler managed to drum up some serious interest in the band for the first time. Jack Baverstock, head of A & R at Philips, offered them the chance to record a single for Philips' associated label, Fontana. Fontana had been sent the demo, but, having considered it unfit for release, they invited the band to make a second recording. Rex Bishop was disappointed that Stewart Brown was not offered the chance to sing the lead. 'I remember we got into the recording studio at Fontana and the guy running the session stopped us as we were playing it and said he wanted Reg to sing it. And I remember being pissed off, because I thought Stu had a really good voice, a lot better than Reg.'

According to Mick Inkpen, the recording didn't run at all smoothly. 'We found ourselves in the Fontana Recording Studio, which is near Marble Arch. We had a go at doing "Come Back Baby" again and it was dreadful, the piano didn't sound right. We spent most of the time trying to mic the piano properly. Even Jack Baverstock, who was really an A & R man, got called down to try, but it wasn't happening at all. So after a lot of expensive studio time they simply grabbed hold of the original master tapes of "Come Back Baby" and fixed them up, and that's what Fontana released.'

The single was released in July 1965 and, unsurprisingly, failed to chart, although Mills Publishing accepted it. Much to the delight of Reg, it was also played on Radio Luxembourg. The band's first publicity photo shows Bluesology standing outside the Tower of London in matching 'cool' attire. Reg Dwight, with pudding-bowl haircut and dark-rimmed glasses, is in semi-profile, the better to reveal his paunch.

That summer of 1965, the band turned professional after entering a talent competition at the State Cinema in Kilburn on the morning of Saturday June 22. 'The State was the sort of Irish dance hall even the Irish were afraid to go to,' says Inkpen. 'It was a rough old place. It was also huge, having been used as a ballroom in the heyday of ballroom dancing. We struggled a bit, as we had equipment that was more suited to small clubs.' Nevertheless, a representative of the Roy Tempest Agency was sufficiently impressed to offer Bluesology regular employment as backing musicians on tour.

What followed were three years of constant live work, playing their own gigs but also working as a warm-up act and backing musicians for a succession of artists signed up for UK tours. Bluesology's first small splash in the music press also came that summer. On July 22, 1965, *Record Retailer and Music Industry News* included a brief interview with the band 'spokesman', who was interestingly neither Stewart Brown or Reg Dwight, but Mick Inkpen. 'The story hung on whether Rex should go for his degree or whether he should persevere with the band,' Inkpen remembers. 'And we had a picture of us shaking hands with Rex. He should have gone to university, but he stayed with us for a bit.'

For now, Bluesology were committed to working unsocial hours for little pay as hired hands for a variety of entertainers of uncertain pedigree. 'Roy Tempest was a curious bloke,' says Inkpen. 'I think he'd been a boxer and now he was a musical entrepreneur and ran this agency. He was bringing over American acts who were in the doldrums or completely forgotten. If they had any mileage left in them at all, he would book them for a two-week tour. Every expense was spared, and they came over with promises of a fairly modest tour sheet. But there was always a clause saying more dates might be added and so when they arrived they found they were solidly booked up for two weeks. In some cases, you found you were playing more than one gig a night, which was just ludicrous.'

Bluesology's career as a backing band did not get off to a particularly auspicious start. Roy Tempest booked Wilson Pickett, who had just had a Top 20 hit in the UK with 'In the Midnight Hour', for a tour. Pickett was used to top session men backing him. 'He sent over his musical director bloke and I think he expected to be provided with a set of session musicians', says Inkpen. 'I got the distinct impression that we weren't considered experienced enough. Reg had all Wilson Pickett's records so he knew his stuff, but we didn't. We weren't used to being taken through a number and learning it in double-quick speed, which is what you are supposed to do. We made a couple of attempts at one of his numbers and his musical director just said no.'

The initial rejection was understandable given the band's inexperience, which was rectified by the addition of two older hands. By late 1965, Bluesology had expanded into a six-piece with the arrival of trumpeter Pat Higgs and tenor saxophonist Dave Murphy. Older and musically wiser than the existing Bluesologists, apart from Reg, they had much more experience in the music business and were not used to rejection. 'All those American acts used to be very organised,' Pat Higgs has said. 'They'd have their song arrangements all written out and expected the backing band to be the same. Bluesology had never used arrangements. Before we went up for the next audition, I had to scribble a few out.'

Bluesology had more success with their second audition, for the soul star Major Lance, famed in the US for 'Um, Um, Um, Um, Um, Um', written by his school chum Curtis Mayfield. Covered by Wayne Fontana and the Mindbenders, it had reached Number 5 in the UK in 1964. 'We were actually doing quite well, [we were] certainly adequate for what he wanted,' says Inkpen. However, Bluesology were soon upstaged by Robin, Major Lance's knockabout musical director.

'Robin was a fantastic guitarist,' says Inkpen. 'He would come on and do a number with the band before Major Lance came on, and then he would introduce him and he'd come on stage in a big flurry. One night we were playing at the Q Club, and Mick Jagger, Keith Richards and

Alexis Korner were in the audience. We did our bit and Major Lance did his bit and went off, and Robin decided he would come out again with us at about 3 o'clock in the morning. He did his speciality number, which was playing the guitar round the back of his head, and with his teeth, and brought the house down. This was long before Jimi Hendrix did the same thing. He got fired by Lance on the last night for being too flash.'

Bluesology underwent the most exhausting of apprenticeships. They toured with Patti Labelle and the Bluebells (featuring future Supreme Cindy Birdsong), backed the Drifters for two weeks, and toured with Doris Troy and with the Inkspots. The Inkspots, big in the 1940s and 1950s with their genteel close harmonies on hits like 'Only You', were clearly incongruous figures on the mid-1960s circuit. 'They were fantastic men. The stories they told were wonderful,' says Rex Bishop. 'They had been in the business for donkey's years. We'd do a warm-up set for them and then they did the main set. It really was a con job, because the kids we were playing to had never heard of the Inkspots. I often thought we would get bricks thrown at us.

'I remember one gig, I think it was in Sheffield. It was in the early hours of the morning and the audience looked somewhat under the weather through either booze or drugs. We did our opening set, and then on came the Inkspots. I remember a lot of uneasiness in the audience, like, what the hell is this? We hit the finale number, the high point of which was a clarinet solo by one of the Inkpots. What he did was he dismantled the clarinet as he played, and as he got down to the reed part the audience started yelling and screaming because they were so high.'

There were no road managers and Bluesology were responsible for schlepping their heavy equipment up stairs, down into cellars and in and out of vans up to three times a night. 'There were clubs we played in that you'd never heard of,' said Elton years later. 'There were posters outside saying things like, "Tonight, the fantastic Patti Labelle and her Blue Bellies".'

Also on the circuit was 29-year-old 'Fat Boy' Billy Stewart, famed for a blues version of the George Gershwin standard 'Summertime' and a man who certainly lived up to his appellation. 'He was a gigantic man. He seemed to be ill, as well, and needed to pee quite a lot,' records Inkpen. 'That meant continually stopping on the way to and from gigs for calls of nature. Despite this, he had a great voice and a knockout act. Unlike some of the "stars" we backed, he was a kind man with a lot of patience with his inexperienced band.'

Patti Labelle was a different kettle of fish altogether. For the only rehearsal they had before the first gig at the Scotch Of St James the very next day, the band were presented with the wrong parts. 'It was a small, cellar-type club, done out in Scottish plaid walls and other Highlands bits and pieces,' says Inkpen. 'One feature was a dirty big stagecoach on the already none-too-large stage. The audience consisted of the Beatles, the Who, the Animals, several big-time record producers and numerous film and show business folk. Terrifying! The girls were a knockout, and the big-time audience went mad. But we never seemed good enough to please Patti.'

Bluesology were by now playing some famous rock 'n' roll venues, including the Whisky A-Go-Go and the Pink Flamingo in London, made famous by Georgie Fame. A gig with Doris Troy at the Cavern Club in Liverpool in 1966 was memorable for the fact that the toilets overflowed. By now, Reg was equipped with a new organ, a Vox Continental, which was painted a disgusting orange colour. During all this time, he had remained a relatively subdued stage presence. Offstage, he kept touring spirits up with his Stanley Unwin, Eric Morecambe and Goons impressions and seemed uninterested in partying after gigs.

The London hipsters used to frequent all the same clubs and pubs and Bluesology were a minor presence throughout the mid-1960s. Gary Osborne, then a teenaged A & R man, and later to become a songwriting partner to the future Elton John, recalls: 'I used to see Elton playing with Bluesology down at the Cromwellian. He was just another guy in a band. We were on nodding acquaintance – if you go to a club regularly, you end up on nodding acquaintance with a lot of people. They were one of the better bands. If you watched Bluesology you came away with the image of the lead singer in your mind – he was a good-looking guy and had quite a strong voice.'

Another musician fated to work with Elton was B.J. Cole. He retains much the same impression of a man devoid of anything that would mark him out from the pack. 'That's the thing about him back then, if you talk to other musicians who knew him at that time, he was one of us really,' he says. 'It wasn't him and us. He was definitely as much a musician as all of us.'

Bluesology's second single, 'Mr Frantic', was released on Fontana in 1966. Again, the B-side, a cover of 'Everyday (I Have The Blues)' by B.B. King, sung confidently by Stewart Brown, was more representative of the band's live repertoire. But it was Reg Dwight's second self-penned effort that was chosen as the A-side. Like 'Come Back Baby', it's a middling effort musically, but with its charming naivety and more obvious soul influence it was hooky enough to possibly be a hit. Lyrically, it was as blandly derivative as their debut single.

Reg sang, 'When you hold me, when you thrill me/ My heart sets on fire' in verse one, adding, 'You know I love you, baby' in verse two, just in case the message isn't getting across. He delivers a reassuringly domesticated 'We could be such a happy pair/ And I promise to do my share' in the penultimate verse, before cautioning in the final knockout blow of a couplet: 'And if you were to go away now/ My heart couldn't stand the pain'. '"Mr Frantic" crept into the bottom half of the charts. Well, when I say into the charts, I mean about Number 150,' recalls Inkpen. 'For a brief moment, it was actually selling a few records.'

By 1966, Bluesology had secured a reputation for being among the UK's top session players. They had experienced, if only vicariously, the adulation, temptations and sheer hard graft that formed part of the mid-1960s club circuit. The promise of a regular income led them to give up their day jobs and Reg handed in his notice at Mills Music. A photograph of him from the time, taken in what looks like a photo booth, shows him staring at the camera, slightly nerdy of countenance like a modern-day alternative comedian, with the photogenic Patti Labelle and Cindy Birdsong smiling sexily in a slightly out-of-focus foreground. For all his musical talent and drive, Reg Dwight still seemed a world away from where he wanted to be.

The Bluesology members were earning £15 to £20 a week from their new professional status. But the relentless pacing of the gigs was hard to get used to. 'There was one famous Roy Tempest booking,' remembers Mick Inkpen, still wincing at the memory of an 18-hour stint backing Billy Stewart. 'We played an afternoon lounge session at an American servicemen's gig in Earls Court. We had to get the gear in through the front door, up two flights of carpeted stairs and into the sergeants' mess bar then set it up. We did our gig, an hour-and-a-half, and then we packed up and drove the four hours to Birmingham for around 10pm. There were two dance halls in Birmingham that had some sort of association with each other and we played both, then we came back into London to do a late-night gig. It was the hardest I'd ever worked in my life. I was just fading away.'

Understandably, Bluesology soon left Roy Tempest and signed to Marquee Enterprises. The Marquee in Soho's Wardour Street had started life as a trad jazz club but had gradually moved over to rhythm and blues and soul music. Among the regulars there were the Spencer Davis Group, Graham Bond, Chris Farlow, Long John Baldry, Rod Stewart and the Rolling Stones. For the band, this was a significant step up the ladder and led to support slots at the Marquee for bands including Manfred Mann. Around this time the band also played on the same bill as a fast-emerging talent, the Who.

'We did a gig with them on Brighton Pier,' says Rex Bishop. 'They smashed the place up, did the lights in and everything. Then we went on and we were tame in comparison. We were also on the same bill as Georgie Fame and Spencer Davis. I was just proud that our band was on the same stage as them. But when you heard a band like the Spencer Davis Group at the Flamingo, you knew they were streets ahead of you. You looked at them and thought, Jesus, that band's got potential. They were writing their own material. You used to think, Christ, they're a much better band than we are.'

Reg Dwight also harboured similar feelings of inadequacy. 'We just did mediocre things,' he was to reflect on Bluesology. 'We never starved, but it was such a mundane experience. I remember seeing the Move in

Birmingham and saying they were going to make it. Sure enough, they made it. You used to see other people coming up and you'd think, here I am, plodding on. I always wanted to make it and I really got pissed off.'

In addition to backing established stars in the mid-to-late 1960s, Bluesology also played their own gigs, including in Sweden, the south of France and that obligatory stopping-off point for the journeyman live band, Hamburg. Bluesology were sent over to tour Germany and once again the working day was soul-crushingly hard. 'We were playing in a place called the Top 10 Club on the Reeperbahn in Hamburg, just round the corner from the Star Club where the Beatles played,' remembers Inkpen. 'We were there for a month, on duty eight hours a night. One hour on, one hour off, for eight hours. You finished at about midnight if you got the early start, but if you were really unlucky you got the late-night start. We had no time off at all. But we certainly knew how to play when we came back – we were so tight. None of the acts had enough material to fill two hours and you simply had to learn enough music to be able to fill four hours, and then repeat it again and again.'

At this point, Bluesology underwent the first of many line-up changes. Already disillusioned, Rex Bishop left after one particularly unlucky gig with the Inkspots in Soho, when an audience member barged into the PA, knocked it over and smashed his guitar. 'It pissed me off no end, because it meant I couldn't play for the rest of the evening. And I went home and thought about it and said, "Screw it, I've had it." I never played the guitar again. I liked everything Bluesology did until we became a backing band and then I just felt the group was going nowhere.'

At the same time, the newer recruits, Pat Higgs and Dave Murphy, were turning out to be not on the same wavelength as the rest of the band. 'They were older than we were, in their mid-twenties, and they could both read music,' says Inkpen. 'I think they thought we should be picking up the ball a bit quicker, so they used to take the mickey out of Rex mercilessly at times. And I was getting much the same treatment as Rex, to be honest. I was young and inexperienced and I didn't think they were being very fair really. It wasn't a friendly atmosphere, let's put it that way.'

Mick Inkpen also found himself surplus to requirements pretty soon afterwards: 'Bluesology were offered another tour with Patti Labelle. I got a phone call from Arnold Tendler, who said that Patti Labelle has told us that we couldn't do the tour unless we found another drummer. They wanted a funky drummer and funky wasn't something I was interested in being. It was a hard life for the two years I was in the band and when I left it took me about six months to recover.'

December 1966 was the most important month in Bluesology's life to date. On the 11th, they appeared on the support bill at the Saville Theatre, Shaftesbury Avenue, for the only London appearance of one of Reg's rock 'n' roll heroes, Little Richard. By now, just two of the founding members – Stewart Brown and Reg himself – remained. David Murphy on sax had been joined by Freddie Gandy on bass, Chris Bateson on trumpet and Paul Gale on drums.

More significant for the band, and, ultimately, for Reg Dwight himself, was the intervention of one of the 1960s' most iconic singers, Long John Baldry. Was he the man who discovered Elton John? 'I found the whole band in the gambling casino on the Cromwell Road opposite the V&A, the Cromwellian Club,' Baldry told the broadcaster Spencer Leigh in 2002. 'The ground floor was Harry's Bar and in the basement there was live music and this night it was Bluesology. Reg was playing keyboards and I gave them a job. They were just off to Sweden to do some dates and I said, "I can start using you as soon as you come back. Meet me at Birmingham University." Their ferry was late, and I was wondering what I was going to do, but Brian Auger and Julie Driscoll were doing a date there, so they did the first set with me, and lo and behold Bluesology then turned up, looking very seasick, and they did the second set.' Mick Inkpen remembers that Baldry had been interested in the band for several months before he left. 'We were playing the Cromwellian on a regular basis, and I well remember the (unwelcome) interest Long John Baldry showed in our Stewart!'

At 25 years of age, six-foot-seven Baldry was already a well-established artist by the time he made the invitation to Bluesology. He was one of the first British artists to sing the blues in clubs. In 1962 he had

performed in Alexis Korner's Blues Incorporated, Britain's first ampli-
fied blues group, an outfit which, at various stages, included pre-fame
Charlie Watts, Mick Jagger and Jack Bruce in its ranks. Eric Clapton
has said that he was inspired to become a musician after seeing a Baldry
gig at the Marquee Club.

In 1963, Long John had also played with a pre-Zeppelin Jimmy
Page in Cyril Davis and the All Stars, before forming Long John Baldry
and the Hoochie Coochie Men in 1965. The singer in this collective
would be none other than 19-year-old Rod Stewart, discovered quite
by chance when, waiting for a train in Twickenham, Baldry spotted
him playing the harmonica and busking a Muddy Waters song. Stewart
joined Brian Auger and Julie Driscoll, becoming the second vocalist and
harmonica player for Baldry's latest project, the Steam Packet. Baldry
was also friends with Paul McCartney and had the Rolling Stones
support him for the Stones' first concert at the Marquee. Quite simply,
Long John Baldry was not only supremely well connected, but also had
an uncanny knack of spotting future talent.

Over the next two years with Long John Baldry, the ever-changing
and expanding collective called Bluesology would see the arrival of,
among others, the singers Marsha Hunt (the future star of *Hair* and the
inspiration for the Stones' 'Brown Sugar') and Alan Walker; the saxophonist Elton Dean, later to work with the Keith Tippett Sextet and
Soft Machine; the trumpeter Marc Charig, who joined on Elton Dean's
recommendation and who later also played with Tippett; the guitarist
Neil Hubbard, who later played with Joe Cocker, Bryan Ferry and Roxy
Music; and Caleb Quaye, the gopher in Denmark Street, now flexing
his muscles as a professional musician.

Reg Dwight was by now 'a frustrated singer', according to Elton Dean.
'His problem was that we already had three regular singers: Alan Walker,
Stu Brown and Marsha Hunt – not that she was a terribly good singer
but she looked great. Bluesology became a bit of a struggle. I remember
being on one tour backing some awful one-hit wonders called the Paper
Dolls.' Relegated to fourth-choice singer, Reg's disaffection with the band
grew and he seemed to be simply going through the motions. He would

present his own songs at rehearsals, but none ever made the live set. According to Long John Baldry, he was now prone to the odd 'screaming fit' too, as his morale dropped. Elton Dean nicknamed him 'Bunter', 'because he was a little bit portly and always used to wear striped blazers'. biographer Philip Norman writes that it was around this time that Reg began taking amphetamines to control his weight.

Live, the band had certainly become technically proficient. 'I went to see them at the Marquee and was very impressed with how tight they were,' says Mick Inkpen. 'They were a really good rocking outfit, in fact, doing just what I would like to have done with them. Marsha Hunt was very impressive, with a great voice for the blues numbers and a truly amazing Afro hairdo.' Bluesology would have one last crack at breaking into the UK charts. 'Since I Found You Baby', backed by 'Just A Little Bit', was released in October 1967 on the Polydor Label and credited to Stu Brown and Bluesology. Both songs were co-written by none other than all-round entertainer Kenny Lynch.

But by the spring of 1967, and with the newly revamped Bluesology failing to match the success of his earlier Steam Packet project, Baldry moved into the cabaret circuit as the John Baldry Show, At the end of the year, Baldry as solo artist would have his first and only UK Number 1 with the big smoochy ballad 'Let The Heartaches Begin'. For the 22-year-old Reg Dwight, this was a turning point. 'I think that's the graveyard of musicians, playing cabaret. I think I'd rather be dead than work in cabaret,' he felt. In the summer of 1967, quite by chance, he was offered a way out.

LIBERTY

WANTS TALENT

ARTISTES/ COMPOSERS/ SINGER-MUSICIANS TO FORM NEW GROUP

*Call or write Ray Williams for appointment or mail audition tape or disc
to 11 Albemarle Street, London W1. Tel. Mayfair 7362.*

So ran an ad in the UK magazine *New Musical Express* on June 17, 1967.

The man behind the launch of Liberty Records was Ray Williams. Already a major figure on the London scene, by 1967 his CV included *Ready Steady Go!* with Cathy McGowan and three years of PR work with artists such as the Kinks and Sonny and Cher. He shared a Mayfair flat just off Berkeley Square with DJ Phil Martin and Simon Hayes, who ran a pop PR company, Ace Relations. Williams was still in his teens when the American label Liberty, who had been part of the British EMI group but were now setting up their own independent label, asked him to be head of A&R.

By the summer of 1967, the climate of British popular music had begun to change dramatically under the force of the counterculture. Music, fashion, the underground press – in fact, the entire spectrum of the popular arts – were undergoing an accelerated maturation. Just four years earlier, the Beatles had serenaded the Queen at the Royal Command Performance, their music a brilliant if undemanding blend of Scouse tunesmithery and American beat music. Now, in mid-1967, they seemed unrecognisable from their earlier selves. *Sgt Pepper's Lonely Hearts Club Band*, released that summer, heralded in a new era. A brilliant collage of high and low art, orchestration and mystical pop melodies, it gave British music a whole new depth. The same year, Pink Floyd seemed to be edging towards an even more radical future, a pop world in which sight as well as sound would work on the minds of a febrile new youth culture. With its crashing volume, trippy ambience, space-age sonic zooms and strobing, psychedelic live show, Floyd's was a music that perfectly matched the fried minds of many an L.S.D user.

Yet perhaps more directly influential on the future Elton John that summer was the sound of Procol Harum's UK Number 1, 'A Whiter Shade Of Pale'. The dreamy, surrealistic lyrics and the saddened, stately organ music were ethereal and unique. Interestingly, the song had developed, according to the generally accepted dictates of popular music, 'the wrong way round'. At a time when the vast majority of pop songs started as pieces of music first, with the lyrics added later, Procol Harum's Keith Reid wrote the lyric first and then the music was layered on top. The possibility now arose for literate and intelligent lyricists, even poets, to become part of the pop world.

Reg was on tour with Bluesology in Newcastle when he read Liberty's ad. Having put pen to paper, he was invited down to speak to Ray Williams at the newly formed label. 'I didn't know what I wanted to do, I just knew I wanted to come off the road,' Elton would later tell Paul Gambaccini. 'I said, I can't write lyrics and I can't really sing well, because I wasn't singing with Bluesology, but I think I can write songs.' Reg was asked to audition five songs in a recording studio. Struggling to find enough songs to attempt, he ended up performing five Jim Reeves numbers that he used to sing at home. He was turned down flat and left with the recommendation from Ray Williams to make some demos and try Dick James Music, the publishers of the Beatles' music.

There was another applicant who couldn't sing and couldn't even play. 'I remember he said that basically he was a poet, but that he thought that some of his work might fit well with music,' remembers Ray Williams. 'However, he didn't write music, so he asked me if I knew anybody who did.' The poet's name was Bernard Taupin.

CHAPTER 3

ONE ROOM

'When we signed with Dick, it was like two years of misery, writing garbage.'

Elton John speaking to *Playboy* in 1976

'Old '67 what a time it was
What a time of innocence.'

'Old 67'; lyrics: Bernie Taupin; music: Elton John

Reg Dwight is lying on the kitchen floor. He has placed his head inside the gas oven, turned it on (low) and, on first inspection, it looks as if he is trying to commit suicide. But this is no ordinary suicide attempt. A pillow has been placed inside the cooker for Reg's head and all the windows have been left open. This would be no Sylvia Plath-like ending for the 21-year-old musician, no real attempt at 'gasphyxiation'. In fact, as suicide attempts go, this one is straight out of a Woody Allen film.

Reg's new friend and writing partner Bernie Taupin finds him that day back in 1968. The only problem is, though, that Bernie can't stop laughing. He has walked out of his bedroom and, smelling gas and thinking the cooker is on, he has come into the kitchen to find the near-farcical scene of a grown man enacting a dummy suicide run. But still, despite the funny side, it's obvious that there's *something* wrong with his flatmate. After all, even comedy suicide attempts are indicative of something other than a penchant for the bizarre.

Reg now lives in Furlong Road, Islington. He is engaged to Linda

Ann Woodrow, two years older and four inches taller than him and, potentially, several thousand pounds richer for, by chance, she is heiress to the pickled onion empire that is America's Epicure Products. Her upper-middle-class schooling has included a select girls' academy in Reigate and a finishing school in Eastbourne. Linda's inheritance is in a trust fund and, in order to provide for herself and her relatively impecunious spouse-to-be, she works as a secretary. The engagement ring on her finger, which cost a whopping £200, has been bought using her own money. The cake has been ordered, the invitations to a June wedding sent out and there have even been discussions about soft furnishings, but the alarm bells are ringing in Reg's head.

Reg is disillusioned. His musical career is marked by frustration. At 21, he sees others catching the train to stardom, but for himself, so long trapped in the relative mediocrity of Bluesology on the club circuit, it looks as if his career is destined to be one of middling success as a journeyman pro. Reg also feels trapped by the new domestic life that lies ahead of him. In truth, he is in denial about his feelings and too stubborn to admit to the impending mistake that would be his marriage to Linda.

It seems that almost everyone he knows is against the wedding. His mum, Sheila, according to Reg always a good judge of character, is hardly enthusiastic. Neither is his now closest friend, Bernie, an aspiring lyricist newly down from his home in Lincolnshire and trying to make it as a songwriter in London. His fiancée sees a more sensible, more conformist future ahead for her husband, one in which the music is to be put on the back-burner in favour of a 'proper' career, a regular income, a place of their own and a family of little Dwights. Nothing wrong with any of that, of course, but Reg knows that the first songs he's written with Bernie show promise. His musical calling is still an unstoppable force. How can he give all that up before it has even properly started?

One night, a few months after the 'suicide attempt', Reg is out drinking at the Bag O' Nails in Kingly Street, near Carnaby Street, with Bernie and Long John Baldry. P.J. Proby is one of the punters that night in a bar that is fast becoming one of the hippest hangouts for the new rock fraternity. It is here that John McVie will propose to his fellow Fleetwood Mac member Christine Perfect and it is also here that Paul McCartney has just met his future wife, Linda Eastman. But tonight the emphasis isn't on making engagements, but breaking them.

Bernie and Reg are hideously drunk. Baldry bites the bullet and lays it on the line to Reg straight: 'Oh, my dear, for God's sake you're getting married and you love Bernie more than this girl. This is ridiculous. Put a stop to it now, Reggie.' It doesn't occur to the incredibly naïve Reg Dwight that Long John Baldry is gay and that he has already probably guessed that Reg is too. 'If you marry this woman you'll destroy two lives – hers and yours.' The advice that Baldry gives is life-changing and, as the singer would so publicly announce seven years later, it 'saves' his life that night, or, at the very least, helps set it along the path it has travelled ever since.

At about 4am, Bernie and Reg stumble back from the West End bar to Linda Woodrow's flat in Islington, setting off a car alarm in their early morning stagger home. Reg enters the flat and tells Linda that the wedding is off. For his fiancée, it's a huge shock. She breaks down and, in a last-ditch attempt to keep him, tells Reggie that she is pregnant, the one scenario that might make him change his mind. Yet even this lie can't change a mind made up. For Reg, a huge weight has been lifted from his shoulders.

The next morning, it's all over. Step-dad Derf comes round and helps Reg move out, back to his parents' maisonette in Frome Court, Pinner. Bernie follows him a few days later. Linda and Reg never speak again. So ends Reg's early brush with heterosexuality. The experience would not be repeated for another 16 years.

* * *

Reg Dwight and Linda Woodrow had met on Christmas Eve 1967, when Reg played a gig with Bluesology at a cabaret club in Sheffield. He had played knight in shining armour to her damsel-in-distress. 'At

59

the time, Linda was going out with a midget disc jockey – he drove a Mini with special pedals and everything,' Elton remembered a few years later. 'But he used to beat her up.' According to this story, Reg 'rescued' Linda from the clutches of the DJ known as The Mighty Atom before any further fireworks ensued.

Linda, however, subsequently told Elton biographer Philip Norman that the DJ was not her boyfriend, just her escort on the night she met Reg. 'We clicked straight away,' she said. 'He asked me to see his next gig. I found him funny and enjoyed his company.' Reg told everyone he was in love and, for the first six months, the two appeared to be happy in each other's company. They spoke frequently on the phone, Linda in Sheffield and Reg in London, until she made the decision to move down to be with him on a permanent basis. Reg moved out of his mum and step-dad's maisonette in Frome Court, Pinner, his home for the whole of his adolescence and teenage years and also, at the time, home to Bernie Taupin. Soon after, Bernie followed Reg to Linda Woodrow's flat in Furlong Road, Islington. 'It was a given that where Elton went, he did,' Linda told the *Sunday Mirror* in 2005. 'Neither of them paid rent. I paid for everything – the bills, the food. But I didn't mind – I was in love and wanted to be with him.'

But there was always something wrong, according to Reg. For a start-off, Linda liked Mel Tormé and found Reg's obsession with the pop music scene to be not quite the thing she had in mind on which to build a future. 'She didn't think that music was a good career move,' Elton was to affirm many years later. 'She was trying to get me to give it all up. She didn't like my songs.'

With hindsight, there was also something not quite right for Linda about Reg, particularly in the bedroom. 'Looking back, and when I'd had other boyfriends after Elton, I realised something was not right with that side of things,' she has said. 'He was inexperienced and lost his virginity to me. But even allowing for that, he didn't show much interest in me sexually and didn't pay me very much attention. We didn't have sex very often. But I just thought that was the way it was at the time.' In fact, according to Linda, Reg didn't seem overly keen on anything much, apart from his own particular interests. 'He never took me out for meals or treated me,' said Linda. 'He spent most of his money on clothes, records and drinking. He seemed to assume I'd pay for everything else.'

After living with his parents, life at Furlong Road was very different for Reg Dwight. Linda insisted that he and Bernie did their fair share of domestic chores. Bernie was to admit to being 'shit-scared' of his landlady. He moaned that he wasn't even allowed to put a poster of Simon and Garfunkel up on his bedroom wall, so strict were her house rules. 'She was odd, very odd,' said one of Elton's friends at the time. 'A very dominating person. And the funny thing was that she never looked the same twice. Every day she seemed to have on a different wig. She always had this dog with her, too.' This dog was allowed to defecate on the newspaper provided in the entrance hall of Furlong Road. Bernie used to enter the house singing under his breath (to the tune of 'Old MacDonald Had A Farm'): 'Here a turd, there a turd, everywhere a turd-turd.'

Yet Reg and Linda's relationship was not as peculiar as all that. It was obvious that Reg, at least initially, had a lot of affection for Linda, and Linda was very keen on Reg. Now a mature 21, the pressure was on for Reg to have some sort of relationship, and the middle-class Linda was not so odd a bedfellow for the well-mannered, shy boy from Pinner. Linda put Elton's difficult moods down to his frustrations in the music business, rather than to any doubts he might have about their future together. With hindsight, though, it was obvious that Reg's sexuality was not what she had thought it was. Reg didn't lack a libido; he just didn't fancy women 'He [Long John Baldry] knew I was gay and told me I had to get used to it or else it would destroy my life,' Elton has said. Reg's reaction to the split, however, was to retreat into his music. Linda 'frightened me off sex for so long that I don't really remember. I think it was probably a good year or two.'

The 1968 'suicide attempt' would be the first in a succession of very real cries for help over the next years. The hissy fits (described by those around him at the time as 'Reg's little moments'), the petulance, the frustration at his relatively low status as a professional musician and, perhaps more importantly, the dawning realisation that he might indeed be gay were overpowering emotions for a naturally shy, still naive man.

In fact, Reg had been living with a man, but in a purely platonic relationship. Eighteen-year-old Bernie Taupin was the brother Reggie had always longed for, but never had. He was born on May 22, 1950, in the village of Anwick, near Sleaford in Lincolnshire. While still a child, he and his family moved to the charmingly-named village of Owmby-by-Spital, where his father, Robert, worked as a farm manager at Maltkiln Farm. His mother, Daphne, was a housewife who had been well educated and had studied French and Russian.

'The county of Lincolnshire, for all its efforts, will never win prizes as one of England's fairest,' wrote Taupin in the 1980s. Yet the lyricist had a happy childhood in a relatively pleasant semi-rural part of England where the North and the East meet. There were cold winters and, initially at least, no electricity, along with the harsh reality of the ration book. Bernie's first memory is of crawling on a rug in front of the Aga as his mother busied herself with the daily chores. 'I was blessed with really great parents, parents who never challenged me, never asked me why I did what I did,' Taupin has said. 'They were always there, backing me up.'

A big influence on young Bernie was his maternal grandfather, John Leonard Patchett Cort, affectionately known to his grandson as 'Poppy'. With an MA from Cambridge, he taught classics, and fired the pre-pubescent imagination with a world of wisdom, words, and fantastic stories. Throughout his early school career, Bernie was one of those students who was strong in one area (English language and litera-ture) but useless in others (for Bernie, mathematics was an unbreakable code). When it was time for him to sit the eleven-plus, an examina-tion designed to sort out the wheat from the chaff in terms of future academic potential, his lack of dexterity with numbers meant that he failed conclusively. This meant schooling, not at the local grammar school that his elder brother now attended, but at the secondary modern in Market Rasen.

Yet Bernie had more than enough to occupy his adolescent years. Boys born in the baby-boom era were fed on a cultural diet, both in the movies and on television, which seemed to consist of just two things. The first was tales of wartime heroism, principally taking as their subject matter the then recently-concluded Second World War, in which common sense, pluck, and the British bulldog spirit always triumphed over the machinations of the evil enemy (played by Englishmen with bad German accents). The second staple of any adolescent's Sunday afternoon was Hollywood westerns and B-movies, the product of an American culture keen to promote its past as a daring battle of Man against Nature, settler against Native American and heroic outsider against the law, all wrapped up in one big thrilling package of shoot-outs, ambushes, massacres and midnight raids.

For the young Bernie, it was the Wild West that mattered. The new songs he heard on Radio Luxembourg in the early 1960s seemed to confirm the mystery and endless imagination of the American Dream. Although he was sold on the native skiffle of Lonnie Donegan (with his English take on American culture, he was also a crucial early influence on Elton) and was a paid-up member of the Joe Brown fan club, it was the likes of 'Ring Of Fire' by Johnny Cash and 'El Paso' by the country star Marty Robbins that set his imagination racing. These were brilliant narratives set in a mythical world. It was all as far removed from the rain-lashed acres of Lincolnshire farmland as he could imagine.

Back at school, and for hours outside it, Bernie consumed literature with an appetite. He poured over the *Oxford Book of English Verse* and fell in love with the great narrative poets. Like his grandfather, who died when Bernie was just nine, his mother used to read to a child with an almost insatiable capacity for all things literary. 'The things I loved more than anything else weren't so much the odes and the short love poems,' Taupin said years later. 'It wasn't about Byron and Shelley and Keats, it was more about Tennyson and Coleridge. They were like adventure stories and that's what I loved. They were really like reading *Boy's Own*, only they were better written. When I first heard Johnny Cash, Johnny Horton and Marty Robbins, the things that excited me were the story songs.'

Horton's 'North To Alaska' together with Marty Robbins' *Gunfighter Ballads And Trail Songs*, captured Bernie's imagination with their patent truthfulness in a way that the B-movie world of the Lone Ranger and Hopalong Cassidy now so evidently could not. 'To write a story and put it to music, I thought that was wonderful,' said Bernie. 'Then I got obsessed with Americana and from there it was a natural progression to country music and people like Woody Guthrie who documented American social life.' Taupin wanted to write story songs and poems and, as a teenager, devoted much of his spare time to writing descriptive poetry.

Here's a sample of the early Bernie from his school magazine of 1966:

'Klu *[sic]* Klux clan the hooded men,
Who kill in packs for segregation
Nail firey *[sic]* crosses to their doors.
In Alabama like starving rats, despite the interegation *[sic]* laws.'

When it came to actual music, British pop idols also had their place in Bernie's record collection, although they seemed to be less loved than their more exotic American counterparts. Unlike the teenage Reg Dwight, Bernie was allowed to wear his collarless jackets and Chelsea boots with Cuban heels, and to attempt his own version of the mop-top hairstyle that was all the rage in mid-1960s Britain, albeit with little success: 'The new hairstyle I had begged the barber to create for me looked a lot like Henry V and not in the slightest like George Harrison.'

Bernie also dated girls and had his normal share of teenage romances and thrills. He drank in a pub in Market Rasen, played snooker and watched, at first hand, as the noisiness of Saturday nights ended in territorial violence and scuffles between gangs of youths fuelled by a liberal flow of beer. After leaving school in 1966 he worked briefly in the machine room at the local newspaper. This menial job wasn't the sort to fire the imagination of a would-be reporter.

'I couldn't stand it,' Bernie later admitted. 'It was one of those horrible, Northern factory-type machine rooms with very high skylights, very dark and gloomy, and little men walking around asking for their sixpence a week to join the union. I just wasn't cut out for that. I got fired in the end for trying to find another job during working hours.' Bernie then enjoyed, or rather endured, stints working as a fruit-machine mechanic and then on a local chicken farm. One of his tasks was to cart hundreds of dead birds to be incinerated after an outbreak of fowl pest. He told Philip Norman: 'I've got a photograph of myself bundled up against the wind, surrounded by all these dead bodies, looking like some scene from *The Killing Fields.*'

Bernie, like any other 17-year-old, looked upon the soon-approaching adult world of jobs, responsibilities and relationships with a certain fore-boding. Like Reg Dwight, he saw the Liberty Records advertisement in the *NME.* Reg had answered the call-to-arms with an application care-fully drafted with the help of his mother. Bernie's mum would likewise play a role – an even more important one – in the future career of her son. 'I had been writing poetry. It was all psychedelic, "Canyons of Your Mind" stuff,' he has said. 'I couldn't play any instruments and I still can't, but I can hear melodies in my head when I write. So I wrote a letter saying I needed someone to do the music for my words… I never mailed it though… just threw it away. My mother found it in a wastebasket and posted it.' Later, however, Taupin was to modify the tale. 'That's sort of like a fairy tale, isn't it?' he told Paul Gambaccini in 1973. 'It didn't happen like that. It wasn't like, "Oh, what's this letter my son has thrown into the garbage? A letter! I must post it!" She prob-ably said, "You should do it, you should do it," but it was never a matter of grappling with the garbage.'

At Liberty, Ray Williams was about as impressed with Bernie Taupin as he was by the audition tape of Reg Dwight. They both had some-thing, yet, as individuals they didn't appear to have what it took to make it in a music business now on the verge of a change that would have been unthinkable just five years previously. The massive success of Bob Dylan and the Beatles, with their self-penned compositions, had changed the way the industry saw the development of new talent. There was, of course, still a place in the music business of the late 1960s for songwriters who wrote to order and produced a portfolio of songs for established stars to record. But there was also a smaller, and far more progressive, wing of the British music scene that was breaking away from this old style of music production. The days of London's Tin Pan Alley, of ranks of underpaid and overworked songsmiths writing to supply a demand, were disappearing fast. The task of writing songs was now being taken over by the performers themselves.

The same Liberty ad from the summer of 1967 had brought to Ray Williams' attention the brilliantly eccentric Bonzo Dog Doo-Dah Band, the singer-songwriter Jeff Lynne (later to find international fame in the Move, Electric Light Orchestra, and Traveling Wilburys), and the songwriter Mike Batt, the voice of the Wombles and writer of dozens of major hits for singers including Art Garfunkel, David Essex and Elkie Brooks and, more recently, the discoverer and sponsor of singer-songwriter Katie Melua. Williams' commercial antennae were nothing if not finely tuned.

Ray Williams had told Bernie that 'if he was up these parts, he should come and see me'. Of course, the idea that Bernie would be 'just passing through' London was somewhat fanciful. To all intents and purposes, Lincolnshire marked the boundaries of all Taupin knew. Williams passed Bernie's sheaf of lyrics in need of a decent melody to Reggie Dwight and, for the first few months of their collaboration, Bernie and Elton wrote separately, Reg Dwight writing music for his as-yet-faceless co-writer. 'We wrote our first 20 songs together before we ever met,' confirms Elton. Bernie then began travelling to London to stay with his Uncle Henry and Aunt Tati in Putney, making frequent trips back up north to his parents in Lincolnshire.

Williams also dealt with the group the Hollies, and band members Graham Nash, Allan Clarke and Tony Hicks would play a small, but not unimportant, part in the breaking of Reg Dwight. Their acronymic publishing company, Gralto, was part of the massive publishing empire of Dick James, the Beatles publisher and a leading light in

London's Tin Pan Alley. At the time, Williams was also championing another writing partnership from the Midlands, Nicky James and Kirk Duncan, who in turn had founded their own company, whose name was, like Gralto, an ungainly amalgamation of their Christian names Nicky, Ray and Kirk: Niraki Music.

Williams did a deal for Niraki with Gralto, and so brought Nicky James and Kirk Duncan, albeit at one remove, under the umbrella of the Dick James music publishing empire. By the summer of 1967, James and Duncan were producing demos at Dick James' own studio, and kindly offered Reg Dwight the chance to use the studio to try out his new compositions, with a view to offering them to Gralto (a deal which, in the end, failed to materialise). Tony Murray, soon to join the Troggs, would play bass on these demos, with Dave Hinds on drums.

Gralto published Reg's earliest compositions and for a while Graham Nash took an active interest in the new singer-songwriter. Reg's first output contained songs like 'A Little Love Goes A Long Long Way', 'Can't You See It' and 'If You Could See Me Now', all original Dwight compositions, and collaborations with Bernie Taupin on songs like 'A Dandelion Dies In The Wind', 'Velvet Fountain,' (on which Bernie asked: 'Do you believe in faeries?/ For the children's rhymes are in my mind') and 'Scarecrow'. The latter's lyrics went like this: 'Like moths around a light bulb/ Your brain is still bleeding/ From visions and pictures of nature's young raincoat'.

'There must be an album lying around of things like "Scarecrow" and "A Dandelion Dies In The Wind",' said Elton, years later. 'We still have all the lyrics. I found them in a suitcase recently, and I was beside myself with laughter for about two days. I mean, we used to sneer at people who wrote bloody psychedelic lyrics, and there we were, writing the biggest load of old garbage you ever read.'

Reg was surprised, if not a little alarmed, to find that the manager of Dick James' studio was none other than Caleb Quaye, the office boy from Paxton Music who had christened him Billy Bunter and had teased him ever since. But this time, there would no teasing. In its place lay a mutual admiration for each other's talents and a bond of friend-ship that would endure for years.

It was also at Dick James' studios that Reg Dwight and Bernie Taupin would meet for the first time. 'One day I was doing a demo session and noticed him in the corner,' Elton has explained. 'I said, "Oh, are you the lyric writer?" and he said, "Yeah", and we went round the corner for a cup of coffee and that was it, really.' Outwardly, the two couldn't have been more different: Reg was the 'town mouse', Bernie the 'country mouse'. Yet their love of music caused them to bond in a way that, with only minor breaks in transmission, has endured ever since.

Dick James – bald, avuncular and immensely charming – was one of the most dominant figures in the 1960s music business. Born Isaac Vapnick in 1920, he had been a 1950s crooner of middling talent. A generation of baby-boomers remember him as the voice of the theme tune for *The Adventures of Robin Hood*, a song that became a Top 20 UK hit in 1956.

Songwriter Tony Hiller remembers James with much affection. Hiller was the man who had welcomed the Chelsea football team to Mills Music when the teenage Reg Dwight was working there, and who had given Terry Venables a few tips on songwriting. He knew Reg Dwight was a good singer, but had no idea he was a songwriter too. 'Had I known,' he says ruefully today, 'I would have signed him and made a zillion!' Hiller would later become a hugely successful song-writer, penning the 1970s smashes 'United We Stand' and 'Save Your Kisses For Me' for the Brotherhood of Man. But back in the 1950s, he, like Dick James, was just a music man during the classic years of Tin Pan Alley.

'I was selling songs on Denmark Street in 1954,' Hiller says. 'Dick James was working for Bron Music at the time, which was run by Gerry Bron, the actress Eleanor Bron's father. That was the greatest time of our lives. You would go down there and see every artist looking for recording material. Then Dick James left Bron and set up on his own.' What came next was a mixture of extraordinary good fortune and extraordinary prescience. For a while in the early 1960s, James struggled along doing middling business. Then, in 1963, he made a decision that would turn him into a music industry legend.

The record producer George Martin had hawked the Beatles around almost every major music publisher in London in 1963 and was shown the door by everyone but Dick James. James took a gamble on the untried quartet from Liverpool and it paid off big time. In 1963, he formed Northern Songs, a publishing company that would handle original material. By default, James managed to position himself very firmly in the vanguard of the new order. He was an old-style operator who had happened upon a new kind of singer-songwriter. After the Beatles, the monopoly of London's Tin Pan Alley would be broken as a new wave of young talent took on the onus of writing their material rather than searching for a song elsewhere.

The offices of Dick James Music (DJM) were situated above a branch of the Midland Bank at 71–75 New Oxford Street. They contained a studio that was hardly state-of-the-art. 'It had an old valve desk which was fantastic,' remembers musician B.J. Cole fondly. 'Although it was fairly lo-tech, people liked the sound. The infamous Troggs tape [of the West Country band bickering and arguing] was made at that studio.'

For the new wave of writer-performers, the likes of Dick James were walking anachronisms. 'Dick James was old school, he was part of the 1950s music scene, which was dying pretty fast but they still really controlled the whole thing,' says Cole. 'In essence, he was part of light entertainment and the old way of looking at the record industry. People like Dick drove a hard bargain and artists didn't get much from what they were signing. Compared with modern artistic rights, the whole scene was fairly unfair.' In the Beatles spoof *All You Need Is Cash*, which memorably told the story of the 'pre-fab four' the Rutles, Barry Cryer's old-school Jewish music publisher Dick Jaws was an obvious 'tribute' to James.

'Dick was always shut away in his office, although occasionally he'd stick his head into the recording studio,' says Clive Franks, a man whose professional relationship with the future Elton John as his live soundman would last well over 30 years. Franks was back then fresh out of school and making his way up the ladder at Dick James Music, a route that would take him from messenger boy to studio engineer. 'Occasionally he would catch us out and we'd be as high as kites – you couldn't see across the control room for smoke.'

Meanwhile, Bernie Taupin had taken the plunge and decided to move down to London on a more permanent basis than occasional stays with his aunt. Sheila and Derf, ever hospitable, said that Reg's new friend could live at Frome Court. So it was then that Bernie and Reg would bunk in together in Reg's bedroom, cramped due to the shared occupancy with Reg's collection of vinyl records. 'He came to me from Lincolnshire with the smallest suitcase you have ever seen,' Elton later said, which was probably just as well given the available space.

A fairly regular visitor to Frome Court over the next couple of years would be Reg's old friend from Bluesology, Mick Inkpen. 'Frome Court was a maisonette, really nothing more than an upstairs flat,' he remembers. 'From the outside it looked like two semi-detached houses, but in actual fact there were four units: two upstairs and two downstairs flats. It was fairly compact. Sheila and Derf only had two bedrooms, so they put bunk beds in Reggie's room and that was that. Bernie lived there for a couple of years until they found their feet. But if it had all gone wrong, he would have just gone back up to Market Rasen, and that would have been the last London would have heard of him.'

Taupin, on the short side, slightly built and certainly more conventionally attractive than Reg, was a self-contained personality. Whereas Reg could play the joker, Taupin tended to remain a quiet but forceful presence sidestage. 'He was a really nice bloke,' remembers Inkpen fondly, 'and very well educated. He'd read very extensively. He put me on to *Lord Of The Rings* – nobody had ever heard of *Lord Of The Rings* before – and Mervyn Peake, which was very trendy at the time.'

The fact that two young men were sharing a room seemed 'fairly innocent at the time,' says Inkpen. Asked many years later if he had fancied Bernie, Elton replied, 'I did. But it was never a sexual thing. I would never leap on him. I just adored him, like a brother. I was in love with him, but not in a physical way. He was the soul mate I'd been looking for all my life.'

Elton's professional relationship with Bernie had started during the last few months of his stint with Bluesology, a stint that came to a close at the end of 1967 when Reg resigned from the band. Now a salaried songwriter at DJM, he didn't need the hassle of life on the road and had tired of being a Bluesologist, seemingly devoid of ambition. Just before his departure, he took it out on his fast-collapsing musical equipment. 'It was all falling to bits,' he explained. 'The organ used to fart and make terrible sounds. At the end, when we were playing the ballrooms, I finally destroyed my amplifier, my Vox 80, by kicking it in during a bingo session.

'We were a second-rate band, trudging up and down the motorway playing "Knock On Wood" for the 115th time,' he reflected. 'Eventually, I couldn't bear the thought of doing that for the rest of my life. But even then I wasn't thinking of becoming a solo artist. I just wanted to get out of the rut and the humdrum boringness of it all.' He developed this theme to *Melody Maker* in 1975: 'I had the courage to leave Bluesology. Up until then I'd always been very weak as far as decisions went. I was always the yes-man at school, frightened of doing something in case I got detention. I was terrified of making mistakes.'

Despite this, looking back at Reg Dwight's lengthy time with Bluesology (about six years in all), it was an invaluable apprenticeship. If nothing else, it had allowed him to 'pay his dues', giving him a certain credibility in the music business of the time. 'I've really had to struggle for what I've got out of life,' he has reflected, 'but when I look back on it now, I honestly enjoyed those early days working for a miserable £15 a week with Bluesology. In retrospect, they weren't the bad times I imagined them to be at the time.'

Towards the end of his stint with the band, whether it was through overwork, the appalling on-the-road diet or, more likely, the fact that he was taking his mother's diet pills, Reg began shedding some pounds. Soon, he was two stone lighter. At the end of a Swedish tour, needing to borrow some trousers, he found he could fit into those of Elton Dean. Mick Inkpen also remembers the image makeover around this time. 'He'd come back from the south of France, I think he'd been there with

Bluesology. He was at a loose end and decided to come and see me. And this was a complete revelation! While they had been in the south of France, there hadn't been that much in the way of food around and they had starved. But he'd also bought a lot of decent clothes for a change. He'd had his hair done, and he was really wearing some quite smooth-looking clothes. I thought, bloody hell, what's going on here?' Gone were the days when, as Elton would later say, he looked like 'a young Reginald Maudling'.

Along with the change of image came another change, one which would probably be the most important of his career. As life-altering changes go, it all happened in minutes. The chance to record a solo single prompted a quick rethink in terms of the name that would appear on the record sleeve. 'Well, I was making a record, and I had to choose a name, because they said, you know, you can't make a record under the name Reg Dwight, because it's never going to – you know – it's not attractive enough. And I agreed with that. I couldn't wait to change my name anyway, because I'm not too fond of the name Reginald. It's a very 1950s name. So I picked Elton because there wasn't – nobody seemed to have the name Elton. And I picked John to go with it. It was done on a bus going from London Heathrow back into the city. And it was done very quickly. So I said, "Oh, Elton John. That's fine."'

In fact, Reg had (with their full approval) taken Bluesologist Elton Dean's first name and combined it with 'John' from Long John Baldry. It was a spontaneous but clever move. Having a first name as your surname wasn't, of course, an entirely new idea in the pop world, as any Cliff Richard or Hank Marvin fan will tell you, but Reg's choice was fresh and distinctive. Moreover, 'Elton John' sounded as if it might be American, again no handicap when it came to selling the singer in the world's largest market.

Dick James eventually signed Elton and Bernie on November 17, 1967. The months of sneaking into the recording studio during dead time and recording late at night were finally over. In the end, it had actually been James' 20-year-old son Steve who had brought the music of Elton and Bernie to his father's attention. He thought it had something and his dad agreed. When Dick invited Elton and Bernie into his office that day in the autumn of 1967, they both thought they were there to be reprimanded for using up studio time. Instead, they would be presented with what they had always dreamt of: a regular wage in return for writing and recording music.

Elton and Bernie were signed to Steve James' record label, This Music ('This' having been chosen because it was an anagram of both 'hits' and 'shit') for a down payment of £50 each, plus £10 a week each as a guarantee against royalties. In return, they were contracted to write at least 18 songs a year for three years. Reg's weekly payment would soon be bumped up to a princely £15.

'I thought, what's so special about this guy?' says Clive Franks. 'I was only earning £7 10s! But I used to go out and get his sandwiches for him and keep him supplied with tea and coffee. He would be sitting in the tiny converted office, with an upright piano, that was now regarded as the Dick James Studio, with egg boxes on the ceiling for soundproofing and cheap Hessian cladding on the wall. It couldn't have been more than 15 feet by 12 feet. The control room was another converted office that was nowhere near the studio. It was halfway down the hall and was connected to the studio via a little black-and-white TV monitor.'

Yet Franks eventually realised there was something special about the newly christened Elton John, something different. To begin with, his knowledge of music was immense. Furthermore, beneath the bubbly, comedic surface, there was a strong determination to succeed. He also looked very different. 'He used to wear lots of different glasses in those days, and quite outrageous clothes for the times,' says Franks. 'It was the hippy era, but he didn't wear the bells and beads like I did. He wore clothes that were different-looking, with bright colours. Of course, back then, one didn't know about the gay scene – or, at least, I didn't. I was living at home with my parents at the time and he used to come over for afternoon tea to play some records. We'd go out to the pictures together. But I could not have foreseen what was coming, the huge international fame. In fact, his music didn't really appeal to me; it was very odd stuff.'

Another member of the team that would go on to launch Elton was Stuart Epps, a friend of Clive Franks who followed his older ex-school chum to Dick James Music. 'There were so many charismatic people around those offices at the time,' recalls Epps. 'There was Graham Nash of the Hollies and, of course, Caleb Quaye. Caleb was probably more charismatic than Elton. He used to play like Jimi Hendrix. But although Elton was just a chubby, funny guy, as soon as I heard his songs and his voice, I thought he was brilliant.'

In late 1967 and early 1968, Bernie Taupin's lyrics were exploring acid-era sensibilities with a childlike naivety. 'His lyrics were very 1960s,' recalls Elton. 'A bit like Traffic, "Hole In My Shoe", and pixies and fairies, and "The Angle Tree" – that was one of the songs we wrote. But I liked the lyrics, in any case.' Those early Taupin creations also included such never-released gems as 'The Year Of The Teddy Bear' and 'Regimental Sgt Zippo'.

However, although it was a time of relatively poor pay, frustration and incredibly hard work, it was also a time of great fun. It was the era before accountants and attorneys took over the music business and turned it into something harsh and corporate. 'Back in 'old '67', as Elton would later sing, people didn't care that much about the money. They really were in it for the fun of making music. It was all very new and exciting for the first wave of post-Beatles performers.

The first Elton John single, 'I've Been Loving You', backed by 'Here's To The Next Time', was released on Philips on March 1, 1968, and was penned solely by Reg Dwight, although Bernie was credited as co-writer. With a reasonably forgettable melody and uninspiring lyrics, it wasn't the best of launches for a solo career. *Top Pop* magazine ran a short article about the single on March 2, under the headline 'Problem: Who's The Star':

Another puzzler. This is Elton John, whose record is called 'I've Been Loving You', on Philips. But the publicity gives equal credit to the writer, Bernard Taupin, and the co-producer, Caleb Quaye, all experienced and highly competent pop men. Come to think of it, it's about time the men behind the discs had more credit. So good for Bernard and Caleb, as well as Elton.

The above might have come straight from the 'jolly good show' school of music journalism which obviously still had a place in the Britain of 1967 (and Bernard Taupin, at 17, might have been surprised to have been called 'experienced'). Nevertheless, it was probably Elton John's first piece of exposure in the music press as a solo artist.

Other songs, lots of them in fact, came and went. 'Baby I Miss You' was a pleasing, if hardly sensational, sing-a-long, while 'You'll Be Sorry To See Me Go' was co-authored with Caleb Quaye. Elton also had the dubious distinction of having a song accepted for the *Song For Europe* qualifier for the *Eurovision Song Contest*, to be aired in January 1969. Unlike today, where the Brits regard the contest with a certain amount of ironic disdain, back in its earlier years Eurovision was taken very seriously indeed. Whole recording careers (and songwriting careers) could be launched on the back of a win or a strong showing in the main contest. 'Can't Go On (Living Without You)', however, finished sixth out of the six songs performed by the UK's entry, Lulu, who went on to be joint-winner of the contest proper with 'Boom-Bang-A-Bang'. 'Thank God!' said Elton years later, fearing the sort of trajectory his career might have taken had he struck gold with his Euro effort. 'My mother was very annoyed though; she sent in reams of postcards. I wrote all the lyrics for it, which Bernie has never forgiven me for. The same as "I've Been Loving You": they're entirely my lyrics, and it's credited to Elton John and Bernie Taupin. But the lyrics are so fucking awful you can spot them a mile away.'

By this time, Elton had accepted that, whatever talents he did possess, they did not include the ability to pen a nifty pop lyric. His previous attempts had been standard clichéd pop schlock. Rather than let his ego take over and pretend that this was something that he could master, if only he had a little time and encouragement, he decided to concentrate on creating winning melodies and vocal lines and, for the most part, let others take care of the words.

According to those who worked at DJM at the time, in 1968 Elton actually produced a whole album's worth of demos. 'They recorded a whole album, but it was never released,' confirms Clive Franks. 'There is a whole album which pre-dated *Empty Sky* sitting somewhere.' Elton co-wrote several songs with Caleb Quaye, an astonishingly talented multi-instrumentalist for his tender years. 'I remember this quote from Eric Clapton from way back,' says Clive Franks. 'The interviewer asked him, "What's it like to be the best guitarist in the world?" Eric answered, "I don't know, you'd better ask Caleb Quaye." Caleb could play anything, but his guitar playing was phenomenal. He was also one of the funniest people around and one of the nicest. He and Elton hit it off, professionally and socially.'

Elton supplemented his income at DJM by moonlighting as guest pianist on several hits around that time. On October 23, 1968, he played piano on comedy group the Barron Knights' single, 'An Olympic Record', a Number 35 hit in the UK released to coincide with the Mexico Olympics. However, the sessions, at Abbey Road, were more significant because of a brush with true greatness. 'In wanders McCartney – he was in Studio 2 and thought he'd pop in and see what the peasants were up to,' Elton has said. 'Me and Bernie Taupin just froze and made some mumbling noises and he said a few things, then sat down and started to play the piano, told us it was the latest thing the band had finished, and it was "Hey Jude". It blew my fucking head apart.'

The pressure was on the new writing team to produce ballad pop material for mainstream acts, the slush-by-numbers material for the light entertainment world catered for by Dick James Music at the time. With its walnut desks and teams of writers, Dick James Music still had the air of a very 'straight' music house. Yet the quality of Bernie and Elton's compositions was not very high. They quickly learnt they couldn't write on demand the commercial offerings that would fit the bill. 'We were writing songs which we knew were crap,' Elton later said. 'And they weren't getting recorded because they were crap.'

With nobody of note covering their compositions, in 1968 Elton John was forced by circumstances to take on the role of performer himself: 'I was sort of pushed into being a singer because nobody recorded our songs. Someone said, "Well, you'd better record them yourself." I never thought when I left Bluesology that I would be a singer or a performer, because I thought, I've had enough of this playing to people eating chicken-in-a-basket, I'll be a songwriter. But once I got a taste of performing, I really liked it.'

What Elton and Bernie needed was some career guidance from a mentor who could tell it how it was. That somebody, the one who provided the much-needed kick up the collective backside, was Steve Brown, a fellow employee of Dick James Music. Brown would emerge as one of the most important figures in the early part of the Elton John story. He was totally committed to Elton's music and offered career guidance at a time when it seemed to Elton and Bernie that they were going nowhere.

'We were so unsuccessful, writing garbage,' was how Elton put it in a 1976 interview with *Playboy*. 'No one ever recorded any of our songs. At this point, we were near to quitting and giving it all up because we were so disillusioned. But Dick had a record promotions man named Steve Brown and we played Steve the commercial stuff we'd written and some of our own stuff. He said, "Well, obviously, your stuff is better than the commercial stuff, you should forget what Dick said," which was a very brave move for him to make, because he was just an employee. He said, "Write exactly what you feel and don't pay any attention to Dick any more."' 'We all thought, who the hell is this guy? How dare he!' remembers Stuart Epps. 'He just walks in and says our top singer-songwriter isn't very good. But he knew Elton was writing to a formula to please Dick, and he was the one who told him to write for himself. From that moment on, Steve really took over Elton's career and I went on to become Steve's assistant.'

There were others at Dick James Music who were equally supportive of Elton and Bernie. Lionel Conway was one of them. Conway had joined Dick James Music in 1964, just after 'Please Please Me' had been a hit for the Beatles. He remembered Paul McCartney coming in one day in 1966 and playing him a song with the working title 'Scrambled Eggs' on the harpsichord. The song would become 'Yesterday'. By the time of Elton and Bernie's arrival on the scene, Conway was head of DJM's publishing division. He managed to place a number of Bernie and Elton originals with artists who had publishing deals with Dick James' empire. The children's TV presenter Ayshea recorded 'Taking The Sun From My Eyes' for a B-side, and the actor Edward Woodward sang 'The Tide Will Turn For Rebecca'.

The writing team of Roger Cook and Roger Greenaway also offered a brotherly arm-round-the-shoulder. By 1968, Cook and Greenaway were one of the most successful writing partnerships in British pop. Their 'You've Got Your Troubles' had been a Number 2 hit for the Fortunes in 1965, and the New Seekers' 'I'd Like To Teach The World To Sing' would be a UK Number 1 in 1972. Cook and Greenaway, like Steve Brown, had witnessed the demoralisation on the faces of Elton and Bernie during the difficult first year of their collaboration when nothing, so it seemed, would go right. 'One day we went into the office at Dick James and we bumped into Reg and Bernie,' says Greenaway. 'They looked so damned dejected because people weren't taking any interest in them. So we tried to get them out of this depression and asked Reg to play us some of their new material. I remember sitting down with them and saying, "Come on, you've got to buck up, play me your stuff." They played three songs: one was called "Skyline Pigeon", and another, "When I Was Tealby Abbey".' And we recorded some of their songs. No one else had ever done that.'

Greenaway recorded 'When I Was Tealby Abbey' using an act he was producing for Bell Records at the time called Young and Renshaw. Paul Young would later go on to find fame as lead singer of Sad Café, and, in the decade before his untimely death in 2000, as a member of Mike and the Mechanics. Roger Cook also decided to recorded 'Skyline Pigeon' as Roger James Cook, and Dick James allowed Cookaway Music to publish the song too. For Roger Greenaway, 'Skyline Pigeon' remains one of Elton's classic records. 'It was so different. I mean, who could write about a pigeon and make it work like a love song? It's fantastic! "Skyline Pigeon" was very much in the right vein. They were writing their own individual songs and they weren't trying to aim them at anybody.'

The first fruit of this new, more single-minded attempt to reach the general public would be the single 'Lady Samantha', a song which was a quantum leap in terms of quality and can be regarded as Elton John's first classic single. Caleb Quaye's guitar riff, which opened and concluded the song, and the strong, sing-a-long chorus (repeated twice, as would so often be the case in future Elton songs in the 1970s) made it a treat. Elton's voice was confident and clear and far less Americanised than it would be in later years. 'All Across The Havens', a whimsical folk-pop song which would prefigure much of Elton's material, was the B-side.

'Lady Samantha' came out in January 1969. Although it didn't reach the charts, it was what was then known as a 'turntable hit', heavily promoted on radio without actually selling that many copies in the shops. Or, as the renowned lyricist Sir Tim Rice puts it, it was one of those records that 'everybody liked except the public'. The tastemakers in the industry, from radio promoters down to record producers, were now aware of Elton John as a name. The success of the single also had the effect of convincing Dick James that Elton should concentrate on writing for himself rather than for others and that the next stage was to record a debut album.

Two months earlier, Elton and his band had begun for the first time to get exposure on national radio. Stuart Henry played them on Radio 1 and Elton performed on the same station for John Peel. Yet even with this progress, his future remained uncertain. In early 1969, he auditioned as a singer for two progressive rock bands, King Crimson and Gentle Giant, but failed both auditions. How different it might all have been.

Steve Brown, who had produced 'Lady Samantha', was asked to take charge of the sessions for the debut album, which would be called *Empty Sky*. A follow-up single, 'It's Me That You Need', was also recorded at Dick James's Studio in April 1969 and released the following month, the first Elton single to be released on the newly formed Dick James Music (DJM) label. With its orchestral arrangement, lead guitar riff and big chorus, it was another sure indication that Elton was more than adept at writing classy melodies. Like 'Lady Samantha' before it, it was, alas, a flop.

With only a limited budget, the tracks for the album proper were recorded swiftly, using the eight-track studio equipment downstairs at DJM. 'The first album, *Empty Sky*, was low budget to say the least,' Elton admitted in 1970. '[Describing it as] stereo was a con; anyone who bought it as a stereo album was definitely conned.'

'The title track rocks so much,' he has since reflected. 'The guitar sound is unlike anything I've heard since. We got it by putting Caleb Quaye out on the fire escape at the top of the studio with a microphone at the bottom to get that incredible echo. That was how things were done then – a wing and a prayer, and a lot of invention. That kind of invention has largely gone, but a lot of what attracts people to those records was the actual use of sounds.'

With little or no time for overdubs or multiple takes, most of the album was played live using the in-house Dick James team. 'It was like a party all the time,' remembers Clive Franks, who was tape operator on the record. 'I remember one day when I came into work and everyone was looking out of the window. I asked, "What's going on?" They said, "We're looking for Elton John ads on the backs of buses." They explained that a couple of dozen buses had been used for advertising space for the *Empty Sky* album and everyone was leaning out the window trying to see one.' Franks also made a guest appearance on a track called 'Hymn 2000'. 'I whistled on it,' he says. 'Reg went to do it and he couldn't. He just kept laughing. He can't whistle to this day. It is hysterical to see him try. He tries, but nothing ever comes out.'

Overall, there was a homespun charm to *Empty Sky*. The title track was a mini-classic of its kind, with a great groove, a great melody, and some phased backwards guitar from Caleb Quaye. The flute, harmonica and recorder also featured, along with some 'Sympathy For The Devil' vocal stylings from Elton before the ending faded amateurishly then reprised itself. And the lyric, about freedom and release, was a perfect late 1960s period piece.

By contrast, 'Val Hala', Taupin's tale of chivalry, was wistful and reflective and, rather anachronistically but no less effectively, set to an Elizabethan harpsichord accompaniment. On 'Skyline Pigeon', Elton stripped the song back to its basics, banished the kit and the rhythm section and, with harpsichord and organ accompaniment, created his first classic ballad. The album was never less than listenable, yet was the product of an artist who was still searching for a style.

In an obvious tribute to the Beatles, the final track, 'Gulliver/It's Hay Chewed/Reprise', incorporated snippets of each of the previous tracks. As bluesy rock rubbed noses with ballads, and folk-pop excursions met crashing white noise that was the very stuff of late-period psychedelia, this song suite was a clear demonstration of a songwriting team more than competent at pastiche but too young yet to have a defining style of their own. It was perhaps hardly surprising that, in the first few months of its release, the album sold only around 2,500 copies.

During those years from 1968 to 1970, Elton was one of the busiest musicians in London. Firstly, he wrote and recorded his own songs. In addition, he stockpiled songs for already established acts to cover. As a talented pianist and more-than-competent backing singer, he hired himself out for session work in the studios. Finally, he was not too proud to sing on the various compilation albums that flooded the market in the late 1960s and early 1970s and which covered chart songs for a fraction of the price of the original.

'I used to do all those *Top Of The Pops* cover records,' he has happily admitted. 'I'm quite a good mimic so I could adapt my voice to whatever act it was. Singing lead on 'Saved By The Bell' by Robin Gibb, I had to sing in this dreadful warble and I couldn't get it so I ended up actually manually warbling my throat.' Indeed, from the comedy of Mungo Jerry's 'In The Summertime' to the reflective 'Lady D'Arbanville' by Cat Stevens, Elton showed that he was able to sing just about anything. Despite the fact that Elton was just a hired hand, and presumably had next to no artistic control over the sessions, his covers are great party fodder.

Elton has fond memories of his days as a jobbing backing vocalist. He appears on many 'classics' of the period if only we know where to look. 'I'm on Tom Jones's "Daughter Of Darkness", "Back Home" by the 1970 England World Cup Squad and even some of the Barron

Knights' stuff,' he has freely confessed. He also recorded a number of demos, such as the original for Tony Hiller's 'United We Stand', before The Brotherhood Of Man turned it into an international hit, and a version of John Martyn's 'Stormbringer'.

Elton also involved himself with a project called The Bread and Beer Band. They recorded an eponymous album at Abbey Road Studios in February 1969, featuring Elton on piano, the Hollies' Bernie Calvert on bass, Caleb Quaye on guitar, Roger Pope on drums, and two Jamaican percussionists by the name of Rolfo and Lennox. The young Chris Thomas produced, with help from Tony King. 'We used to go down the pub in the afternoon, have a few beers and go back to the studio in the evening', King has said. 'Then we'd turn down the lights and get all moody. The Beatles had been using a lot of coloured lights while they were recording. We thought this was terribly avant-garde, so we used to steal them and use them during our sessions.' However, King's vision of creating a British equivalent of one of the great American backing bands of the age was destined to fail. Despite a whole album of instrumental tracks being cut (including covers of 'Woolly Bully' and 'Zorba's Dance'), the album was pulled when a single, 'The Dick Barton Theme (The Devil's Gallop)', sold poorly.

Elton also sang backing vocals on that classic single 'Lily The Pink', the Christmas Number 1 of 1968 that was the work of that motley collection of Liverpudlian comedians, poets and photographers-to-be, the Scaffold. He also played piano on several Hollies tracks from the late 1960s, including the classic tearjerker 'He Ain't Heavy, He's My Brother'. 'I think that I first met Elton on the "He Ain't Heavy" session at Abbey Road,' says Hollies drummer Bobby Elliot. 'He seemed a little shy, but he was outnumbered by us lot, the producer Ron Richards and various engineers. I heard him make a *Goon Show* voice to himself, which made me think that he must be an OK kind of guy.'

In 1969, Elton also began working at Music Land Records on Soho's Berwick Street, serving behind the counter. How many people can claim to have been sold a Beatles LP or a Rolling Stones single by a future pop music legend? 'If I didn't want to be a recording star, the best thing I could imagine would be to have a record store and serve behind the counter,' Elton later said. Bernie and Elton would be regulars at the shop in their free time. 'We both spent all our money on records. We used to go to Music Land in Berwick Street and listen to Joni Mitchell, Hendrix, Dylan and the Beatles. Both of us would have headphones on and would be lying on the floor looking at the gatefold sleeves.'

One visitor to that shop in 1969 was to play an important role in exposing Elton John's music to a wider audience. The broadcaster Bob Harris was at the time co-editor of *Time Out*, the weekly London listings magazine. 'We were probably on the second edition, and one of my favourite shops in London at that time was the Music Land record shop in Berwick Street, which is where I used to buy all my imports,' says Bob. 'We were looking to place the magazines in shops around London on a sale-or-return basis, so we took them to Roundhouse, the Arts Laboratory, all the hip book shops that we knew in London and One Stop Records in South Bond Street.

'I was really keen to get them into Music Land. In those days they still had the listening booths that you could take an album into, so you could spend two or three hours with a pile of albums in a listening booth. It was very civilised. I even bought an HP Lovecraft album from there. When I went to pay, I had copies of the magazine with me. I said to the chap behind the counter, "Would you be prepared to stock the magazine on a sale-or-return basis?" He said, "I'll do that for you if you promise to review my new album in your next edition." I asked, "What album is that?" and he gave me a copy of *Empty Sky*.'

Little by little, progress was being made. Mick Inkpen and his girlfriend would regularly visit Elton at Frome Court. 'Reg had one wall just covered with records, hundreds of them, all filed away and neatly catalogued,' says Inkpen. 'If you wanted a night's entertainment, you just went round there. He was extremely interesting and amusing company. We would play our way through his record collection while Derf and Sheila watched telly in the other room.' One night in November 1969 was particularly memorable. 'I went round there one night after *Empty Sky* had come out and "Lady Samantha" was the first song that had got anywhere. The phone rang and Reg went out in the hall to answer it. There was a lot of mumbling away in the background, and a lot of laughing and giggling. He came back in and said, "I've just had this most amazing phone call. That was Three Dog Night in the States and they're going to record 'Lady Samantha.'" There was a lot of jumping around and celebrating.'

Throughout 1969, Elton and Bernie continued to live at his parents' home. The pair would continue to consume music and film with a passion. 'We went to see *The Party* by Peter Sellers when it was on at the Rex in Northwood Hills,' recalls Elton. 'It was a B-film, the film on before the main feature. You remember things like that. There was just an explosion of ideas going on then, not only the music but the visual arts, with clothes, with everything. It was just *the* most exciting era. You could buy at least ten great albums a week and be inspired. We were listening to bass sounds, drum sounds, piano sounds, which started really with the Beatles and *Sgt Pepper*, and sort of exploded over to America with Blood, Sweat and Tears. We were listening to the first Blood, Sweat and Tears album [*Child Is Father To The Man*, 1968] on our headphones and on our £65 stereo system, and we were filled with wonder. They were magical times.'

By 1969, Elton had begun the routine of keeping a diary. The snippets published to date make for excellent reading, particularly given the nature of the beast that Elton would soon become in all his superstar glory. The entries reveal the singer's pre-fame sense of wonder at the world. On March 29, he wrote: *'Watched the Grand National and then went to see Owmby United win 2-1.'* As if that wasn't exciting enough, on April 22 he recorded that he *'got home tonight to find that Aunty Win and Mum had bought me a car – Hillman Husky Estate – superb!'* Then, on May 28, came the account of his very own ballad of John and Yoko: *'Pinner Fair. Went up to get paid. Went to the fair with Mick and Pat. I own a coconut and two goldfish!! – John and Yoko.'* The journal entry for the very next day carried sad tidings: *'My goldfish died tonight – very upset!!'* Fortunately, the entry for May 30 reported a happy end to the drama: *'Went to get some more goldfish. Got a tank and four fish. Played tennis with Tony's friend Mark – won 6-2 6-4 2-6 4-6 6-0.'*

But it was the events described in the entry for October 27 that year that would, in the fullness of time, change his life forever: *'Session [at] De Lane Lea [Studio] 9:00. Bobby Bruce. Stayed home today. Went to South Harrow market. The session was hilarious. Didn't do anything in the end. Wrote "Your Song".'*

CHAPTER 4

IT'S A LITTLE BIT FUNNY

'Is this the year of Elton John?'

Melody Maker *writer Richard Williams, April 1970*

'"Your Song" was such a fucking misrepresentation of me, although it's become almost a trademark. From the first time we went on the road, we were rockers at heart and on stage.'

Elton John, 1976

No country in Western Europe does bad weather quite like England. Summers seem to have an endless capacity to disappoint. It is the middle of August and Elton John and his new band, comprising Nigel Olsson on drums and Dee Murray on bass, have just taken the stage at the Yorkshire Folk, Blues and Jazz Festival in Krumlin, near Halifax. The weather isn't merely disappointing, though. It is appalling. Huge raindrops have already pounded into the sodden turf, which is soon to morph into a viscous mass of mud. In this summer of 1970, far from letting it all hang out, it's more a case of wrapping it all up warm.

The gloomy weather is matched by the dismal mood of the music scene of that year. In truth, 1970 will prove a year of closure, featuring few new beginnings and many major endings. The Beatles, for almost a decade the central players on the world pop scene, have just imploded in unseemly acrimony and legal bickering. The vigour and sense of the new that was 1967 appears, in 1970, to be exhausted. There is a vapidity about so much of the music scene of the new decade, with

86

its terribly earnest singer-songwriters and acid rock retreads, and the endless noodling of the new guitar 'virtuosos'. The giants of the counterculture appear to be foundering, while there seems to be no new wave to take their place. In darkest Yorkshire, almost a year to the day since the opening of the legendary festival in upstate New York, Krumlin is no Woodstock. But little though they know it, the fans braving the English summer cold in August 1970 are about to witness a changing of the guard.

Krumlin Festival starts five hours late as the acts, having struggled to reach the venue, proceed to squabble over the running order. The Humblebums, featuring the Scottish folk and Glaswegian wit of Billy Connolly and Gerry Rafferty, are due to play the following day, but decide to take the stage a day early and kick off the whole festival. Elton John and his band are second on the bill. They play with such passion and abandon that even the coldest heart is cheered. Elton opens with 'Bad Side Of The Moon'. 'Border Song' and 'Sixty Years On' follow and, by the time of a cover of the Stones' recent UK Number 1, 'Honky Tonk Women', the audience are clapping like seals at feeding time. There are only three musicians up there, but the commitment is unmistakable. With Elton's crashing bluesy chords, Murray's poetic bass fills and strummed chords and Olsson's exemplary rock drumming (which means several broken drumsticks along the way), this new three-piece appears to possess a certain magic. 'He is like a white, male Aretha Franklin,' one member of the crowd is overheard saying.

Apart from the show-stealing performance from Elton John, the three-day festival at Krumlin is a musical, personal and environmental disaster. The rumoured big-name appearance by Pink Floyd never materialises. 'Pink Floyd are fogbound in Paris,' proclaims an announcement over the tannoy on the Saturday, although most doubt that the band ever agreed to play in the first place. Yet the organisers must surely have suspected that a three-day festival on the Yorkshire moors was not exactly a brilliant move, even in August, particularly with oil drums serving as unisex toilet facilities for the weekend.

'They were carting the audience away with exposure,' recalls the singer-songwriting legend Richard Thompson, who was on the bill that weekend with Fairport Convention. 'Everyone was dressed in those bin-liner things. It was great fun.' By the end of the weekend, the weather was so bad that the stage had virtually blown away. 'I looked at the scene of total destruction,' says one fan, recalling the moment he woke up the morning after the night before. 'It looked like the corporation rubbish tip.' 'The rain were absolutely ferocious – you could hardly stand up', says another fan. 'Everyone bought these big orange plastic bags. You put your sleeping bag in that and just watched the bands, half asleep, in the rain. It's just as well the bags were there. They probably saved a lot of people from exposure. We abandoned our tents on the Saturday nights as we couldn't keep them pegged down. You could hardly stand up in the wind and rain. We went into one of the big marquees. I remember it was full of steam from all the wet bodies. I believe the other big marquee fell down in the middle of the night and people were injured as a result of this.' In all some 330 fans are treated for exposure and 70 people hospitalised. There were unconfirmed stories of the promoter found several days after the event, wandering round the Yorkshire moors in a confused state and suffering from exposure.

It has all gone wrong for several of the artists there too. The Move turn up but can't play. So bad are the Somme-like conditions, they can't drive close enough to the stage to unload their equipment. Several performers are incapacitated by drink. Fairport Convention's set is particularly memorable in this respect. The violinist Dave Swarbrick is caught short mid-gig. 'There was a hole in the canvas on the stage,' remembers fellow band member Dave Pegg. 'He went over to the side of the stage, stuck his chopper through the hole and had a piss. Unfortunately, the press area was on the other side of the hole. Consequently, we were never popular with *Melody Maker* after 1970.' Pegg himself suffers an even worse eventuality: 'I was wearing a pair of white trousers. I had rather too much to drink and when I got on stage, I shat myself, which was very embarrassing as the back of my white trousers changed colour very quickly. Behind me were all the other acts that were on, including Elton John, who wasn't very famous at the time, and the Move. I was a laughing stock.'

One journalist there, *Melody Maker*'s Chris Charlesworth, is seriously impressed by Elton John, and says so in his review the next week. 'The first time I met Elton was backstage at Krumlin,' says Charlesworth. 'He was in a caravan sharing a drink with Sandy Denny. On the bill with him were the Pretty Things, Juicy Lucy and the Groundhogs. It was the first time I ever saw Elton perform. On he came, dressed up very flash, and he pounded hell out of that piano for an hour or so. I had never heard his music before, but I thought he was absolutely fantastic. All those miserable people in that field… by the time he had finished his set, they were happy. He got some bottles of brandy and loads of plastic cups and he handed out brandy to the people in the crowd, saying, "Sorry about the weather. It's not my fault, but I'll do the best I can to keep you warm, so, there you go, some brandy." That went down extremely well.

'After the show I went backstage to ask him the names of the songs he had played as I didn't know them at all. He welcomed me into his caravan with open arms, obviously delighted that someone from the music press was interested in him. He was very humble.'

Little do these music fans know, but, within the next six weeks, two icons of their era, Jimi Hendrix and Janis Joplin, would be dead. Those major stars of the 1960s, the Rolling Stones, would continue their massive success into the new decade but they would be one of the few acts from the previous decade to do so. The fans at Krumlin, however, had just witnessed one of the first live performances of a solo act that would in two years go some way to filling the gap left by the Beatles.

*   *   *

So 1970 might have been a lacklustre year for pop music in general, but for Elton John it was *the* key year of his career. It started off with the recording of his second album. Elton had demoed a new ballad, 'Your Song', and this, together with several other new compositions, made it clear to Steve Brown, his in-house champion at DJM, that Elton needed a 'proper' producer.

Elton had already cut tracks for the sophomore record at Olympic Studios in Barnes, with Hookfoot as the backing band. Hookfoot – featuring Caleb Quaye on guitar, Dave Glover on bass and Roger Pope on drums – had backed Elton the previous year on occasional live outings such as his gig at the Royal College of Art in London. They also featured on a number of recording sessions for radio programmes like Johnnie Walker's Radio 1 programme. Hookfoot remained Elton's live band until April 1970 and a session for Dave Lee Travis.

However, Steve Brown was big enough to see his own limitations, and, in effect, fired himself from the job of producer. He knew that somebody else could do better, and that the songs themselves, already very good, could – with the help of a more professional team – become something very special indeed. In another crucial step in the career development of Elton John, Brown convinced Dick James that Elton needed a bigger, better team around him in the studio.

The step-up in quality was unmistakable. Just over two years into their collaboration, Elton and Bernie were writing not just good songs, but excellent ones. It seemed almost certain that they would make it – it was just a question of how big. Throughout 1969, Elton was to amass an impressive body of work. Bernie would seek the solitude of the bedroom, scribbling down lyrics as he sat on the bottom bunk before presenting them to Elton, who would create the music on the piano at Frome Court. Several songs were then road-tested before his extended family of mother, stepfather, aunts and grandmother.

Yet it was 'Your Song' that made it plain to everyone at DJM that Elton had the capability to write a hit single. At one stage, even the Hollies were interested in recording it, as Bobby Elliot recalls. 'Tony Hicks and I went in to Uncle Dick – that's Dick James – and said that we'd like to do "Your Song". He said, "No, I'm thinking of putting an orchestra on it, and it'll put Elton on the scene." The fact that the Hollies wanted to do it helped Dick realise what a good artist Elton was. We missed having it, but it shows we could spot a good song.'

The task of finding the right production team was high on the list of priorities for Steve Brown. According to Brown's assistant, Stuart Epps, several names were suggested and several people sounded out, including Denny Cordell, the producer for the Moody Blues and Procol Harum. In November 1969, at Ronnie Scott's club in London, Brown introduced Bernie and Elton to the arranger Paul Buckmaster. Buckmaster was one of Britain's most talented arrangers and performers, having struck up a relationship, both personal and professional, with the jazz great Miles Davis in the late 1960s and early 1970s. He had played cello since the age of four, and, like Elton, had attended the Royal Academy of Music in London, in Buckmaster's case on a full-time scholarship.

'I was at Ronnie Scott's to hear Miles Davis play,' recalls Buckmaster. 'David Bowie's "Space Oddity", which I had arranged, had come out in the summer of 1969, and I had done a number of recordings that had been noted in reviews in the pop press. Elton had heard those things. Steve Brown sent me an open-reel, two-track quarter-inch tape of demos after the meeting at Ronnie Scott's. I listened to the songs and immediately was attracted to the material and wanted to work on it. Elton was quiet. Not shy – just quiet and reticent in a nice way. Bernie was very quiet too – taciturn is the word that springs to mind. He struck me as a bit dry to begin with, but that is just his external quietness. He was very self-contained.'

Around the time that the initial approach was made to Buckmaster to arrange the new record, the Beatles' producer George Martin was asked to produce it. However, the vastly experienced Martin wanted, perhaps understandably, to arrange the record as well. Having already found Buckmaster, the Elton John management team were unwilling to lose an arranger whose work they admired so much and so they took the almost unprecedented step of turning George Martin down. They then went to work to find someone to produce alongside their first-choice arranger.

In retrospect, this decision looks like something of a high-risk strategy. George Martin was, after all, a recording legend. However, the person they eventually found fitted the bill perfectly: Gus Dudgeon. 'They asked me whom I would recommend as producer,' continues

Buckmaster. 'I had done several sessions with Gus Dudgeon and I got along very well with him, so I suggested him.' 'We had heard "Space Oddity", which for me was one of the best records of all time, and we learned that it was produced by Gus Dudgeon,' said Elton. 'And we knew then that we had to get him to produce my second album.'

Gus Dudgeon would go on to play a crucial role in Elton's career. In fact, it would be no exaggeration to say that, without him, the Elton John sound as we know it might never have existed. Dudgeon was one of the most assiduous, hard-working and likeable producers in the business. His attention to detail was sometimes infuriating for those who worked with him. Yet the detail of his productions speaks for itself. Already a name in 1969, by 1976 he was unequivocally one of the world's top producers.

After several false career starts, Dudgeon had entered the music business as a tea boy at Olympic Studios in Barnes. 'Actually, I had eleven jobs in four years after I left school,' he has admitted. 'I got fired from every one of them without fail. Some of them only lasted a week. In fact, at one point, I was three jobs ahead of my P45, which meant I had to slow down or my P45 would never fucking catch up with me.'

For Dudgeon, the music business provided the perfect outlet for his creativity. 'It was the 1960s. You couldn't be in anything better than music, fashion or the arts,' he said. By 1964 he had established himself as an engineer, working at Decca on the classic hit 'She's Not There' by the Zombies. With Mike Vernon producing, Dudgeon went on to engineer many other acts on Decca, including John Mayall, Ten Years After and Savoy Brown. 'Mike and I were a bit of a team and we were having success, bizarrely, in two entirely opposing fields of music,' Dudgeon reflected. 'One was the blues area and the other was in the pop field.' His professional relationship with David Bowie led to him engineering Bowie's debut album. Indeed, Dudgeon was one of the two gnomes on Bowie's 1967 novelty record, 'The Laughing Gnome', which he was to dub 'my own personal Troggs tape'.

By 1968, he was working as a producer in his own right, scoring a major hit single with the Bonzo Dog Doo-Dah Band's 'I'm The Urban

Spaceman', produced with Paul McCartney under the pseudonym Apollo C. Vermouth. Yet it was his astonishingly detailed production on David Bowie's epic 1969 single 'Space Oddity' that would make him one of the UK's best young producers. 'Arrangement has always been a crucial part of what I do,' he said in 1998. 'The presentation of the song is all-important.'

Dudgeon knew of Elton's work, particularly 'Lady Samantha', before he was called in to be his producer. 'I was aware of him as a name,' said Dudgeon. 'I remember seeing ads on the backs of buses, saying "Elton John".' Dick James's office was just a five-minute walk from Dudgeon's own, and Elton and Bernie came over to play 12 demos to him. 'I just couldn't believe it,' said Dudgeon. 'All of them floored me. My prayers were answered. Although I'd had four hits prior to this, it was with four different artists. What I really wanted was an artist that I could work with on a consistent basis. So I said, "Yeah, I'm going to do this."'

The first meeting between Dudgeon, Elton and Bernie revolved, for the first 20 minutes at least, around a case of mistaken identity, confessed Dudgeon. 'When we had the first meeting, I thought Bernie was Elton. Because no one had actually introduced him, I got them completely arse-about-face. Bernie had long hair and he was slim and he looked more like a singer.'

Dick James had budgeted around £6,000 for Elton's second album, although extra money was pumped into the project due to the relatively high costs of the orchestra introduced after the recording had commenced. 'You could get a semi in Pinner for that,' Elton would later quip. It was certainly a step up from the *Empty Sky* recording, as well as something of a gamble for Dick James. 'We cut the album in a week and I never stopped grinning from beginning to end, because it all fell into place so brilliantly,' recalled Gus Dudgeon in 1997. 'In fact, that album wasn't really made to launch Elton as an artist; it was made as a very glamorous series of demos for other people to record his songs. It was kind of like Jimmy Webb making an album and everyone rushes in and covers all the songs on it. That was the plan.'

The sessions for the album, which was to go by the prosaic name of *Elton John*, were held at London's Trident Studios. The studio piano, a Bechstein, produced a distinctively aggressive and hard sound, with a very bright timbre, and was quite unlike the rather timid piano sounds normally found on records today. 'Trident Studios was one of the deadest rooms I have ever been in,' says Buckmaster. 'You walked in and your ears sort of sucked inwards, it was so dead. The air and ambience was created by Gus and Robin Geoffrey Cable, that brilliant engineer who worked on the record using large plates and chambers for the reverb.' The Trident environment had a similar impact on Clive Franks. 'I couldn't believe how much more professional it was than the stuff Elton had recorded at Dick James Music's studio. You could see the musicians though a glass window instead of on a broken-down TV. Gus was amazing – he knew what he wanted and he knew how to communicate with the engineers. He was such a great personality and such a strong character. That was important for Elton, because he was a very strong character too and he needed someone to guide him.'

The sound of the album was one of invention and a far greater maturity. 'We'd started writing a different class of song. We grew up,' is how Elton later succinctly put it. At just 19, Taupin in particular had matured to a remarkable degree. His fondness for Bob Dylan's lyrics, with their rich allegorical allusions, was an obvious lyrical influence. Yet there was a figurative power to his writing too, and a new, simple way with words that served to balance the more self-consciously cryptic moments. With his early flower power fancies banished from his repertoire, Taupin's new work was altogether more serious.

The hiring of Paul Buckmaster would prove to be a masterstroke. In his hands, and in collaboration with Dudgeon, Elton's songs came alive with bright, sometimes brash orchestral arrangements that were light years away from the syrupy strings of the popular music of the day. Buckmaster brought drama, menace and action to Elton's music, as orchestral figures based on the central theme of each song interwove brilliantly with the singer's piano and vocal line. 'We were very, very fortunate in the fact that Buckmaster was available,' said Elton. 'We did three tracks in a session. To play with a live orchestra was extremely intimidating. It was quite a fearsome task, but we did it. Gus Dudgeon produced and the team was born. It was just like Bernie and me; it was fate basically.'

Elton also revealed an interesting influence: 'The biggest influence on me from a production standpoint and a songwriting point of view was Brian Wilson. I love the Beatles, but I don't actually think they influenced me as songwriters. The Beach Boys' production, sound, way of writing and melodies were a much bigger influence. Brian Wilson was a genius and always will be. Production-wise, his idea of initially using echo vocals on a track and then using dried vocals completely changed the face of recording vocals as well.'

'"Your Song" was the first thing I heard and it immediately locked me into wanting to do this record,' says Buckmaster. 'I was totally in love with the material. With each song I heard on the demo, my level of enthusiasm just went up and up and up. I was just bopping with excitement to be involved in this project. Elton had decided not to be at all involved in the creative process of how we were going to arrange these songs. He put it entirely into my hands and Gus's hands, so Gus and I had two meetings where we went through all the material we were going to record. We each had a copy of the lyric sheet and went through each song, on his desk with a fine-tooth comb.'

Discussions for the album continued round at Frome Court, too. 'My wife Pat and I went round one night,' remembers Bluesology stalwart Mick Inkpen. 'Elton was working on orchestral arrangements. Paul Buckmaster and Gus Dudgeon were sitting in his little room with him discussing the new album, which was interesting. Paul Buckmaster was a very serious musician and he wanted to talk shop, I think, but Gus Dudgeon was full of fun, a good laugh. We got out the Merrydown cider and we had a great time.'

The album sessions took place in January 1970. Elton retained Quaye and Pope from Hookfoot and drafted in a team of top session musicians including Barry Morgan on drums and Herbie Flowers on bass, both from Blue Mink. The guitar duties were shared between Roland Harker, Colin Green, Clive Hicks, Blue Mink's Alan Parker and

Caleb Quaye, always a positive presence in the recording studio with his good-humoured banter. One cut, 'Border Song', featured Madeline Bell of Blue Mink along with Tony Burrows, a singer who had had the honour of performing for three different acts – Edison Lighthouse, White Plains and The Brotherhood Of Man – on one single episode of *Top Of The Pops*.

Despite his anxiety about singing to a full orchestral arrangement, Elton acquitted himself with a maturity beyond his 22 years, as Paul Buckmaster remembers: 'Elton was right there, excellent, right on the money all the time, confident and powerful.' Sessions proceeded at a brisk and orderly pace, using the studio's eight-track machine. 'We worked from 10am to 1pm, 2pm till 5pm, and 6pm until 9pm. The standard length of a recording session was three hours with union breaks: either two ten-minute breaks or one twenty-minute break. I think we did two songs in every session.'

The album kicked off with 'Your Song'. 'It was written in five minutes, recorded in two,' Elton has joked. In fact, according to Elton lore, it was born one morning at Frome Court, over a breakfast of scrambled eggs. It's a love song of quiet innocence, with a lyric written by a teenager with very little experience of women. 'I've always said that number sounds like a song about a 17-year-old guy who is desperate to get laid. Which, at the time, it was. [We were] so naïve,' reflected Taupin, years later.

Despite this, 'Your Song' had a timeless, cross-generational appeal and was in many ways the defining Elton John song of the period. Its structure was one that Elton repeated, with variations, on several well-known songs from around this time. A piano introduction ran into two verses, leading to a chorus. This build-up, the delay, before the pay-off of the chorus, meant that the chorus itself made more of an impact, as it occurred much later in the song than the listener anticipated. Deferred gratification is the hallmark of Elton's best melodies. What made 'Your Song' work, though, was Elton's delivery of Taupin's conversational lyrics. The pauses and hesitations brought a sense of authenticity to the uncertainty of the lyric. 'If I was a sculptor, but then again, no,' sounded as if Elton was externalising his innermost thoughts. 'And so excuse me forgetting, but these things I do/You see I've forgotten if they're green or they're blue' conjured up the intimacy of a private conversation.

Interestingly, 'Your Song' was not chosen as the first single from *Elton John*. That honour went to 'Border Song'. 'I wrote the last verse of "Border Song",' Elton was to reveal to *Q* magazine in 1986. 'And that's why I don't write lyrics any more!' (Sample: 'There's a man over there/ What's his colour?/ I don't care'). An uplifting, gospel-tinged song, it failed to chart in the UK, despite featuring on Elton's first *Top Of The Pops* appearance in April 1970. Released in the US in the summer of 1970, it reached Number 92.

Such is the stature of 'Your Song' that it is very easy to forget about some of the other material on the album, which was arguably as good and certainly now sounds fresher to the ears after the over-exposure of the big hit single. 'I Need You To Turn To', for example, was one of Elton's best ballads. 'Most of the cash went on the orchestra – we had to record three songs per session because they cost so much,' he was to reflect. 'Recording "I Need You To Turn To" was a really nervous moment. I was playing the harpsichord and, while it looks very similar to the pianoforte, there is a delay to how its mechanism works so it is very easy to fuck it all up if you're not thinking ahead. This song is very Leonard Cohen-influenced because Bernie and I were both huge fans.'

Another lyrically direct song was 'The Greatest Discovery', a simple piece of descriptive writing with none of the catches or opaque references that are so much a part of Taupin's usual style. But perhaps the most impressive song on the album was the dramatic 'Sixty Years On'. 'That was one of the demos, and I knew from the beginning that I didn't want it to have piano,' remembers Buckmaster. 'So I sat down with Gus and said, "Look, we've got piano on everything here, let's think of something different." My suggestion was to replace the piano with harp, so that now the whole intro is harp with strings, with the harp replaced by a nylon-string acoustic guitar, which plays under the first verse.'

'Take Me To The Pilot', was a riotous blues-rock-gospel hybrid that still baffles its creators. 'I don't think either of us knows what that one's about,' Elton confessed in 2003. The final cut, 'The King Must Die', was another moody piece of orchestral pop that brought gravitas to the album, while 'First Episode At Hienton', written by Taupin two years earlier, was a reflective song about a love lost. Diana Lewis's glissando on the Moog synthesiser gave this piano-based ballad an eerie edge. The metaphysical lyric surprised with its directness: 'For your thighs were the cushions/ Of my love and yours for each other'.

The immediate effect of the album was to convince Dick James that Elton had a very promising future ahead of him. Two months after the recording sessions, Dick James renewed his contract with Elton, increasing his royalty to around four per cent of the record's retail price for the first two years of the contract, rising to six per cent thereafter. According to Philip Norman the terms of the contract would last for five years, during which Elton would be required to release six sides of music a year. Gearing up to launch Elton on a major scale, James also created a full-time post of press and publicity officer at DJM, the first incumbent being Helen Walters.

The *Elton John* album appeared during a very self-absorbed phase in the history of popular music. In 1970, it seemed every new artist wanted to tell you his or her innermost secrets while playing acoustic guitar and staring misty-eyed to the camera. Furthermore, the album cover photo shoot revealed what at the time felt like a major problem. Simply put, Elton John did not photograph well. In fact, he had the misfortune to be naturally extremely un-photogenic. 'Elton wasn't particularly attractive at that time. When we went through the photos, they were all terrible, to be honest,' says Stuart Epps. 'On one photo you could hardly see him because it was so dark, so that was the one we used.' As a result, the second Elton John album is often referred to by fans (and by Elton himself) as the Black Album.

Elton was 23, the ideal age for a pop singer, but no one at DJM was under the illusion that Elton could sell his music through his looks. Yet, as the years rolled by, this initial disadvantage became an important asset. His very normality made him appeal to an audience that had tired of the preening, wasted, self-regarding iconography of so many 1970s rock stars. A look at the archive footage of *Top Of The Pops* from the era reveals a parade of tank tops, printed cardigans and hideous lapelled blouses, not to mention lank long hair, comb-overs, mullets and perms. Elton, in his at times frankly appalling outfits, was only reflecting the distressingly unfortunate fashion statements of virtually everyone else. Indeed, there were times when he seemed to be lampooning them all with costumes that were so over the top as to satirise those rivals who might actually believe that what they wore was in any way commendable. Most of all, though, Elton's costumes were fun for everyone.

The album did not meet with uniformly encouraging reviews. *Rolling Stone* sniffed: 'The main problem with *Elton John* is that one has to wade through so much damn fluff to get to Elton John. Here, by the sound of it, arranger Paul Buckmaster's rather pompous orchestra was spliced in as an afterthought.' Meanwhile, a new, non-album single was prepared for release. 'Rock And Roll Madonna', backed by the superior 'Grey Seal', came out in the UK in June 1970. Despite effusive reviews ('He is probably Britain's first real answer to Neil Young and Van Morrison,' said *Record Mirror*), the single, like all those before it, failed to chart.

In 1970, Elton John was still a jobbing musician, forced to take whatever paid work was on offer. He would gig as a pianist on dates with Simon Dupree. He would sing backing vocals on *Top Of The Pops* for Brotherhood Of Man and Pickettywitch. He recorded a duet with Cat Stevens, 'Honey Man', which would remain unreleased for 30 years. Yet another project that he undertook was intended to popularise the songs of singer-songwriter Nick Drake. Recording took place at Sound Techniques Studios in Chelsea in July 1970. With covers of 'Saturday Sun', 'Way To Blue' and 'Time Has Told Me', Elton's brief was to make the fey originals into commercial hits. 'An impossible task, really,' he admitted in 2004. 'I needed the money, so I did it.'

Elton also recorded with a group of instrumentalists who, under the name Mr Bloe, secured a Number 2 UK hit in 1970 with the instrumental 'Groovin' With Mr Bloe'. The single '71–75 New Oxford Street' (the address of Dick James Music) credits Elton as the writer. Some fans have also speculated that Elton was actually Mr Bloe.

At the time of the *Elton John* album's release, Elton had not played live for nearly two years and was, at least initially, a reluctant performer. 'We were told we would have to get a band together,' said Elton, 'which was the last thing I wanted to do. The last thing I thought was that I was a singer. But they told me I was going to have to do it.' Seemingly sapped of confidence after the latter years of Bluesology, in those early years as a solo artist Elton cut a rather forlorn figure. 'He seemed to have terrible problems communicating,' said Dick James's son, Stephen. 'He'd just sit at the piano, play six to eight songs, then say, "There it is. That's it." For a long time, I don't remember him saying more than two words during his set. My father and I had to go on and on at him about loosening up and projecting.'

Elton had always admired the great pop trios such as Cream and the Jimi Hendrix Experience, so he decided to tour with just a drummer and a bassist, with the piano taking the lead role normally reserved for the guitar. Nigel Olsson became Elton's drummer, and Dee Murray, the bass player, joined Elton after a stint working in the Mirage. The striking, elfin-like Olsson had played in a band called Plastic Penny who were affiliated with Dick James. They had a 1968 Number 6 hit with 'Everything I Am' but failed to follow it up. 'We were one of the original one-hit wonders,' he admits. 'But it put me in the right circle. Elton would be making demos and if I was available I'd do drumming on them.'

Olsson had auditioned for the newly formed Uriah Heep and played a handful of concerts with them before Elton invited him to join his tour. 'He said he had a one-off gig to do at the Roundhouse in London and asked if I would play it with him and Dee,' the drummer recalls. 'We went into Dick James' studio and within the first 16 bars of music I knew that it was what I wanted to do. It hit me in the heart, in the head, everywhere. Before then, I had no direction. It had been very Keith Moon-like; get a load of drums and bash anything in sight! Elton said, "This is great. Let's call this the band and go out and do a couple of dates." And every time we went onstage it was amazing.'

The Roundhouse gig was part of a six-night festival called the Pop

Proms. Hosted by John Peel, the line-up included Tyrannosaurus Rex, the Pretty Things, Traffic, Mott The Hoople, Fairport Convention, Matthew's Southern Comfort and Fleetwood Mac. Admission was 25 shillings per night. By now, Elton had become a more confident live singer. The days of feeling unsure about his voice had gone; three years of session work and recording had seen to that. There were still doubts about his stagecraft but soon these, too, would be permanently dispelled. At the Roundhouse, as Ray Williams told Elton's biographer Philip Norman, '[Elton] accidentally kicked his piano stool over. It got a terrific reaction from the audience. So, at the next gig, he kicked it over on purpose.'

Throughout the summer of 1970, Elton and his new band played gigs in the London area at venues such as the Marquee and the Lyceum, interspersed with the odd trip abroad, such as to the Knokke Festival in Belgium (a gig that turned out to be a music contest, which Elton won). By now, the *Elton John* album had entered the UK charts. Debuting in May 1970, it would eventually climb to Number 5, spending 22 weeks in the listings. Although still without a hit single, Elton John had established himself. Fans were surprised at what they got when they saw Elton live. The dark and self-consciously serious cover design for the album was a perfect match for the serious contents within. Live, however, these songs rocked, with Olsson, Murray and Elton reinter-preting them in a completely different way. In a live setting, the music, which on the album was very much a product of the studio, took on a new lease of life.

Dick James was certain that the time had come to launch Elton John in the US. For the previous 18 months, trying to get anyone interested in him had been a thankless task. DJM had a licensing agreement with New York's Bell Records, but Bell's Larry Uttal had passed on *Empty Sky*. However, in 1970, with the second album as a tempter for would-be suitors, Elton finally got his American record deal in the United States. Roger Greenaway, who had already championed Elton in the music industry, would play a significant part in how the deal was done.

'In those days, I used to go to America four times a year, plugging Cook and Greenaway songs,' he says. 'One time, I was with the guy who then ran DJM in the States, Lenny Hodes. Lenny used to "get me through the door" and on this particular day, we had an appointment with Russ Regan at Universal. At that time Universal was on Sunset Strip, just down by the Hyatt House Hotel. I had had quite a few hits in America by then. I played Russ a few of my latest demos and he passed on all of them. We then listened to some of Elton's material, and he said, "I kind of like it, but it's a bit too esoteric for my tastes. I don't think it is right for America."

'We were about to leave when he looked at me and said, "What do you think of that guy, Roger?" I told him, "Well, it's not really my business, but I tell you what, if you don't sign him, you're going to be the sorriest A & R man who ever lived, because he's a great writer. I have seen him perform and he is a sensational performer too. So, if I were you, I'd sign him."'

The clincher was that Universal was also strongly interested in another Dick James Music act, Argosy. Stephen James told Hodes that Universal could have Argosy only if they took Elton as well. The eventual deal saw Argosy sign to Universal for $10,000. Elton they got for nothing. Argosy sank without a trace. Elton John, however, was on the brink of becoming a global superstar.

CHAPTER 5

A NEW MESSIAH IN TOWN

'I feel more American than British. Really.'

Elton John, 1970

'In open arms we put our trust they put us on a big red bus
Twin spirits soaking up a dream,
Fuel to feed the press machine.'

'Postcards From Richard Nixon'; lyrics: Bernie Taupin;
music: Elton John

They've finally made it. Made it over to the United States, that is. It's Elton and Bernie's first visit and at long last they are setting foot in the land that has enchanted them since they learnt how to turn on a radio. For two of the biggest vinyl junkies in the world, America is paradise. Not only is it the land that makes the best pop music, it's the land that *packages* pop music best, in the best-quality record sleeves. None of your flimsy British cardboard here: American record sleeves are made of sturdier stuff. It is the land of Elvis, Bob Dylan and the Beach Boys. It is also the land of Steve McQueen, of Hollywood, of the ghosts of Martin Luther King and JFK. It is the land of motels, Holiday Inns, drive-ins and the never-ending freeways of 'Lucille', 'Maybelline' and 'Peggy Sue'. In 1970, it is the land of every serious pop musician's dreams.

Elton and Bernie walk through passport control at LAX, expecting to find a uniformed driver with impeccably shiny shoes and a stretch limo with onboard bar, waiting to whisk them away to some air-conditioned palace on the Strip. What they find, however, is something surreally out of place. In a double-take moment of cartoon surrealism, what they actually see as they leave the airport terminal is a red double-decker bus – the sort that jams the streets of London. The super-saturated LA sunshine bounces off its gleaming, deep-red surface, an all-too-graphic reminder of the roots they had hoped to leave behind. Along with warm beer, roast beef and Yorkshire pudding, repressed attitudes to sex, and the bowler hat and brolly of the middle-class man about town, the red London bus is a sign of Englishness for those who aren't English. And English is the *last* thing Elton and Bernie want to be right now.

There is also a banner that reads 'ELTON JOHN HAS ARRIVED'. Several onlookers wonder if it is advertising a new type of toilet. The captain and the kid are ushered aboard and taken through the streets of sizzling Los Angeles. It feels as if the whole of LA is ogling them incredulously as their bus rolls on down the highway, at least two of its passengers squirming with with embarrassment.

* * *

'I thought it would be nice to make him feel important, not as a hype to promote the album, but just to make him and his entourage feel welcome,' said Norm Winter, Elton's American publicist. 'So we got this English bus, and then we thought, "Well, shit, we might as well go one step further," so we put "ELTON JOHN HAS ARRIVED" on the top. He was in the baggage area when he saw the thing and his eyeballs bugged out. We all rode the bus to Hollywood. Later he told me that he had expected to be greeted in a big Cadillac limousine and to really enjoy the luxuries of life. And here he is riding in this bumpy red bus that couldn't even climb a hill – they're terrible buses, English buses.' 'I found it extremely embarrassing,' Elton was later to say of the double-decker-sized welcome. 'Everyone was sort of getting into a crouch and trying to hide below the windows. I don't know – it seemed like a cheap trick. I really could not believe it.' There would be plenty more that week that Elton could not believe.

Norm Winter was an important figure in the early career of Elton John. As a teenager he had moved from New York to LA, where he worked as a fanzine photographer before getting involved in PR. By 1970, he was head of publicity at MCA/Universal (commonly known as Uni). That same year he would also break Andrew Lloyd Webber and Tim Rice's *Jesus Christ Superstar* rock opera, helping to turn the composer and lyricist into huge stars in their own right. The week that Elton arrived, Winter had really gone to town on the promotion. Every record store carried Elton John window displays. The airwaves were primed and stoked for Elton activity.

Six nights had also been booked for Elton to perform at Doug Western's Troubadour club. Founded in 1957 on Santa Monica Boulevard in West Hollywood, the Troubadour had began its life as a folk club, but in recent years helped to establish such singer-songwriters as Joni Mitchell, James Taylor and Kris Kristofferson. Neil Diamond, also an MCA artist, recorded his live album, *Gold*, at the club in 1970. Here it was that MCA/Universal chose to launch their newest signing.

The stakes for Elton and Bernie were high. As Elton remembers, Dick James had told them, 'OK, this is it, boys: make or break.' Before the first night, Elton wobbled. Morose and clearly in a state of shock about the importance of his fast-approaching big night, he declared that he was leaving for home. Ray Williams, the man who had brought Elton and Bernie together in 1967, was still Elton's personal manager, even though relations had by now started to fray. He arranged a day out in Palm Springs: Bernie took up the offer, but Elton stayed in the hotel and sulked. For Bernie, it would be the day he started to fall for a pretty LA blonde by the name of Maxine Fiebelmann. For Elton, it was the day that he felt abandoned. It took a transatlantic phone call from Dick James and some straight talking from Ray Williams to pull him round.

Before they set out for the States, Elton had embarked upon a process of further jazzing up his increasingly wacky wardrobe. So the London tailor Tommy Roberts, who traded under the pseudonym of Mr Freedom, had knocked up a completely new set of outfits for the US tour.

'He came in one day and said he wanted a few things to take with him to America,' Roberts told Philip Norman. 'I remember I made him a yellow boiler suit with a grand piano appliquéd on the back. And some white boots with green wings. Just normal-size heels, those first ones had.'

For the first-night performance, Elton, now bearded and with a hairstyle that made him look like a human coconut, wore bell-bottomed jeans and a red t-shirt with the words 'Rock And Roll' in white lettering. David Ackles, a performer much admired by Elton and Bernie, was on the bill as support, something which so shocked Elton that he asked for the running order to be changed. It was to no avail: Elton was the headliner.

On that opening night of August 25, at the hot and steamy Troubadour, Elton looked out from behind his piano to see Quincy Jones at the front of the audience with most of his family. Dave Crosby, Graham Nash, Henry Mancini and Beach Boy Mike Love were there, and Neil Diamond, already something of a music legend, having made the successful transition from songwriter to performer, stepped up to introduce the new act from England: 'I know the album and I love the album and I have no idea what these people are about to do. I just want to take my seat and enjoy this with you.' During Elton's six-night residency, other celebrities who joined the audience included an Everly Brother, Gordon Lightfoot, more Beach Boys, Bread, and Elton and Bernie's particular hero, the singer-songwriter Leon Russell. Norm Winter had his photographer, Pierre, take as many photos as possible of the executives and stars paying homage to the new kid on the block. The hype could not – and would not – stop.

It seemed as if every interested journalist and important A&R man in the States had flown to LA to witness the coming of Elton John. Norm Winter greeted them at the door and thrust a press pack into their hands. They all made the acquaintance of the star himself, as Elton later reflected: 'The week at the Troubadour should have been called The Million Handshakes. That was all I did. I couldn't tell you who I met. So many people wanted to meet me. I just stood there, and Norman Winter would say, "This is a very heavy cat, from the *Detroit*

Evening Puddle, and he's flown out to see you," and I would say, "Oh, really nice to meet you."'

The reviews were not just positive; they were positively ecstatic. The tactic of extending hospitality to dozens of newspapers and magazines, flying them in for the shows and treating them with respect paid off big-time. 'From the moment we arrived it was pandemonium all the way,' Elton reflected. 'The first night at the Troubadour was hype night, [with] all the record company people and the press, and the first set was incredible and it stayed that way. We got unbelievable reviews – I didn't see a bad one.'

Kathy Orloff of the *Chicago Sun Times* wrote, 'He was a major star before the end of his first set'. John Gibson of the *Hollywood Reporter* gushed, 'It's not often that someone gets a standing ovation at the Troubadour, but Elton John did – twice'. Perhaps the most vociferous and influential review came from Robert Hilburn of the *Los Angeles Times*: 'Rejoice. Rock music, which has been going through a rather uneventful period lately, has a new star. He's Elton John, a 23-year-old Englishman whose United States debut Tuesday night at the Troubadour was, in almost every way, magnificent'. 'Well, I honestly can't remember a thing about the first week in America,' Elton later said. 'All I can remember is that they have artificial turf on top of the Continental Hyatt House. And I went to Disneyland. But I was suspicious of all the excitement in LA. Maybe people were just coming to see me because of a glowing review in the *Los Angeles Times* by Robert Hilburn.'

Elton's relative obscurity was a major advantage. 'I thought I was signing a singer-songwriter,' said Uni's Russ Regan. 'At that stage, I hadn't had the luxury of seeing him in person. I was basing it on the music and the artist who was singing. The Troubadour was the first time I saw him as an entertainer, and then I knew we were going all the way. I just felt it.' It was 'like an Exocet missile', said Elton. 'I went to the Troubadour and I had the *Elton John* album, which looked, if you remember, very dark and [had] the face in profile with the glasses and the hair, and of course I went on stage and played 'Sixty Years On' in flying boots and hot pants.'

Nobody expected the version of Elton John they saw that August night: the flamboyant dresser, the powerhouse performer, the extrovert piano man. On vinyl, Elton was all about introspection; on stage, it was as if the spirit of the early rockers, of Jerry Lee Lewis and Little Richard, had found a new home. 'I was leaping on the piano, standing on it, doing handstands on it, and people went, "Fuck! What's that?" For the first time in my life, I felt released,' said Elton. 'The piano I play is a nine-foot instrument and it's a wooden object. It doesn't go anywhere and I didn't want to be someone who just sat there and played that. I wanted to be all around it, over it, in it, the way a guitarist can do anything with his instrument.'

The reception he received from these established stars of the American scene was both warm and generous. Neil Diamond invited Elton, along with Roger Greenway, round to his LA home. One LA radio station took out a full-page ad to thank Elton for the shows. Meeting Leon Russell, who had attended Elton's second night at the Troubadour, was especially moving. 'He's my idol as far as piano playing and there he was sitting in the front row. My legs turned to jelly. I mean, to compare my piano playing with his is sacrilege. He'd eat me for breakfast,' Elton told *Melody Maker*. 'He said that he wants to record with us, and he told me he'd written "Delta Lady" after hearing one of our songs, which was a gas.'

After the week-long residency at the Troubadour, Elton performed a gig at the Bay Arena in San Francisco before flying to the East Coast for more concerts, this time in New York. 'When I first saw New York, it terrified the crap out of me. It actually scared me,' Bernie has admitted. 'It took me quite some time to understand and enjoy the city.' His first appearance in the city would be at the Playboy Club. 'Of all places,' said Elton. 'How ironic is that! All I wanted to do was to go to the Apollo Theatre. It was dangerous for people to go up into Harlem, but Bernie and I wanted to go. Being white guys from England, it took us quite a few taxi drivers before we found one to take us up there. I just wanted to stand outside that theatre and look at it and think of all the great music that had come out of it. We stayed on Eighth Avenue, and the first night we were staying in a hotel called Lowe's Midtown. There was a gunfight in the street and we were terrified.'

By the time he arrived in New York, where Dick James had flown in just to congratulate the singer, news of Elton's success was already being beamed around the country. 'It was the fastest breaking of anyone in America, because he was unknown the day he arrived in Los Angeles,' says Roger Greenaway. 'Nobody could have predicted it. I did the first two tours with the Beatles and nobody realised what they might go on to become. Reg was the same. Brian Epstein didn't have a clue what he had with the Beatles, but I think, to be fair, Dick James did with Elton and, because of that, he was prepared to spend a lot of money.' Greenaway was driving back to LAX airport in Los Angeles when he happened to hear an announcement on the local radio. The DJ said, 'Ladies and gentlemen, there is a new Messiah in town. His name is Elton John.' I just thought, 'It's going to be giant,' says Greenaway. 'Reg is going to be a great star in America.'

Yet it might all never have happened. Elton had been doubtful about whether it was the right time to go to America. He wasn't yet a household name in his own country and thought it was too soon to try to break the States. However, James had cut a deal whereby he and MCA would share the costs of the promotional visit. MCA were insistent that, having signed the singer, he should be seen in a live context. Elton had shrugged his shoulders: 'The only reason I had agreed was because I thought that at least I'd be able to buy some records.' He wasn't expecting anything to happen, other than several trips to Tower Records.

In fact, just weeks before his date with destiny at the Troubadour, Elton had almost settled for a role as a sideman again. 'Before we got the offer to go, I was on the point of packing it all in and joining Jeff Beck, believe it or not,' he has confessed. Beck had originally seen Elton live and had offered to join his band as lead guitarist and tour the States with them. Obviously, Jeff Beck was a big catch and Elton was, at first, adamant that the tour should go ahead. 'The *Elton John* album was receiving a lot of attention on American radio and I'd just been signed by MCA, so they told me it would be good to play the Troubadour. At one point, the idea had been for me to play the Troubadour with Jeff Beck; I had met him in London and got along with him fantastically well.

'Jeff's manager stepped in and said that, because he was already big in the States, I'd get 10 per cent and Jeff would get 90 per cent. He was telling Dick James that Jeff got $10,000 a night in some places and that it would take me six years to build up to that. So I was sitting there, thinking, $10,000 a night, wow! I heard Dick saying, "Listen, I guarantee you this boy will be earning that much in six months." I said to myself, Dick, what a dippy old fart you are! You would be picked immediately in a Cunt of the Month competition! What a schmuck... So the Jeff Beck thing fell through and I was sulking.' However, Dick James was perfectly right to back his instincts. His prophecy about Elton's future selling power would come true.

With its orchestrated sections, piano and largely American-friendly themes, Elton's music seemed to fit the American music scene of the day. Indeed, in Britain, he was thought a bit of an oddity. Apart from Cat Stevens, whose Lothario curls and classic Greek good looks made female hearts flutter alarmingly, Elton was perhaps the only major singer-songwriter in the country. Although he and Bernie shared the composing tasks, Elton was very soon bracketed in the singer-song-writer category, spoken of along with the likes of David Gates, Neil Young, Tom Paxton, Tim Buckley, David Ackles, Leon Russell and James Taylor. So to the American public, Elton seemed new, but not strangely so. His sound was not too far removed from the close harmonies of Crosby, Stills & Nash or the gospel and soul-derived down-home sound of The Band, and had echoes of the meticulously crafted melodic pop of the Hollies and the piano-led ballad style of late-period Beatles. In short, he reminded the Americans of themselves and, simultaneously, of the palatable parts of the British pop scene. His musical DNA was perfectly understandable.

Elton John was the first British superstar of the 1970s in the USA. His American fame pre-dates that of David Bowie by three years. While

Marc Bolan would be the bigger singles artist in 1971 and 1972 in Britain, the T Rex man's profile in the States was comparatively low and would remain so. It was highly unusual for a British artist to make it big in America first, the notable exception being blitzkrieg bluesers Led Zeppelin. Despite this, two other songwriters on Elton's American record label were experiencing a similar phenomenon: the lyricist Tim Rice and the composer Andrew Lloyd-Webber.

'We were thrown together somewhat with Elton in the early days as we were both on the same record label, MCA, although he was technically with Uni to begin with, and were on Decca,' says Sir Tim Rice. '*Jesus Christ Superstar* and Elton's album came out at roughly the same time in America and both went to the top of the charts there without having any success whatsoever in England. We even featured on the same *Cashbox* cover as MCA's new stars: Elton, Andrew and myself.'

Before the 1970 trip to the States, Elton had begun recording a follow-up to *Elton John*, then still a month away from its UK release. *Tumbleweed Connection* would see him use the same team of Dudgeon and Buckmaster, and the same London studio, Trident. The sound, however, would be quite different. With a greater country influence in evidence, the orchestral flights of fancy were toned down in an effort to capture an earthier Elton. *Tumbleweed Connection* would be 'so different from the last one', he enthused to *Melody Maker* about an album still months from release. 'I wanted to get away from the orchestral thing and one cut is just me and the piano, recorded live. It's all much simpler and funkier.'

Although Buckmaster came up with some wonderful arrangements again, he was less conspicuous sonically. 'I was trying to re-create those Civil War brass band sections,' he remembers. 'There were tubas, trombones and flügelhorns on some tracks.' It was a measure of Elton's growing stature within the business that no less a figure than Dusty Springfield can be found on backing vocals. Ever gracious, Elton dedicated the album to his fellow entertainer at the Troubadour, David Ackles.

This album would give full rein to Bernie's vision of a land that he had at the time still not yet visited: America. In interviews, Elton was now citing James Taylor and Randy Newman as his main influences, but for Bernie, Robbie Robertson of The Band had usurped even Dylan as his lyricist of choice. The Band had very limited commercial success in the UK, scoring just one Top 20 hit single with 'Rag Mama Rag'. Their debut album, *Music From Big Pink,* regarded by many as one of the most influential records of the era, failed to chart at all in the UK, yet they seemed to have a dogged purchase on the hearts and minds of those British musicians who looked to the States for inspiration. Eric Clapton credited The Band with his move from the blues rock of Cream to the more laid-back music that he made with Blind Faith and on his first solo record in 1970.

'We'd all been listening to The Band at that point,' says the eminent pedal-steel guitarist B.J. Cole. 'For musicians in the early 1970s, The Band were probably our biggest influence at the time. They had a line to the American myth in the fact that Levon Helm came from the South, yet the rest were all Canadian guys who were just living the American myth. They had a similar approach to it as English musicians. They were observers in a way, so they got to it more effectively than people like the blues or country artists who were American and rather took it all for granted.'

Taupin's writing didn't focus on the America of the day – the political intrigues, the foreign policy disasters, the Cold War tensions and the battle between the counterculture and the Establishment on the student campuses. Nor did it discuss the American past as such. There is nothing much about abolitionism, the Gilded Age, the Depression, the New Deal or the civil rights movement. In fact, his view of America seemed to be largely one seen from horseback. It was really the America of his childhood and adolescence in 1950s and 1960s Britain: the America of the Western, the gangster flick and the novel.

Like so many other artists growing up at the time, Taupin saw in America the dream of endless improvement, adventure, and danger. And this dream, although essentially a myth, was endlessly fascinating. He was in a state of permanent wonder at it all. 'It all began with watching TV as a kid,' he has confessed. 'It stemmed from very plastic things like *The Lone Ranger*. I started reading about it then and I now have shelves of books on the subject.' Yet Bernie was no dilettante. In 1972, he revealed to the journalist Steve Turner that he had sought out such historical artefacts as *The Bad Men*, a record containing authentic cowboy songs and an interview with Wyatt Earp's girlfriend.

Taupin's source material was nothing if not knowledgeably researched. Reacting tetchily to the criticism that he was merely living the events in these songs from a distance, having never set foot on American soil at the time they were written, he snapped, 'I think it's a stupid thing to say. If people don't use their imagination, where would they be? People have been writing about things they have never seen for years. I think we captured the atmosphere very well on *Tumbleweed Connection* – without name-dropping, Robbie Robertson thought it was great! It seems that people accept it much more in the States.'

Tumbleweed Connection made more sense if viewed as a concept album, made up of a series of narrative songs based on one central theme. It produced no hit singles and was best listened to in its entirety as a collection of short stories rather than as an unconnected series of individual songs. The zenith of the album was undoubtedly 'Burn Down The Mission', a song which was also the highlight of Elton's live set. It featured an astonishingly powerful pounding by Elton as the music swelled and climaxed in an orgiastic frenzy. There were other strong cuts too, including 'Amoreena' (named after Ray Williams' daughter, who was Elton's goddaughter), 'Where To Now St Peter?' and 'Come Down In Time', which showcased Buckmaster's gently romantic string arrangement and harked back to the previous album.

Throughout the record, Bernie's lyrics expressed a youthful exuberance but dealt mainly in American stereotypical figures. There were Confederates and Yankees in 'My Father's Gun'; there was rich romance in the tale of the wanted man that is 'Ballad Of A Well-Known Gun'; and there were the melodramatic recollections of the battle-scarred figures in 'Talking Old Soldiers'. Then there was the carefree lady in the cornfield in 'Amoreena'; the 84-year-old grandma who needed her barn fixing in 'Country Comfort' and the riverboat that was sailing to New Orleans in 'My Father's Gun'.

From the sepia-tinted cover artwork and the image of Elton in black tie, suit and hat (perhaps an echo of Robert Mitchum's attire in the *noir* classic *The Night Of The Hunter*) to Elton's much more Americanised vocal delivery (something the producer Gus Dudgeon would call 'almost cod'), this was an astonishingly English view of American life. The album seemed to be as much about Taupin's adolescence in Lincolnshire as it was about the reality of lived experience in the American West. Despite this, as a package of ideas it has attained an elevated status within Elton's canon. Elton himself regards it as his finest work from the 1970s.

One of the songs, 'Country Comfort', would be covered by Elton's friend and contemporary Rod Stewart on his 1970 album *Gasoline Alley*, an effort that, at least at the time, failed to fry Elton's onions. 'We're really pissed off about it. He sounds like he made it up as they played,' he complained. 'I mean, they couldn't have gone further away from the original if they'd sung "Camptown Races". It's so bloody sad, because if anyone should sing that song, it ought to be him. Such a great voice, but now I can't even listen to [Stewart's] album; I get so brought down. Every other word is wrong.'

Tumbleweed Connection was released in the UK on 20 October 1970 (and the following January in the US), with a press launch at London's chic Revolution Club in a mews off Berkeley Square. Chicken wings in cream sauce and honeydew melon were on offer, and Elton's close friends were still calling him Reg. He had been back from the States for just over a month and his astonishing industry meant that he had already recorded yet another album, a soundtrack to the movie *Friends*.

The film, directed by Lewis Gilbert and written by him along with Vernon Harris and Jack Russell, took as its central theme the romance between an English boy and a French girl. It generated quite a controversy, given the full-frontal nudity of the girl, played by 17-year-old Anicée Alvina, who was supposed to be just 14 in the film.

The soundtrack, which was commissioned in early 1970 before Elton's Troubadour success, was recorded in double-quick time and was not one of his finest works. The songs contained few memorable episodes, and the lyrics from Bernie had a rather perfunctory feel.

'They sent me the script, and I just kind of skimmed through it,' Bernie later admitted. 'I think I spoke with the director's son, John Gilbert, who was doing the music, and he told me what it was about. I was too lazy to read the script, so I wrote all the songs for it having never seeing a cut of the film. It had to be done in four weeks; it was such a panic session, really a drama.' While Bernie's writing was, in its generalisation, akin to a critic penning a book review based on the jacket blurb, the real task of putting together much of the *Friends* music fell to Paul Buckmaster. Finding himself in the position of not having enough music to fill up the album, he took some of the central musical motifs of the movie and expanded upon them to create the eleven-minute orchestral suite 'Four Moods'. As for the artwork, Stuart Epps is damning: 'The sleeve was pretty horrible. Nobody was really happy with it.'

Elton himself had been keen to be involved in designing the artwork and had sent Paramount the *Tumbleweed Connection* album only to be told that they could come up with something better. In the end, what they came up with was a rather cheap pencil drawing of the lovers in black and white set against a pink background. Elton would later call it 'that fucking pink massacre'.

Meanwhile, the real buzz was about *Tumbleweed Connection*. Back at the Revolution Club launch, Elton spoke with obvious pride to *Rolling Stone*'s Robert Greenfield about his 'new country album' and about how he might now be able to make $500 a week at the Troubadour and $750 in San Francisco. The album was played to an attentive audience and, when the final note of 'Burn Down The Mission' ended, there was spontaneous applause. Elton graciously took to the microphone: 'If you listen to the album, if you dig it, you should know it's Steve Brown as much as me, Gus Dudgeon as much as me, Paul Buckmaster as much as me.'

Chris Charlesworth was among those who attended. 'When I left,' he recalls, 'I was waiting for a taxi and Elton was nearby with Helen Walters. I don't know why but I started singing "Your Song" quite quietly... "It's a little bit funny..." and Elton was obviously within earshot. "Not so fucking funny if you have to sing it every fucking night," he said. He was laughing but I got the distinct impression he was fed up of singing it all the same.'

Elton was by now keen to present himself as a serious singer. He did not want to be seen, as he suspected he was in some areas of the media, as a pop star, part of the 'Radio One hype', as he put it: 'At the moment, I am still struggling to get rid of this image that media people like Radio One have built up for me. You know, people think that I'm all cuddly and lovely and beautifully pop star-ish. I'm not, really I'm not.' The launch of *Tumbleweed Connection* confirmed that he was, indeed, now being taken seriously. 'I moved in to my new flat yesterday, they want me to live in town now,' Elton said at the end of the launch party, as the punters filed away. It would be the start of a very different life for hip new star Elton John.

In fact, Elton had gone to Geoffrey Ellis at DJM with a request. He needed help with buying a new property and was unsure what to do. Apart from the six months with Linda Woodrow, he had always lived at home. At 23, Elton paid very little attention to business matters. When the time came to renegotiate his management, publishing and recording contracts with Dick James and James honourably told him he should get a lawyer, Elton famously asked, 'Can't I use yours?' According to his biographer Philip Norman, James had manoeuvred Elton's personal manager, Ray Williams, out of the equation by quite ruthlessly tearing up his contract and goading Williams into suing him. Williams would surely have had good grounds to sue, as he was in no way in breach of contract, yet James knew that he did not have the resources to fight a long legal battle. Williams was stunned. The man who had found Elton John was being removed from the scene.

Williams and Elton had, in fact, already agreed in September 1970 that the relationship wasn't working. 'I could see the kind of manager he needed and it wasn't someone like me,' said Williams. 'Another thing was that, with his success, he was starting to get away with murder. He was very quick, very witty, very funny, and people just let him do anything he liked. I'd been standing up to him and that hadn't been going down well.' Williams still had nine months of his contract to run, a period that would have been extremely lucrative, given Elton's newfound recording success. Two months later, however, and he was out, eventually securing a £1,500 pay off. 'At least it was enough to pay my back rent and put some food in the fridge,' he said.

When Elton came to buy his new property, a flat in the relatively exclusive, newly built Water Gardens complex off the Edgware Road, Geoffrey Ellis accompanied him to Chesterton's estate agents. 'They were clearly not impressed by Elton,' Ellis remembers. 'Even then, he was not what could be described as a conservative dresser. In addition, he was yet to become famous in the circles in which these estate agents moved.' However, Uncle Dick was to sort it out. Teddy Barnes, Dick James' solicitor, knew some of the top people at Chesterton's and after a quiet word in their shell-likes, the purchase went through.

Elton, however, would not be living alone at 384 Winter Gardens. His new flatmate would be 21-year-old John Reid, a small and striking man from Paisley, Glasgow, whose slender build housed a terrier-like mentality. Born in 1949, the son of a mill worker, Reid had as a child lived for a brief period, in New Zealand, where his father worked as a welder, before the family returned home to Clydeside because of Reid's mother's homesickness. After school, he went on to study marine biology at Glasgow's Stow College, but by 18 he had dropped out of academia, moving to London to seek his fortune in the music business. He sold shirts at Austin Reed and sang at the Locarno before eventually being hired as a song plugger for EMI's publishing company, Ardmore and Beechwood. By the age of 19, Reid had been promoted within EMI to become the UK label manager of Tamla Motown Records. It was a precipitous ascent for the assiduous, stylish and hard-working young Glaswegian.

Not long after arriving in London, Reid became the escort of the shapely *Carry On* actress Barbara Windsor, who was 12 years his senior. 'I met a diminutive but good-looking young record plugger just down from Paisley in Scotland,' Windsor remembered in her memoirs, *All Of Me*. 'John Reid was only 18, but he had a drive and ambition I found very attractive. He was ballsy and had a sparkle, a twinkle in his eye. He wanted it all and you could see he had the chutzpah to go out and get it. We soon fell madly in love; more importantly, we liked each other and remain great friends.'

John Reid was aware of Elton John as the singer used to pop into EMI's offices when Reid worked there. He was 'a dumpy little guy in a funny jumpsuit who put his head round the door and asked to borrow some records,' he remembers. Reid had received a white-label test pressing of the *Elton John* album but couldn't be bothered to play it. The first time he saw Elton perform, however, he couldn't believe what he was seeing: 'He was something I hadn't seen before, or since really. He is just a one-off.'

The two became romantically involved during Elton's first tour of the States in 1970, when John Reid was working in San Francisco. Reid was to recall: 'He was bubbling over with what the critics had said and dying to tell someone about it. I was the nearest Englishman – or the nearest thing to an Englishman.' Just two months later, the singer and the Scotsman were an item, both professionally and in private. Reid was to become Elton's manager. Dick James had long realised that Elton needed a full-time manager and DJM's Steve Brown, although a more-than-efficient operator and wise counsel within the company, couldn't devote all of his time to him. 'Dick James invited John Reid to his office and, after discussion, agreed to employ him, on a fairly ordinary salary, specifically to look after Elton John and generally to carry out the functions of a hands-on manager on Dick's behalf,' says Geoffrey Ellis. 'I found [Reid] perfectly charming and clearly anxious to make a good impression.'

Elton's parents accepted his sexual coming out with their typical tolerance, love and understanding. 'They were fabulous, because they were the very first people I told,' Elton was to reflect. 'My mother has always said how hurt she'd be if I was ever deceitful and so when I confided in her that I might be gay she was very understanding about it. I was very lucky in that respect. My family was very accepting. I'm in an industry where it's not unusual for people to be gay, or whatever.' The relief was palpable. Elton had finally summoned up the courage to accept himself for what he was: 'I didn't accept the fact that I was gay and didn't come out of my shell until I was about 24. But that wasn't only sexually; that was all round. I was so naïve it was pitiful.'

Bernie Taupin was perfectly happy that Elton was finally in a serious relationship. Rather than there being any jealousy, or rivalry for Elton's affections, it seems that, from the very outset, he was comfortable with the situation. After all, he had never been Elton's lover. Dick James could also see the merit in the new set-up: 'If he's living with his manager, at least he'll have someone to get him up in the morning.'

For others, however, John Reid was simply a necessary evil. He was a man who would fight for Elton tooth and nail, but the problem was that he often reserved his most biting sarcasm and sometimes violent temper for those who were as committed as he was to the cause. 'He was never unfriendly to me, but it seemed like he didn't trust people, or he looked at people with a good deal of suspicion, as if they were trying to get to Elton,' is how the former *Melody Maker* journalist Chris Charlesworth puts it. 'I don't know if this was gay jealousy, or whether he was worried that Elton might go off and be managed by someone else – although that didn't seem likely as Elton seemed very dependent on him at the time. John Reid was also a very ill tempered man. He could fly off the handle at the slightest thing, and go wild like a little terrier.'

'I remember going to see them in their new flat at the Water Gardens,' recalls Mike Inkpen. 'It was modern and luxurious. A lift took you straight into the flat; there was no going up the stairs. It was quite small, but perfectly formed and in a very expensive part of town. John cooked the meal. I hadn't realised that their association went beyond the manager/client relationship, but he was exactly what Elton wanted and Elton was exactly what John needed. John was absolutely dedicated. He knew Elton was star material and he knew exactly how to develop him. But he was a ruthless man, very tough.' 'I met John Reid when he was at EMI,' reminisces Bob Harris. 'He was amazing. "Sparky" would be the way to describe him. There was certainly always something happening when he was around.'

Chris Charlesworth's rave report from the Krumlin Festival led to a casual friendship with Elton around this time and he remembers him as a quite unaffected and friendly guy. As Charlesworth was a vocal supporter of Elton in *Melody Maker*, the singer's management team were always affable and co-operative, particularly after the Krumlin review. 'After "Your Song" was a hit, I bumped into him everywhere,' he says. 'I went to a London show and met him and he started saying, "Oh Chris, thank you so much," and hugging me. Then it turned out he was living in a block of flats off Edgware Road not far from me. I bumped into him in the dry cleaners so we went and had a beer in the pub. I started going to more Elton John concerts. He was really nice, affable and charming. He had an astonishing knowledge of rock and pop music. It was obvious that he was a real record-collecting buff. He was the sort of guy who, if you mentioned a record, would say, "Oh, that was on the MGM label: it was yellow". He would know the B-side and who had sung backing vocals. He sounded like he'd studied pop, as if he'd taken a degree in it almost.'

Bernie Taupin's life was also about to change. He had fallen head over heels for Maxine Feibelmann, to be immortalised by Bernie later that year as the 'seamstress for the band' in the classic song 'Tiny Dancer'. Maxine would indeed make running repairs to the band's outfits on tour. The two were married in April 1971 in Market Rasen. 'Bernie wore a white velvet suit, a lilac shirt and earrings,' said one local newspaper report. 'Elton John, Bernie's pop-star partner, was also in white as the best man, outshining all the Rasen best men who ever were. He had a top hat of silver silk and his white-silk, 250 guineas wedding suit was embroidered with large blue, red and yellow flowers made of rhinestones. In the congregation were familiar figures of the world of pop, giving the scene an appearance almost of showbiz unreality. With three policemen outside directing the traffic and with many Rasen people lining the pathway up to the church, it was about as far away as you could ever get from the traditional type Market Rasen wedding.'

John Walters, the BBC producer, went up to Bernie and joked: 'If I were a bridegroom… but then again, no.' Mike Inkpen remembers the wedding day as being quite a bash. 'We went with all the people from Dick James Music. They hired a coach and picked us up in London. After the wedding, we all went back to the racetrack, where they had the reception. And of course, with Maxine's dad being a champagne importer, he had laid on unlimited champagne. So you have got a room full of about 150 musos and unlimited champagne. I don't need to paint you a picture, really, do I?'

Bernie bought a house in nearby Tealby. Beck Hill was a two-bedroom semi-detached stone cottage said to be the home, a hundred years earlier, of the Tennyson d'Eyncourt family, relatives of the Poet Laureate, Alfred, Lord Tennyson. Many of the early Elton John classic songs were to be conceived in this hideaway.

Fired up by their sudden success, Elton and his band just kept on keeping on. They flew out to Boston for the second US tour in three months and Bernie Taupin was permanently changed by the American experience. 'For us, arriving there was life-changing,' he marvelled. 'It was the garden of Eden – musically, culturally and sexually.' The fairytale land of his childhood and adolescence was suddenly there in front of him, in all its grandeur. 'At the first opportunity, I rented a car and drove through Arizona, through the heartland. It was a dream come true, because I got to experience a country which had excited and inspired me since practically the day I was born.'

On the road, it was a time of camaraderie. 'It's a real band now,' Elton told *Melody Maker* in 1970, during the break in the UK that followed those first American dates. 'And the boys have helped me quite a lot. It is so tight now, but in a year's time it'll be unbelievable. America did our confidence a lot of good and I don't ever have to tell them what to do, because we all know what we're doing. There are some songs with very broken rhythms and they just play them without having it explained to them.'

A handful of UK dates were squeezed into the touring schedule, including a concert at the Royal Albert Hall in October and a charity gig supporting the Who at the Roundhouse in December, at which Pete Townshend dedicated his band's performance of their *Tommy* rock opera to Elton. It was the last time the Who performed the piece in its entirety until their reunion tour of 1989. Elton's main concern for the rest of 1970 was America. 'I returned to the States for another tour. And what do you know? In six months I'm earning $10,000 a night!' said Elton. 'I was really furious, because Dick had been right.' He played Boston, Philadelphia, the Fillmore West in San Francisco, Santa Monica Civic in LA, the Fillmore East in New York – just over 20 gigs in the lead-up to Christmas. His showmanship was coming more and more to the fore. One journalist, David Felton, noted: 'At Santa Monica, Elton wore a Jagger top hat, cape and purple jumpsuit… During "Burn Down The Mission", he kicked away the piano stool, ripped off his jumpsuit and finished with a series of giant bunny kicks in purple pantyhose. The crowd, to use Elton's term, went mental.'

At the Fillmore West, Bernie and Elton were introduced to a certain Bob Dylan. 'I've met Dylan… and I really haven't given a fuck,' was how Elton put it in 1971 when asked how it compared with meeting his real hero, Leon Russell. Yet with the passing of the years, Elton was to remember the encounter a tad differently: 'Bernie and I were just like, fuck! Dylan has an aura about him. It's not frightening. It's just… blimey!' 'I didn't even recognise him,' confessed Bernie. 'Elton said, "This is Bob Dylan." I wasn't ready for it, what can I say? I mean it was like, "Oh God," or "You're God," or "My God."'

News of Elton's success started filtering back to the UK through the music papers. 'Dylan Digs Elton' ran one *Melody Maker* cover that autumn. Such a ringing endorsement from the iconic US songwriter of the day confirmed Elton's newly won stature as a major player. There would be other high-profile admirers, too. 'I remember hearing Elton John's "Your Song" in America,' John Lennon said in 1975. 'I remember thinking, great, that's the first new thing that's happened since we happened. It was a step forward. There was something about his vocals that was an improvement on all of the English vocals until then.' Lennon was not the only former Beatle to be impressed. 'When I first came to America and the *Elton John* album was, like, Number 18 or 19 on the charts, and I was pinching myself, looking at all the records on the charts by my heroes, I got a telegram from George [Harrison] congratulating me. I still have it somewhere. It was just a very thoughtful thing for him to do. It meant the whole world to me.'

Elton was not, as yet, a big enough star to have his own personal retinue, mode of transport and schedule. For now, he was just one of the band: the most important one, obviously, but touring still felt like a team effort. 'We had our differences on the long tours, especially when we did those bus tours,' says Nigel Olsson. 'They were Greyhound buses with no telly or catering on board. We were very worn out and tempers got frayed. But they were the golden years. In those days, the money wasn't that good: it was just that surge every time you went on stage.'

It seemed that, with every performance, Elton grew in stagecraft: grimacing and pouting, bashing a tambourine against his bum, cracking jokes, dropping in the odd funny voice, pounding the piano keys with his head thrown back in ecstasy, jumping atop the keyboard performing mid-air balances as if it were a pommel horse. 'The outrageousness is very much a part of me, which is why I admire people like Jagger and Zappa so much,' he reflected. The climax number, 'Burn Down The Mission', was always the opportunity for Elton to cut loose. 'Elton turned it into a sporting event,' reported journalist David Felton. 'He spun away from the piano and clapped his hands, like a center breaking from the huddle. He leaped and ran across the stage, shaking random hands with the crowd that had zoomed forward. At one point he actually leapt on top of the grand piano.'

While some rock performers turned the pop spectacle into something cool and detached, for Elton John, it was all about entertainment, good music played to the best of the band's ability, and connection with the audience. Explaining why he shook hands with the audience at the end of the show, Elton explained: 'With me, it's as if the kids think I'm the boy next door who's fat and podgy, who's got no right to be a rock and roll star. That's my image, and that suits me fine.'

'He decided that he didn't want to be ignored any longer,' says Stuart Epps of Elton's abrupt change in stage persona in 1970. 'He decided he would rise to the occasion when he went on stage. He wanted to be big. He was the one who wanted to go beyond what we imagined him to be. That was purely him.' Yet, on the inside, despite flashes of flamboyance offstage and his almost demonically possessed persona on it, there was still a deep insecurity. After shows, he would sit quietly, lost in thought. Polite to the point of timidity when approached, Elton has admitted: 'I was comfortable onstage, but not very comfortable off it. Although I was having a ball, I was still stuck with the insecure, nervous person inside. And just being successful doesn't cure it.'

Throughout this period, Elton was almost constantly on tour. He followed up his autumn American tour with a New Year UK jaunt, playing small urban venues and university halls. A live album, *17-11-70*, came out in May 1971, making it four albums in 12 months. 'That was done as a radio broadcast up at Phil Ramone's studio in New York, to an audience of maybe 100 people,' said Gus Dudgeon. 'It was being bootlegged like mad, so Dick James rang me up and said, "Look, if I send you a tape of this broadcast, do you think there is an album there?" So I managed to find about 20 minutes to fill each side, and Dick said, "Go ahead and mix it and we'll put it out as an album."' 'It is a fucking amazing album, that,' Elton has said. 'One of the best live albums I've ever heard.'

As a snapshot of Elton's early years as a live solo artist, *17-11-70* is invaluable. The playing and singing was fresh and unselfconscious. A version of 'Burn Down The Mission', checking in at over 18 minutes, it interpolated Elvis's 'My Baby Left Me' and the Beatles' 'Get Back'. It also included a live favourite of the period, a cover of the Stones' 'Honky Tonk Women' which – much to the audience's amusement – begins with a three-part harmony.

Around this time in 1971, the folk singer and future stand-up comedian 'Big Yin' Billy Connolly witnessed Elton John live for the first time. 'A piano-playing pop star?' he marvelled. 'The last one of those we'd had was Neil Sedaka. But here was this amazing guy so different from all that, yet at the same time not afraid to be showbizzy in a venue that was all joss sticks, marijuana and alternative lifestyles and trousers. Like everyone, I was just blown away.'

Elton's music was now selling fast. The *Elton John* album, which had sold 10,000 in the UK, stormed up the charts into the Top 10 in the USA, selling 100,000 copies. *Tumbleweed Connection* would reach Number 2 in the UK and Number 5 in the US. In the States, the two albums would remain in the charts for 51 and 37 weeks respectively. Then, finally, the big singles breakthrough came. Although there was initial reluctance to release 'Your Song' as an A-side in the States (it was originally the B-side to 'Take Me To The Pilot'), radio pluggers soon moved to back the ballad. In the UK, it was released as an A-side, and in early 1971, it became a hit on both sides of the Atlantic, reaching Number 7 in the UK and Number 8 in the USA. With its romantic melody and tinkling piano, 'Your Song' was perfect for the times. Later in 1971, John Lennon's 'Imagine' and the popularity of Gilbert O'Sullivan would confirm that piano pop was in vogue.

The promotional video for 'Your Song' might be primitive even by the standards of the mid-1970s, but it was nevertheless quite charming. Filmed in the countryside, Elton lip-synched the song to camera, uncertain at first, but with a genuine tenderness that made it a classic of sincerity. And not just that – Elton actually looked cute. A whole generation of teenagers were about to take him to their hearts.

Throughout 1971, Elton continued to tour to the point of exhaustion. The spring UK tour preceded a third US tour, which would run almost without a break from April 2 to June 13. The show would begin with Elton playing solo on piano before the band joined him for the second half of the set. The live album, re-titled *11.17.70* for its American release that May, reached Number 11 on the Billboard charts. Elton also helped out his old friend Long John Baldry, working as producer and session musician on Baldry's album *It Ain't Easy*. In a novel move, Baldry had Elton work on one side of the record while another of his ex-singers, Rod Stewart, produced the flip side.

Bernie was also by no means idle, producing David Ackles's *American Gothic* record. He was also coaxed into the studio by DJM to make his own album. Long-deleted in reality, it was apparently also deleted from the memory banks of its creator shortly after its release at the end of 1971. 'To be honest, I'm not that interested in my album any more,' he told Paul Gambaccini two years later. 'I made it for my own ends and for personal satisfaction. I just got a few friends, went into the studio and did some poems I wanted to get down on record. I can't even remember what's on it.' His studio 'friends' included most of the normal Elton John team, with Gus Dudgeon producing, Clive Franks engineering, Steve Brown co-ordinating and Caleb Quaye on guitar. One new addition was a blond-haired acoustic guitarist named Davey Johnstone, who was soon to become the fourth member of Elton's band and, eventually, Elton's longest serving sideman.

Johnstone was born in Edinburgh in 1951 and at the age of 17 moved down to London to play on the folk circuit. Under the unlikely pseudonym of Shaggis, he played banjo with Noel Murphy as Murf and Shaggis, before briefly upsizing to a three-piece, Draught Porridge, with the addition of Ron Chesterman from the Strawbs on double bass. Davey left Draught Porridge to join the folk outfit Magna Carta, whose producer happened to be the one and only Gus Dudgeon. Dudgeon kept on mentioning Elton to Davey, saying that if he ever got the call to work with him, he should jump at the chance.

Sure enough, fate duly intervened and Davey was asked to add acoustic guitar, mandolin and sitar to *Madman Across The Water*, Elton's fifth studio album, at Trident Studios. Most of the album was recorded in just a few days that August. Although Dee Murray and Nigel Olsson were now established as Elton's touring band, back in the studio, Gus Dudgeon was still far from convinced that the three-piece could work. A crack team of players was assembled, including Roger Pope, Barry Morgan and Terry Cox on drumming duties and Dave Glover, Brian Odgers and Herbie Flowers on bass. The session percussionist Ray Cooper, a man who would also come to play a huge part in the Elton John story, but was then a session musician, was called upon to flesh out the rhythm section. Rick Wakeman also made an appearance on the organ. Caleb Quaye returned on guitar and Dee and Nigel were asked to play on just one track, 'All The Nasties'.

Madman Across The Water was arguably Elton's most experimental record. With a European orchestral aesthetic married daringly to American blues, country and rock and roll, its sound harked back to *Elton John*, yet there was something more strident and aggressive about this record. At times the strings surged wildly, casting ominous shapes on Elton's melodies.

Ken Scott worked on the album as an engineer. At just 24, he had already worked on many classic Beatles sessions, including the *White Album*, and, by the summer of 1971, was also established as David Bowie's producer. 'Those arrangements by Buckmaster really pulled people in,' Scott says. 'He was unlike any other arranger at that time. There was a lot less schmaltz and a lot more of the Beatles' edginess.'

'When you finally got into the studio, all of a sudden you would hear this orchestra running through the parts, and you could actually hear it being played by 20 or 30 people.' said Gus Dudgeon. 'I would be thinking, wow, this is just magic, because that would be the first time anybody had actually heard it. Then you would finally marry the string parts up with the orchestra and it was such a buzz. It was such a white-knuckle ride. There's nothing like hearing an orchestra play a great arrangement.'

Under the guidance of Buckmaster, the title track of the new album became a brilliant piece of orchestral rock. Its opaque lyrics by Taupin had people thinking that the madman in question was Richard Nixon, although Bernie subsequently denied any political intent. The original 'Madman Across The Water', featuring David Bowie's guitarist, Mick Ronson, had, in fact, been recorded for the *Tumbleweed Connection* sessions and then discarded. As ever, Ronson was on inspired form, lending the track a mildly unhinged heavy rock atmosphere that would never be repeated in Elton's long and illustrious career. Gus Dudgeon, for one, thoroughly enjoyed the original version. 'It's a loony version, completely crazy. I think it's funny, especially the bit where I'm slinging sound effects on all over the bloody place. It's Mick Ronson just going completely crazy.'

The true classic cut, however, is 'Tiny Dancer'. 'Steve Brown rang me up at about 10pm one night and asked me if I could come into Trident Studios,' says the pedal-steel player B.J. Cole. 'The studio was full of musicians. Elton obviously had the seeds of the song and he was putting it together while we were in there. Then the song just evolved from that. I remember by the time I got out of there it was daylight, which was fantastic. It's a great way to record. I was very pleased with what I'd done on it, and I still am.'

Taupin's narratives were both engaging and yet strangely cryptic. Some decoded 'Indian Sunset' as a protest song, yet Elton was quick to disavow such hidden meaning, saying that the song was simply an American Indian narrative. Yet it's undeniable that *Madman Across The Water* revealed greater maturity to Bernie's writing. It was broader, more rounded and certainly more abstract.

One reason for this was that Elton, although not the author of the songs, was the team's editor and director. Confronted with pages of new lyrics, he would perform the necessary surgery to turn them into living pop songs. Taupin was still very much learning his craft. With only a rudimentary idea of how a song might work in terms of its structure, where the verses and choruses and middle-eights ought to be, his songs were sometimes formally quite odd and therefore unique and inspiring. 'Bernie's lyrics, if you saw them, they weren't iambic pentameter at its best,' Elton was to reflect. 'They were like seven lines, then three, then four, then nine, and I did a lot of crossing out. He didn't interfere with melodies; it was just purely on that basis. But I know what he was writing about most of the time because we were like brothers. So it was very easy to interpret his songs.'

The early Elton John albums have gone on to become cult classics, particularly among fellow musicians. Indeed, two of the songs on *Madman Across The Water* would be revived 30 years later. 'Tiny Dancer' would be featured in the film by the former *Rolling Stone* writer Cameron Crowe about the early 1970s music scene, *Almost Famous*, while Eminem cunningly interpolated 'Indian Sunset' into 2pac's post-humous 2005 UK Number 1 single, 'Ghetto Gospel'.

In its intimacy and companionability, Elton's music spoke to both sexes. And while other more perfectly formed rock stars attracted more open shows of female adulation, Elton nevertheless always had a very sizeable following of girls. The teenage Kate Bush, for example: 'At one point I had a bit of a crush on Elton John,' she has confessed. 'I thought he was fantastic. It was before he got really famous... around *Madman Across The Water*. I'd play the records and dream of being able to play like him, those fantastic hands. I was really crazy about him, his music, everything he did. I knew classical pianists from records, but he was the first great popular piano player I had heard. I wrote [to him] saying how much I liked him. I quoted some of Bernie Taupin's lyrics and told him how I played his music when I was low and how much better I'd feel. I took [the letter] round to the BBC [because] I didn't know where else to send it. I don't suppose he ever got it.'

Despite its quality, *Madman Across The Water* underperformed, at least in the UK. In America, it sold relatively strongly, reaching Number 8. But on the other side of the Atlantic, it was a different story alto-gether. Released on November 5, 1971, it got no further than a lowly Number 41. Elton's career was once again in something of a lull as the 'Friends' single also failed to chart.

Elton John had not seen any action in the British singles charts for over a year when, driving to his parents' house one day, Bernie came up with the first lines of a new song, almost fully-formed. Repeating them over and over again in his head until he could get hold of a pen and paper, he quickly scribbled down the first couplet:

'She packed my bags last night pre-flight
Zero hour 9am...'

CHAPTER 6

A CAT NAMED HERCULES

'I want to be a legend.'

Elton John speaking to filmmaker Bryan Forbes

'I'm gonna grab myself a place in history
A teenage idol, that's what I'm gonna be.'

'I'm Gonna Be A Teenage Idol'; words: Bernie Taupin;
music: Elton John

Spring 1972. Elton John and John Reid are taking in the morning air as they look about their new surroundings in the heart of the English stockbroker belt. They have just moved into their new home, an exclusive and spacious bungalow at 14 Abbots Drive, Virginia Water, Runnymede, Surrey. Windsor, Ascot and Eton are all nearby. London is still but a short commute away. It is one of the most affluent areas in the whole of the British Isles.

The pair's new home is just off the A30 on the edge of Wentworth Golf Course. It has its own swimming pool and spacious lawns in front and, at a cost of £50,000, is an oasis of opulence befitting the *nouveau riche*. Several cars stand on the drive, among them the obligatory Rolls Royce. In the front of the property is a well-stocked kitchen, a games room including a pinball machine, a table-tennis table on which visitors vanquish their super-competitive rock star host at their peril and a jukebox stacked with 7" singles. A cavernous main dinning room is situated further towards the back of the bungalow, full of *objets d'art* and ornaments. Elton's gold discs hang in the bathroom.

Elton John's new circle of friends includes people like the film-maker Bryan Forbes and his wife, the actress Nanette Newman. In the space of a little under 18 months his income has catapulted him from the two-bedroom maisonette he shared with Bernie, Sheila and Derf into the sort of postcode in which proper entertainers like Bruce Forsyth are domiciled. Indeed, Elton's mum is a frequent visitor to the house, which her son has christened Hercules. He has just bought her a £15,000 house in Ickenham and a white MGB sports car. In fact, Elton has just this month signed Sheila and Derf's marriage certificate; his mum has finally remarried. On the certificate are the two witnesses, John Reid's mother, Elizabeth, and Elton Hercules John.

* * *

Although some people round the DJM offices still, on occasion, called him Reg, they would, as of January 6, 1972, be technically incorrect. That was the day that Reginald Kenneth Dwight changed his name by deed poll to Elton Hercules John. Many rockers have adopted stage names, but Elton's transformation was more complete than most – Reg Dwight was legally banished forever to the annals of history.

As late as the 1990s, Eric Clapton was still referring to Elton as Reg, something that did not go down too well with the star. 'Reg is the unhappy part of my life,' Elton told the interviewer Tony Parsons. 'I can't bear people calling me Reg. If people send me letters as Reginald Dwight, I don't even open them. I've been Elton John for 33 years. If my mother can call me Elton, then everybody else can.' In 2006, much to the delight of the show's host and the production team on Channel 4's *New Paul O'Grady Show*, Elton told a tea-time UK television audience that 'Reginald Kenneth Dwight made me sound like a banker... or a wanker, one of the two.'

Elton's new middle name, Hercules, had a comedic, not heroic origin. It was the name of the horse in one of British television's most famous sitcoms, *Steptoe And Son*, a long-running saga about a father-and-son rag-and-bone-man team. The pathetic son, nearing middle age, tried hard (but failed miserably) to rebel against his Victorian father, all bad teeth and beggar-man's clothes, as the two played out a classic, if improbable, rivalry against the backdrop of a London which was changing more quickly than either of them could comprehend. Yet the status quo never changed and the son always remained Steptoe's servant. It obviously appealed to Elton's sense of humour that his mythological middle name had such scrapheap origins. Just how often does a grown man take on the name of a fictional horse?

Yet the glam rock world would have been a much more boring place without such acts of wilful silliness: 'Metal Guru' by Marc Feld, 'School's Out' by Vincent Furnier, 'The Jean Genie' by David Jones, 'I'm The Leader Of The Gang' by Paul Gadd, 'Dancing On A Saturday Night' by Barry Green, 'Rock On' by David Cook, 'Get Down' by Raymond O'Sullivan, 'Sugar Me' by Lynsey Rubin, 'My Coo-Ca-Choo' by Bernard Jewry and, indeed, 'Crocodile Rock' by Reginald Dwight – none of them have had the same ring to them.

By 1972, just as so many inhabitants of the pop world were changing – dressing up and putting on the lipstick, powder and paint – so the promotion of popular music was also on the verge of a dramatic change. Through advances in media and television, pop could be heard, seen and bought in a far greater range of locations throughout the world than ten years previously. The advent of the transistor radio and the cassette meant that popular music was now being consumed in the car and the workplace, as well as in the home. Advances in technology in the recording studio, notably the spread of first 16-track and then 32–track recording, also enabled music like Elton's (detailed and with high production values) to flourish on FM radio and on the home hi-fi.

The demand for, and love of, popular music was as strong as ever. British television's *Top Of The Pops* was, in its early-to-mid-1970s heyday, regularly watched by upwards of 16 million viewers. That's well over a quarter of the entire British population, all watching the same songs every Thursday – an astonishing figure by today's standards. Singles might sell over 250,000 copies and still not even reach the Top 5. BBC Radio One DJs were genuine 'superstar DJs', almost as popular, and in some cases actually more so, than the acts they presented. The cast of stars that dominated the glam rock era – Bolan, Bowie, Roxy Music, Elton, Alice Cooper, Slade, Sweet, Wizzard, etc – were joined in the public imagination by Jimmy Savile, Noel Edmonds, Tony Blackburn and the self-proclaimed hairy cornflake, Dave Lee Travis. Elton John found himself, whether he liked it or not, lumped in with the other glam rockers. Five-foot eight Elton, with his receding hairline, joke glasses and budding paunch, was suddenly a teen idol.

Although 1972 and 1973 saw frock 'n' roll became a deeply rooted part of the music scene of the day, it would be very wrong to think of that time as one big roller coaster of fun. The 1970s were, for the majority at least, a troubled time. In the US, 1973 was the year of the deepening disasters of Vietnam and Watergate. In Britain, it was the era of the three-day week and the industrial unrest that would lead, in February 1974, to a change of government. Glam rock was the *un*reality of the times. It provided a sense of spectacle and fun at a moment in British society when ordinary people's lives were hard. Children would get home from school to find the electricity cut, no hot food and the prospect of completing their homework by candlelight. Unemployment and inflation began spiralling out of control. The hitherto hegemonic ideas of the National Health Service and equal educational opportunities for all were coming increasingly under attack from the New Right. In short, the political consensus that had dominated British society for almost 30 years was being broken up by increasingly polarised views of how society should be run: either State-controlled or deregulated and at the mercy of the market.

Yet in Britain, this increasingly radicalised political and social climate was the catalyst for some impressive pieces of popular culture, as young people reflected these turbulent times through artistic endeavour. It seemed to be a golden age of literature, film, fashion, popular music, the theatre and television. Virtually all the great situation comedies were invented in that 1970s, as was so much of what was unique and great about popular music. Behind the strident silliness of much glam rock, there beat a far more serious heart of change. The original Roxy

Music with Bryan Ferry and Brian Eno set a new, post-modern agenda for popular music. But, more importantly, there was David Bowie.

In the summer of 1972, Bowie appeared on *Top Of The Pops* singing 'Starman'. In one of the defining moments of early 1970s British pop, he looked so different – scarily different in fact – with his wan complexion, red hair and gamin beauty. Bowie had a gay following, but also a massive following among straight teenage boys and girls. His music told weird tales of multiple personalities and sexualities and predicted multiple futures for popular music as a whole, as each album release switched styles in a dizzying blur of the new. The moment when Bowie put his arm round his hulking guitarist Mick Ronson to sing the chorus of 'Starman' on *Top Of The Pops* looks tame by today's standards but in the context of the era it was a little piece of history, a moment of male bonding; a queering of popular music. Thereafter, for a man to wear make-up was no longer necessarily a signal that he was either effeminate or a transvestite.

How ironic, then, that Bowie (predominantly heterosexual, with a wife and child) should make the first move in this game of sexual politics. In January 1972, he had announced to *Melody Maker* that he was '… gay, and [I] always have been'. Because Bowie's fans were expecting and accepting of shock and outrage, his admission simply made him more *other*. In actual fact, in early 1972, Bowie didn't have that many fans to shock. His fame was to explode later in the year with the release of *The Rise And Fall Of Ziggy Stardust And The Spiders From Mars*.

By contrast, Elton John, living with his male partner and almost exclusively homosexual by orientation, was pretending, in public at least, to be straight. There was nothing in the slightest unusual about this. Society was still almost overwhelmingly intolerant as a whole towards homosexuality. For a man who had only recently found himself sexually, we can guess that it was hardly an appealing prospect to go public about his orientation. Furthermore, Bowie's admission had merely added levels of mystique to his already highly charismatic persona. Elton's audience was rather different.

Elton John's music did not appear to represent the deep aesthetic changes within society that the music of Roxy Music and David Bowie seemed almost innately to reflect. For Roxy and Bowie, their music was art. For Elton, his music was about entertainment. It became so enormously popular because it was escapist. In the troubled 1970s, for the vast majority of music buyers, escapism was exactly what they needed. 'My music – I'm very into what I'm doing,' Elton was to say. 'But even that you can't take too seriously. I've never regarded pop music as an art form: I think it's just entertainment, and I think that is why pop groups are coming back because people are fed-up with moodies *[sic]* and they'd rather go out and have a good time.'

The singer was also tiring of what he called 'the Elton John syndrome'. 'I'm getting a bit fed up with singer-songwriter records. They drive me mad,' he was quoted as saying. 'I was labelled a singer-songwriter and did four LPs in that syndrome. But I've always fought against the Elton John syndrome. People take it too seriously. I'd like us to be a band. On the first albums we used a lot of session men, but we could never do it that way now, planning it down to the last flute.' 'If people deny that they're writing pop music, I think that's their own ego,' Bernie Taupin agreed. 'Weren't the Beatles a pop group? That's what we all need – a bit of simplicity. I just like a good pop record. I like T. Rex and I think the Kinks are amazing. As far as musicianship goes – I don't give a shit as long as I enjoy it.'

Elton's next album, *Honky Château*, in June 1972 was to see both a change of locale for its conception and a shift in musical direction. 'It's going to be a really funky album,' Bernie promised early that year. 'It will shock a few people. I think we've gone as far as we can on the grand scale with string arrangements and that. We just want to get back to the roots.'

The new member of the band, Davey Johnstone, turned the Elton John trio of drummer, bassist and singer-pianist into a more much more versatile outfit. The addition of a fourth instrumentalist gave colour and depth to the older material and meant that Elton didn't invariably have to shoulder all the responsibility as the soloist; now

Dave's lead guitar lines could trade musical motifs with Elton's or could take on the role of focal point in the sound.

For Johnstone, it was something of a change of tack. He had hitherto mainly played acoustic folk guitar, but it's remarkable how quickly the 21-year-old grew into his new job. He was also a talented singer and, together with Nigel and Dee, formed a trio that would provide some of the best backing vocals in pop. Long-haired, blond and lean, Johnstone was also an added visual attraction on stage. For the rest of the band, the recruitment of Davey as a permanent member came out of the blue. 'I wanted Mick Grabham in there, because he was my buddy from school,' admitted Olsson. 'But we found he was the wrong type of player. Davey fitted because of his folk background.'

Engineer Ken Scott remembers that *Honky Château* was conceived as the start of a new page in the musical history of Elton John: 'The decision had been made that *Madman Across The Water* was the end of Chapter 1 and that it was about time to move on and do something completely different, and that something different was *Honky Château*.' Shorter songs, less complex arrangements and a lighter touch were the order of the day. The new material lacked the furrowed-brow profundity of previous albums, but it more than compensated with its pop quality. 'I was just about ready to give up,' claimed Elton in 1973, rather melodramatically. 'I got very depressed with all the bad reviews of *Madman*.' *Rolling Stone* summed up the disappointment felt by some reviewers: '*Madman* is a difficult, sometimes impossibly dense record. America is worthy of a better story than this record and Elton John needs a better story than this to sing.'

It had also been suggested to Elton that, for tax reasons, he needed to record outside of the UK. At the time rock stars were moaning about what they regarded as the excessively high levels of taxation imposed by the government. The Rolling Stones, for example, took their mobile recording unit to Nice to work on tracks for 1972 album *Exile On Main St*. Elton also chose France, looking for as secluded a haven as possible. He found it at the Château Hérouville, also known as Strawberry Studios, 25 miles north of Paris in the countryside close to the town of Auvers-sur-Oise, the resting place of Vincent Van Gogh. It had been built in the seventeenth century and came complete with a medieval moat. At the time Elton discovered it, it was owned by the French film composer Michel Magne and was, it seemed, in a state of permanent restoration. In the mid-nineteenth century, the château had been home to the composer Frédéric Chopin and his lover, the novelist George Sand, and the two studios at the complex were named after them. Their ghosts were said to haunt the building. After working there four years later with David Bowie, producer Tony Visconti confirmed the rumours: 'It felt like it was haunted as fuck, but what could Frédéric and George really do to me, scare me in French?'

The summer before Elton's first stay there, another rock group had made its mark on the local population with a never-to-be-forgotten free show. In June 1971, the Grateful Dead had been booked to play a festival, but when the gig was cancelled due to poor weather, they simply set up on the lawn and played. Legend has it that either the food and drink or the actual water supply was spiked with acid. A fireman was seen swimming fully clothed in the pool, while a schoolteacher and a priest danced the polka. 'Yes, the Grateful Dead spiked everything with acid,' affirmed Elton's engineer, Ken Scott. 'They even had the police drinking the stuff. Afterwards the local gendarmerie were extra vigilant concerning the château and the sort of people there, and the drug use that could go on, so you had to be very careful. The phones were supposedly tapped too. At least, that was the story that went round.'

There were two main wings to the château. The right wing housed the Sand Studio and the owner's accommodation and office, whilst the left side contained the living quarters for the musicians and their entourage, as well as a suite for the 'name' artist. This area also included a games room and a room that was also allegedly haunted and was always kept locked. 'We're totally out of our environment,' said Elton, 'And there are no hangers-on there, no phone calls.'

Life at Strawberry Studios was one of communal living and hard work but plenty of relaxation. The leisure time was spent enjoying the studio's folksy charm, excellent cuisine, ample French wine exclusive to the château and the tennis court and swimming pool. Sitting round after breakfast, the band would begin work with Elton in the kitchen area. He would compose and the band, equipped with rudimentary kit and amps, would learn the songs as he created them. Working quickly, Elton would read through Bernie's latest lyrics, selecting, editing, changing a line here, deleting a line there before producing two, maybe three melodies which would then be laid down later in the day in the studio proper. Astonishingly, melodies seemed to be springing from Elton fully formed.

'I saw Elton write "Rocket Man" in ten minutes right in front of me whilst I ate breakfast. It was unbelievable,' recalls Ken Scott. 'Bernie would go up to his room after dinner every night at around 9pm. He would come down the next day with several sheets of paper and give them to Elton. Elton would look at them and say, "Oh, that one looks good," and put it to one side and he'd keep going through them until he'd come up with two or three that he really liked. Then he would go over to the piano and start working on them. The one that really stuck out was "Rocket Man", because in just ten minutes it was there. Elton would take Bernie's lyrics and he would change them all round. Where Bernie might have written something as a verse, Elton would take a couple of lines from it and turn it into the chorus. It was very impressive.'

It soon became apparent at these January 1972 sessions that both Elton and Bernie were in superb songwriting form. The resultant album would prove the most consistently excellent Elton John album to date and transform him from a mere star to an international superstar. '*Honky Château* was a really important album for us,' he later reflected. 'We'd made it but we still had one final bridge to cross, which was to make a great album.' Two songs in particular confirmed this upward shift in quality: 'Rocket Man' and 'Mona Lisas And Mad Hatters'.

'Rocket Man' was released as a single in April 1972, reaching Number 6 in the US and Number 2 in the UK. Sounding quite different from just about anything he had done before, it was confirmation that Elton had now fully moved into pop. Like the record that had clearly inspired it, David Bowie's 'Space Oddity', 'Rocket Man' was a pop song about an astronaut on a space flight. The similarities between the two singles were inescapable: they had the same producer (Gus Dudgeon), the same childlike quality to the lyrics ('Mars ain't the kind of place, to raise your kids/ In fact, it's cold as hell', sang Elton) and the same use of space as a metaphor for personal alienation (Bowie's Major Tom is 'sitting in his tin can, far above the moon'; Bernie's astronaut is also cast adrift, 'burning out his fuse up here alone'). 'Nobody but Elton could have sung that line from "Rocket Man" about being as high as a kite without getting banned from the radio,' said Taupin, 20 years after the single's release. 'It was a drugs song.'

'Rocket Man' was beyond a doubt one of Elton John's most brilliant singles. The musicianship was outstanding. Davey Johnstone's space-age guitar work, with its upward slides, provided the sonic zooms that fitted the material so well, while David Hentschel played ARP synthesizer. Hentschel had joined Trident Studios as a tea boy during a year out between public school and university, but soon decided that the music business was for him. As an engineer, Hentschel would be Gus Dudgeon's right-hand man on this and several other Elton John recording sessions, before moving on to become a top producer in his own right with Genesis.

'The modern incarnation of synthesizers started to appear on recordings around the time I started working at Trident,' remembers Hentschel. 'The Beatles flirted with a Moog. Since I was the only person at Trident there with a formal musical education, I was elected as the programmer/session player. I fell in love with this seemingly infinite array of sounds, which seemed like pure imagination coming to life. Gus had heard a couple of my demos and was keen to use these new sounds – "Rocket Man" was the perfect subject matter for this new space age technology.' For 1972, this was a groundbreaking sound. It sounded great on the radio too, as Dudgeon's production gave it plenty of treble, especially on the acoustic guitar and high vocal harmonies.

'Rocket Man' would return to the charts in 1991 as a cover version by Kate Bush, although perhaps the most famous cover of all dates back to 1978 and an appearance by *Star Trek*'s William Shatner at the Science Fiction Film Awards ceremony. Shatner, introduced by Bernie Taupin himself, spoke the lyrics in a classic piece of ham over-acting which, it has been suggested, brings out the druggy references rather more clearly than the original. Commenting on the footage years later on YouTube, one perceptive viewer was to call it 'the worst non-harmful thing I've ever heard or seen'.

The other standout track on *Honky Château*, recorded roughly in the middle of the sessions, was 'Mona Lisas And Mad Hatters'. Although by no means as well known as 'Your Song' and never released as an A-side single, it deserves to be thought of as one of Elton's classics. The pared-down arrangement with piano and mandolin but no drums gave the song a hymn-like effect. The lyric encapsulated Bernie's feelings on his first visit to New York that sense of being a very small fish in a very large pond, where everything is more vivid and more different than expected. 'Until you've seen this trash can dream come true/You stand at the edge, while people run you through.' Cameron Crowe used the song in *Almost Famous* to express the idea of an individual being 'just one story in the big, big, big world of the city'.

Another highlight was the goofy melody to 'I Think I'm Going To Kill Myself'. Bernie's lyric was a witty exploration of teenage self-absorption while Elton's vocal was perfectly pitched – slightly under-played and arch to mock the superficiality of a teenager planning to kill himself for the sole reason of getting his death reported in the papers. Elton turned the song into a classic by taking the process to a logical, absurdist conclusion. Undercutting any hopes of the song being taken seriously, he couched it in a quite wonderful music-hall honky-tonk piano romp. The chorus sounded like a pretty accurate parody of the theme tune for *The Goodies*, one of the least cool but most popular UK TV comedy shows of the 1970s. In fact, with their ludicrous but hilarious sketches including giant cats, black puddings used as martial arts weapons, grown men with Union Jack undergarments and plenty of Buster Keaton-type visual gags, Bill Oddie, Tim Brooke-Taylor and Graeme Garden were arguably the comedy equivalent of Elton's early 1970s music. Elton was no satirist or intellectual; he played the silly card for all it was worth. And he would no doubt have approved of Union Jack underpants.

'I Think I'm Going To Kill Myself' also boasted a suitably eccentric musical contribution from a famous guest at the overdub sessions, 'Legs' Larry Smith of the Bonzo Dog Doo-Dah Band, who added a tap dance solo at the end of the track. 'He brought his own floor, I think,' laughs Ken Scott. It was also rumoured that Elton's step-father Derf would be asked to play spoons on the track, though the idea was apparently vetoed before things got any sillier.

The album's jaunty, if undemanding opener, 'Honky Cat', replete with cod-oriental beginning and sax-driven honky-tonk, was issued as the follow-up to 'Rocket Man'. While it performed well in the US, reaching Number 8, in Britain it peaked at Number 31, a more accurate reflection of its merit. 'Slave' was memorable purely for Elton's alarmingly accurate parody of Mick Jagger. The last track, 'Hercules', showed Elton was sensitive to the undercurrents of the 1950s revivalism about to break into the UK charts two years later with Mud and Showaddywaddy. But his version not only pre-dated them – it was also superior.

Once Elton had written a song and recorded his vocal and piano to the backing track, his role in the process was to all intents and purposes over. It was left to Gus Dudgeon to work with the band on backing vocals and other production sweeteners. Elton's boredom threshold was incredibly low and rather than kick his heels round the studio getting on everyone's nerves, he would go out for the day. 'He would take himself off to Paris when all the "boring bits" of the recording were being done,' says David Hentschel. 'He would indulge himself in all the designer fashion houses of the Left Bank and return with one of every item in every colour. A sign of things to come, maybe.'

Over the next 18 months, Strawberry Studios would be used for three further Elton John albums. After the recording of *Honky Château*, the star approached the band with an offer. 'Elton came to see me and Davey and said, "Man, this is such a great album. You guys are going to get royalties from now on",' remembered Nigel Olsson in 2000. 'That was unheard of. It still is to this day.'

Life at the château with Elton was never dull. 'John Reid had gone into Paris one day and he'd brought Elton back this bottle of port which was 100 years old,' remembers Ken Scott. 'He must have spent a thousand bucks on it, and Elton finished it off that night. We didn't do much work that night, surprisingly enough. Elton had us in hysterics. He was phoning people he knew in England, at two in the morning, waking them up, and in this strange mock-German accent he was saying, "I want to lick your body! I want to lick your body!" We were falling about all over the place.'

Inevitably, there were further practical jokes. 'My bed was in the hallway between two bedrooms,' says Clive Franks. 'One morning I woke up to find Elton and the band leaning over me and laughing. They picked me up, still wrapped in my bedding, and took me down the stairs and outside. They chucked me and the bedding into the swimming pool. I nearly bloody drowned because I was still wrapped in these sheets. I think I had my pyjama bottoms on, but when I got out of the pool, of course they were soaking wet and very revealing. The partner of the owner, who was an absolute babe, she was around too, so I was pretty embarrassed by it all. I was pissed off at the time, but I guess I can see the funny side to it now. They always picked on the quiet ones for the practical jokes. They used to do the same to Dee Murray.'

Some felt that there was a chill atmosphere at night in the château. 'The room that is usually reserved for the producer is supposedly haunted and Gus or Sheila saw something in there, I can't remember what,' says Ken Scott. 'Ken's wife held a séance one night at the foot of the stairwell,' says Clive Franks. 'There was me and Stuart Epps and a few others, but we couldn't stop laughing and she was getting so pissed off. I think she did get in touch with somebody, but I don't actually know as by that time Stuart and I had left the circle. We had to. I was doubled-up with laughter.' Ken Scott himself had nothing to do with such antics, and buried himself in the studio.

The new *Honky Château* material was given its first airing at the Royal Festival Hall on February 5, 1972. The speed of Elton's creative process was astonishing. He was able to perform just-written songs without fear and so played the entire record. Opening the concert solo, Elton was joined by Dee, Nigel and Davey (making his live debut in the band). Alan Parker of Blue Mink was on guitar, while Madeline Bell, Lesley Duncan and Caroline Attard provided backing vocals. For the closing 11-song section, comprising early work like 'Your Song', 'The Greatest Discovery' and 'Madman Across The Water', he was accompanied by the Royal Philharmonic Orchestra, conducted by Paul Buckmaster.

In March 1972, Elton teamed up with Marc Bolan, one of his closest friends in the music business, to record tracks for Marc's forthcoming rock film, *Born To Boogie*. In early 1972, Bolanmania was at its height in Britain. A teen idol, and arguably the most charismatic and sensual rock star of the decade, Bolan was also the first post-Beatles superstar. 'I grew out of that British variety, music hall, pantomime era and we were all larger-than-life,' Elton was to reflect in 2004. 'Marc Bolan was a dear friend; he was completely from another planet. I do like my rock stars to be a little larger-than-life. I don't mind the earnest ones at all, but I do like a bit of individuality.' Bolan also had a fantastic knowledge of music and an enthusiasm for it. 'In those days, Marc and Elton used to compare notes about their record collections,' remembers the broadcaster Bob Harris. 'They were both deeply knowledgeable and big record collectors. I used to go round to Marc's place to play old singles, rock 'n' roll things or Phil Spector, and it was – and is – the same with Elton.'

Bolan was nothing if not original. With his cheeky bleat of a vocal and teen-titillating amalgam of 1950s boogie, 1960s folk and 1970s attitude (woven seamlessly together with the help of American-about-London-town producer Tony Visconti), he became the premier singles artist of his day. In 1971, when T Rex performed 'Get It On' on the *Top Of The Pops* Christmas edition, Elton had appeared with them playing piano. For Bolan's film, Elton recorded a storming version of 'Tutti Frutti' plus Bolan's 'Children Of The Revolution' at Apple Studios. Ringo Starr on drums completed the all-star line-up. In one surreal moment in the film, Bolan is implanted inside Elton's piano. His head pops up to be photographed by the bizarre apparition of a mullet-sporting Ringo Starr dressed as a clown. A version of Bolan's 'The Slider' and a cover of another Little Richard classic, 'Long Tall Sally', were also apparently recorded, but cut from the final edit of the film.

For long periods in 1972, Elton John and his band found themselves on the road. The poster for the 1972 tour depicted a goofy, bare-chested Elton, in a fedora, pulling his best stupid face for the camera. The contrast between him and the other glam icons of the day such as Bolan, Bowie or Ferry could not have been more striking. Elton's brand of stardom came with ample doses of comedy and self-mockery.

On its way to Number 1 in the USA (his first) and Number 2 in Britain, *Honky Château* had only been in the shops for a matter of weeks when it was time for Elton to record a follow-up. His contract at DJM stipulated that he had to record two albums a year, an astonishingly punishing schedule by today's standards, but one which Elton would stick to relatively easily, such was his and Bernie's productivity. However, this time round, Elton initially wanted to delay recording. He had contracted mononucleosis or glandular fever and was feeling distinctly below par.

'I made *Don't Shoot Me I'm Only The Piano Player* really on the verge of a nervous breakdown,' he reflected years later. 'I was so ill. I didn't know it, but I had glandular fever and was very slow. When we first went over to make it, *Honky Château* had just gone to Number One in the States and I said to Gus, "I can't make this album," so he said, "All right, we'll do it in September." Then I said, "Wait, I'm going on holiday in July, it would be nice to have it over by then." It's a terrible way to look at it. So we did it, although I was very ill and had some terrible rows. I don't think Dick James and I spoke to each other for four months after that.'

The new material was in a similar vein to that found on *Honky*

Château: superior pop music, this time with a lighter, more retro feel. The title, *Don't Shoot Me, I'm Only The Piano Player*, has an interesting place in Elton lore. Elton had met comedy giant Groucho Marx whilst on holiday in Malibu with Bryan Forbes and Nanette Newman in 1972. At one party, Groucho turned to Elton and said, 'They tell me you're Number One, but I'd never heard of you until I went into my office this morning and said I was having dinner with Elton John. They all fainted. After that I lost what remaining respect I had for you.'

According to Elton's biographer, Philip Norman, the man who cracked arguably the funniest one-liners in the world gave Elton a hard time about the sequence of the two parts of his name, claiming he had them the wrong way round, and insisting on calling the singer John Elton. Elton's retort to Groucho after one evening of constant ribbing was to hold his hands aloft and say in defence, 'Don't shoot me, I'm only the piano player.' The cover of the album, depicting a small-town cinema with the name of the album illuminated as if it were the name of the film being shown, also features a hoarding for the Marx Brothers' 1940 MGM classic *Go West*.

The album contained two big hit singles, 'Crocodile Rock' and 'Daniel'. 'Crocodile Rock', still an integral part of the Elton live experience three decades later, was a fine piece of nostalgia with a vamping Farfisa organ melody and a classic 'Lah, la, la, la, la, lah' chorus. 'I wanted to do something that was a send-up of the early 1960s,' Elton was to claim. 'I wanted it to be a tribute to all those people I used to go and see as a kid. That's why I used the Del Shannon-type vocals and that bit from Pat Boone's "Speedy Gonzales". We also tried to get the worst organ sound possible.'

The Calypso-tinged 'Daniel', meanwhile, had none of the simplicity of 'Crocodile Rock', at least lyrically. Musically, it was another piece of soft rock with a memorable pop melody. 'David Hentschel and myself spent lots of time experimenting with the ARP 2600 at Trident,' says Ken Scott. 'While I was in the middle of mixing "Daniel", producer Gus Dudgeon decided Davey Johnstone's solo didn't "pop". So I actually doubled the part on synthesizer.'

The lyric gave rise to a certain amount of speculation as to the identity of the song's protagonist, with some assuming that Daniel must be the narrator's gay partner. However, the ambiguity in the lyric comes from the fact that the final verse, which revealed Daniel to be a Vietnam veteran, was cut from the song by Elton himself. The reason he gave, according to writer Robert Sandall, was that the final verse 'struck Elton as too American for a lad from Pinner in Middlesex to sing with real conviction'. 'I was reading *Newsweek* in bed, late at night, and there was a piece about the vets coming home from Vietnam,' recalled Bernie. 'The story was about a guy that went back to a small town in Texas. He had been crippled in the Tet offensive. They lauded him when he came home and treated him like a hero. They just wouldn't leave him alone but he just wanted to go home, go back to the farm, and try and get back to the life that he led before. I just embellished that and like everything I write, it probably ended up being very esoteric. It is a song that is important to me because it was the one thing I said about Vietnam. I arrived in this country [America] at the time it was going on, and I was here when it was over. But when I give things to Elton, it's very important that I don't lay a big message or my innermost feelings on him, because I'm putting words in his mouth. In some ways, I had to hide it a little. Maybe in "Daniel", I hid it too much.'

The absence of the final verse meant that Elton had to repeat the third and first verses to hit the necessary length, yet this repetition does not seem to detract from the song. Still, it does have a curiously unfinished and unresolved air about it, which adds to its charm and mystique. 'Daniel' would be the second major hit single from the album in early 1973 and would be promoted in the UK with the help of another appearance on *Top Of The Pops*. Dick James was so adamantly against releasing the track as a single that he would only do so on condition that Elton paid for all the advertising. If the record charted in the Top 10, Dick said he would concede and pay up. According to the thinking of the day, a second single off the album would seriously affect the performance of that album. A decade later, Michael Jackson would release seven singles off a nine-song studio album, *Thriller*.

However, the best song on the album was never a single. 'High Flying Bird', with its anthemic melody, was Bernie's favourite and, unlike 'Crocodile Rock' and 'Daniel', has not been over-exposed on radio and stage. It's 'a cross between Crosby, Stills & Nash and Irma Franklin,' Elton said. Bernie's lover, his 'high flying bird' who 'has flown from out of my arms' mistakes affection for control: 'She thought I meant her harm/ She thought I was the archer'. Continuing in the avian mode, Elton also recorded a beautiful, and superior, version of one of his earliest songs, 'Skyline Pigeon', which can be found as a bonus track on the CD reissue. Another strong cut was the thumping 'Elderberry Wine', while 'Blues For Baby And Me' seemed to deliberately pastiche the psychedelia of Love's 'Alone Again, Or' from their classic *Forever Changes*.

Continuing in the vein of nifty musical borrowings, 'Have Mercy On The Criminal' seemed to re-invent the main riff from Derek and the Dominoes' 'Layla'. 'Teacher I Need You' started with one of Elton's trademark musical motifs, the quick repeat of triplets on the piano, before he embarked on a tale of a pupil whose fantasy of the school curriculum extends to a one-to-one practical demonstration by his teacher of 'the birds and the bees' (a theme famously visited seven years later by the Police's 'Don't Stand So Close To Me', although in the latter song, the lust is directed from teacher to pupil). Here, Elton's voice again seemed to deliberately pastiche the American teen idols of the very early 1960s, as Elton himself acknowledged: 'I thought of every Bobby Vee record I'd ever heard'.

The mixing and matching of musical styles continued on 'Texas Love Song', a track with echoes of the electric folk of Fairport Convention. On 'I'm Gonna Be A Teenage Idol', Bernie appears to be alluding to Marc Bolan with his depiction of a singer who sits 'cross-legged with my old guitar'. 'We played it to [Bolan] and I think he liked it,' said Elton in 1973. 'He didn't hit me, anyway.'

The release of *Don't Shoot Me, I'm Only The Piano Player* was held back for over six months in order to give *Honky Château* a clear run in the charts. During the second half of 1972 and the first few months of

1973, it was obvious that Elton was becoming a very major star indeed. Some of his early fans might have bemoaned the transition from sensitive singer-songwriter to what Elton himself described as 'Cher on an acid trip', but the mainstream pop punters loved the result.

In late August and early September there would be a seven-date British tour, with Linda Lewis in support. From September 26, Elton toured America again for two months, this time with 'Legs' Larry Smith as special tap-dancing guest and with Family, featuring the dusky growl of Michael Chapman, as support act on many of the dates. 'Smith tapped his way onto Elton's stage during "I Think I'm Going To Kill Myself" wearing a flimsy bridal gown,' remembers journalist Richard Cromelin of the guest appearance of the Bonzo man. 'He then returned in Gene Kelly drag to do a "Singin' In The Rain" song-and-dance act with a raincoat-wearing Elton amidst, at the LA and New York dates, a bevy of dancing girls and an endless downpour of confetti.'

During that autumn US tour, Elton met up with the other defining icon of 1972, David Bowie. Elton was a great admirer of *Hunky Dory* and *Ziggy Stardust*, and had employed Paul Buckmaster as his arranger on the strength of Bowie's 'Space Oddity'. However, the two seemed too dissimilar, both as artists and as people, to really become firm friends. '[Elton] invited me over for tea,' says Bowie in his book about the Ziggy period, *Moonage Daydream*. 'I'd met him only once before and although he was cheerful and quite friendly we didn't exactly become pals, not really having that much in common, especially musically. This meeting was even more awkward. His entire living room was barricaded with huge stacks of record albums. He sat, small and bewildered-looking, in the middle, as if in some kind of bunker. He had, apparently, a deal with all the major record companies to supply him with their latest releases. I couldn't see how anyone could keep up with the amount of vinyl with which he was ensconced. We had tea and cakes and we asked each other how we found America and after a polite half-hour I made my apologies, declining a further cuppa, and went for a wander down Sunset.'

As Elton's engineer and Bowie's producer, Ken Scott was perhaps in a better position than most to compare the two icons. On the surface, the two singers seemed to share a common heritage of sorts. Almost the same age, both were suburbanites, both extrovert stage performers, both in love with British and American music. But, although there were similarities between David Bowie records such as 'Starman' and some of Elton's work, they remained two very different recording artists. 'Bowie never became poppy. There was always an artistic bent to him,' is how Scott puts it. 'Elton was a pop singer. That's why he had such great success, because you can sit there with your grandmother and you both like him. Bowie was with the kids fighting against the Establishment. You wouldn't sit there with your parents and watch Bowie.'

The only interruption to the US tour schedule was a dash across the Atlantic to appear on the Royal Command Performance Variety Show at the London Palladium, where Elton again performed 'I Think I'm Going To Kill Myself' with 'Legs' Larry. It would be the first performance of a rock act on the Royal Command Performance since the Beatles in 1963, an indication of Elton's broad appeal, although the choice of song cannot have been what the organisers had in mind as suitable musical fare for the occupants of the Royal box. 'It was so embarrassing, it was frightening,' is how Nigel Olsson remembers the peculiar appearance with the famed Bonzo. 'We were performing for Her Majesty and this bloody twit came on with a crash helmet with bride-and-groom wedding figures glued on the top. I looked at Dee and said, "I hope this is a dream."'

Also on the bill that night in November was the balladeer Jack Jones and the supreme showman Liberace. Elton had always had a genuine admiration of the Number 1 populist entertainer of the day. Liberace and his glittering suits, lacquered hair and unstinting cheesy smile to camera were a staple of Anglo-American light entertainment throughout the 1950s and into the 1970s. With a chintzy candelabrum as a prop and a repertoire of easy-listening sing-along melodies, Liberace hammed it up on the piano to such an extent that his mannered flourishes and exaggerated hand movements caused many to think that he was all style and no content, yet he was an extremely gifted pianist technically. Elton too was to fall foul of media who failed to realise that his own showmanship was just one aspect of who he was as a performer.

By the beginning of 1973 and the British tour to promote the *Don't Shoot Me...* album, Elton was riding the crest of a wave of popular approval. For the first time in his career, he would take the stage to find himself drowned out by the screams of a largely female teenage following. On its January release, *Don't Shoot Me...* became Elton's biggest-selling album to date by some distance, despite the fact that, on reflection, the star himself found it lacking: 'I really like some of the things on *Don't Shoot Me...* but as far as a continuous flow, it doesn't hold up. It's really a bubblegum album.'

The album artwork, by Michael Ross and David Larkham, confirmed the public's perception of Elton as a complete pop star. Gone was the studied seriousness of the *Elton John* album, the Americana of *Tumbleweed* and the simplicity of the *Honky Château* cover (a still shot of Elton from his first US tour in 1970). In its place were colour-tinted iconic studies of master showman Elton in cape, black hat, pink suit, straw boater and platform shoes, and Bernie exuding film-star good looks. 'Bernie was so subdued. He should have been a movie star,' reflected Nigel Olsson. 'On some of the pictures on the early records, he looks like a Brad Pitt or a Tom Cruise or a James Dean.'

Buoyed by the success of 'Crocodile Rock' and 'Daniel', *Don't Shoot Me* became Elton's first Number 1 album in the UK and stayed there for six weeks. It also reached Number 1 in the States, and would remain on the Billboard charts for a staggering 89 weeks. 'Crocodile Rock' was his first US Number 1 single, staying atop the charts for three weeks. Elton John was no longer just heading towards superstardom: he had arrived.

CHAPTER 7

E - L - T - O - N

'It was magic; that creative period of my life will never come back again.'

Elton John

'Flamboyant? Bizarre? Ridiculous? You better believe it! Rock has gone Hollywood.'

Albert Goldman, writer, academic and controversialist, 1974

Septembe 7, 1973. Huge searchlight beams light up the night sky. It's show time at the 18,000-capacity Hollywood Bowl in Los Angeles. Linda Lovelace, star of the porn film *Deep Throat*, takes the stage. Behind her is a gigantic backdrop featuring a painting of a smiling Elton John in profile. He's dressed in top hat and tails and, in the best tradition of the musical, he comes complete with white carnation and cane. His likeness is flanked by a chorus line of dancing girls, five on each side. It's the same image that adorns a billboard on Sunset Boulevard announcing a show that has been talked about and hyped for weeks. It is a classic image from a musical of the 1930s or 1940s, that golden Hollywood era of Fred Astaire, Busby Berkeley, glamour and glitz. This isn't rock 'n' roll as we know it – loud, scruffy, made by people with a point to prove or sung by smouldering, sexually predatory singers. This is pure entertainment.

Of course, the gig is a complete sell-out. On the morning of the concert, tickets are being sold on the black market for a staggering $500 dollars each. On the stage, which is bathed in glittering light, stands an illuminated staircase with palm trees on either side. The set includes five pianos painted orange, yellow, blue, purple and pink, to give a partial rainbow effect. 'Ladies and gentlemen,' begins Lovelace. 'In the tradition of old Hollywood let me introduce you to… the Queen of England.' And down the glittery staircase walks Elizabeth II. Well, a reasonably realistic look-alike. The Queen is followed by the King – Elvis Presley – and he in turn comes before Batman and Robin, Frankenstein's monster, Groucho Marx, Marilyn Monroe, Mae West and the Beatles. 'Now,' announces Lovelace, 'the co-star of my next film.' Down the staircase walks the Pope. Then she introduces the man himself: 'The gentleman you have all been waiting for. The biggest, most colossal, gigantic, fantastic, Elton John!'

Elton appears at the top of the staircase, more outrageous, more showbiz, more of a superstar than any of the rich and famous doubles that have walked down the star-spangled path before him. Groucho Marx and Frankenstein's monster wave to him as he approaches the stage dressed in a white-and-silver jumpsuit, with an outrageously plumed wide-brimmed hat. The Twentieth Century Fox Cinemascope theme tune blares out over the PA. As he arrives on stage, the lids of the five pianos lift to reveal the letters E-L-T-O-N and, as each piano lid opens, 400 white doves are released into the night sky. Well, that is the intention, at least. In the event, several dozen petrified birds refuse to co-operate. Inside one piano, hidden from view, is none other than Bernie Taupin, desperately heaving reluctant birds into the air so that the effect is not lost. The audience gaze in wonder at the spectacle. Then the first crashing chord of 'Elderberry Wine' fills the LA night air. 'It was the most spectacular entry on to a stage I and probably everyone else at the Bowl had ever seen,' was how Chris Charlesworth sums it up in *Melody Maker* the following week. Elton is now officially H-U-G-E.

*   *   *

So many of the most significant events in Elton John's career have occurred not on record but on stage. The Hollywood Bowl gig was undoubtedly among the most memorable of his career. 'The band shared a dressing room with Linda Lovelace,' remembers sound man Clive Franks. 'That was quite outrageous in itself.' Franks also recalls a piece of unscripted fun during the second song of the night, 'High Flying Bird'. 'All the doves we released returned, except one. They had been trained to do a circuit of the Bowl and then fly back into the wings. Apparently they got 399 of them back, so there was one missing. Elton was in the middle of "High Flying Bird" when the last dove came back. It hovered around the stage and the lighting engineer picked it out and followed it with the spotlight as it flew around as though trained to do so. And at the end of the song, it flew into the wings backstage.'

Towards the end of the set, Elton was scheduled to play one of his major hit singles, 'Crocodile Rock', his first and thus far only US number one. Clive Franks had a trick of his own up his sleeve. '"Crocodile Rock", as you know, has this vamping Farfisa organ part which, of course, Elton needed someone to play while he was on piano. So I would leave the mixing desk for this one song when we played it live. Normally I would be wearing a silver lamé teddy boy jacket that I borrowed from him. But at the Hollywood Bowl I decided to do something different. I rented a crocodile head and a huge black cape that I tied to the head so it looked like the head was appearing out of nothing. I didn't tell anybody in the band I was doing this. I came on stage and Elton turned round to find me and all he saw was this huge crocodile head. He could hardly sing a word he was laughing so much. And when we got to the "Lah, la, la, la, la, lah" chorus, there was a string inside the cape which I pulled and the jaws of the crocodile head opened and closed as if I was singing along.'

'There was a big party afterwards at the newly opened Roxy Club,' recalls Chris Charlesworth. 'It was a must-have invite. Elton and his entourage stayed at the Beverly Hills Hotel and there was a luncheon there a day or two later to celebrate John Reid's birthday. Elton gave him this brass sculpture of an erect cock and balls, which John opened in front of everyone, and it was passed round so everyone could examine it. I recall Elton's mum laughing her head off when she held it… good bawdy humour.'

By 1973, Elton John had turned himself into the most extravagant performer in rock music. Central to the fun was his seemingly unlimited capacity to mock himself. 'I'm not trying to come on heavy,' he freely admitted. 'It's all done for fun, the glasses and all the ultra-pop stuff. Really all I'm saying is I'm a dumpy 26-year-old guy who's going bald and I sell millions of records, so I'm going to enjoy myself when I perform, no matter how ridiculous I look.'

Yet from the outset of his career, Elton John as a live performer was handicapped in one very crucial respect. He had to spend 99 per cent of his stage time 'at stool', hidden behind a grand piano. He has, as a result, evolved a unique sense of bad taste and self-deprecating flamboyance. 'The clothes were important. And I developed all those glasses I wore, and people developed glasses for me, and they became funnier and funnier and wilder and wilder at a time when glasses were really boring, I hasten to add. It was kind of like, listen, I'm not David Bowie. I'm not Mick Jagger and I'm not Rod Stewart. I'm not sexy. I don't move around in front of the mic. But here I am, and I'm making the best of what I can do with myself, and I'm just saying, "Yeah! Let's go for it! Throw all the rules out the window!"

'I felt that changed me. It changed my thoughts. When I put my costume on, that's when I know I'm ready to go onstage. It's such a necessary thing for me. I'm putting on a show for people and I not only want to give them something to listen to, I want to give them something visual to look at as well.'

Central to the fun, of course, was Elton's astonishing array of glasses. His usual nerdy white Joe 90 specs would soon be augmented by a catalogue of the absurd, the centrepiece of which was undoubtedly a pair commissioned for $5,000 which, in the appearance of a billboard, spelt out the letters E-L-T-O-N in coloured red, yellow, blue, green and orange capital letters made up of 57 flashing light bulbs powered by a six-volt battery pack. Elton seemed to have all bases on the road to immortality covered through ever more ludicrous specs. In the early Seventies the collection would include outrageous offerings such as glasses that spelt out 'Z-O-O-M' (an infamous photo shows Elton, wearing those, picking his nose). There would be those in the shape of a piano. Then there were the feathered glasses, which gave the effect of a peacock's display. There would be heart-shaped glasses and glasses covered in fluffy white trim. Then there were those in the shape of a sea horse and the ones that made him look as if he had a compound eye like a bluebottle, as well as big square ones and huge round ones encrusted with beads. As the 1970s progressed, the glasses became Elton's biggest stage gimmick. On the autumn 1973 tour, one pair had battery-operated windscreen wipers. The situation was obviously getting rather silly, sillier maybe than Bernie Taupin would have liked, as he watched the poetry/verse he had toiled over for weeks on end being sung by a man wearing a pair of glasses which, in the words of Philip Norman, 'lit up his face like the rings of an electric stove'.

Elton made wearing glasses pop fun. Hitherto, they had tended to look terrible, reaching a nadir in the calamitously un-hip specs worn by Nana Mouskouri. Only in cinema had anyone looked even remotely alluring. Michael Caine, in the guise of Harry Palmer, actually looked sexy portraying what was known, in the nation's playgrounds at least, as 'a four eyes'. Elton's quest for the oracular spectacular became a serious mission in the second half of 1973, when he began commissioning LA's Optique Boutique on Sunset Strip to provide him with a full range of the strange.

The supplier of so many of Elton's on-stage spectacles was Dennis Roberts, a man who would go on to win Glasses Man Of The Year. The famous 'Elton In Flashing Lights' specs were a Roberts creation, and 'a bitch to design'. His other musician clients included Elvis Presley, Sammy Davis Jr, Andy Williams, Barbra Streisand, Diana Ross and the Osmonds. In 1975, Elton won the American Optical Society's 'Eyes Right' award. Dennis Roberts presented the singer, who wore star-point glasses, with a certificate in recognition of his 'worldwide influence in encouraging people to wear glasses and his achievements in the world of entertainment'.

On a more serious note, he would go on to play charity shows
– including one at the Troubador – to publicise and raise funds for Dr
Jules Stein's renowned eye clinic in Los Angeles.

That night at the Hollywood Bowl, Elton debuted four songs from
his soon-to-be-released double album, *Goodbye Yellow Brick Road*. The
record, released in October 1973, arguably marked the highpoint of
Elton's entire recording career. Of the 17 songs arranged on four sides
of musical magic, around half were Elton classics. Bernie Taupin has
said that the album is, in some way, 'the karmic root' for Elton John
fans, for everything that came before it and everything that came afterwards. Almost every song painted vivid filmic pictures in the mind of
the listener, as sweet painted ladies of the night, real-life screen stars
Marilyn Monroe and Roy Rogers and a fictional glam rock band,
Bennie and the Jets, took the stage along with an array of gangsters,
lesbian lovers and brawling mods and rockers. For almost every image
created by Taupin, there was an extraordinary melody by Elton. There
were four major hit singles off the album, but there might easily have
been half a dozen more.

Yet many of the songs might never have been created, had not fate
played a small but crucial part in the record's birth. Elton had been keen
to record at Byron Lee's Dynamic Sound Studios in Kingston, Jamaica,
having heard that the Rolling Stones had recently worked there on their
Goats Head Soup album. Bob Marley and the Wailers had cut *Catch A Fire*
there, so the studio had some pedigree. However, when the Elton John
band arrived, they found that 'dynamic' was a bit of a comical misnomer.
To the highly professional unit that the Elton John band had become in
1973, it was obvious that the studio was seriously unsuitable.

'We get in there, the first day, and I'm trying to get a drum sound,
and I couldn't get any guts out of it, it was all very thin,' says Ken Scott,
who was again engineering the record. 'So we used a test record and
found that the low end completely cut off.' 'The first time we knew we
were in deep shit was when the guy who ran the studio said, "Carlton,
get the microphone." We used 20 microphones on our drum kit even
then,' recalls Davey Johnstone.

'It sounded amazing when I'd previously been there,' said Dudgeon. 'It had exactly what we were looking for, this massive bottom end. Things were looking great until we set all the equipment up. Then it sounded fucking terrible. The Stones had just been there and they were checking out as we checked in. They told us a few slightly scary stories, like don't open the piano lid too fast or you'll upset the cockroaches that live in there.'

In addition to having to work in a studio with virtually no equipment, the circumstances surrounding the trip were hardly conducive to rampant creativity. 'We were driven from the hotel to the studio in this van and there were hordes of people banging on the van as we went in,' remembers Ken Scott. 'The studio was in the middle of a record plant and this American union was trying to get all the workers into the union and on strike. They were attacking us going in as technically we were trying to cross a picket line. It was pretty scary.'

'There was barbed wire around the studio, machine guns, and people yelling obscenities at us in the streets,' were Bernie's memories. 'There wasn't a positive vibe in the place.' 'We decided to leave early,' reported Elton. 'That didn't go down too well, so they impounded our equipment and our rental cars. As we were being taken to the airport, I just thought: "They're gonna kill us!"'

According to Ken Scott, it was he who suffered most from the enforced holiday in Jamaica. 'A couple of weeks later, I was told by the management at Trident that John Reid had booked time back at the Château to record, but would I not charge for Jamaica. Now I had no control over whether I charged for it or not. It was up to the management of Trident Studios, because I was still staff at that point and they said it was ridiculous. They said it was Gus's fault. You just don't go blind into a studio. So I ended up not doing the album because John Reid said I was too expensive. Now, at that stage I think I was on £100 a day. So that would have been £700 and that was too expensive. I never worked with Elton John again.'

Overall, however, the Jamaica debacle had more positive than negative effects. Holed up for days waiting for the studio to be readied,

Elton and Bernie wrote additional songs for the album and, by the time they reached the Château, they already had more than enough material for a single album. When further songs appeared, once ensconced in France, including 'The Ballad Of Danny Bailey', it was decided to make Elton's eighth studio album a double.

Goodbye Yellow Brick Road was Elton's pop zenith. Furthermore, it all came to Elton and his team so naturally. 'It wasn't hard,' Elton was to reflect. 'It wasn't an effort; it was a pleasure.' The band intuitively seemed to know what to play. 'The way we recorded was to go away and stay at the studio. We heard the songs being created,' says Nigel Olsson. 'There was never a time when Elton would say, "Nigel, I want you to play this like this and, Dee, I want you to play this like that." We were on the same wavelength before we sat down to cut the songs. We never did more than three or four takes of any song. If it wasn't there in the first few takes, we'd go on to the next song.'

The album's most famous song is 'Candle In The Wind'. However, its legendary (some would say infamous) status would only be confirmed in 1997 following the death of Diana, Princess of Wales. Although initially released as a disappointing live single in 1988, Bernie re-wrote the lyrics as a tribute to 'England's Rose' and, after Elton sang the new version at Diana's funeral in Westminster Abbey, it became the biggest-selling CD single ever. At the time, though, it was seen as just another admirable component in a portfolio of very strong songs. It was, in fact, only the third single off the album, behind 'Saturday Night's Alright For Fighting' and the title track. On release in early 1974, it only reached Number 11 in the UK singles charts. 'I don't remember writing it,' Bernie has admitted. 'I don't remember him playing it to me, and I don't remember hearing it for the first time.' 'I can't really remember writing it, I can't remember much about it,' an equally vague Elton has concurred.

'Many songs were composed at breakfast before being recorded later the same day,' says David Hentschel. '"Candle In The Wind" I remember particularly. Bernie Taupin would give Elton the lyric, who would then write the music at a piano in the large dining area while everyone else was eating breakfast. It was quite magical. The band would be listening as this happened, and then we all went over to the studio and laid the track down.' 'I had always loved the phrase', says Bernie. 'Solzhenitsyn had written a book called *Candle In The Wind*. [Record industry mogul] Clive Davis had used it to describe Janis Joplin and, for some reason, I just kept hearing this term. I thought, what a great way of describing someone's life.'

Although the song's lyric took the life and death of Marilyn Monroe as its overt subject matter, it would be simplistic to say it was a straightforward tribute to the movie star. 'Candle In The Wind' was about Hollywood fame in general. It was a song about the pressure stardom brings, about unfulfilled potential, about being cut off in one's prime and misrepresented in the press. 'The song could have been about James Dean, it could have been about Montgomery Cliff, it could have been about Jim Morrison,' Bernie has conceded. 'Anyone whose life is cut short at the prime point of their career, and how we glamorise death and how we immortalise people.' In fact, it's a song that speaks to anyone, famous or not, who had known someone who died before their time and whose life has been misrepresented. However, whether the song deserves the status of undisputed Elton classic is debatable. It could be argued that there are at least half a dozen better tracks on this album alone.

'Candle In the Wind' appeared on the first side of the album – arguably the finest side of music Elton had ever produced. The title track, a major hit in the autumn of 1973, had one of Elton's most beautifully wistful melodies and his singing is so high-pitched that Dudgeon has often been asked if it had been speeded up. Over the years, Elton's vocal range has understandably been transposed down in live performance. Bernie's reflective lyric is an early and telling indication that fame was becoming all too much for the lad from Lincolnshire: 'I should have stayed on the farm/ should have listened to my old man.' It's a song about disillusionment and was the first by Bernie to reveal a road-weariness and a desire for something post-fame, 'beyond the Yellow Brick Road'. The Emerald City of fame and fortune was evidently bringing as many hardships as benefits. Bernie wanted out: 'I'm going back to my plough.' There would be many, even darker-themed songs from Bernie as the 1970s unfolded.

The opening piece of music on the album was one of Elton's finest musical creations. 'Funeral For A Friend', a sombre instrumental, segued perfectly into a classic Elton riff-rocking masterpiece, 'Love Lies Bleeding'. It's a song sequence which is still used by Elton in concert to this day. 'If I remember correctly, *Goodbye Yellow Brick Road* was originally going to be called *Silent Movies And Talking Pictures*,' says David Hentschel. 'Gus had wanted to use the MGM movie jingle to start the album, but there were licensing problems with that. Following that, the idea was to do a kind of "overture" to the album. I took several of the melodies from the songs, changed them round to join them up gracefully, then added a couple of bits of my own for good measure. We knew that the piece would segue into "Funeral For A Friend" proper, hence the wind and funereal tone of the early bars.'

The original vinyl first side also contained a song which nobody in the band, including Elton, saw as a single, but which went on to become one of his biggest sellers in the US: 'Bennie And The Jets'. In Bernie's tale of this fictional glam rock group, Elton's vocal leapt from deep soul jiving to castrato squealing. It was, however, Dudgeon's production fairy dust that turned the song into something both odd and spectacular. Dudgeon took himself off to the record archive to dig out both an earlier Elton John concert, recorded at the Royal Festival Hall in London, and Jimi Hendrix's performance at the Isle of Wight in 1970. Slapping on applause from these two shows in order to create the impression of a live audience, he then dubbed in whistles and, comically, some handclaps 'doing the wrong beat, because English audiences always clap on the "on" instead of the "off" beat, which drives me crazy,' said Dudgeon in an interview shortly before his death in a road accident in 2002.

Although 'Bennie And The Jets' would not be released as a single in Britain until 1976, when it fared disappointingly, in the US in 1974,

ABOVE: A young Reg Dwight (far left) acts as page boy at the wedding of his uncle, footballer Roy Dwight.

LEFT: Town mouse, country mouse: Elton and songwriting partner Bernie Taupin on the verge of stardom.

```
       J O H N        }   THIS CHANGE OF NAME DEED (intended to be enrolled at the Central
                      }   Office) made this 8th day of December 1971 By me the undersigned
       (DWIGHT)       }   ELTON HERCULES JOHN of 14 ABBOTTS DRIVE, WENTWORTH, SURREY now
                      }   or lately called REGINALD KENNETH DWIGHT a citizen of the United
          A           }   Kingdom and Colonies by BIRTH - - - - - - - - - - - - - -
                      }
  D E E D    P O L L  }   WITNESSES AND IT IS HEREBY DECLARED as follows:- - - - - -
                      }
     50p.       13    }   1.   I absolutely and entirely renounce relinquish and abandon
                      }   the use of my said former name of REGINALD KENNETH DWIGHT and
                          assume adopt and determine to take and use from the date hereof
                          the name of ELTON HERCULES JOHN in substitution for my former
                          name of REGINALD KENNETH DWIGHT - - - - - - - - - - - -

  2.   I shall at all times hereafter in all records deeds documents and other writings and in
  all actions and proceedings as well as in all dealings and transactions and on all occasions
  whatsoever use and subscribe the said name of ELTON HERCULES JOHN as my name in substitution
  for my former name of REGINALD KENNETH DWIGHT so relinquished as aforesaid to the intent
  that I may hereafter be called known or distinguished not by the former name of REGINALD
  KENNETH DWIGHT but by the name of ELTON HERCULES JOHN only - - - - - - - - - -

  3.   I authorise and require all persons at all times to designate describe and address me by
  the adopted name of ELTON HERCULES JOHN - - - - - - - - - - - - - - - - - -

  IN WITNESS whereof I have hereunto subscribed my Christian or first name or names of ELTON
  HERCULES and my adopted and substituted surname of JOHN and also my said former name of
  REGINALD KENNETH DWIGHT and have affixed my seal the day and year first above written - -

  SIGNED sealed and delivered  }   Elton Hercules John                    L.S.
  by the above-named ELTON      }   ELTON HERCULES JOHN
  HERCULES JOHN in the presence }   formerly known as
  of                            }   Reginald Kenneth Dwight
                                    REGINALD KENNETH DWIGHT
  Michael Oliver,
  40, Piccadilly,
  London, W.1.
  Solicitor.

  Ashley Lawrence,
  40, Piccadilly, W.1.
  Solicitor.

  Declaration filed  Birth Cert. Produced  H.W.

                         Enrolled in the Central Office of the Supreme
                         Court of Judicature the 6th day of January
                         in the year of Our Lord 1972.
```

ABOVE LEFT: Elton on stage in 1976, with carrot accessory.

ABOVE RIGHT: Acrobatics on the piano, London 1972.

LEFT: Reginald Kenneth Dwight becomes Elton Hercules John via deed poll dated 6 January, 1972.

OPPOSITE ABOVE: Elton in his Bluesology days: 'I looked like a young Reginald Maudling'.

OPPOSITE BELOW: Bluesology playing at the Ricky Tick Club in Windsor.

TOP: On stage with his guitarist Davey Johnstone, 1976.

ABOVE LEFT: The classic line-up. Left to right: drummer Nigel Olsson, Legs Larry Smith ('borrowed' from the Bonzo Dog Doo-Dah band to perform a tap-dance routine!), Elton, bassist Dee Murray and guitarist Davey Johnstone, in November, 1972.

ABOVE RIGHT: Elton with percussionist Ray Cooper, in 1979, during their successful two-man show.

OPPOSITE TOP: Elton John aboard *Starship 1*, their private Boeing jet used for the 1974 US tour.

OPPOSITE BOTTOM: Elton and Bernie pose in front of *Starship 1*. Behind them are some of the 35 musicians, roadies and other personnel who accompanied the tour.

ABOVE: One of the most iconic photographs in rock: Elton at Dodger Stadium, Los Angeles, autumn 1975.

OPPOSITE TOP: The biggest boots in rock history: Elton with Roger Daltrey in the 'Pinball Wizard' sequence from Ken Russell's Who epic, *Tommy* (1975).

OPPOSITE BOTTOM: On stage with John Lennon, Madison Square Garden, New York, 28 November, 1974. This would be Lennon's last-ever concert appearance.

Elton John and his then manager
John Reid at Reid's birthday
party, London, 1990.

Producer Gus Dudgeon,
co-creator of the classic
Elton John sound.

when Elton was already the biggest pop superstar in the country, it
was an immediate success. Pat Pipolo, head of promotions at MCA
Records, had a hunch it might break Elton into the R&B charts and
urged Elton to release it as a single. Elton was sceptical, but agreed,
and the single duly went on to top both the Billboard and R & B
charts. Elton thus became the first white UK artist of his generation
to break big and be accepted on black radio stations. His success in
this area pre-dated that of Bowie, the Bee Gees and the Average White
Band by over a year.

The first single off the album was the classic Elton rocker
'Saturday Night's Alright For Fighting,' a track that is surely Davey
Johnstone's finest hour. Elton has often bemoaned the fact that
composing on piano often means that there's a tendency to over-
elaborate and use too many chords, when a songwriter strumming
a few chords on a guitar is more likely to come up with something
livelier and more direct. Elton has recorded very few all-out-attack
rock numbers; the few that he has done, however, have usually been
worth waiting for.

Johnstone's riffing turned 'Saturday Night' into one of the finest
rock songs from the 1970s. Recording the song was problematic,
though. An aborted attempt was made out in Jamaica, with Elton
playing with the band. 'We just couldn't get it down right with just
the four of us as a band doing it live in the studio,' Elton was to
report. 'It kept running away with itself or speeding up or disintegrating into an unruly mess.' When the time came to cut it back at the
Château, Elton told his band: 'Right, you three just play the fucker
and I'll sing it and we'll do the piano later. I'd always sung at the piano
but this time I did the vocal standing up like most singers do and it
worked. I was there waving my arms about, really getting into it, just
going totally crazy.'

The song reached Number 7 in Britain a couple of months before
the October release of the album. It was one of the few Bernie Taupin
tracks of the time that did not have an overtly American theme
running through it, which made a refreshing change for a lyricist who

was, perhaps, beginning to repeat himself somewhat. For 'Saturday', Bernie delved back once again into his teenage years, to the days of the Mods and the Rockers, when a Saturday night out in the North Midlands could easily lead to a bout of beer-fuelled fisticuffs. To this day, Elton fans still travel to Market Rasen to visit the Aston Arms pub in the market place, thought to be the main inspiration behind the song.

Goodbye Yellow Brick Road was a concept album in all but name. It was Elton and Bernie's cinema show, with Bernie at his most filmic and Elton at his most melodically flexible. Of the 17 cuts, only four failed to deliver: 'Your Sister Can't Twist (But She Can Rock 'n' Roll)' showed that, after 'Crocodile Rock' and 'Hercules', the novelty had worn off when it came to early 1960s nostalgia, while the kindest thing that could be said about the white reggae of 'Jamaica Jerk-Off' is that it was catchy, if transparently slight. On two tracks there were signs that Bernie was getting bitter. 'Sweet Painted Lady', a song about prostitution, was relatively tame in its lyrical content, but 'Dirty Little Girl' is certainly more problematic for today's listener. Lines like 'Someone grab that bitch by the ears/Rub her down, scrub her back' and 'So, don't show up round here 'til your social worker's helped' are not among Bernie's most enlightened lyrics.

Elsewhere on the album, though, there was real quality. 'Harmony', a simple melody much-admired by Elton fans, was the single that never was. 'This Song Has No Title' also boasted a simple arrangement, as Elton accompanied himself on keyboard and synth. 'All The Young Girls Love Alice' was an unequivocal lyric about lesbianism that seemed to have completely bypassed those in the media of a censorious bent. 'Social Disease' carried on the lowlife imagery in a stupor of drunken imagery. In real life, it wouldn't be long before Bernie was drinking as much as his fictional star, who was 'juiced on Mateus'.

'Roy Rogers', a joyous tribute to a childhood film hero, fitted perfectly into the album's song sequence of villains and heroes. 'The Ballad Of Danny Bailey (1909–34)' saw Bernie invent his composite gangster, his own creation to match the real-life Al Capone and John Dillinger (name-checked in the song). The melody from Elton was one of the album's finest, too; the bass guitar work, high up on the fretboard from Dee Murray, was highly inventive, as was the closing orchestral section scored by Del Newman. 'I've Seen That Movie Too' represented the thematic root of the album, which was that of life as a film set. Then there was 'Grey Seal', a 1970 B-side scored by Paul Buckmaster, which was re-invented as an uptempo pop song with Elton's trademark rapid triplets on the piano and Newman's sweetly soaring strings. Bernie was to admit that he didn't have a clue what the abstract lyrics actually meant.

Goodbye Yellow Brick Road managed to remain consistently musically inventive while being one of Elton's most accessible albums. He had delivered his best record at the beginning of the peak period of his global popularity. 'If it's not *the* classic, then it's certainly one of the top few of his career,' says David Hentschel. 'Firstly, though this is always subjective, it is due to the songs themselves, many of which I think are among his finest. Secondly, it is very hard for any artist to make a double album and even more so to make it hold up and keep the listener's interest throughout. *Goodbye Yellow Brick Road* managed that in my opinion, and I can only think of maybe three other albums in the history of contemporary music that achieved that.'

Goodbye Yellow Brick Road would reach Number 1 on both sides of the Atlantic. In the UK it stayed on top of the charts for two weeks at the end of December 1973, rounding off a year which had seen glam rock rule: in the album charts in that one calendar year, Slade, David Bowie, Elton John, Alice Cooper and Roxy Music accounted for 27 weeks at Number 1 between them (make that 30 weeks if Rod Stewart is allowed into the glam rockers' club). In America, *Goodbye Yellow Brick Road* sat astride the Billboard Top 100 for 8 weeks and would go on to sell six million copies in all.

One of the ongoing themes in the Elton John story is his willingness to give something back to the music business. In the press, Elton was a vocal supporter of the work of others and even in 1972, with his own position in the pop firmament only very recently secured, he wanted to use his power and money to promote the talents of others. During the recording of *Don't Shoot Me...*, Davey Johnstone was discussing his own solo work and bemoaning the fact that he didn't have a record label. One night, after one too many glasses of the Château's red wine, Elton blurted out that they should start up their own record company. The next day, when someone remembered through the fug of the morning hangover that the idea had been mooted, Elton seized on it with gusto.

On September 16, 1972, Elton had announced the formation of his own label, Rocket Records, with a full-page ad in *Disc*. Gus Dudgeon, Steve Brown, Bernie Taupin and John Reid would also have shares in the company, which was committed to the support of new talent. 'What we are offering is individual love and devotion, a fucking good royalty for the artist and a company that works its bollocks off,' Elton told *Disc*.

'It was a great family,' says Gary Farrow, who now runs a PR firm, but was then a teenage runner for Rocket Records. 'It was like a little family that used to go to work every day in this little house at 101 Wardour Street. It wasn't like proper work. You went in through the front door and it was like a house with comfy settees.' Steve Brown managed the office: his own room, according to Philip Norman, boasted a mural of 'steam trains, fields and cows'. Steve's younger brother, Pete, was his assistant. John Reid would commute to the Soho office from his own office in South Audley Street, Mayfair, home of the newly established John Reid Enterprises.

Over the next year, the roster of acts signed to Rocket Records would include Longdancer, featuring Nigel Olsson's brother Kai, Steve Sproxton, Brian Harrison and a certain Dave Stewart, later to find fame as a member of the Tourists in the seventies and the Eurythmics thereafter. They also signed folk outfit Stackridge, the first act to perform at the first-ever Glastonbury Festival in 1970; singer-songwriter Colin Blunstone, late of the Zombies; vastly experienced American veteran Neil Sedaka, and the singer who would become Rocket Records' first chart success: Kiki Dee.

Kiki was born Pauline Mathews on March 6, 1947 in Little Horton, near Bradford. Possessed of one of the most natural and impressive voices in pop, she had spent the best part of a decade being feted but largely unbought. At the age of 17 she had recorded an album for Fontana and later in the 1960s she became the first European singer to be signed by Motown Records. 'Rocket were interested in Dusty Springfield, but for some reason that didn't happen,' she says. 'I knew John Reid because he was head of Motown EMI London in Manchester Square. I always got on well with John. He was about 18 at the time and I was 21. I'd done this Motown album and nothing commercially had really happened, although I think I did a good job. So I said to John, "I'm a bit stuck as to what to do next, so I thought I'd just give you a ring." And he said, "Well, I'll introduce you to Elton."'

Kiki was invited to meet Elton while he was still living in the flat at Water Gardens. She remembers how she made a move that broke the ice rather too literally. 'Neil Young was coming over the same night, so I got to meet him. Elton asked me to go into the kitchen to bring some wine glasses. It was probably one of his first sets of good quality stuff. I opened what I thought was a glass door and knocked all the glasses on the floor. Elton thought it was hysterical. I demolished them opening a glass door that was already open.' Elton impressed Kiki as a charming man 'with a shoulder bag wrapped across him and Cuban-heeled boots. He was boy-next-door cute, I'd say. He wasn't a sex symbol, but he had this persona and a presence about him. I think a lot of women still think he is cute.'

Elton decided that, for Kiki's debut on Rocket, he would cut his teeth as a producer. At the urging of Steve Brown, Kiki had written several songs for the album, including the one that would give the album its title, *Loving And Free*. 'Elton had by now moved to Wentworth. I went to his house and I had to play him this song. I was absolutely petrified. He said he had a guitar at the house, but when I picked it up it only had five strings on it and I wasn't a guitarist in the first place. I started singing this song, "Loving And Free", and at the end he kind of looked a bit like he didn't know what to say. I thought, "Oh, he hates it." But he said, "It's really good, Kiki, but you can't start a song with "Bound, I am bound, like an ox in a stream." I told him the lyric was, "Bound, I am bound, like the knots in a string," and we collapsed in laughter.'

Kiki's *Loving And Free* album was released on Rocket in April 1973 but she would have to wait almost six months for her first hit single, 'Amoureuse', the English lyric for which was penned by Gary Osborne. Osborne was to become one of Elton's closest friends in the 1970s and, eventually, a songwriting collaborator. In the overpopulated musical genre of the love song, in which so many sound trite and/or hackneyed, or deal in the currency of bland emotional cliché, 'Amoureuse' was remarkable in that it talked of intimacy, loving and sex in a way that seemed utterly real. 'Apart from it being my first hit, it was Elton's first hit as a producer, Rocket's first hit as a label and Kiki's first hit as a singer,' says Osborne. 'You always remember the first time, which, of course, is precisely what the song is all about.'

The song garnered some very high-profile admirers. 'The first time I met Pete Townshend was on the sessions for the movie of *Tommy*,' says Osborne. 'I went with my brother-in-law Kenney Jones, who was deputising for Keith Moon. Kenney introduced us and Peter told me he thought "Amoureuse" was one of the finest love songs ever written. A few months later he did a solo gig at the Roundhouse. In the middle of the show he put down his guitar, walked to the piano and played "Amoureuse". I lived nearby in Hampstead and had intended to go to the gig, but something came up. Just as well, as I'd probably have fainted.'

'Amoureuse' was not an instant success, bubbling under the Top 40 for months before charting and reaching a respectable Number 13. 'It was during that bubbling-under period that I gradually became friends with Elton,' says Osborne. The son of the respected bandleader, composer and arranger, Tony Osborne, Gary had between the ages of eight and eleven attended an Arts Educational School with academic lessons in the morning and acting, singing, tap, ballroom and ballet in the afternoon. 'Those are the schools where people go when they want to put kids in shows. So, I was a star of knitting pattern books, a Siamese twin in the West End production of *The King And I* and an extra in the *Tom Thumb* movie. I was the kid in the *Lucozade* advert who was too sickly to go and play football with his chums. I was in the *Milky Bar* commercials before there was a Milky Bar Kid. My dad at this stage was MD-ing for all the big acts of the day, Shirley Bassey, Johnny Mathis, Judy Garland and that sort of people, he was also conducting for Dorothy Squires so her husband Roger Moore would be round the house a lot. He gave me my very first capo so I could play guitar in different keys. It was a very showbizzy upbringing really. At that point it suddenly occurred to my parents that I hadn't actually ever seen a football, let alone kicked one, and they thought they'd better butch me up a bit, so I was sent to the Lycée Jaccard, an international school in Lausanne.'

At 15 Gary first discovered his songwriting talents, penning the English lyrics to a French hit of the day. 'I soon realised that you couldn't translate it literally and still make it lyrical, but you could translate the idea.' The lyricist Hal Shaper, who had his own publishing company, started commissioning him to write the English lyrics to French songs and then Osborne started writing his own melodies too. 'I took one of my own tunes to my dad and they took it to Germany and gave it to Nana Mouskouri,' remembers Osborne. 'So now I was doing English lyrics to French tunes, Germans were putting German lyrics to my tunes, I was 15 years old and it was the summer holidays. I was getting advances of fivers and tenners. A tenner back then would be like a ton now.' Osborne also co-wrote 'Say You Do' with his father for the film *Every Day's A Holiday*, starring the Mojos, Freddie and the Dreamers, Mike Sarne and John Leyton. 'I went to the session and there on drums was Kenny Clare, the greatest drummer in town. Big Jim Sullivan was on first guitar, Jimmy Page on second guitar, and John Paul Jones, or John Baldwin as he was known then, on bass. So I had half of what was to become Led Zeppelin playing in the rhythm section on what was my very first track!'

Osborne left school at 15 to seek fame and fortune in the music business. 'You weren't allowed to leave school at 15, but because I went to school in Switzerland, nobody knew I had.

'When I was 15, my sister Jan, who was 13, and I had a brother-and-sister act recording for Pye. Then I went to work for Hal Shaper's publishing company as a plugger before moving to RCA as an A & R Man. When I wasn't busy doing A & R I did a bit of plugging for them. This was 1969 so the acts I was plugging were Nilsson, Mama Cass, Steppenwolf and Richard Harris. In my spare time I was doing a music-based magazine programme for the BBC World Service called, 35 years before the term became popular, *Cool Britannia*.'

In the early Seventies Osborne did the rounds as a backing singer and also made a name for himself as the singer and writer of hundreds of jingles for ads. 'Apart from singing stuff like The Abbey Habit I was singing about five beers at the same time: Carling, Worthington E, Tennants, Younger's Tartan and Bass Export. I also did the Gas and Electricity ads in competition with each other.' He knew all the other singers on the London circuit and became one of the top bookers. 'For one Smarties ad I had Linda Lewis on vocals. David Essex did Pledge polish for me and Julie Covington did Blue Band margarine.'

Later in the Seventies, Osborne would also sing backing vocals with his partner, Paul Vigrass, on the UK Number 1s 'Sugar Baby Love' and 'Gonna Make You A Star'. In 1973, Vigrass and Osborne had a hit in Japan 'we took a Lego toys commercial that we had done with Jeff Wayne (the jingle king of the day). We put lyrics to it, put it on our album, and it was No 3 in Japan. It was called "Forever Autumn". Five years later, the song would become an international best-seller, covered by Justin Hayward, when Osborne was given the commission to pen the lyrics for Jeff Wayne's *War Of The Worlds* album, a record which went on to become one of the biggest-selling albums of all time.

'I remember that I got locked out of my flat when I was living in Hampstead and Gary and his wife Jenny took me in for the night,' says

Kiki Dee. 'We've been best friends ever since. In 1973 Gary was very, very good-looking, with long blond hair in a sort of Justin Haywood look. He was a great lyricist, lovely to work with and warm-hearted. He was very flamboyant, with a lot to say.'

Rocket Records was officially launched on April 30, 1973. Invitations were designed in the form of a train ticket. From Paddington, a train transported the partygoers to the Cotswolds village of Moreton-in-Marsh. The onboard stock of champagne was soon drunk dry. 'I organised the day,' says Stuart Epps. 'I booked the hall and the catering. When everyone arrived they were drunk out of their minds. I hired a brass band, and, to the tune of "Hello Dolly", we marched to the village hall, where a stage and PA had been set up and Longdancer played. It was a brilliant night.'

Signed up later in 1973 was a 13-year-old singer-songwriter from Swansea by the name of Maldwyn Pope. 'I'd done a radio session for John Peel in July and had interest from two record companies,' remembers Maldwyn – now Mal – Pope. 'One of them was Virgin, but John Peel and [his producer] John Walters thought it was a fly-by-night operation and said Elton and Rocket was a better bet. I come from a very "chapel background" and although my parents were supportive they were terrified about the world I was entering. I'd made a tape of my songs for John Peel and sent them without them knowing. The main reason they allowed me to sign for Rocket was that Steve Brown's dad had been a major in the Salvation Army.

'Steve Brown came to Swansea to record some songs and bring a contract for me to sign. I was met at Paddington station and, chaperoned by my elder brother David, was taken in Dee Murray's Rolls Royce to Mayfair studios for my first session. Elton was on tour in the US, but there was a telegram from him delivered to the studio. It was addressed to Madwyn rather Maldwyn, which was a bit of a disappointment. He had trouble with my name early in our relationship and often referred to me in interviews as Blodwyn Pig.'

Maldwyn would, however, soon meet his chief benefactor. 'The first time I met Elton was right at the end of my half-term holidays. I'd been recording in London and he was flying in from the US after a 48-date tour. I was with my dad, and remember arriving at 101 Wardour Street and seeing an enormous brown Phantom 5 Rolls outside. I remember climbing the stairs feeling incredibly nervous and excited. Elton was seated in one of those 1970s cane chairs that had an enormous back like a butterfly. He had pink hair and spent most of the time talking about gardening to my dad, who was a headmaster and Sunday school superintendent. After signing my autograph book, he told his driver to take us to Paddington in the Rolls, where we caught the train back to Swansea.'

With a share in a record label with a vision liberal enough to include on its books both a Welsh child singer and an established pro like Neil Sedaka, and a career that seemed unstoppable on both sides of the Atlantic, it seemed that Elton John had reached his peak. His spending-power certainly announced his arrival in the league of the super-rich. Elton spent £40,000 on a Francis Bacon painting and £18,000 on a Rembrandt sketch as well as lavishing gifts on others. He had already given away his white 1910 A-Day upright piano to his neighbours, Bryan Forbes and Nanette Newman. An inscription on the piano read:

'To Bryan and Nanette, Sarah and Emma with love, Elton John, May 31, 1972, original piano, lots of success with it.'

'Within this piano lays [sic] the ghosts of a hundred songs. Take care of them, they love you. God Bless from the one who writes the words, Bernie Taupin.'

In 1972, Forbes had begun filming an Elton John documentary entitled *Elton John and Bernie Taupin Say Goodbye To Norma Jean and Other Things*. Some of the footage is included on the *Goodbye Yellow Brick Road Classic Albums* DVD. It shows Elton, his hair dyed turquoise one day, orange the next, confident and happy. He was, if he had but known it, at the very height of his personal satisfaction with his music career. Having reached the top in terms of his creativity, and with it seeming hardly possible that he could get any bigger, he still retained an enthusiasm for his job.

This enthusiasm and commitment was showcased in an interview which would, in future years, be rightly regarded as one of the finest ever with the singer. As *Rolling Stone* magazine's chief London correspondent, 23-year-old Paul Gambaccini thought it was high time Elton received proper coverage in the paper. 'I met Elton under circumstances I would now not wish to repeat with anybody,' recalls Gambaccini. 'I was so keen a fan of music myself that, as a writer for *Rolling Stone* while still a student at Oxford, I had the most wonderful carte blanche. Our much-loved editor, Andrew Bailey, was fairly unmotivated and he was very happy for me to interview anybody I thought was worth being in the paper. It was a tremendous opportunity for me, because in the home office in San Francisco they were all fighting to get the plum assignments and here I was in London where more of the stars appeared.

'I went to a Bee Gees concert at the Royal Festival Hall and Elton was in the audience. I thought, well, you know, all the press are falling over themselves to say how wonderful Stevie Wonder is and he is wonderful, but while they're not looking, Elton has become the best-selling male vocalist. It's time he had what was called The *Rolling Stone* Interview, which was the big magnum opus. So, during the interval, I followed him into the gents and, while he was at the urinal, I asked him if he would like to do the *Rolling Stone* Interview. Of course, looking back now, it's beyond believability on the scale of rudeness. And he would have been forgiven if he had just whirled around in my direction. He was a great gentleman and he looked and me and said, "Call Helen Walters at DJM, she's in charge of things like that." We didn't shake hands.'

Gambaccini met Elton again shortly thereafter, having been chauffeur-driven to his home in Virginia Water. Bernie Taupin also came up for the interview. 'I loved them,' says Gambaccini. 'I don't know anyone who dislikes Bernie. This was a miracle match and they fit together perfectly.' The extensive interview – candid, funny and intelligent – was later published as a book, with an update taking the story into 1974. For Gambaccini, a writer and broadcaster who was to go on to become a personal friend of the singer's one of the reasons behind Elton's huge success was his comparatively ordinary social status: 'There is almost nobody who becomes a pop star who is from the social elite, that is to say, from a top university or rich, or people who you think would be the best trained musically, because in fact those people either aren't hungry enough to create prodigiously, or rock 'n' roll is not their natural language.'

The year of 1973 ended with Elton at his most carefree. On the final Iggy and the Stooges tour, in December, *Creem* journalist Ben Edmonds, who was helping the Stooges at the time, managed to set up an astonishing piece of rock pantomime involving Elton, a gorilla suit and the Stooges. 'I believe that was the last Stooges tour, the one that culminated in a near-riot in Detroit,' says Iggy Pop. 'I was very stoned from some sort of debacle the night before and I wasn't even in shape to stand up. I shuffled out to the stage, just trying to get through 50 minutes. I look to my left and a great fucking gorilla is lumbering towards the stage. I was scared. For all I knew it was a crazed biker on methedrine in that gorilla suit. He lucked out, because I don't know why one of us, probably me, didn't take him out. We didn't, but I was very annoyed though. Elton was smart enough to know that and took his head off to let people know who he was. He picked me up and danced round in a benign fashion. I think he had a crush on James [Williamson, the Stooges' guitarist]. James was the hottie.'

The fun also continued on vinyl. A Christmas single, 'Step Into Christmas', made the Top 30 in the UK and filled the airwaves along with Slade's 'Merry Christmas Everybody' and Wizzard's 'I Wish It Could Be Christmas Every Day.' A tribute to that great fixture of the Yuletide scene, Phil Spector, its sleigh-belled good humour was infectious. However, it was to mark the end of the first phase of Elton's career and the end of innocence for Elton John. Soon the freshness, the pioneering silliness and the unselfconsciousness of 1973 would be turned sour by the excesses of superstardom that were waiting in the wings.

PART 2

THE BREAKING OF A
SUPERSTAR 1974–1987

CHAPTER 8

ELTON IS TWO PER CENT
OF THE WORLD

'I could fart and reach Number 1.'

Elton John

'We've been living in a tinderbox
And two sparks can set the whole thing off.'

'Tinderbox'; lyrics: Bernie Taupin; music: Elton John

It is November 28, 1974. John Lennon is being sick into a bucket. It's a matter of minutes before he is due to take the stage at one of America's most prestigious entertainment venues, Madison Square Garden in New York, and he is consumed with stage fright. And it is all because of a stupid bet.

Elton and Lennon's off-stage friendship has graduated into a full-blown studio collaboration. Elton has sung backing vocals and played piano on a new Lennon classic, 'Whatever Gets You Through The Night'. Elton has laid down a challenge to the former Beatle: if the song gets to Number 1 on the Billboard charts, Lennon must perform it on stage with him.

'Seeing that it's Thanksgiving, we thought we'd make tonight a bit of a joyous occasion by inviting someone up with us on stage,' says Elton. (There's no turning back now. It is going to happen). 'And I'm sure he will be no stranger to anybody in the audience when I say, it's our great privilege and your great privilege to see and hear Mr John Lennon...'

The audience, stunned by the presence of Lennon, seems to know instinctively that they are witnessing a major piece of rock history. The wave of emotion is overwhelming. Some of Elton's band are in tears at the response. They play just three songs: Lennon's 'Whatever Gets You Through The Night', Elton's cover of 'Lucy In The Sky With Diamonds' and, finally, something completely unexpected. 'We're trying to think of a number to finish off with so I can run out of here and be sick,' Lennon tells the audience. 'And we thought we'd do a number by an old, estranged fiancé of mine called Paul. This is one I never sang; it's an old Beatles number and we just about know how to play it.' The band crash through 'I Saw Her Standing There'. It is John Lennon's last live concert performance.

* * *

'We did "I Saw Her Standing There", which was great and I was so glad we did that,' Elton later said. 'Originally I said, "Let's do two numbers, but you'll have to do another. Why not do 'Imagine?'" He said, "Oh no, boring. I've done it before. Let's do a rock 'n' roll song." So I thought of "I Saw Her Standing There", which was the first track on the first Beatles album. And he had never sung it. It was McCartney who sang it. John was so knocked out because he'd never actually sung the lead before.'

'I remember Lennon asking Davey Johnstone to tune his guitar,' says sound man Clive Franks about the historic performance. 'John came out on stage and I don't think anyone in history has ever had an ovation like that. It must have gone on for eight to ten minutes. I was like everyone else; I was shaking. There was an outrageous party after the gig. It was here that John and Yoko got back together again. I remember them sitting with Uri Geller and Geller was bending one spoon after the other.'

'I was moved by it but everybody else was in tears,' Lennon reflected in 1975. 'I felt guilty because I wasn't in tears: I just went up and did a few numbers. But the emotional thing was Elton and I together.

Elton had been working in Dick James's office when we used to send our demos in and there's a long relationship musically with Elton that people don't really know about. He has this sort of Beatles thing from way back. He'd take the demos home and play them and… well, it meant a lot to me and it meant a hell of a lot to Elton, and he was in tears. It was a great high night, a really high night… Yoko and I met backstage and somebody said, "Well, there's two people in love." That was before we got back together. But that's probably when we felt something. It was very weird.'

As a teenager, Elton had seen the Beatles in concert in London, an event he would later describe as 'like seeing God'. To be actually sharing studio and then stage space with a living legend was therefore one of the highlights of his life. 'I was terrified of meeting him because of his biting wit and musical genius,' confessed Elton in 2005. 'But it was like meeting an old friend – he was warm, sweet and very funny. He was so kind to my family, my band and my friends. There was no swagger, just humility and warmth. It was as if for two years the sun shone directly on me and that heat has stayed with me forever. I loved him and will never forget.'

'Elton sort of popped in on the session for *Walls and Bridges* and sort of zapped in and played the piano and ended up singing "Whatever Gets You Thru the Night" with me. Which was a great shot in the arm,' said Lennon. 'I'd done three quarters of it, "Now what do we do? Should we put a camel on it or a xylophone?" That sort of thing. And he came in and said, "Hey, ah'll play some piano!"'

John Lennon spent a good deal of time with Elton in 1974. He would be a regular backstage on tour and he would visit Elton with his temporary escort May Pang when Elton was recording at Caribou Ranch Studio in Colorado. In July 1974, Elton cut a fine version of 'Lucy In The Sky With Diamonds' and Lennon guested on guitar. Davey had to re-teach John Lennon the chords because the man himself had forgotten them.

'Then I heard he was doing "Lucy" and I heard from a friend – 'cause he was shy – would I be there when he cut "Lucy"? Maybe not play on it but just be there?' said John. 'So I went along. And I sang in the chorus and contributed the reggae in the middle. And then, again through a mutual friend, he asked if it [Whatever Gets You Through The Night] got to be Number One, would I appear onstage with him, and I said sure, not thinkin' in a million years it was gonna get to Number One. Al Coury or no Al Coury, the promotion man at Capitol. And there I was. Onstage.'

Elton described working on 'Whatever Gets You Through The Night' as 'a fucking dream. I really did think I'd died and gone to heaven. He put the vocal down first and I had to sing backing vocals, double-tracked, to someone else's phrasing. Now, I'm very quick but that took a long time because Lennon's phrasing was so weird. It was fantastic but you start to understand why he was a one-off. We did two vocal harmonies in the studio based around his one lead vocal and it was quite nerve-wracking.'

Lennon was on his famous 'lost weekend', that period of time when he had left Yoko Ono and was in a relationship with May Pang. 'John was just the nicest man deep down; genuinely a great and quite humble person,' Elton was to reflect. 'The time we spent together – what I remember of it – is just one laugh after another. John was the kind of man who would walk into a room full of people and, instead of going up to the biggest celeb, he would go round the room talking to everyone one by one, a real man of the people. He took my parents out to dinner once; John got up to go to the toilet and when he came back my dad had taken his false teeth out and put them in the water glass. Lennon just pissed himself laughing.'

It was a measure of Elton John's colossal stature in the pop world of 1974 that he was one of perhaps three or four rock icons of the day big enough not to seem completely out of his depth on stage with a former Beatle. By the end of the year, Elton was entering a phase in his career in which everything was he did was simply on a massive scale. Just as it seemed that the huge successes of 1973 couldn't be topped, Elton's popularity seemed to soar into the showbiz ionosphere.

At the end 1974, the *Elton's Greatest Hits* compilation spent 11 consecutive weeks at the top of the UK charts and also reached

Number 1 in America. In June 1974, Elton had re-signed to MCA in America. *Billboard* magazine quoted label president Mike Mailand as saying that it was 'the best deal anybody ever got'. Reportedly, Elton would receive increased royalties on his catalogue, plus an advance on future earnings to the tune of a whopping $8 million. Despite the outlay, the record company obviously still thought that Elton's colossal status would mean that the financial pie would be big enough for everyone to gorge on greedily.

Then, inevitably, the critics began sniping away at Elton. He was suddenly *too* popular. 'There was a thing at that time where, if you were in progressive music, you took your "music", in inverted commas, seriously, and of course Elton never really completely did that,' is how broadcaster Bob Harris puts it. 'He was having a lot of fun on stage and for this reason some people felt it was easy to dismiss it, because he's not taking it seriously or it's not meaningful.' 'Credible artists were those who audibly suffered or were rebellious, and he was neither,' adds Paul Gambaccini.

Elton tended to be regarded by some critics as an irrelevance, or at best a sales rather than a musical phenomenon. 'It was precisely because Elton John was great fun and guaranteed to give a good time in concert that Americans loved him,' wrote Paul Gambaccini in 2002. 'They were living through the era of Nixon, Vietnam and Watergate, and they desperately needed a break from the relentless unpleasant news. He could not have been more socially relevant! At one point his discs accounted for 2% of the world's records sales.' Elton's music was dominating the global arena to an astonishing degree. It helped define what the academic Dave Laing has called 'the trans-national sound'. It spoke across cultures, across nations. It was a universal language of music, as intelligible in Japan as it was in Europe. Its melodies and themes were inclusive and understandable.

As a result, the Elton John brand became massive. By the mid-1970s, it was quite possible for the top earners in the music business to become millionaires many times over. A new professionalism was making itself felt within the business. Just ten years earlier, groups such as the Beatles were still playing comparatively small-scale gigs with a meagre managerial and promotional support network. Now, the new superstars could play to 60,000 people on a fairly regular basis. They had entourages to do their bidding – musicians, accountants, lawyers, managers and personal assistants, as well as wardrobe, catering, sound and lighting people.

A world tour was now a massive operation, especially the US leg on which dates visited gigantic arenas built originally for baseball. Groupies, hangers-on and drug dealers also came as standard for many rock acts. While this was a still an era before the accountants took over, before stylists and conceptualists tried to push music into the background and commerce to the fore (that would come in the 1980s), the music scene of the mid-1970s was certainly moving rapidly away from the amateurish state that had existed a decade earlier. By 1975, stadium tours in impersonal but lucrative sports venues throughout the US were where the big bucks were made. The artist might be virtually invisible, the sound almost inevitably substandard, but that didn't matter. Rock shows had become events, spectacles, and you had to be there. Even for the half-serious fan, to miss the tour was to miss one of *the* events that year, musical or otherwise

In the summer of 1974, Elton decided for the first time in his career to make an album in the United States. *Caribou*, also a transatlantic Number 1 album, was recorded at the Caribou Ranch studio in the Rocky Mountains. 'It was recorded under the most excruciating of circumstances,' Elton admitted to Allan Jones of *Melody Maker* in June that year. 'We had eight days to do 14 numbers. We did the backing tracks in two-and-a-half days. It drove us crazy because there was a huge Japanese tour, then Australia and New Zealand, that could not be put off. It was the first time we had recorded in America, and we couldn't get adjusted to the monitoring system, which was very flat. I never thought we'd get an album out of it.'

One of the album's most puzzling moments was 'Solar Prestige A Gammon'. Apparently tired of his lyrics being pored over by fans and critics seeking to tease out deep, Dylan-esque profundities (or even, according to Elton, anti-religious or anti-Semitic messages), Bernie was urged by Elton to write a piece of nonsense. It might have been a bit of a laugh on Bernie's part, but the joke was obviously on the audience this time. The lyric itself was nothing more than a mix of gibberish, puns and poor piscine allusions: Elton sang 'Kool kar kyrie kay salmon/ Har ring molassis abounding/ Common lap kitch sardin a poor floundin' over a jaunty Euro-beat in the chorus and a mock Italian tenor in the verses.

Much of the rest of *Caribou* continued in this playful but ultimately slight fashion. The country-inflected 'Dixie Lily' lacked in all respects the sort of heartfelt take on Americana found on earlier classic Elton albums. Several cuts also came with added horn sections from Tower of Power: that autumn, Elton would tour with the Muscle Shoals Horns. But the addition of the honking horn section seldom worked as successfully as planned.

Elton and Bernie appeared to have gone into the recording studio with nowhere near the powerful collection of songs they needed to follow up *Goodbye Yellow Brick Road*. The exception, though, was the closing number 'Ticking', one of Elton and Bernie's finest creations from the 1970s. It told the tale of a lonely, troubled son who succumbed to a time bomb of deep emotional anxiety within him and went on a murder spree in a bar in Queens, New York. The narrative was chilling and Bernie's lyrics explored the psychology of the killer in a totally convincing fashion. Elton's unadorned piano melody and David Hentschel's synth were the only musical accompaniments.

The album was further rescued by the inclusion of two brilliant singles. 'The Bitch Is Back', cut in January 1974, is one of Elton's most iconic songs. Along with his enormous generosity of spirit came a seemingly endless candour. Read almost any interview with Elton John and there will be (usually good-humoured) swipes, asides and bitchy comments about everyone, from his closest friends to his more distant rivals. It's what makes Elton so endearing to so many, the fact that he can not only take himself to task, but also say what we all think about the arrogance of others. The lines, 'I can bitch, I can bitch, 'cause I'm better than you/ It's the way that I move, the things that I do' are a perfect summation by Bernie of the arrogance within the pop world, but also a clear piece of self-analysis relating to Elton's own frequent tizzies and 'artistic temperament'. Not many pop stars have this self-mocking capacity. The track's other charms included brilliant zapping guitar work from Davey Johnstone, a blasting tenor sax solo from Lenny Pickett and Dusty Springfield sharing backing vocal duties. It was released as the second single off the album in the autumn of 1974, reaching Number 15 in Britain and Number 4 in the US.

The other major song on the album was the ballad 'Don't Let The Sun Go Down On Me'. Elton's debt to, and love of, the Beach Boys was dramatically captured here in a song which was obviously a tribute to the band's classic sound of 'God Only Knows' and 'Good Vibrations'. Beach Boys Carl Wilson and Bruce Johnstone supplied sweet backing vocals along with Toni Tennille, who as one half of the duo Captain and Tennille was shortly to score a Number 1 hit in the US with 'Love Will Keep Us Together'. 'Don't Let The Sun Go Down On Me' fared disappointingly at home on its release in the early summer of 1974, reaching only Number 16, but in Elton's commercial homeland, the USA, it was Number 2 for two weeks. Elton, however, found recording his own lead vocal a bit of a strain. As Nigel Olsson reports, 'He got so frustrated that he couldn't get this one line [that] he screamed to Gus Dudgeon, "Screw this! Send it to Lulu, and if she doesn't like it, send it to Engelbert [Humperdinck]!" But five minutes later it was fine.'

The *Caribou* album was significant in that it saw the formal addition of Ray Cooper to Elton's band. Cooper was already vastly experienced as a musician and had played jazz, rock and roll, and pop. He had played with the Who and the Stones and would remain one of the top session musicians for the next two decades. His interest in film (Cooper was also an actor and music producer and would later work in various capacities on such distinguished films as *Popeye*, *A Private Function*, and several films with Terry Gilliam including *Brazil* and *The Adventures Of Baron Munchausen*) and the arts in general, meant that Elton had a genuine cultural polyglot within his ranks.

Specifically, Cooper brought two new dimensions to Elton's world. As a brilliant and powerfully theatrical stage presence, he added a visual counterpoint to Elton's own performance. His timpani rolls, vibraphone solos and manic tambourine bashing were performed with a unique sense of style. A tall, balding man in a three-piece suit with waistcoat and fob chain, he looked like Elton's slightly older, and slightly madder, brother; part visual humorist, part slightly unhinged mortician. 'Ray's the greatest,' says Ken Scott. 'Believe me, when he's up there, you can't keep your eyes off him; he becomes the star of the show, he's so animated up there.'

But the main reason Ray was now in Elton's band was his musicianship. 'I was given the credit (or discredit perhaps, from a classical point of view) for being one of the first people to bring classical percussion instruments into rock 'n' roll: timpani, tubular bells, vibraphone, all that stuff which looks spectacular in classical orchestras,' he says. 'It was incredibly instinctual. I didn't sit down and plan it. One of the many joys about being a percussionist as opposed to a *kit* drummer is that, whereas the primary task of the drummer is to produce the driving force behind the music, the percussionist, who is also an integral part of that "force", can also have the ability to be a musical colourist. As a percussionist I have before me an incredible range of sound colour to orchestrate or illuminate lyrics or certain nuances of music, I can, therefore, generally, be more liberated than the kit drummer. Gus Dudgeon, Elton's record producer, realised and understood this, and gave me the freedom to punctuate, colour and embellish many of Elton and Bernie's songs. Gus gave the percussion sounds "air, space and dignity." I'll always be grateful to him for that.'

The support for Elton's 1974 tour was the Kiki Dee Band. Kiki was busy making her second album for Rocket Records, called *I've Got The Music In Me*. 'Kiki's a lovely person and an amazing singer, but also the world's most paranoid person,' recalls Clive Franks. 'She doesn't have the confidence that you think that she would have. When she was trying to record her vocal for "I've Got The Music In Me", she was actually in tears because she couldn't get it.'

'It was in New York, at the Ladyland, Jimi Hendrix's studios,' recalls Kiki. 'Cissy Houston was there doing the backing vocals with these two black women. They were absolutely fantastic singers. And I just bottled it, I lost confidence.' 'Elton was in the studio at the time and he ripped his clothes off and ran around her as she was at the microphone and totally freaked her out,' continues Clive Franks. 'Well, it would freak anyone out. Anyway, it broke the ice and she started laughing, so the next take she got it, probably because she was scared that he would come and do it again.'

If Elton's own version of 'The Streak' showed him to be in tune with the zeitgeist, his 1974 tour, in its splendour and general vastness, perfectly represented rock celebrity mid-1970s style. He had at his disposal *Starship 1*, the plane of choice for elite rock stars, a full-sized Boeing passenger jet whose regular seats had been ripped out and replaced with comfy seats and sofas, a bar, an office and a bedroom. 'It was so glamorous,' says Kiki. 'It was very 1970s. There was a chill-out room with a fluffy rug and they had a bar where you could sit and have a cup of coffee. And they'd have these – so American, so early 1970s – packets of vitamins on the bar so that you could get your daily supply. What we did in America was that we'd stay in one hotel for the week so you could unpack and make a little nest and then each day you'd fly to the gig and then back to the hotel. It was like family. I knew all the crew, I knew the sound engineers and I got on really well with Elton's band. We weren't treated like some support bands, who are not considered part of the family. I had the confidence to know that I could do 45 minutes before Elton came on and people wouldn't be calling: "We want Elton! We want Elton!"'

Kiki's closeness to the Elton touring band led to romance with one of the band members. Between 1974 and 1978, Kiki and Davey Johnstone would be an item. 'I think a lot of people thought I was gay for a time, but although I have never married, that is definitely not the case,' says Kiki. 'I've had an interesting single life, I have to say!'

One of the features of the touring life was the John Reid's overly protective stance towards his client. Like so many managers before him, and so many since, Reid had developed a style under which the artist came first, at almost any cost. His prime objective was to make sure everything ran as smoothly and professionally as possible and when, due to normal human failings, it didn't, his reaction was almost inevitably irrationally explosive. 'I guess he was a good manager, but he had a very aggressive streak,' affirms Clive Franks. 'He was a Jekyll and Hyde character; very similar to Elton in that respect. That's why they got on so well together. From one day to the next they were different people. There were times when John was a friendly and loving person, but that doesn't excuse that other side. That other side was horrendous. I've seen him almost strangle a hotel receptionist because his room wasn't ready.'

Despite being one of the more placid members of the touring party, Franks also fell foul of Reid's bullying moments. There was some history between them. Franks had co-produced Kiki Dee's second album with Gus Dudgeon and, according to Franks, Reid had been 'really nasty about it, and hadn't liked what I had done. I got a credit in tiny letters and I didn't get a penny from it'. One night, during a concert in Alabama, when Franks was, as usual, mixing Elton's live sound, he felt a finger prodding the back of his neck. 'It was John Reid,' continues Franks. 'He said, "Turn up the piano." And I said, "The piano is the loudest thing in the mix, what do you mean, turn it up?" "Turn up the fucking piano," came the reply. I said, "Well, with all due respect, John, if I turn up the piano, then I'm going to lose the voice." He said, "If you don't turn it up, you're fired and you'll go home tomorrow." I couldn't believe it, so I said, "Why wait until tomorrow, I'm going home now."

'I left the console to my second-in-command and went back to the dressing room. John Reid found me backstage and he went mental: "Don't you ever leave the mixing desk in the middle of a gig again." I reminded him: "You just fired me, and you can stick the job up your arse anyway, I don't want it." John couldn't handle this. He was holding a glass of champagne and he threw it in my face. He grabbed me by the throat and ripped my favourite embroidered Beatles T-shirt off me! And he had his fist clenched to punch me. I know it wasn't a very gentlemanly thing to do, but I kicked him in the balls with all my might and knocked him out. He was lying flat on his back in the dressing room. I thought, "Fuck, I've killed him." The floor manger whisked me away.'

Franks understandably thought that his career with Elton John's band had reached an abrupt ending. However, there was a surprise in store. Instead of being fired, when the band reconvened for the next gig in LA, Elton called a 'house meeting'. 'I had brought everything to a head,' continues Franks. 'Elton said to John, "Cool it. Start being nice to people, and if you're not, I'll fire you." They were still lovers at the time, but it was getting pretty tense between them by now. John Reid had the good grace to come up to me after the LA show. I was pretty worried about seeing him. He was holding a glass of champagne and for one moment I thought he was going to throw it over me again. But he just said, "Enjoy the party." That was his way of apologising.'

There were further incidents. In February 1974, during an after-noon Maori reception at Parnell Rose Garden in Auckland, Reid was arrested and subsequently had to serve a custodial sentence for assaulting a journalist, Judith Baragwanath. According to Philip Norman, Reid had behaved violently towards the party's organiser Kevin Williams when, having asked for whisky, he was told their supplies had been consumed and would he take a glass of champagne instead. Rebuked by the forthright Baragwanath, Reid hit her in the face. Later that day, at an after-show party for a David Cassidy concert attended by Reid and Elton, David Wheeler, a friend of the injured female journalist, had told Elton's entourage that they were all 'marked men'. 'The threat was communicated to Elton, who reacted with unusual truculence, marching up to David Wheeler, grabbing him by the shirt front and asking him who he thought he was threatening,' reported Norman. 'John Reid then intervened, knocking Wheeler down and kicking him as he lay on the floor.' Reid was arrested by Auckland police and charged with assaulting both Baragwanath and Wheeler. Elton was also arrested for his assault on Wheeler at the nightclub.

According to Norman, Reid apologised to Baragwanath, offering to settle out of court. In the subsequent trial Elton was asked to pay a meagre NZ$50 in costs, while Reid was given a custodial sentence. Elton, distraught at the imprisonment of his manager and lover, initially refused to play the scheduled gig. During the trial, Baragwanath admitted calling Reid a 'rotten little bastard' but denied she had used the word 'poof'. Clive Franks recalls: 'I travelled in the car with John to the reception, and this very outspoken journalist [Baragwanath] came up to him with a tape machine and a little microphone. She said something which must have caused John great personal offence, and he looked at her and smacked her right between the eyes.'

After Reid had been found guilty, the level of local antagonism towards the whole Elton John operation reached a new level. 'There were death threats issued against anyone connected with the shows,' confirms Clive Franks. 'I was at the mixing desk with two cops with rifles, who were looking out into the audience in case there was anyone out there planning on doing anything silly. The next day our plane was delayed by three or four hours because people had rung the authorities to say a bomb was on board. John Reid stayed with a prison warder and his wife for the time of his sentence. He wasn't actually in jail as such but he was under detention.' Asked about the incident in 2001, Reid said, 'Well, she was very aggressive and I'm not defending myself, but it was a knee-jerk reaction.'

The problem by the mid-1970s was that John Reid had a foul temper when he was drinking heavily. 'I was very young when I started, learning on my feet almost daily. I always seemed to be getting into trouble and got a reputation,' he has admitted. Elton was also no stranger to the odd glass or five and, sometime around the mid-1970s, became a drug user. For Elton, a man who liked a drink, but who had hitherto been uninterested in drugs, this was a new and, as it turned out, disastrous development.

The drug of choice was, of course, cocaine. 'Glam was the first musical style to flow directly from the use of cocaine,' was how the pop impresario Simon Napier-Bell put it in his autobiography, *Black Vinyl, White Powder*. 'The pop publicist Tony Brainsby summed it up perfectly: "Coke was the 'fuck-you' drug. You didn't give a damn what other people thought. You put on your spangled costume, slapped up your face, threw back your shoulders, shoved more coke up your nose and strutted on stage... You could see that cocaine arrogance in all of them – Bowie, Bolan, Elton...'"

'I joined the record industry and I got a desk and a drinks cabinet. I ended up on two or three grams of cocaine a day. It was always there,' John Reid would later admit. 'I am not proud of these fights. But in my part of Scotland we have an aggressive way of life. Though I know that more can be achieved by well-chosen words rather than violent actions.'

Unlike heroin, cocaine was a drug that, statistically, did not prove fatal very often. But over a prolonged period of septum-destroying use, it ultimately wreaked havoc on its victims. It was the perfect drug for the world of film, fashion and music. A natural appetite suppressant, unlike alcohol it would not leave you moving up a dress size at regular intervals. Cocaine primarily gives the user a sense of indestructibility. It produces a sensation of supreme (over-)confidence, allowing users to stay up for days in a state of over-alertness. For some, it enhances sexual euphoria and the appetite for sex. It also makes the addict gabble and lessens the immediate effects of alcohol (though not the following morning's hangover). Shy people became over-loquacious and part-time philosophers are soon imbued with a new assuredness in their values and visions. Cocaine users are irrational people to be around and, what is worse, they couldn't care less who they hurt along the way.

It wasn't just Elton who succumbed. Bernie Taupin was drinking heavily as his marriage to Maxine Feibelman hit the rocks and he too began using cocaine. 'The whole thing about being jacked up on coke is that you become this paranoid maniac,' Bernie reflected in 2006. 'You're nailing towels to the windows and you're getting freaked out by the phone going off and the doorbell ringing.' John Reid would succumb a little later, at around the age of 28. 'At first it's a lot of fun and gives a lot of energy, for the first couple of years. Then it becomes not so much fun and then it becomes completely destructive. I do not recommend it.'

In the mid-1970s music business, cocaine use was so widespread that it was in danger of becoming the norm. 'Everybody was doing it, it was no big deal,' remembers *Melody Maker* reporter Chris Charlesworth. 'If you were a rock star you did coke, full stop. The journalists did it, the roadies did it, the record company people did it; everybody did it. The fact that it was illegal was irrelevant, because people hardly ever got caught. People even wore their tiny coke spoons around their necks advertising the fact. And there was loads of it about. You wouldn't think any worse of anyone for smoking joints and doing coke.'

Meanwhile, although the *Caribou* album might have been a disappointment, it didn't stop its inexorable rise up the US and UK charts, where it reached Number 1. There were plenty of other 1974 highlights too. In April, at Rampart Studios, Elton filmed an outrageous cameo for the Ken Russell film of the Who's classic rock opera, *Tommy*. Elton's frantic version of 'Pinball Wizard', recorded at speed in the Who's studios in Battersea, was easily a match for the original. The new version came with maniacal triplets on the piano in the intro, trademark Elton John aggressive and trebly acoustic guitar, Ray Cooper's equally wild percussion and Davey's pristine rock guitar (which interpolated 'I Can't Explain' towards the end). In the film itself, Elton's performance, for which he wore arguably the tallest platform boots of the glam rock era, was as bravura a moment as any in his career. Elton would release the song as a single in early 1976 in the UK, scoring yet another Top 10 hit. In real life, his huge heels sometimes garnered more than the odd raised eyebrow or two. On one tour, he was reportedly stopped at customs by airport officials concerned that there might have been a stash of illegal drugs hidden in his footwear.

On May 4, 1974, Elton played a benefit concert at Vicarage Road, Watford. One of the constant themes running through Elton's long career has been his willingness to fund things he holds dear. There was no bigger fan of Watford Football Club than Elton John. At the time, Watford, under the managership of Mike Keen, were languishing in the Third Division. Also on stage that May day was one of Elton's closest friends in the rock fraternity, Rod Stewart. It's a measure of their respective commercial standings at the time that Rod Stewart, along with the hard-rocking Nazareth, were Elton's support for the day.

Rod and Elton formed a friendship in the 1970s that was both competitive and affectionate. Rod trusted Elton's judgement. His publicist at the time, Sally Croft, said: 'Rod used to send for Elton whenever he was doing a record because Elton was wonderful at saying which notes were wrong or a bit off. He and Rod were very close friends.' Elton would lavish gifts on the singer. According to Rod's most recent biographers, Tim Ewbank and Stafford Hildred, Elton arrived at Rod's Christmas dinner party in 1974 with a Rembrandt, *The Adoration Of The Shepherds*, as a gift. Rod would refer to Elton as 'Sharon' and, in return, Elton called Rod 'Phyllis'. John Reid was, of course, 'Beryl', after the British actress Beryl Reid. (Just to complicate things, Clive Franks and Elton always called each other Sid.) 'Bar none, he's the best singer I've heard in rock 'n' roll,' Elton was to say of Rod. 'He is also the greatest white soul singer.'

Two weeks after the Watford show, Elton played another charity gig, this time in the rather more rarefied atmosphere of the Royal Festival Hall, for the Invalid Children's Aid Society Benefit. The reception was mostly one of polite applause as Elton delved into his musical past to produce songs such as 'Skyline Pigeon' and 'Burn Down The Mission'. A crazy 'Honky Cat' featured that most rare of birds, a duck-call solo on a kazoo-like instrument by the resident absurdist Ray Cooper. Tracks from this concert would form the first side of Elton's second live album, *Here And There*, with the famous US Madison Square Garden Show from Thanksgiving Day 1974 providing the music for the flip side.

If the Madison Square Garden gig with Lennon was a piece of rock history, for British fans it would be Elton's *Old Grey Whistle Test* appearance on Christmas Eve that year which would live longest in the memory. The show's presenter, Bob Harris, had been a longstanding admirer and supporter of Elton, and saw Elton, or rather, the Elton

John Band as they were then briefly known, as the perfect artist to bring a dose of festive fun to BBC 2's late-evening line-up.

'It was one of the greatest music experiences of my entire life,' says Harris, who came on dressed as Father Christmas to introduce the main act. 'That was Elton at his absolute peak in terms of energy, flamboyance, stage presentation and warmth. We were at the Hammersmith Odeon and I was at the side of the stage throughout most of the concert. Most of the audience were bathed in light, partly from the lights from the stage but also because of television lights used so that the cameras can pick up people's faces. So I was looking out across the stage towards Elton and then out across the whole crowd into the auditorium, and everyone had a smile on their face. The warmth that was being generated towards Elton that night, you could cut it, you could hold it. Everybody was mouthing the words to every one of his songs, swaying from side to side, arms in the air. Elton also had a smile on his face. It was when he was at his most impish. He was up on the piano, jumping down again, running right up to the audience, smiling, talking. It was one of my greatest nights of music ever.' During the show two bunny girls walked on stage to present Elton with a Christmas cake and, for the encore of 'White Christmas', Rod Stewart and a fur-coat-wearing Gary Glitter briefly joined Elton. Fake snow fell on the audience in such quantities that Elton couldn't sing for laughing.

The Hammersmith Odeon Christmas shows were a regular feature of Elton's touring schedule for many years. One night in particular goes down in Elton lore as one of the most hilarious ever. 'They had a wire suspended from the upper balcony to the opposite side of the stage where Elton sat, stage left,' says Clive Franks, who watched it all from behind the mixing desk. 'They dressed a mannequin in the same stage clothes as Elton was wearing, along with the hat, glasses and platform boots. This dummy would be hidden from the audience and, when the house lights went down, it would be uncovered and pushed from the balcony. A spotlight would illuminate its as it came hurtling down the wire to disappear offstage. A split second later – Ta-dah! – Elton would come out as if he'd done the trick. It was very effective until one night the mannequin got stuck halfway down the wire. A stagehand started shaking the wire to get it moving again but in doing so caused its trousers to fall down. Hilarious! This thing bounced all the way down to the stage with its pants round its ankles.'

Elton's first single of 1975 would see something of a change of musical direction. 'Philadelphia Freedom' was obviously influenced by the Philly Sound of the mid-1970s. Although not a big hit in Britain, where it failed to reach the Top 10, it inevitably stormed to Number 1 in the US and remains in Elton's live repertoire to this day, such is its fresh exuberance. Elton's phrasing on 'Philadelphia Freedom' was perfect, and ample evidence of his supreme skill as a vocalist. The way in which he punched out the five syllables of 'Phil-a-del-phi-a' brought to mind the ra-ra chant of the baseball cheerleader. The music – replete with the high-register sonics of the strings, cool horns, Doobie Brothers-like rhythm guitar, booming bass drum, and judicious use of the sweetest of sweeteners, the flute – provides the basis for one of Elton's best songs.

The song's title was a tribute by Bernie and Elton to Billie Jean King, the legendary sportswoman who later that year would claim her sixth, and last, Wimbledon Singles title. King's tennis team were the Philadelphia Freedoms. An all-round sports fan, Elton took particularly to tennis and received some tuition from Billie Jean herself. 'Elton is crazy about tennis,' says Gary Osborne. 'He's a fanatical player, far better than you'd expect from his bulk. He is not as short as people imagine. People have this idea that he's short because of the shoes, and they assume that the shoes were a cover-up, but he's about five foot eight-and-a-half, which is average height. He's fast, and that competitive spirit is always in evidence.'

Well before the release of the single, however, Elton already had another studio album in the can, its release delayed by the huge success of the *Greatest Hits* released at the end of 1974. In fact, work on the new album had begun as far back as the early summer of 1974. In July, Elton had taken the *SS France* from England to New York, chaperoning 11-year-old Julian Lennon who was visiting his father. During the trip,

Elton sought out a piano and got to work on a new set of lyrics by Bernie. This new collection was a weightier and more considered collection of songs than those on *Caribou*. Of a mostly autobiographical nature, they examined Elton and Bernie's life together in London as struggling music business neophytes between 1967 and 1969. Bernie wrote the songs in order and Elton did the music in the same way. It was not only Elton and Bernie's most personal work to date, but also an important piece of rock industry criticism. Bernie's lyrics maturely – but with some bitterness – critiqued the final days of Tin Pan Alley in London. They marked the passing of the old guard and triumphantly told of the time the new guard arrived.

If *Goodbye Yellow Brick Road* is the classic Elton John pop album, a record tumbling with images and melodies, then 1975's *Captain Fantastic And The Brown Dirt Cowboy* is a musical novella, a piece which works brilliantly from start to finish. 'That album was about the two of us, the things we'd been through together and what it all meant thus far,' Elton has said. 'It felt so good to be writing songs that I not only understood the lyrics to, but was a complete part of. Before, I was singing stuff that perhaps didn't directly relate to me.' 'For me, *Captain Fantastic* will always remain an entirely satisfying work, possibly the only album we have ever made where every track fits into a cohesive pattern free of any corrupting elements,' says Bernie. 'It's time in a bottle, a potent capsulated snapshot of a crucial period in our lives that helps to remind me that nothing comes easy.'

The album cast the central figures as fictional cartoon characters. Elton was Captain Fantastic, Bernie the Brown Dirt Cowboy. Yet in the period of time covered by the album, from their meeting in 1967 to the release of their first album, *Empty Sky*, neither member of the team had achieved what they had set out to become. Elton in 1969 was by no means Captain Fantastic, and the closest Bernie had come to a cowboy was at a children's fancy dress party. So although the album looked back, it also predicted a future for both of them. *Captain Fantastic* was as much about prophecy as history.

There really was not a weak link in the chain of songs that forms this album. The title track was one of Elton's loveliest melodies, its gentle country winsomeness much loved by Bernie. 'Bitter Fingers' was perhaps the best lyric, as Bernie recalled the time when the fledgling songwriting duo were stuck in a rut, writing trite pop for unwilling takers: 'It seems to me a change is really needed/I'm sick of tra-la-las and la-de-das'. The closing sequence of the song, when Davey repeated the main melody on lead guitar in the fade-out, was a classic Elton moment. Another standout track was 'Better Off Dead'. Elton took Bernie's tale of depression and wrote a melody that totally undercut the song's seriousness with its Gilbert and Sullivan-like mock-operatic music. Dudgeon's recording of Olsson's drums, crashing and thudding throughout the song, was another moment of high innovation. The last number, 'Curtains', was a perfect ending for the album, building in a wall-of-sound-like crescendo of vocal harmonies, as the lovely melody soared away into the distance.

Two songs showed Elton at his most emotionally raw. He has always loved 'We All Fall In Love Sometimes': 'it's just a beautiful fucking love song,' he told *Mojo* in 1997. 'But it's not, as has been suggested elsewhere, about sexual love, but the kind of love that can exist between two people that is, in so many ways, above plain sexual love or lust. Bernie showed me things and ideas that I had never encountered; he was the big brother I never had. In most ways we were so completely different, but we had the kind of relationship that if he liked something, I thought there must be something in it. For instance, I'd listen to Dylan because Bernie thought he was the greatest writer ever.

'I hear "We All Fall In Love Sometimes" now and listen to the lyrics and I can cry, because I remember the closeness that we had then. In a wider sense, it also has some relevance to my past. I've fallen in love with the wrong people so many times. I used to go to clubs and I'd see people at the bar and by the time I managed to get to talk to them I had already planned our entire lives together. Even if I did manage to will a relationship out of them, it always went wrong and I'd end up getting hurt. It always ended up in tears.'

The biggest moment on the album, however, was 'Someone Saved My Life Tonight'. 'I thought about Brian Wilson and "God Only Knows",' Elton said in 2005. 'From the first chord you can tell that.' The song is one of the most dramatic moments in his vast repertoire, yet during the actual recording producer Gus Dudgeon apparently called over to Elton to ask him to give his performance a bit more emotion, not realising the subject matter centred round a very dark time indeed for the singer.

The song depicted the night in 1968 when Long John Baldry 'saved' Elton's life by urging him to ditch his misguided wedding plans. Its target was clearly Elton's jilted fiancée Linda Woodrow. Woodrow was depicted 'Sitting like a princess perched in her electric chair' while Elton cried: 'I'm strangled by your haunted social scene/Just a pawn outplayed by a dominating queen'. Seldom had a pop song been so poetic, so perfect and yet so blistering in its attack on one person's psychological and emotional dominance over the other. This was a very public retaliation.

Paul Gambaccini remembers being present when the album was played to journalists that summer of 1975 at Marquee Studios, close to Rocket Records in London's Wardour Street. He considered the album 'brilliant' on first hearing and over 30 years later his opinion hasn't changed. '*Captain Fantastic* isn't poppy. *Goodbye Yellow Brick Road* is an ultra-pop album,' says Gambaccini. '*Captain Fantastic* is a serious album; it's not for laughs. Not for nothing was the booklet for *Goodbye Yellow Brick Road* accompanied by illustrations, because Bernie had a way of conjuring up the visual. You can see it as well as hear it. *Captain Fantastic* wasn't image-driven, it was autobiographical, so it's almost as if part of the dimension of Elton John was not there. As a strictly musical achievement it is at least its equal, but it doesn't have the pop culture plusses that *Goodbye Yellow Brick Road* has.'

The final piece in the jigsaw was the album's artwork. Elton asked graphic designer Alan Aldridge to work on the project. Aldridge had created the *Beatles Illustrated Lyrics* book and his style, as the *Guardian* reported in 1969, was 'lavish and rounded, reminiscent of

Art Nouveau, images soaked in psychedelic colours that leapt out at the viewer'. His album design did not disappoint. Dressed in goggle-like spectacles, headphones and top hat, Elton clutched what could be a conductor's baton in one hand and a pink rose in the other, sitting astride a piano surrounded by a surrealistic menagerie of birds, snakes and fish. Beneath him, a half-opened capsule depicted, presumably, the life of clock-time city and industry.

'Town mouse' Elton was contrasted with 'country mouse' Bernie. The back cover depicted a seated Bernie, contentedly smiling and reading a book, still hermetically sealed inside his own bubble, a rural idyll of hares, snails, beetles and sheep for company. Outside his personal capsule was a rather more sinister underworld of Lewis Carroll-esque images, including a top-hat-wearing character clutching a key, a statue of a woman with the head of a bird and several worms and skeletons. In the distance, Davey, Dee, Nigel, Ray and a final, tiny figure, thought to be John Reid, float towards the figure of Bernie in their own specially drawn 'bubbles'. One of the barmiest – but also one of the most brilliant – record sleeves ever designed, it linked the colossal figure of Elton John in 1975 to the heritage of the Beatles.

Before the release of *Captain Fantastic*, Elton made a move that he would later call inexplicable and which, at the time, caused a great deal of resentment. After five years in the band, Nigel Olsson and Dee Murray were told that their services were no longer required. 'When he first let Dee and me go, it was both a kick in the pants and a total shock,' remembers Nigel Olsson. 'He hadn't told us what was going on. In fact, he called me the week before and he was raving about the fact that we were going to do Dodger Stadium [in Los Angeles]. It was a sold-out gig and nobody played at Dodger Stadium, especially rock 'n' roll bands. The next week I got this call from Steve Brown, saying, "Elton doesn't want you guys involved in gigs or recording any more, what are you going to do?" all in one sentence. I was floored.'

'They were sickened and I was very upset,' says Clive Franks. 'Even though the guys who were coming in were friends of mine, I thought, why break up a successful formula?' Many years later, Elton expressed not a little regret at the decision. 'I can't really understand why I did it,' he told the BBC DJ Johnnie Walker in 2005, before attempting to explain it to himself: 'In retrospect, it was part of me trying to change things musically. Maybe we had gone on as far as we could.'

The new line-up would see two old colleagues recalled in the drummer Roger Pope and the guitarist Caleb Quaye, and a second keyboardist was found in the guise of James Newton Howard. Jeff 'Skunk' Baxter was 'borrowed' from the Doobie Brothers to play guitar and steel guitar, while Kenny Passarelli came in on bass duties. 'It was the closest Elton had to a real zapping rock 'n' roll band,' says Ray Cooper. 'This was a hard-edged band. Caleb doesn't take any prisoners. The addition of James Newton Howard was also an important development. James was an academic, classical musician, almost a concert pianist.'

'I've always wanted to be part of a good driving rock 'n' roll band,' Elton confessed in June 1975. 'The old band never used to drive – we used to rattle on. Whenever we played anything live, it was always twice the tempo of the recording and it was a bit off-putting to me. I want to chug rather than race.'

Caleb Quaye was delighted to be back in the fold, although his participation came with a condition. 'Elton assured me that he wanted to take a looser, funkier approach with his music. I let him know what he already knew – that I despised some of the mainstream pop songs he had recently produced. In fact, I set one condition on my returning to his band: I would not play "Crocodile Rock".' During rehearsals for the *Captain Fantastic* tour in Amsterdam, Keith Moon and Ringo Starr dropped by. Quaye admits that, at this point, his own drug use went 'up to the next level'. 'At one point I went on a four-day cocaine binge, during which I asked Ringo a question about *Sgt Pepper's Lonely Hearts Club Band*,' Quaye recalls. 'Ringo was so stoned that he couldn't remember the album.'

The new band's first gig would be at Wembley Stadium. Elton had lost weight after a period at a tennis camp in Scottsdale, Arizona, where he was tutored by Billie Jean King. The band came to the show well drilled. They played brilliantly but, as Elton later admitted, they died a death. Elton had taken the brave and, as it turned out, foolish decision to perform the whole of his new album, a set of ten serious and mostly downbeat songs that nobody had ever heard before. 'I handpicked the bill,' recollects Elton. 'It was Stackridge, Joe Walsh, Rufus & Chaka Kahn, the Eagles, the Beach Boys and us. It was £2.50 to get in!'

'The Beach Boys came on when the afternoon was at its peak,' explains Paul Gambaccini. 'It was hot and sunny, Beach Boys weather, and everybody grooved and danced and, after they had finished, everyone was knackered. Elton came on when the adrenaline level was falling.' 'We came on at about 8pm and played a whole album that people had never heard,' marvels Elton. 'It was something we should have done in a club, or a small venue, not to 75,000 at Wembley Stadium. You could feel by the third number that people were starting to fidget.' 'Elton got booed and people walked out. It was a total mistake,' was Clive Franks' even franker assessment of the day the Beach Boys stole the limelight.

Nevertheless, the album would be the first in recorded history to debut at Number 1 on the Billboard charts. Elton was featured on the front cover of the July 7, 1975 edition of *Time* magazine, billed as 'Rock's Captain Fantastic'. He had become so huge that he was now not only a living, breathing human rock star, but an icon in the form of a cartoon figure. There would also be a *Captain Fantastic* pinball machine, with original artwork from Alan Aldridge. 'New from Bally', ran the ad, 'full-size, commercial quality home pinball featuring rock giant ELTON JOHN'.

'Once, in 1976, I visited Elton in Toronto and in his hotel room he had a prototype of the *Captain Fantastic* pinball machine,' recalls Paul Gambaccini. 'He said, "Let's have a game." After four balls I was ahead and I was thinking, What do I do now? Dare I win? Dare I beat this guy on his own machine? It would have been Regicide. Elton was so competitive; he just turned it on. I didn't have a bad last ball, but he just went into overdrive. The guy just can't stand to lose.'

Later in July, Elton found himself on stage with the Rolling Stones at a concert in the Hughes Stadium in Colorado, having been introduced by

Mick Jagger as 'Reg from Watford'. He joined the Stones for their opener, 'Honky Tonk Women', a song that he had featured in his own earlier shows as a tribute. But now the former Reg Dwight was up on stage with the band as their equal, even if, as it turned out, there was a little bit of an atmosphere. 'We should have kicked him off the stage, but we didn't,' Jagger apparently later complained. 'It's because we're both English.'

Meanwhile, the money kept pouring in. By the autumn of 1975, there were press reports that Elton was about to fork out nearly £400,000 for a 37-acre estate complete with gardens, swimming pool and, according to the *Daily Telegraph*, 'a coach-house block with garaging, stables, a staff cottage and groom's flat'. That property was Woodside, between New Windsor and Englefield Green on Berkshire/Surrey border. The estate is close to Windsor Great Park, his occasional neighbour therefore the Queen of England, and Runneymede where King John signed the Magna Carta in 1215. Over the years, the property would be developed, redesigned and restyled with loving care and attention. It was Elton John's country estate and is a home he still has to this day.

Throughout 1975, as Elton the workaholic kept up an almost insanely busy schedule of touring and recording, it became apparent that he was beginning to suffer from exhaustion. The buoyancy of his interviews of just two years previously, when fame was new, had been replaced by a more reflective, even darker tone. It came to light that, even after so many years, Elton continued to be disturbed by his relationship with his father and by his parents' painful divorce. 'I was terribly bitter at the time but I see my dad now, sometimes. And I feel really sorry that we didn't get closer,' he told one journalist. 'He has four kids now who he loves, but I don't feel that he's a shit. I just wish he could have loved me like that, too.'

If there was one week in Elton's career that might be seen as the absolute pinnacle of his superstardom, then that week came in the autumn of 1975. Paradoxically, it was also a week in which the pressures of superstardom became so great that Elton would collapse under the crush. He had just released yet another studio album, the eleventh in six years, and it was now time for the promotional treadmill to start up again. *Rock Of The Westies*, a typically Elton-esque wordplay on 'West of The Rockies', was recorded at Caribou Ranch in the summer of 1975. It was the first of his albums since *Honky Château* to see a significant change in musical direction. Elton's new band might have lost Olsson's dependable drumming, Murray's inventive bass runs and the trademark Davey/Dee/Nigel backing vocals, but what it had gained was more of a groove and more funkiness. 'I'm literally the worst musician in the band,' Elton was to claim. 'I've got to work hard to keep up with them, which is going to make me play harder and better.'

The only problem was that, just as *Caribou* appeared to be underwritten compared with *Goodbye Yellow Brick Road*, so most of *Rock Of The Westies* seemed distinctly second rate compared with the triumph that was *Captain Fantastic*. The result was a pleasing collection of, at times, brilliantly played songs, not a million miles from the sort of laid-back LA sound produced by the Eagles. The boogie of the opening track 'Medley: Yell Help/Wednesday Night/Ugly' was one of the standouts, the hyperactive 'Grow Some Funk of Your Own' another. 'Island Girl' was the first single off the album and, while the lyrics were not Bernie's finest, it had a great melody and was yet another huge US Number 1 hit.

'Dan Dare (Pilot Of The Future)' and 'I Feel Like A Bullet (In The Gun Of Robert Ford)' also had their moments, but with so many of the musical reference points from Elton's past missing, the album sounded reactive rather than innovatory. *Rock Of The Westies* was the sound of a British artist with an Anglo-American band, recording in the US with an overwhelmingly American sound. To all intents and purposes, it could have been made by an American act.

At around the same time, a major change had taken place in Bernie's life. His wife, Maxine, had moved in with the bassist Kenny Passarelli. 'Bernie was there in the studios along with Kenny,' recalls Caleb Quaye. 'But if there was any tension, I don't remember it. I do know that Bernie was drinking pretty heavily during this period and that he was keeping himself to himself more than usual.'

A London Weekend Television film crew headed by the presenter Russell Harty filmed Elton, his family, friends and business colleagues on what, on the surface, was a week of unparalleled success. Sheila and Derf, along with Aunty Peg and assorted relatives and neighbours, were seated with John Reid's parents, Gus Dudgeon, Bryan Forbes and Nanette Newman in luxurious splendour on the *Rock of The Westies Express* plane. They dined on Steak Diane and glugged champagne as an in-flight movie played. When they arrived, they found Elton preparing for two sell-out shows at the Dodger Stadium on October 25 and 26. The mayor of Los Angeles proclaimed 'Elton John Week' and the singer himself was present to see the official unveiling of his star on Hollywood Boulevard.

The gigs at Dodger Stadium were an astonishing triumph for Elton. The home of the baseball team the Los Angeles Dodgers, the venue had not been used by a rock act since the Beatles a decade earlier, a gig that had ended in a near riot. The Elton John concert would be immortalised in stunning photography by Terry O'Neill. His stage clothes had been designed by Bob Mackie as a tribute to the LA Dodgers. He would perform in blue baseball cap and glittery lamé costume with ELTON and his team number (1, of course) emblazoned on the back. He opened with 'Your Song' and later performed another classic slowie 'Goodbye Yellow Brick Road', endearing himself to the crowd by changing the words to: 'It'll take a couple of tequila sunrises/ To set you on your feet again'. Billie Jean King joined Elton on stage, dancing along to 'The Bitch Is Back'.

Yet despite the massive success, Elton was beginning to tire of life as a star. For those few months in the autumn of 1975, he took up a temporary residency in LA. Philip Norman claimed the reason was part of a plan worked out by John Reid after problems with the US Internal Revenue Service over Elton's tax liabilities on his huge American income of over $7 million a year. Elton bought a mansion in Beverley Hills, formerly owned at various times by the film legend Greta Garbo and David O. Selznick, the legendary producer of *Gone With The Wind*.

It seems that Elton very quickly became ensnared by the siren call of cocaine around the time of making *Rock of The Westies* in the summer of 1975. Surrounded by so many drug takers in the music business and in the second-half of '75 based in LA with a new entourage, Elton's original motivation was probably no more than seeming to want to fit in. His addictive personality, however, meant that, once he had opted in, it was impossible to opt back out.

Sharon Lawrence, who had worked at LA's Rocket office until the end of 1974, told Philip Norman that the change in Elton was both speedy and dramatic when he saw Elton again later in 1975. 'I remembered this person who was mildly temperamental, who could be a bit neurotic and difficult, but who was basically happy and organised. Now he looked ghastly, he was incredibly strung up, anxious and panicky. In the few months since I'd seen him, he seemed to have become a complete wreck.'

The atmosphere in the house was dark and sinister. Elton looked pale and unwell. Russell Harty interviewed him for LWT the day after the first Dodger Stadium gig and Elton spoke half-disconnectedly, his eyes barely open behind his glasses. During 'Elton John Week' in Los Angeles and a few days before his two sell-out shows, Elton took what he later claimed were 60 Valium tablets and jumped into the indoor swimming pool shouting, as he remembers, 'I'll be dead in two hours!' 'My grandmother, who was on her first trip to the States, said, "Oh well, I suppose we'd better go home now!" he later confessed. Elton remained in a coma for two days after this, his first serious suicide attempt.

'It was a terrible, terrible time, those days,' said his mother, Sheila, reminiscing with Elton for a 1996 television documentary, *Tantrums And Tiaras*. 'It's an awful thing to see someone you love unhappy. I couldn't get near him at all. It was a different lifestyle and he'd got in with a different crowd of people. There were drugs, which he denied frantically, but I'm not daft. I knew he was taking drugs, but what can you do? I didn't see him all week until backstage before he went on, and I remember his hands were just split from playing the piano so hard and he was putting this stuff onto his skin.' At this point, Elton's mum began to sob at the recollection of the image.

'He looked terrible. I thought he was going to die. Russell Harty filmed us and [later] everybody said, "We saw you crying," and I thought, You don't know; you've got no idea. They thought I was crying with joy, but I was so worried. And that was only the start of it.'

CHAPTER 9

THE FIRST FINAL CURTAIN

'I just think people should be very free with sex – they should draw the line at goats.'

Elton John's words of wisdom to *Rolling Stone*, October 1976

'There's a lot more to me than playing on the road.'

Elton's valedictory speech, Wembley Arena, November 1977

It is a cold and blustery winter Saturday afternoon and Watford are playing away in the north of England. Normally, the chairman of the visiting club takes his seat without much in the way of fanfare, but this time is somewhat different. Elton is spotted and the chants are going up. As he's sitting down, he's wondering what on earth the travelling Watford board will think. The opposing team's supporters' full-throated vocal swells to a crescendo and, to the tune of 'My Old Man Said Follow The Van', 1,500 of them sing in unison:

'Don't bend down, when Elton's around
Or you'll get a penis up your arse.'

And a little later, another chant goes up from another corner of the ground, to the tune of 'Glory, Glory Hallelujah:

'Elton John's a homosexual!'

The singer chuckles to himself as he waits for the kick-off. But the chants keep on coming. Elton is now, officially, a 'poof'.

* * *

Elton John has a sense of humour and a very forgiving nature. To him it was all water off a duck's back. Of the chants that used to greet him on a regular basis, he has said: 'I found that very amusing and quite inventive, although very embarrassing I have to say. I remember the vice-chairman's wife sitting next to my mother and asking what they were singing. My mother was like, "Oh, nothing." If my fellow directors were embarrassed, and they must have been at times, they were extremely cool about it.

'You have sit there and grin and bear it. They're doing it to test you out and if you get uptight about it, that's the wrong thing to do. You've got to sit there and take it. The British public have been very supportive of me. I never had any trouble at football matches, apart from the odd insult. But they've been very loving and supportive.'

Elton's formal association with Watford FC began at the end of 1973. Having been informed that the club would welcome any investment, even from a pop star, Elton had held talks with the Vicarage Road board and bought shares in the club. In return, he was given the honorary title of Vice President of Watford FC. Elton proved himself to be no part-timer. Whenever he was in the country and his diary permitted, he supported his beloved Hornets (so-named, rather unsurprisingly, because of their black and gold home strip) with fervour. He would publicise the club in interviews at every possible opportunity, famously brandishing his membership card to camera midway through his promo for 'Step Into Christmas' in 1973, and was prepared to back his team with hard cash. In April 1974, he became a director of the club. On the field, however, the club were going nowhere, suffering relegation to the Fourth Division at the end of the 1974/75 season. Then, in the spring of 1976, Elton was elected chairman, his election ushering in a period of intense involvement in the club. He had already invited John Reid onto the board of directors and a plan for continued investment into the club was discussed. It came at just the right time, as Elton's musical career, for half a dozen years in the ascendant, had peaked and he needed a new challenge. For the foreseeable future, football was to become as important to him as his music.

It was one thing having a celebrity as big as Elton as one's chairman. The fact that he was gay was something else again and made him something of a sitting duck for endless barracking from the opposing team's fans. Football grounds in the 1970s and 1980s were verbally – and often physically – threatening places to be. 'You're going home in a St John's Ambulance' and 'You're gonna get your fucking head kicked in' were regularly sung by home crowds to visiting supporters at football grounds up and down the country. How much greater the potential for intimidation was when the chairman was gay. In the homo-social and at times homophobic world of 1970s football, an out-gay owner of a football club was unheard of.

These were the days when David Bowie fans, straight or gay, were called 'poofs' in the street, when television sitcoms such as *Are You Being Served?* dealt with homosexuality as a grotesque caricature, when gays in the media were figures of fun or to be pitied. The idea that a professional sportsman could be a homosexual was almost inconceivable. Even a full decade later, when the striker Justin Fashanu admitted he was gay, he would be shunned by many in the football community and would eventually commit suicide aged just 37.

Elton John, Britain's most famous pop celebrity, had let the cat at least part way out of the bag in an interview for *Rolling Stone* on October 7, 1976 entitled 'Elton's Frank Talk – The Lonely Love Life of A Superstar'. After some preliminary, non-controversial questions, the *Rolling Stone* interviewer, Cliff Jahr, asked: 'Can we get personal? Should we turn off the tape?' Elton replied, 'Keep going.' Jahr, sensing perhaps that Elton was in the mood for revelations, asked: 'What about Elton when he comes home at night? Does he have love and affection?' Elton replied, 'My life in the last six years has been a Disney film and now I have to have a person in my life. I get depressed easily. Very bad moods. I don't think anyone knows the real me. I don't even think I do.' He then made the following admission: 'I've never talked about this before. Ha, ha. But I'm not going to turn off the tape. I haven't met anybody that I would like to settle down with – of either sex'. 'You're bisexual?' asked Jahr, looking for confirmation. He found it, easily enough. 'There's nothing wrong with going to bed with somebody of your own sex,' answered Elton. 'I think everybody's bisexual to a certain degree. I don't think it's just me. It's not a bad thing to be. I think you're bisexual. I think everybody is.'

It was time for Elton to tell the world about his true self. The problem was that 'the world' – or, more accurately, that sizeable portion of Middle America that bought his records and adored him in concert – didn't understand or sympathise. In a letter printed in *Rolling Stone* on November 4, 1976, Lisa Crane of Provo, Utah wrote:

> *As a highly devoted Elton John fan, I regret being needlessly informed that my 'hero' is bisexual. The effect is shattering. He needn't have revealed his moral midgetness [sic]. I regret facing the fact that he is a gross perverter of the sacred (ignorance was bliss). Luckily, his decrepit morality hasn't affected his musical abilities, although it may take an exercise in 'separating the man from the music' to enjoy him again. My disgust is matched only by my disappointment, while both are overshadowed by pity; I pity him for his sexual illusions and perversions.*

However, Elton himself was of the opinion that his admission had had very little effect on his career. At the end of 1976, he told the now-defunct British music paper *Sounds* that his revelation had been '… the anti-climax of the year. More people wave to me than before, that's all. Nobody seems to harbour a grudge against me, especially within the football club. Though there has been a bit of shouting from the terraces: "You big poofter" and such.'

It may, of course, just be a total coincidence that Elton John's 'coming out' coincided with a commercial slump. Perhaps it was inevitable, given six years of forward momentum, that some kind of levelling off would take place. However, at the time, there were those around him who thought the display of candour a mistake. By the mid-1970s, John Reid and Elton were coming to the end of their personal relationship, but they were still extremely close and Reid simply thought the admission was likely to do more harm than good. 'In those days, it was uncharted territory; nobody ever asked and there was no need to talk about it. Everybody in the business knew we were together. And then the *Rolling Stone* chap asked the question, and Elton answered and it became an issue. I had no problems with it, but then I wasn't a public figure.'

'I was working with him in 1976, 1977 and 1978 and, although he stayed popular on the coasts, in Middle America his sales suddenly slumped dramatically,' is how Gary Osborne remembers it. 'And, in fact, it was one of the things I was most proud of him for doing, because he didn't have to make that admission. He wasn't outed. People who knew about his sexual orientation didn't see any reason to out him.'

At the time, an admission of bisexuality was a halfway house, a code that homosexuals tended to use to admit they were gay. In interviews around the time, however, Elton gave the impression that his sexual orientation was genuinely bisexual. 'I eventually would like to have a family, but I've seen so many marriages hit the rocks,' he told *Playboy* early in 1976. 'How can you have a kid and be gone for six months of the year? I had such a horrible childhood, I'd want it to be more pleasant for my kids.'

'To be honest, I don't believe that I'm 100% gay, because I'm attracted to older women and therefore I can't dismiss that side of my character,' he was to further reflect in 1978. 'Basically, I think I'm a loner and I always will be. See, I'm not the kind of person who's gonna get married, get tied down. But then, I can't predict anything. In ten years time I could be married to Shirley MacLaine and we could have six dwarfs.'

The only other recent example of a rock star 'coming out' had been David Bowie, but close observers believed this was a career move designed to grab early headlines and increase his appeal to the liberal-minded, discerning rock fan. After all, there was plenty of evidence, not least a son, to suggest Bowie was heterosexual. Elton, on the other hand, had a massive mainstream and far more conservative fan base than the Thin White Duke. Elton appealed less to the cultist and rather more to the average teen and twenty-something who looked to music for entertainment without the sort of strangeness that Bowie naturally seemed to embody.

In fact, according to Gary Osborne, Bowie was always a bit of a sore point for Elton. 'Elton did feel a sense of rivalry towards Bowie,' he admits. 'Most of these rock stars have somebody that they feel more rivalry towards than the others. It's because they're on similar territory. I think Elton slightly resented the fact that Bowie, who is substantially straight, made it partially by pretending to be gay, by courting a gay following, by propagating a gay mystique, whereas Elton, who is substantially gay, had for so long had to conceal his real orientation from the public. From Elton's point of view, here was this guy who had made it as a pretend poof, and here was he, a real poof, having to be a pretend straight. I think that got up his nose a bit. Elton is such a music fan, such a connoisseur of music, that he could not fail to notice how talented Bowie was and that was a little worrying. Because he could look around and say, it's easy to dig Marc Bolan because Marc's only got three songs. It's easy to be a fan of Bryan Ferry, because he really isn't as good a singer as me. But here's a contender about whom he could wonder, maybe this guy's as good as me; maybe, on his best day, he's even better?'

In 1976, there was a minor war of words between the two defining pop icons of their day. Bowie had made a tart comment to an interviewer in *Playboy*, referring to Elton as 'the Liberace, the token queen of rock'. 'I consider myself responsible for a whole new school of pretensions,' Bowie continued. 'They know who they are. Don't you, Elton?' 'He was obviously a little high when he did it,' Elton then told *Rolling Stone*. 'His insults to me go by the board. I think he's a silly boy.' Later, *Playboy* asked Bowie once again about the 'spat'. 'How is your relationship with Elton John these days?' 'He sent me a very nice telegram the other day,' replied Bowie. 'Didn't you describe him as "the Liberace, the token queen of rock?"' asked *Playboy*. 'Yes, well, that was before the telegram. I'd much rather listen to him on the radio than talk about him.'

This Bowie/Elton 'rivalry' was picked up on by one journalist as a recurring theme among Elton's British fans around the time. In the spring and summer of 1976, Elton was on the road again, this time on a world tour named *Faster Than Concorde... But Not Quite As Pretty*, a reference to the recently launched plane of the same name. Covering the tour for *Street Life,* Nigel Fountain interviewed several Elton fans. 'He's better than Bowie,' said one fan by the name of Frances. 'You get a lot of boppers at Bowie. You know, they all come along with "David we love you" and all that. The audiences at Elton John are almost all over 18, aren't they? Bowie is maybe more distinct *[sic]* but Elton has better tunes.' Another fan, Chris, opined: 'Bowie's a bit odd. Elton John sings songs like they are from human beings. Bowie gives the impression of coming from another place.' 'Bowie and *Yellow Brick Road* are two continuous reference points among the audience,' concluded Fountain. 'Bowie is disturbing. *Yellow Brick Road* is the yardstick of John's successes.'

However, the *Street Life* journalist was ultimately deeply unimpressed by Elton's actual music. Like many other journalists at the time, he regarded Elton as not much more than a sales phenomenon. 'It is similar to watching Ford Cortinas being produced: competent, efficient, noisy. Or some grotto, illuminated by coloured lights, with digital gnomes banging away with hammers and chisels. The star walks, trots amongst the musicians like a foreman ensuring the team are doing a good job. A friendly fellow, ready to have a drink with the lads afterwards.' He went on: 'The star's outfits are like garish paint on a semi-detached; you notice it, but it is still a semi-detached.' Elton was nothing more than a peddler of sentimentality, he concluded, 'not firsthand experience but second-hand emotions. So song after song goes into Yellow Bricked chorus of "Ahs and Ohs." A mind drifting from a sob story about Monroe in bathetic reverie. It is like looking at a kitten on a Christmas card. It is safe.'

Despite this, there were plenty of satisfied customers on the 1976 tour. The Elton look had been partly 'de-glammed' compared with previous tours but still carried a distinctive streak of trademark madness.

'Elton stomped round the stage, wearing a groovily-striped jacket, blue lurex plimsolls and a giant gold banana (subtle touch) flapping round his knees,' reported *Sounds* of Elton's May concert at the Grand Theatre in Leeds. 'The audience were decked out in bowler hats with appropriate graffiti round 'em, scarves to be waved in the air like a football match, elaborately constructed facsimiles of the man's old ZOOM glasses, top hats made out of *Capt. Fantastic* posters, the works… They knew all the lyrics, mouthing silently all the way through, and they were reverent. Hip to the fact that Elton running around on planks set out into the audience, shaking hands like a madman all the time with people in the front row, was coming on really sincere, not a trace of arrogance, hipper-than-thou-ness. He's still one of them. Appreciative.' The tour's highlight was to be a concert at Earls Court on May 12, a gig that raised, in what was the year of the Montreal Olympics, £40,000 for the Sports Aid Foundation.

Elton also played to packed houses in his homeland of support in the US. Dressed again in an oddly matching array of stage garments, including a matador jacket with big bars down the sides in the shape of black and white piano keys, dungarees, Uncle Sam hats and stripy T-shirts, for comic effect he would dangle a toy carrot, strawberry or banana between his legs. On July 4, Elton marked America's Bicentenary by taking to the stage at Foxborough's Schaeffer Stadium dressed as the Statue of Liberty. The tour ended with a seven-night residency at Madison Square Garden in September. There would be special guest stars, including on one night, the oversized drag act, Divine. Madison Square Garden would go on to play a huge role in his live career. It's Elton's favourite venue, big enough to create a fantastic atmosphere, but, at 20,000 capacity, still relatively intimate compared with the stadia and 'enormodomes' that were by then a commonplace fixture in the touring schedule of any pop superstar.

The 1976 version of Elton had been toned down since his excesses of 1973 and 1974. 'I think if I'd been a miserable sod and come onstage in jeans and t-shirt, I'd have got much better critical acclaim throughout the 1970s than I did by wearing the clothes. But as far as

I'm concerned, I don't really care, because I was having such a good time,' Elton told the BBC DJ Steve Wright in 2004. Bernie was known to be less than enthusiastic about Elton's more 'imaginative' costuming and the chorus of disapproval would be added to by John Reid: 'I'd try to strike some balance but, the more you'd tell him not to, the more he'd go after the most outrageous Bob Mackie and Bill Nudie creations.' 'I've done nothing that I wouldn't do all over again,' said Elton defiantly at the end of 1976. 'I've done everything in all innocence and with a sense of humour,' adding: 'I never took much interest in what I was wearing; just had someone design something preposterous and laughed when I saw it.'

Chris Charlesworth, then resident in New York as *Melody Maker's* US Editor, accompanied Elton on some of the US dates on the *Faster Than Concorde* world tour. 'I joined in Chicago and went to Cleveland. I remember ringing up and asking to travel in the plane with EJ and the PR was very snooty at first. "You'll be put on a list with the 100 other similar requests," she said. So I said, "It's Chris Charlesworth from *Melody Maker*. Just ask anyone close to Elton." Half an hour later she was back on the phone saying sorry. And I was on the plane. So no matter how big he was, EJ hadn't forgotten me. He was always loyal.'

'After one of the concerts,' continues Charlesworth, 'we flew on somewhere after the gig, and we were all really hungry. I remember Elton getting very excited because he'd sent some crew guys off to get Kentucky Fried Chicken. They came back with these huge cartons of it, loads of it, which we ate on the plane. Elton absolutely adored Colonel Sanders' Kentucky Fried Chicken.'

Charlesworth managed to pull off a scoop on the tour when, in his interview with the star, Elton let slip a very important piece of information. 'He told me he was retiring!' said Charlesworth. 'Elton said, "I've done it for six years and I'm fed up with it. Not fed up with playing so much as having no base and constantly roaming around. I don't want the pressure of having to tour for another two years or so."'

In another interview around the same time, Elton admitted that he could envisage a time when he might give up rock music altogether. 'I won't be doing "Crocodile Rock" in six years' time,' he vowed. 'I don't want to become a pathetic rock 'n' roller and take a slow climb down, like a lot of people do. I don't want to be a Chuck Berry. When I'm 40, I don't want to be charging around the country doing concerts. I'd rather retire gracefully, get out when people least expect it and live semi-detached in England, become part of something else.'

Elton John was exhausted. Between 1970 and 1976 he had played around 500 concerts and recorded 11 studio albums and two live albums, not to mention his work as a producer and his guest slots with other artists on stage and on record. The travelling, the airports, the hotels, the waiting around, the press, the sound checks, the meals, then the concert, the after-show, and the wait for the adrenaline to stop pumping and the serotonin levels to rise sufficiently to induce sleep, all of which would be repeated the next day – even the healthiest person would at some point have to succumb to the jetlag, the disruption, the tiredness, and the irregular meal times, resulting in a personal biology that was fragile and an emotional geography that was unhinged by the relentless round of hours with nothing to do followed by periods of intense stress during performance.

In one *Playboy* interview, Elton confessed to a bad diet ('I do like garbage food, I must admit'), drinking too much ('When I'm making an album at Caribou, I drink a lot of wine. And I started drinking 100% proof liquor and getting really out of it – for no reason') and suffering bouts of depression ('I sometimes get depressed for no reason whatever; just stay in bed and get really miserable. Usually they're one-day jobs, just out of the blue'). The drug intake, which was even more debilitating, was never mentioned in interviews, by interviewer or interviewee.

These were not good times for Bernie Taupin either. *Playboy* asked Elton: 'He hasn't become a recluse, has he?' To which Elton replied: 'If you call staggering out of some place at six-thirty in the morning with a bottle of wine a recluse…' Taupin was rumoured to have been dating the British singer Lynsey de Paul, but his closest relationship in 1976 was with the bottle. He stipulated that he would only drink Coors beer while on tour and any venue which had the cheek to supply him with any of the other almost identically tasting beverages which are the staple of the North American market would be asked to seek out the real Coors deal. He would start the day with a beer topped with vodka. He piled on the pounds.

In June 1976, Bernie's collection of lyrics, *The One Who Writes The Words For Elton John*, edited by Alan Aldridge and Mike Dempsey, was published in the UK by Jonathan Cape, priced £2.45. Taupin had always maintained that pop lyrics should never be read as poetry, yet the process of detaching them from the music and reprinting them as silent words on a page only invited that very comparison. While the array of images (collages, drawings and photographs, assembled by Aldridge and featuring contributions from the likes of David Larkham who designed Elton's album sleeves, renowned artist Peter Blake and rockers such as Alice Cooper, Charlie Watts and John Lennon) were never less than engaging, it didn't stop one critic at least from dismissing the book as 'an ego trip for Taupin, a collector's item, a set of thoughts and fantasies and illustrations for a rainy day. Nothing more'.

Despite the road-weariness and burn-out, Elton and Bernie would achieve a first during that baking hot UK summer of 1976: their first UK Number 1 single. 'Don't Go Breaking My Heart' by Elton and Kiki Dee occupied the top spot for six long summer weeks.

'We were in Barbados for Christmas, and he came to me and said, "I really want to write something up-tempo, like a disco-soul thing,"' remembers Bernie. 'So I went upstairs and started banging away on the typewriter. In five minutes, I'd done something, came downstairs, and just gave it to him. In the next five minutes, he finished it and it was great. It was just one of those things that sparked off immediately. As soon as he played it, I said, "Well, that's gonna be the next single. That's a hit!"'

In fact, Elton wrote several of the lines in the song, making it one of the few numbers to have any lyrical input from the star himself. At the time, duets were pretty unfashionable, so the idea of making it a duet was quite unusual. 'We talked about the possibility of doing a duet because we grew up with Motown and we loved all the Marvin Gaye and Tammy Terrill stuff,' recalls Kiki. 'From what I heard Gus Dudgeon say, Elton initially wasn't going to give me that many lines to sing. I think it was going to be a sort of guest appearance by me. It was Gus who urged Elton to divide the lines up equally. Elton did his recording in America and I did mine in London. I remember Elton sent over a demo with my parts sung in a high voice as a guide, so I could work out with Gus which parts were mine. That was quite funny.'

The promotional film reinforced the childlike innocence of the song, with Kiki dressed in pink dungarees and Elton in a baggy checked suit. 'Mike Mansfield, the producer of the TV pop show *Supersonic*, did the promo video for it,' says Kiki. 'It was all done in one take. You look at videos today and they're so produced, directed and themed, but that promo was just a performance, pretending to be in a studio and larking about. My hair was really shiny and I had *that* fringe.'

For Dee, it would mark the commercial highlight of her career. Yet, in a funny way, it was also something of a typecasting moment: 'I was 29 when that song was a hit and I had been singing professionally since I was 17. I'd been waiting a long time for something big to happen and then that song defined me in the British public's mind. That can be difficult to get away from. There have been times in my life when I have tried to get away from that song, but I finally realised that, firstly, I won't be able to, and secondly, why should I? I'm proud of the song and proud it did so well. It's made so many people happy.'

The single would also reach Number 1 in the US and was nominated for a Grammy for best pop vocal performance (duo) or group. However, its huge success would also mark the end of Elton's period at the top of the rock tree. From 'Rocket Man' in 1972 to 'Sorry Seems To Be The Hardest Word' in 1976, there had been 14 Top 10 singles in America and seven in the UK. Each studio album from *Honky Château* to *Rock Of The Westies* had reached Number 1 on the Billboard chart. That his next album, *Blue Moves*, only made Number 3 was a surprise and the first indication of a downswing in public support. Nevertheless, one estimate put Elton's total sales by 1976 at 42 million albums and 18 million singles, with ten of his albums recording sales of over a million in the US. A likeness of Elton now stood in Madame Tussaud's Wax Museum. The first rock figure since the Beatles to be recognised in this way, Elton John was, in 1976, the most recognisable pop icon on the planet.

By 1976, Rocket Records, Elton's other main business interest outside of Watford FC, was going from strength to strength. Steve Brown had left the company in 1974, at the time a major blow but, as it turned out, not a fatal one. David Croker replaced him as boss and Clive Banks was headhunted from DJM to work in promotions. After the success of 'Amoureuse' for Kiki Dee, a steady stream of hits would follow for other artists, including, most notably, an American Number 1 for Neil Sedaka's 'Laughter In The Rain'.

Still on Rocket's roster was Maldwyn Pope, the teenage prodigy from Swansea. 'I had had a bit of a difficult time at Rocket,' admits Mal today. 'Steve Brown had walked out. Steve was a very forceful character and I can imagine how he would have influenced Elton, because he made you believe he was right. I spent a lot of time during my summer holidays at Steve's house in Kent. I rang up Rocket one evening after coming home from school to check on how things were going and they told me that Steve didn't work there any more. Apparently he had been driving into the office when he realised he didn't want to be going there, so he simply turned round and went home. Elton rang him a lot, but Steve wouldn't return his calls. I think that hurt Elton a lot.'

With his career in limbo, Maldwyn sought out Elton's help in earnest. 'I wrote to Elton saying I felt like a 15-year-old failure, so he rang me at home and said he was going to take control. I recorded with him at the New Year, but it took until the summer to get into the studio. The week before, he got me tickets for the FA Cup Final. I walked into Abbey Road to be greeted by Eric Morecambe. He was making a charity record and was really nice.

'I also stayed at Woodside and there were even more things lying around there than in Virginia Water. Elton had the dress worn by Judy Garland in *The Wizard Of Oz* in a presentation case just resting on the stairs. We spent the evening talking about music. I'd just been to a concert by Andrae Crouch, a black gospel singer. Elton just went to his record collection and pulled out every record Crouch had made. We went through a lot of different artists that night.

'I suppose a lot of people would question the appropriateness of Elton having a teenage boy staying at his house, particularly in the light of Michael Jackson today. I have always been heterosexual and we are talking about a time when being homosexual was not well accepted. He was always very kind to me and I never felt the slightest bit uncomfortable in his company. What I have told many people since is that he was gay, not a paedophile. I found out years later that all the people at Rocket had had a meeting about me and decided that they should respect my age and not even swear in front of me. I think Elton did want to be a big brother character. He even took me training with Watford FC.'

John Reid's business empire was also growing fast. After he and Elton split, Reid moved out of Hercules and bought himself a stylish house in Montpelier Square in Knightsbridge. Never as ostentatious as his client and former lover, Reid began investing his money in a number of ventures outside of the music business. He started up a restaurant called Friends and bought shares in Edinburgh's Playhouse Theatre. He also extended his business interests within the music industry and for a short period managed Queen. He also moved John Reid Enterprises from Soho to a plush suite of rooms at 40 South Audley Street, off Grosvenor Square in Mayfair.

During this time, Reid poached many of DJM's staff, including Geoffrey Ellis, who had spent seven years with Dick James. Ellis remembers one example of Elton's largesse: 'A few days before Christmas, he arrived at John Reid's office with a large cardboard box being carried by a minion. He had previously made it known that he was not going to make any effort that particular Christmas, so we were all surprised when we proceeded to unload from the box a small package for every single member of the staff. All the gifts were from Cartier in Bond Street, where he had been on a spending spree. Most people, me included, received a Cartier watch, while a few of the very juniors got a handsome wallet.'

Thus began the tradition of Elton John's extreme generosity to those who worked for him. True, he could explode into a rage and be irrational, but one thing all his employees have said is that, on a personal level, he always cared. He would commit to memory the names of his employees' spouses, their children's birthdays, their anniversaries and suchlike, and he very rarely forgot them.

Ellis remembers that John Reid, on the other hand, could on occasion be rather erratic. One morning, Reid had returned from a business trip to LA to find that his chauffeur, Gary Hampshire, was not at the airport to meet him due to some crossed wires. On his arrival at the office, Reid flew into a rage and sacked the entire staff. 'He ordered them all into the street, a move that attracted the attention of at least one tabloid newspaper,' recollects Ellis. 'Over the next few days, all the staff returned to the office. No more was said of the incident.' According to Ellis, Reid was 'living life to the full'. 'It was some time before I realised that his lateness to work and quite frequent inattention to important meetings and details were the result of over-indulgence in alcohol and pills. Shades of Brian Epstein although, unlike him, John was eventually able to overcome his demons.'

Elton John's next studio album would be released in the autumn of 1976. It would be the first to be released on Rocket Records, Elton's recording contract with DJM having expired. *Blue Moves* was a quantum leap forward in quality compared with the slightly facile *Rock Of The Westies*. While it was several songs short of being able to pose as a credible double album, there was certainly enough on it to suggest that the Bernie/Elton partnership was still able to conjure up occasional moments of brilliance. Its sound was very different from that of *Rock Of The Westies*, being much more intricately produced, and, while downbeat, was nevertheless able to throw up some moments of sublime quirkiness, not least on the three excellent instrumentals. The best known of these 'Out of The Blue', was used as the end music for the perennially popular BBC2 car programme *Top Gear*. Taking its name from the quiz show *University Challenge*, then hosted by Bamber Gascoigne, 'Your Starter For...' a one-minute 22 second instrumental penned by Caleb Quaye, was another great track.

By the middle of 1976, Bernie Taupin had reached a personal low. His almost exclusively downbeat lyrics about doomed relationships, unrequited love and hurt also suited Elton's own fragile state. 'While we were making *Blue Moves*,' remembered Elton, 'a friend of mine gave me the gold disc of l0cc's "I'm Not In Love" because I played it everywhere, in the car, at home, and I'd sob like a baby because someone or other had taken my fancy and it was totally wrong.'

Some of Bernie's lyrics seemed to be intensely personal. In what is a very thinly veiled rebuke to his estranged wife Maxine, now sharing the bed of Kenny Passarelli, who was playing on this very track, he wrote on 'Between Seventeen And Twenty', 'I wonder who's sleeping in your bed tonight/ Whose head rests upon the bed/ Could it be a close friend I knew so well/ Who seems to be so close to you instead?'

So raw were the emotions in the set of lyrics that Bernie submitted for *Blue Moves* that Elton felt uncomfortable singing some of them: 'I never rejected one of his lyrics before but some of the stuff he did for *Blue Moves*! I said, "Taupin, for Christ's sake, I can't sing that." They were just plain hateful, three or four of them.' One song, 'Snow Queen', which had been the B-side to 'Don't Go Breaking My Heart', led to a pre-emptive apology from Elton to its high-profile addressee, Cher. 'It was so cutting I had to tell her in advance and apologise in advance,' Elton has confessed. 'She was OK about it.'

The album's strongest musical moment was 'Tonight'. Close to eight minutes long, it contained one of Elton's most melancholically beautiful piano melodies and another superb orchestral arrangement by James Newton Howard. It was, in fact, almost two songs in one. An opening all-instrumental section almost three minutes in length gave way to Bernie's desolate world of a relationship breaking apart in slow motion: 'I'd like to find a compromise/And place it in your hands/My eyes are blind, my ears can't hear/Oh and I cannot find the time'.

'One Horse Town', co-written with James Newton Howard, continued the pattern of long orchestral openings to songs, courtesy of the recalled Paul Buckmaster. Other standouts included two tributes – one to Edith Piaf ('Cage The Songbird') and the other to Elvis Presley ('Idol'). Bernie and Elton had met Elvis, self-medicated to the point of stupefaction, backstage in the US 1976. 'He's not long for this world,' Elton was reported to have said as he left his idol to all intents and purposes being propped up by his entourage of minders.

'Sorry Seems To be The Hardest Word' has become a classic Elton song, covered even by Frank Sinatra. Yet at the time it reached only Number 11 in the UK and Number 6 in America. 'Most of the lyrics on "Sorry" are mine,' Elton was to tell *Sounds*. 'I was sitting out there in Los Angeles and out it came: "What have I got to do to make you love me?"' Years of over-familiarity have tended to distract us from the power of the original song. The arrangement was perfect for the song: an accordion brought a touch of Parisian romance, Ray Cooper's vibes lent an incongruous melancholy, Elton's piano part was plaintiveness personified, and James Newton Howard's orchestral arrangement was discreetly beautiful. But the album's emotional roots were perhaps to be found on another, less well-known cut, 'Someone's Final Song', which told the graphic story of man putting pen to paper before taking his own life: 'He died when the house was empty, when the maid had gone/He put pen to paper for one final song'.

The cover of *Blue Moves*, released in October 1976, was a reprint of one of the pieces of art that were now hung in Elton's house in Woodside: *The Guardian Readers* by Patrick Procktor. Elton wanted to reflect the serious content of the new, moody record by using a similarly serious cover design that did not have him as its focal point. Some critics considered the cover art to be significant in that the painting depicts only men and the album was released just after the *Rolling Stone* interview in which Elton had admitted his bisexuality. (Not without humour, one Elton fan recently posted on a discussion forum that an anagram of the album title was 'Love's Bum'.)

Yet was the cover chosen with any ulterior motive? David Costa, again in charge of artwork for the record, doubts it. 'If that were the case, I was unaware of it, but little with Elton happens by chance. Elton had the painting in his possession and – as with many such things – in hindsight it married so well with the overall feel of depth and substance and not a little mystery. I'm not sure whether the expression "Guardian Reader" to suggest "gay" was current at the time. I remember meeting Patrick Procktor at some point in the proceedings. He was the tallest, thinnest, Noel Coward-est artist I'd ever come across, all elbows and cigarette holders. The painting, too, was surprising, executed in enamel paint from memory. The launch of the album was at a renowned art gallery in Savile Row. We had a limited edition run of signed lithos prepared for it, plus blue drinks – Curaçao, I guess – and, somehow, blue food.'

Blue Moves would be the last time Elton would work with Caleb Quaye. A brilliant guitarist, he was affectionately described by his fellow band member Nigel Olsson as 'a total nutcase'. Quaye's life had changed irrevocably one day on tour in 1978. Sitting in a lonely hotel room, drugged up on cocaine and marijuana, he was at his lowest ebb. 'And then I heard a voice, and it told me that from that day forth, my life would never be the same. I heard it so clearly I actually thought someone was in the room, but I was alone.' Two years later, after a second 'visitation', he decided to enter the ministry. Quaye is now the National Worship Director for the Foursquare denomination, ministering all over the United States and Europe. He also teaches music and 'worship leadership' at LIFE Pacific College in San Dimas, California.

By the end of the *Blue Moves* album, two further crucial people had dropped out of Elton's musical world. Gus Dudgeon, the producer of all his albums save *Empty Sky*, left the camp. 'I haven't fallen out with Gus,' Elton was to tell *Sounds*. 'He left the company after a board meeting, a dispute over shares – a political matter. He just got up, said, "That's it, I'm off," and walked out. But I honestly believe that after 14 albums we needed a break from one each other. Also, by now I know exactly what I want.'

'Funnily enough, my falling out with Elton was not a falling out with Elton, it was a falling out with Rocket Records, which is a different thing altogether,' confirmed Dudgeon in 1998. The issue for Gus, then a director of Rocket, was a lack of vision for the label. Getting Elton, John Reid and Bernie in one room at any given time to discuss company policy was almost impossible. The result, according to Dudgeon, was that the company was losing direction. Dudgeon had unsuccessfully lobbied for the label to sign the rocker Dave Edmunds and the comedian and writer Barry Humphries. One of their biggest stars, Neil Sedaka, was unhappy with the label. 'And I was very dissatisfied with the way the accounts were being kept,' Dudgeon told Philip Norman. 'I said, "Things have got to be a lot better, or I'm quitting." I realised that no one was saying, "Don't go, Gus" – and I was out.'

Dudgeon's departure certainly weakened Elton's hand in the studio. To a large extent, the Elton John sound was the Gus Dudgeon sound. 'He was passionate and he cared about detail so much,' says Stuart Epps, who would go on to work with Dudgeon for many years at Dudgeon's new recording complex, the Mill, in Cookham, Berkshire. Yet Dudgeon's exacting style of production came a price. 'Gus could be a very difficult guy to work with,' admits Epps. '"Gus Difficult" should have been his name. He just did everything and was in charge of everything. After *Blue Moves* I think Elton had had enough, really. Elton's not into recording particularly, it is just a means to an end. He just writes the songs, gets it down, gets it out, sells it, asks, "Where's the money?" then goes out and buys something. He just wants to get the whole recording process over with. Also, Elton never got on with Gus's wife, Sheila. She was a bit of a nightmare. I loved Sheila to bits, but she could fall out with anyone, let alone Elton.'

Although Gus would go on to produce records by Joan Armatrading, Lindisfarne, Elkie Brooks and Chris Rea in the years immediately after departing Elton's inner circle, it wasn't an altogether successful situation for him. 'We all get pigeonholed,' Dudgeon said. 'When I quit working with Elton, all I got offered to work with were piano players.'

The second, and even more momentous, decision taken by Elton was to end his working relationship with Bernie Taupin. There was no spectacular falling-out but there was no intention for the split to be temporary. It was simply the fact that, after nine years of working together, both felt the time was right to move away from one another. Elton encouraged Bernie to do some writing with other rock performers and he was to work on the Alice Cooper record, *From The Inside*, released at the end of 1978 and co-wrote its sizeable US hit single, 'How You Gonna See Me Now'.

In Elton's eyes, the partnership had been in danger of becoming stale. He too needed a fresh musical challenge. 'I've made the mistake of writing too many albums in the same key,' he told a journalist. 'The wrong key for my "poofy little voice", as Rod Stewart calls it. You spend half an hour on a song then sing it in the key you wrote it in. It's very easy to get into a rut. In the early days, [Bernie and I] shared a flat, knew what one another was listening to, had a rapport. But it had fallen away. Ever since *Honky Château* and except for *Captain Fantastic*, we have been writing without meeting. He sent me words through the post. We were drifting along in our own sweet way like Dial-A-Date.'

Furthermore, Bernie had lost all of the buoyancy of his teenage self. Still only 26, he was entering a life-changing period. Resident in Doheney Drive, LA in the immediate aftermath of his failed first marriage, he was still drinking heavily. He began dating Loree Rodkin, who freely admits that Bernie was her first true love: 'Give me a guy who writes for me, and be still my beating heart!' Rodkin was a young LA scenester who would, in the fullness of time, become a friend to the stars. She would design homes for Rod Stewart and Alice Cooper, manage Brad Pitt and Robert Downey Jr and design exclusive jewellery for the likes of Catherine Zeta-Jones, Madonna and Elton John himself. However, after a routine medical check-up, Taupin was strongly advised to stop drinking. He took himself off to Acapulco, where he spent some time in a house in Horseshoe Bay, his mind slowly un-fogging as his body detoxified.

It was also a difficult period for Elton John in other areas of his life. In the very early 1970s he had been hip for a few years and had then become a massive star. By the start of 1977, however, he just looked worn out, on the verge of what looked like premature middle age. He was now no longer just thinning on top but visibly balding. He blamed the acceleration of his chrome dome not on completely normal male-pattern baldness, but on chemical intervention: 'It was bad dye. It was when I had my hair pink and green. I used to have it done at Smile in London and it was never a problem. Then I had it done somewhere in New York and next time I took a shower I glanced down at my feet and it was like the murder scene from *Psycho*: pink water and great tufts of hair everywhere.' Sadly, Elton remained the opposite from Bryan Ferry. Ferry could make a £10 t-shirt look good; Elton could make a £1,000 suit look like it had different-length arms.

Instead of accepting baldness, Elton raged against it. His first tactic was to grow his hair long at the back and cover up his pate with a cap. This had the reverse effect of what was intended in that it made him look even older. Later in 1977, Elton decided to go for a hair transplant. In a painful procedure, the surgeon 'harvests' hair follicles from the back of the head, where there is normal hair growth, and then punctures holes in the area of baldness, where the grafts of living hair are then inserted, in the hope of giving an impression of normal growth. Elton's first hair transplant garnered a whole page of coverage in one UK daily newspaper while the return of Bob Dylan to the concert stage got a few lines tucked away on an inside page.

Elton was 30 and looked it and this made him a particularly vulnerable target in the year punk rock became headline news in America and Britain. The suggestion that punk destroyed the very foundations of the rock establishment and replaced it with a totally new set of acts, values and music, although still indulged by some cultural commentators, is, in fact, fanciful. In America, which has always been more musically conservative than Britain, at least since the 1960s, the commercial impact of punk was minuscule. In Britain, punk *was* a more significant event, particularly at a local level. Yet a glance at the UK charts of 1977, when punk's reign of terror was at its height in London and other major cities, reveals Abba, Boney M, Rod Stewart, Paul McCartney and Leo Sayer all enjoying Number 1 singles. It wouldn't be until 1978 and

1979, when punk morphed into the more media- and tune-friendly New Wave, that the movement produced genuinely commercially successful acts in the Boomtown Rats, the Police, Blondie and Elvis Costello and the Attractions.

Elton, never a music snob and always open minded, was a great admirer of many of the punk acts. Speaking in 1995, he said: 'The whole era was brilliant in its way. The first time I saw punk was on the Janet Street-Porter Saturday morning show when she did an interview with the Sex Pistols, Siouxsie and the Banshees and the Clash. I sat there in my bed in Windsor watching it and I got slagged off by one of them. But it was kind of endearing. God, I thought, you cheeky buggers.'

That Elton John's record sales fell by 75 per cent at this time is more to do with his own lack of drive and consistency as with a mass boycotting of his records by a hipper music-buying public. There was no intrinsic reason why Elton John couldn't survive the punk era in much the same way as Rod Stewart, Mick Jagger or any of the other established acts of the pre-punk years. His natural record-buying constituency were likely to be his age or older, hardly the people who would naturally turn their attention and their spending power onto the likes of the Damned and the Jam. Elton's fans would continue buying in the musical middle ground, whatever was happening at the cutting edge. Of Elton's contemporaries, only David Bowie managed to maintain his critical kudos with the new wave and that was by transferring his muse to decadent Berlin and his music into wildly leftfield territory on *Low* and *Heroes*, both released in 1977.

'The late 1970s was not a good time for Elton,' remembers Bob Harris. 'With the whole punk thing there was a new generation of [music] writers coming through who were much more aggressive and much more willing to criticise. I'm drawing a parallel with myself here because, once punk had arrived, irrespective of my opinion of it, it formed a very strong opinion about me, and all the journalists that were coloured by that became aggressive, and this is something that then sticks. If you were unfashionable in 1976, God knows what people will say about you in 2006. It was very fashionable to knock the Elton Johns, Rolling Stones, Led Zeppelins and Bob Harrises of this world.

'Elton took me to see the Eagles at Wembley in 1976 and we had an absolutely wonderful evening together. This was at the outset of punk and we were both conscious of the fact that where we'd always sat and felt comfortable with just liking music, suddenly all of it was under attack. With the Eagles, the songwriting and the production and all the strengths that they had at the time were being subjected to such vitriolic criticism. I remember Elton looking at me and saying, "But this is wonderful. They write great songs, they play beautifully, what more do you want from a band?"'

At the same time, Harris became acutely aware that Elton had changed quite dramatically as a person. 'As the evening went on, I remember that the vibe off Elton wasn't quite the same and from then on it was completely different. That was the weird thing, because Elton was always such an open and lovely person, and suddenly that wasn't happening any more. He wasn't in a good mood, and other people round him were saying, "Oh, Elton's busy" when I tried to reach him.'

In most cases, however, the vitriol of the punk rockers was more justified. By 1977, many of the established acts of the previous decade had become of questionable validity. The tax-exiled, supermodel-fixated, easy and unquestioning misogyny of many rockers combined with the long hair, crap flares and clubby showbiz vibe all pretty much stank. But what annoyed the punks and their apologists even more was the musical complacency of society in the mid-to-late 1970s. It seemed as if the rock aristocracy had absolutely nothing to say about the social conditions in which millions lived. In the 1960s, groups like the Who and the Kinks had articulated what it was like to live through their decade. In the mid-1970s, Rod Stewart seemingly had nothing to say about anything other than Rod Stewart.

Having announced his retirement from live concert tours to Chris Charlesworth, Elton began to busy himself with matters outside music. He took the leading role in selecting, and then enticing, a reluctant young manager by the name of Graham Taylor to occupy the managerial hot seat at Watford FC. Taylor, just three years older than Elton, had played full back for Grimsby Town and Lincoln City before being forced out of the game at just 28 with a serious hip injury. Starting his managerial career at the latter club, he led Lincoln to the Fourth Division title in 1976. A straight-talking but friendly Lincolnshire man, he would form a bond with his new chairman that Elton later likened to that between two brothers.

Taylor looked at Watford and saw a team woefully lacking in direction and work ethic. When he took over for the 1977–78 season, he let it be known that he expected his players to live within a ten-mile radius of the ground and be part of the local community. 'Elton used to turn up at the club dressed in really outrageous clothes,' remembers the former Watford player Arthur Horsfield. 'The first time I met him he had a white boiler suit on. At a pre-season meeting, Graham Taylor was telling me how he expected us to behave and that stuff, and then he finished off saying something like, "Don't step out of line because I've got enough on my plate teaching Elton John how to be club chairman." He was right, because you can't go into other clubs' boardrooms dressed like Elton used to.'

For the first time in years, Elton was beginning to live a life that at least approximately resembled reality. 'At the start, I was glad to be protected because I was frightened of something. I don't know what of. But then it got so that everything was done for me. The only thing I did for myself was get in the shower and wash,' he told *Sounds*. 'Royalty probably weren't treated as well as I've been for the last five years. But I'm suddenly beginning to realise that the life I have lived in that time has been totally irrelevant to what's going on in the outside world. I was being completely locked away like a prize tiger... In fact, I know it's boring, but being involved in the soccer club has brought me down to earth. Mixing with the same people who used to go to the pub I played in when I was 17 or 18... This will sound ludicrous, but the other day, I actually went to Carlisle on my own. And I went to Rome with the English football team, stayed in a hotel on my own, made my own phone calls and came home on my own. Daft, isn't it? And yet, for me, it was, "Phew, what an achievement!"'

That interview with Phil Sutcliffe of *Sounds* was one of the most revealing of Elton's 1970s career. Today, Sutcliffe is one of the most respected of British music journalists, well known for his even-handed approach to his subject. Back in 1976, he was on the receiving end of a quite unusual piece of generosity from Elton John that gives a very clear insight into the star's lack of ego. 'One of the strange things that happened in that interview,' says Sutcliffe, 'is that I felt able to tell him something that I wouldn't say normally, but there was something about his manner that made me feel able to say out loud fairly early in the interview that my position in relation to his work, as far as he cared about it, was that I liked about one in ten of his tracks.' With other rock stars, such an admission by an interviewer might lead to friction, or even tantrums, but not so with Elton. A little later, Elton appeared on Capital Radio, where the DJ, the smooth-talking star of *Adam Adamant* Gerald Harper, offered each of his guests the chance to send a person of their choice a bottle of champagne. Elton chose Phil Sutcliffe. 'The message went something like: "Thanks for doing a fair job on the interview." So, he had obviously taken completely in his stride the fact that I wasn't a great fan, and he just appreciated a square deal, which was nice.'

Musically, Elton used his period of downtime in 1976 and 1977 to foster the career of the Glasgow band Blue, who played Beatles-inspired pop and who scored a Top 20 UK hit in the spring of 1977 with 'Gonna Capture Your Heart' on Rocket Records. Elton himself experimented musically by recording tracks in Sigma Sound Studios in Philadelphia and Kay Smith Studio in Seattle with the legendary producer and architect of Philly Soul, Thom Bell. Bell had been involved in creating the sound for such soul luminaries as the Delfonics, the Stylistics and the Spinners. His most important piece of advice when recording Elton was to ask him to lower the register of his voice and sing in a slightly deeper, more soulful timbre. The tracks from the sessions wouldn't be officially released until 1979 and it would take a further quarter of a century for the standout track 'Are You Ready For Love', reissued after exposure on Sky TV, to become a UK Number 1.

One of the songs from the session was 'Shine On Through', Elton's first collaboration with Gary Osborne, the man who, for one album, would take over from Bernie Taupin as Elton's sole collaborator and remain as a contributor to Elton John albums for several years thereafter. 'We were acquaintances for a year or two and then became very close friends,' says Osborne. 'Elton became very close with my wife in particular. We used to go round to his house, just like normal people, and he would come round to ours. I think he spent the Queen's Silver Jubilee round our house going through my record collection.

The first Elton/Osborne collaboration came about naturally and unplanned. 'He was round my house watching telly,' says Osborne. 'Then he sat at the piano and said, "Listen to this," and he played me this lovely tune. "Would you write a lyric for it?' I said, "What about Bernie?" "Well, he's over there working with Alice Cooper, he's tried this song…" Now, I don't know whether he was telling the truth on that, I think he was trying to make me feel better. I don't think Bernie had tried and failed on it. Anyway, he said, "No, he's had a go at it, and he hasn't come up with anything. So I said, "Oh, if you really insist," and then of course the minute he left I got my pen out and worked all night. So I wrote the lyric and took it to him and he said, "Oh that's lovely." We then went in to do the demo and while we were doing the demo he sat at the piano and wrote another tune and said, "Will you give me one for that?" We went back to demo that one and then he did two more and suddenly we had enough for an album.'

The first ever performance of an Osborne-John song was given on Christmas Day 1977 on *The Morecambe And Wise Christmas Special*. This hour-long programme has gone down as a piece of television history. It was watched by nearly 28 million people, over half the population of the UK at the time, the largest ever audience for any British TV show. Even the Queen was rumoured to have put her turkey dinner back by an hour in order to see it.

'At the beginning of the show, Eric and Ernie said, "Elton John's coming on the show but he's very expensive, you know,"' remembers Gary Osborne. 'Elton then went around with a bit of paper trying to find the *Morecambe And Wise Show*. He stumbled into a room where Kenneth Kendall was reading the news and they showed him the door and it was a river – it was all that kind of gag. I had told every member of my family and everybody I'd ever met to watch this show to see this song that I had written with Elton. I couldn't bear to be in the same room as them while the programme was on, and I was in a sweat because I thought they had fucking cut the song.

'The credits rolled and you saw two cleaning ladies, who were Morecambe and Wise in drag, tidying up the studio. Elton came in and said, "Ladies, ladies!" and they said, "Yes?" He said, "I'm Elton John," and they said, "Oh, sorry about that." "I've come to do the *Morecambe And Wise Show*." And they said, "You've missed them, they were very good." "Oh dear," said Elton. "I was going to do a new song." They said, "Oh dear." Elton says, "Well, I'm here now, do you want to hear it?" And they looked at him and they both shrugged. And he sat down and played the song, just him at the piano. As the last chord fades away, he said, "That was what I was going to do on the *Morecambe And Wise Show*," and Eric said, "It's a good job you didn't!"'

Elton John wasn't entirely off the road in 1977. In May, he performed six charity concerts at the Rainbow in London, just him on piano and Ray Cooper on percussion. Yet the unlikeliest gig, perhaps in his entire career, would take place on June 17 that year at Shoreditch College Chapel in Egham, south London. It was the college's valedictory ball and the planned musical turn for the night had cancelled at short notice.

'A bunch of us were sitting around and somebody mentioned that Elton John lived nearby,' one former student, Paul Davies, told *Q* in 1995. 'We didn't really think he'd play, but it was worth a try.' A delegation of students went to Woodside and explained their plight via the intercom at the gates of the estate. 'Elton was apparently lying on his bed watching the tennis. It was Wimbledon week,' remembered Davies.

'We were stunned because, right away, via his housekeeper, he asked what time he would have to be there. He also asked that we didn't get in touch with the press and said he had to have a grand piano.' Elton appeared bang on time at 9.30 pm, scribbled down a six-song set list on a Barclays Bank cheque book and rehearsed in the chapel. He was taken into a tiny anteroom, the sacristy, and then announced as the evening's star entertainment. 'Even then we still thought it must be a joke. I really expected somebody to come in dressed up as Elton John,' marvelled another student, Tom Watson. 'But then he came in through the side door. We were no more than ten feet from him.'

Elton played the chapel gig to a disbelieving audience. 'He didn't ask for a penny, although I gather he could get about £70,000 for Madison Square Garden at the time,' recalled Davies. 'We felt we had to recognise what he'd done in some way, so the next morning we took him a cut glass goblet inscribed with the college colours and a shield with the badge on. We could see him over the other side of the garden fiddling with the lawn mower. The housekeeper thanked us and took it in for him.' 'I wasn't doing anything that night, so I thought, "Why not?"' Elton reflected later. 'I admired their nerve.'

At the end of 1977, Elton was also forced into fulfilling an important obligation. He had agreed to play a charity gig on November 3. The beneficiaries would be the Royal Variety Club and the Goaldiggers, a charity committed to providing football facilities for underprivileged children. Earlier that year, Elton had produced a limited-edition charity single, 'The Goaldiggers Song'. The B-side, 'Jimmy, Brian, Elton, Eric', consisted of a conversation between the pundit Jimmy Hill, the commentator Brian Moore, Eric Morecambe and Elton. On November 3, Davey Johnstone's new group China would be Elton's live band at short notice, with Gary Osborne among the backing vocalists.

'He's in a foul mood, keep away; I wouldn't talk to him if I were you,' Elton's people told anyone hoping for a pre-gig chat with the man himself that night. He took to the stage alone and played the piano melody of 'Better Off Dead'. The night began in a sombre, low-key fashion matching Elton's black mood. He appended 'Candle In The

Wind' with the following intro: 'This is dedicated to someone in the audience who really likes Vera Lynn – Mr Graham Taylor. He hasn't been to one of these before, but he likes this because it's slow and soft you see. Just like it used to be when he played right back for Lincoln.'

But this was to be one of the very few moments of Elton humour that night, as Ray Cooper remembers. 'He was dressed in a black beret and a motorcycle jacket and he looked very white,' remembers Cooper. 'Then he played some strange chords on the piano.' 'I would like to say something,' said Elton. 'It's very hard to put into words. I haven't been touring for a long time and it's been a painful decision whether to come back on the road or not. I've really enjoyed tonight, thank you very much, but I've made a decision that this is going to be my last show. All right? There's a lot more to me than playing on the road. And this is the last one I'm going to do.' 'I was tuning the timpani and thinking, where's the mortgage coming from?' says Ray Cooper. 'And I could see John Reid saying, "Stop him! Grab him!" It was totally out of the blue.'

'He fired the new band when they were performing their first gig,' recalls Clive Franks. 'They were in shock, and I was in shock. The band had to continue to play the rest of the set.' Not even appearances by Kiki Dee for 'Don't Go Breaking My Heart' and Stevie Wonder for 'Bite Your Lip (Get Up And Dance)' or a rousing reception from the fans could lift Elton. It was the first of many final curtains.

CHAPTER 10

A SINGLE MAN: FROM
WATFORD TO MOSCOW

'There were good days and bad days, and very little in between.'

Clive Franks on Elton in the late 1970s

'There's not one track of his on the new album. He'll probably feel extremely hurt but it'll give him a much-needed kick up the arse.'

Elton on the absence of Bernie Taupin from the
A Single Man album, 1978

Billy Connolly is lying flat out on the floor of Gus Dudgeon's studio, the Mill, in Cookham, Berkshire. He's not moving, he's not responding, he doesn't stir when shaken. If he is joking (and why wouldn't one of the most convincingly nuts stand-up comedians of his day be doing just that?), he's doing a very convincing job.

Elton has invited him down to the studios for a premiere of songs from his new album and Billy needs no second invitation to party. Just a few moments earlier, he was fine: laughing, chatting and drinking. He has already consumed copious quantities of alcohol and cocaine, a substance to which, according to his wife Pamela Stephenson, he had been introduced by one of Elton's roadies a couple of years earlier. Billy certainly likes a drink and, at this stage, he is imbibing so much that he may as well have an intravenous drip linking him to the nearest wine cellar. According to Stephenson, one night Billy was so drunk that he couldn't find his way out of a London telephone box.

Billy and Elton have been friends for several years. Billy had opened for Elton on one of his US tours. It wasn't a happy experience. 'Hearing them announce my name was like someone saying, "Ready, Aim, FIRE!"' Billy later admitted. At a gig in Washington, he told TV chat-show host Michael Parkinson, someone threw a pipe at him, which hit him between the eyes: 'It wasn't my audience. They made me feel about as welcome as a fart in a spacesuit.'

However, tonight Billy is still spark-out. It is now when panic breaks out. An ambulance is called and there are very real fears that the Big Yin may be about to start haranguing St Peter with a willy joke. Before the ambulance arrives, Billy suddenly comes to and gets up as if nothing has happened. Unsurprisingly, he asks for another drink. 'Whenever I bump into him now,' says Gary Osborne, one of those worried people who peered into his face that night for signs of life, 'Billy always asks, "Remember the time I died?"' In the late 1970s, being a star, with all the concomitant temptations and pressures, is a life-threatening profession.

* * *

At this stage, Elton John, too, was at a low point in his life. His support network of professional friends had gone and he himself was entering a period of sustained self-abuse, a 'mission' on which he was joined by many of those around him. For someone who, up until 1975, had never taken hard drugs and had warned others as to their evils, it had been a speedy descent into the world of addiction.

'Elton was drinking a bottle or two of brandy every day and smoking joint after joint, so there was a lot of laughter on those sessions. We were all pretty stoned,' says Clive Franks. 'The obvious problem seemed to be that Elton was drinking a lot,' says Gary Osborne. 'He was drinking a lot because he was doing a lot of coke and you need the booze to calm you down and keep you level. You don't even realise how much you're drinking. You don't get drunk. If you're up all night and for most of the next day too, instead of stopping drinking after four or five hours, like most people would, you're drinking solidly for ten or twenty.' It would be in this state that Elton recorded his thirteenth studio album. Astonishingly, it didn't seem to stem the flow of musical ideas. However, not all of them, perhaps, were as good as he imagined them to be.

Having dropped Gus Dudgeon as producer, Elton had decided to cushion the blow by recording the new album in Dudgeon's new studio, thus ensuring that Dudgeon would still be rewarded financially despite the loss of his production income. The Mill, situated in Cookham, Berkshire, was a brand-new complex, with plush carpets and a state-of-the-art console. It wasn't the first time Elton had used the studios. Earlier that year, he had used them to cut a Taupin song, 'Ego'. Hailed as a tour-de force comeback single, it came with a lavish promotional film, at the time the most expensive ever made. Elton, with short hair and contact lenses, his face thinner, looked quite different, altogether more dramatic and serious. According to the writer Elizabeth Rosenthal, 'Ego' was 'a rare collaboration in which the music came first'. Elton called it 'one of the best lyrics Taupin's ever written. It was based on a few superstars that I know, but again it was done tongue-in-cheek.' Pressed to name them, Elton said. 'Well... it's the David Bowies... the Neil Diamonds... the Barbra Streisands of this world.' Interestingly, it was widely believed that Bernie himself had earlier been the target of a similar rock-star swipe: 'Johnny come lately, the new kid in town/Everybody loves you, so don't let them down' the Eagles had sung in 1976.

'Ego' began with a slightly unhinged silent-movie piano refrain and the toot of a steam-train whistle, reminiscent of scenes of Lillian Gish being tied to a railway track at the mercy of the oncoming express. It continued on its way with odd time signatures and dramatic stop-starts in the action. While it might have been one of his most groundbreaking songs, it was certainly one of his least commercial, reaching a lowly Number 34 in both the American and British charts, much to Elton's bitter disappointment.

The new album, recorded in the summer of 1978, was called *A Single Man*, an apt title, bearing in mind that Elton had been denuded of his old support system. "He didn't have Gus, he didn't have Davey, he didn't have Dee, he didn't have Nigel, he didn't have Bernie; all he had was me and Clive,' recalls Gary Osborne. 'So I had a far greater role. Remember, Bernie very rarely hung in the studio. I'm a studio cat – I love the studio. I was the extra pair of ears. I would be the one to say, "Oh, that's good," or "Why don't you move it up an octave?" or "Why don't you repeat that line?" And, of course, I could sing backing vocals, I could play a bit of guitar and say "That note's out of tune," where Bernie didn't have those musical attributes. He's a words man, whereas I am a musician, with a very small "m". So I was there for every minute of every session. Very early on in the making of *A Single Man*, I said to Elton, "If I can suggest anything I like, without you being offended, you can ignore all my suggestions without me being offended." And he said, "That sounds like a good system." So throughout our entire working relationship I always felt free to say exactly what I wanted. I would make suggestions about the melody, the chords, the arrangements or the producion and of course Bernie hadn't done that. By the time Bernie heard the song it was finished. When I came back to Elton with a lyric to his tune we'd talk it though – it was very much a collaboration.'

Clive Franks took on the role of producer, somewhat reluctantly. 'How do you follow the work of Gus Dudgeon?' he asks. 'That was always on my mind. It was very difficult for me because Gus was there, and sometimes Gus would come into his recording studio. And I really would rather have not played bass because I wanted to focus more on the production. All I could hear throughout that album when I listened back to the tracks was my below-par bass playing. But I thought it was a pretty decent album in the end.'

Elton John decided to sing many of the vocals lying on the studio floor, declaring that he found it less of an effort that way. Such was the quantity of songs which tumbled effortlessly out as melodies for Gary Osborne to write lyrics for that many more songs were recorded than were needed for the album, resulting in several tracks being used as B-sides over the next four years. Nevertheless, in the search for a track listing and a running order, Dudgeon was perhaps missed. As an editor of ideas, Dudgeon had proved himself to be a master. On *Blue Moves*, he had been out-voted when he argued that the album didn't contain enough strong tracks to make a double. *A Single Man* certain lacked the pacing and drama of Elton's best work.

B.J. Cole, who had provided pedal steel guitar all those years ago on 'Tiny Dancer', was asked to join the sessions. He immediately noticed the change in Elton's character. 'I got the very strong feeling that he was coming down the other side of his fame and it was all rather decadent,' he admits. 'He was probably doing too many drugs at the time. In fact, I know he was. It was nice to work with Elton again, but there was a distance that hadn't been there before. But that's understandable, because he'd been living a lifestyle that separated us all. I'd been around a number of well-known people who had had dependencies, such as Steve Marriot, and they may be professional enough to keep it out of the picture while they are working, but it still affects their judgement and their attitude towards you and what's being done.

'I always felt like Elton was the kind of person you could talk to as a mate, though, whatever my impression of him the second time I worked with him. You never felt intimidated. There were some artists I've worked with who have a certain reserve and you have to be on your best behaviour. Some artists have an insurmountable barrier, as much as they would probably hate to think that they had. Unfortunately Sting is like that, which is a real problem for him, whereas Elton was never like that. He may have been fucked up, but he was always a mate.'

The first single from *A Single Man*, 'Part-Time Love', is one of those songs that Elton has long since fallen out of love with. Released as a single at the end of 1978, it would peak at a relatively modest Number 15 yet hang around in the UK charts for an impressive 13 weeks. The promo film, intended as a nostalgic homage to the more innocent pop world of the mid-1960s, featured *Ready Steady Go*'s Cathy McGowan. In truth, it's an absolutely fine single, catchy, lightweight, but no worse for that and surely a better song than many of the more mawkish ballads which Elton would play on stage in the decades to come. 'The funny thing about that [song] was that, although I liked it a lot at the time, I have grown to dislike it over the years,' says Osborne. 'It seems too poppy. I'm not mad about the backing vocals, which I organised, but I like Davey Johnstone's guitar. Davey happened to be in town, staying with me, and I said to Elton, "Davey's in town, why can't we get him on this track?" Their relationship was slightly strained, but I liked what Davey played, particularly the little deviations off the main riff.'

One of Osborne's main ideas was to put more of Elton into the actual songs. 'The song "Big Dipper", which was a bit of fun, was very definitely a gay song,' he says. 'What happens in that song is that Elton meets a young lad, goes up on a big dipper and is given head. It had to be slightly disguised because, firstly, it was 1978, and secondly, we wanted the Watford football team to sing on it and we couldn't have them singing words that were… too puffy. I was trying to put a bit of Elton's wicked sense of humour into his songs. Elton had said that it was about time that he wrote a gay song, so that was what that was about. Graham Taylor and the whole team and whoever else was in the studio sang on the track. It doesn't take a wild leap of the imagination to see that "Everybody's got to do their thing/ Everybody's got their song to sing" means live and let live. In my mind it was them [Watford FC] giving their approval to his "saucy" ways. There wasn't a single one of them that didn't know he was gay and none of them cared. He was paying wages and he was turning up and supporting them whenever he possibly could.'

Osborne's lyrics contained other knowing references to Elton's life and personality. For the song 'Georgia', the lyric 'Give me 35 good acres, Lord, and let progress take the rest' wasn't written at random. 'The reason I chose 35 is because that's the amount of acres he has at Woodside,' says Osborne.

'Bernie and I have totally different ways of working,' he goes on. 'I am a lyricist while Bernie's essentially a poet. Now, I'm a lyricist who could knock you up a poem and I'm sure if you gave Bernie a tune he could knock out a lyric. But the way Bernie works is he writes a poem and gives it to Elton and Elton turns it into a song by being totally ruthless and brutal with that poem. He'll cut out a word here, a line there, a whole verse here. If you look at the lyric that Bernie sends and then look at the lyric that Elton does, half of it has been expunged. Now, along with what's gone, have gone some of the rhymes, some of the streams of the thought, some of the things that connect one idea to the other. Elton doesn't care about that, they've gone because the words will now better fit his melody. What you then get is a lyric that is more mysterious than it was when it was written, because there are bits of it missing. But it all seems to work, and that's a fantastic way of working.

'Elton sometimes subtracts the bit that joins the ideas, so sometimes the ideas are coming at you from leftfield, which is part of their charm. Now with me, Elton gave me a tune and I decided what I would try to write. When he gave me the tune he would sing whatever first came into his head. And then I would say, right, I'll keep that title, I'll keep that line, and join them together and try to put a little bit of you into the song.'

Overall, *A Single Man* was a solid, underrated album. Clive Franks did a sterling job as producer and on bass while Osborne's pop lyrics fit the mood of the music snugly. Yet its sound was very different from the work of Dudgeon and Taupin. Once the listener accepted this and didn't try to compare it with Elton's earlier music, the album worked quite successfully. This wasn't Elton at his very best but the album could certainly hold the attention with songs such as 'It Ain't Gonna Be Easy', the ballad 'Shooting Star', a stripped down version of 'Shine On Through' and 'Madness', a description of the London IRA bombing campaign of the time.

'I particularly like "Madness",' says Osborne. 'I felt it was serious; it was describing something that was very important to us at the time. There were bombs going off all through the 1970s. I remember one blew up in a shop in Hampstead. I heard it explode and I thought, "Oh God, it's getting a bit near now." I got a letter from a policeman from Dundee saying the song meant a lot to him because he had attended the aftermath of a bomb blast. The song meant a lot to him, and the letter meant a lot to me.'

One of the most melodic songs was 'Return To Paradise'. 'The interesting fact about that track is that Elton gave me the tune and when I went to write the lyric I suddenly realised that the chorus was a complete pinch of an old Caribbean song called "Jamaica Farewell" that goes "I'm glad to say, I'm on my way..." I'm trying to write the thing and I'm thinking, oh dear, the track is really cool and he'll dump it when he realises it's a nick, so I took a complete liberty and I wrote a new chorus melody. A week later we were in the studio, and he wants to cut the vocal, and I say, "Can we go in a room on our own for a minute? I want to play you something." So we went off to an office and I explained that the chorus was a dead ringer for "Jamaica Farewell". Elton said, "Christ, so it is." And I said, rather nervously, as this is Elton John after all, "But I have written a new tune." So I played the track on the cassette while singing him my new chorus and, when it finished, he just turned the tape recorder off and said, "That's it", then walked into the studio and sang it. So on that song I wrote the chorus melody as well as the actual song, which is fair enough because quite a lot of the words I am credited with are his words, so it works both ways.'

The big hit off the album, though, was a semi-instrumental track named 'Song For Guy'. Released at the end of 1978, it eventually reached Number 4 in the UK. Reportedly, one of the reasons it failed to top the charts was that Phonogram, who were now in charge of Rocket's UK distribution, decided to push another of their big singles of the post-Christmas period, the Village People's 'YMCA', instead.

'Song For Guy' was a response to a real-life tragedy. During the making of *A Single Man*, Guy Burchett, a 17-year-old dispatch rider for Rocket Records, was killed in a road accident. 'He used to drive around on a moped,' says Osborne. 'He was a bit of a mod, I think. He came off his bike in the rain. That morning I turned up at the studio and Elton was really down. He told us what had happened and the mood of the day was really sombre, obviously. The song wasn't exactly written about Guy Burchett but it was a little thing he had been tinkering with in the studio on the day he died: there was no words and no title. When the news came through, Elton said he was going to dedicate the song to that lad.' 'I was nearly in tears when he played it,' admits Clive Franks.

The version on the record was meant to be no more than a run-through of the song prior to actual recording and yet Elton ended up using it, hence the presence of rhythm box drum machine originally intended as a guide. Franks and Stuart Epps, Gus Dudgeon's assistant at Mill Studios, looked at each other in horror when, just as Elton was building to the song's emotional climax, they noticed the tape was about to run out. In fact, it did run out at the very last moment, but a judicious fade solves the problem. The track is one of Osborne's favourites: 'He came up with this wonderful circular line, where he sings at the end: "Life isn't everything". And the way that goes round, it becomes: 'Life isn't everything, isn't everything life?' which is rather poetic and sweet.'

Elton had problems selecting the songs to go on the album. 'He had recorded about 18 songs, and it was very hard to choose which ones to use,' says Franks. 'Elton invited Paul Gambaccini, Kenny Everett and loads of other people for a playback. They were all given pen and paper and asked to rate their favourites. It was a bizarre situation.'

For those involved in making the album, the sessions would be equally memorable for what became known as the 'Morrie tape'. As an in-joke, Elton would punctuate the recording by imitating two ficti-tious Jewish musicians, Morrie (with a deep voice) and Isaac (with a high one). 'When he's doing his vocals, Elton tends to chortle on,' says Stuart Epps. 'On this occasion he was impersonating these two charac-ters, and slagging off everyone: Gus, Sheila, the studio, everything.'

The sombre album cover depicted Elton dressed in a black knee-length overcoat and top hat and carrying a walking stick. Behind him was Windsor Castle. 'I don't think that picture helped sell many copies,' says Gary Osborne. 'He looks a bit funereal on it, which leads into "Song For Guy" but not much else on the album.' 'As always, Elton's mood was the driving factor,' says David Costa, who was again respon-sible for the cover artwork. '"Song for Guy" had left him very reflective. We did the shot with Terry O'Neill and it was absolutely what Elton wanted; he arrived for the shoot dressed like that. I can't remember if the location at the end of the Long Walk behind Windsor Castle was Terry's idea or Elton's. I remember it was freezing, though. The sleeve got a *Music Week* award and the pose stuck.'

Perhaps for the first time since he lived at Frome Court all those years ago with Bernie, Elton had found, in Gary Osborne, not just a musical collaborator but a close friend whom he could hang out with. 'I often stayed at his home; and he often stayed at mine,' says Osborne. 'He was in Windsor and he didn't have a place in London at that stage. If my wife and I went to Woodside to spend the evening, we would very often find ourselves not in any fit state to be driving home. Elton, of course, had a driver, but several times he crashed on my couch when he came to see us in London. We didn't have a spare room because Kiki Dee was in it. When she split up from Davey in 1978 she moved in for a month and stayed for a year.'

When the album was released in October 1978, the knives came out for Osborne. The big news, of course, was that the album contained not a word from the maestro himself, Bernie Taupin. 'Taupin is now a tax exile living in Los Angeles, which Elton John hates,' proclaimed Thomson Prentice of the *Daily Mail*. 'They claim to be still close friends, but the working relationship is over.' In a review in *Rolling Stone* entitled 'Elton John: No Future? Apathy in the UK', Stephen Holden called the album a 'debacle', adding: 'If John and Taupin's final collaboration, *Blue Moves*, was a disastrous exercise in inflated pop rhetoric, *A Single Man* is an equally disastrous exercise in smug vapidity. The songs here are barely songs at all, but childish Neil Sedaka-style ditties with characterless little nursery rhymes for lyrics.' Holden went on: 'Even the best tune, "Shine On Through", is marred by hopelessly trite words and a dull slogging arrangement.' 'Song For Guy' was belittled as 'a synthesized instrumental of the sort you might hear in a dentist's office'.

'I'm used to being dismissed. It's easy to be thought of as lightweight when you're compared with Bernie, who is thought of as being so very clever and heavyweight,' reflects Osborne. 'I knew I was on a hiding to nothing and Elton John fans would have a resistance to me. It was completely understandable. No matter what I did, they would feel I was usurping Bernie, who was part of the legend. And people who didn't like Elton John would use me as a stick to beat him with. I knew that I was going to get it from both sides, and I just thought, well, still, lucky me, what a gig! If the downside is that I would be pretty much slated from the left and the right, then that was going to have to be outweighed by the fact I was making a lot of money and selling a lot of records.'

'Can TV's Mr Jingle Rock Elton Back To The Top Of The Hit Parade?' read a headline in the *Daily Mail* on September 5, 1978. Osborne, photographed in front of a branch of the Abbey National Building Society – just one of the dozens of companies he had written jingles for – issued forth: 'I want to be taken seriously. I want to be one of the best lyricists in the world.' 'Actually, the first assumption was that I was gay and I was his new boyfriend,' admits Osborne. 'The fact that I lived with a woman and I was just about to have a kid, and the fact that Elton never fancied me – which, of course, is quite hurtful – were all overlooked. When they looked at what I'd done in the past, they could say I'd been a top jingle singer. So here I was, the man who sings the Abbey National "I've got the Abbey Habit" ads.' What the world didn't know was that Osborne had also just finished writing the lyrics for Jeff Wayne's *War Of The Worlds*, containing the major hit 'Forever Autumn' by Justin Haywood. 'That year in the Capital Radio Awards there were five albums nominated: Kate Bush, Ian Dury, Elvis Costello, *A Single Man* and *War Of The Worlds*. Out of the five, I had written two of them. *A Single Man* won.'

Shortly after the November 1978 release of *A Single Man*, Elton John was taken ill at his home in Woodside. A report in the UK music weekly *Record Mirror* explained: 'Elton John collapsed yesterday morning shortly after leaving his Old Windsor home to travel to Paris. But the singer had recovered consciousness when he was later admitted to a coronary unit at a Harley Street Clinic in London.' The diagnosis was 'exhaustion'. Only the previous weekend, Elton had played in a five-a-side football match organised by the Goaldiggers charity. The star of that particular day would be the Stranglers' Hugh Cornwell, who played in goal wearing a plastic mac, black tights and ballet shoes. The Stranglers won the day, beating off the challenge of a motley collection of teams including the Rubettes, whose team featured the West Ham United legend Trevor Brooking, and Elton's All-Stars, including Rod Stewart, Bill Oddie, Billy Connolly and the actor Denis Waterman.

Despite his increasingly fragile physical and emotional state, Elton decided to come out of live retirement and play some shows in 1979. This time, however, he wanted to tour on a much more intimate scale, with just him on piano and Ray Cooper on percussion. He was tired of playing large and impersonal stadiums. 'I like to share things, I really do and it's not easy when you're the big megastar,' he had admitted to Phil Sutcliffe at the end of 1976. 'When you look at 70,000 people, how the fuck can you share things? That's another thing that depressed me on the last tour: it suddenly struck me it was like a Nuremburg rally.'

For the 1979 comeback, Elton demanded smaller halls and more unusual places. 'When we originally thought of doing a tour, John Reid, Ray Cooper and I sat down and said, "Let's go to places that we haven't been to before – places, for example, that I wasn't very popular in, like Israel, Switzerland or France. We had never played Spain or Ireland. Then John said, "What about Russia?"'

Elton John would become one of the very first Western pop artists to appear in Soviet Russia. Boney M and Cliff Richard had played there in recent years, but Elton was a potentially much more explosive proposition. Vladimir Kokonin, an official at the Soviet Ministry of Culture, had attended one of Elton's new style band-less shows in Oxford and had been impressed. 'Even so, right up to the very last moment, I think we felt it would be a "No" or a "Nyet", as they say,' admitted Elton, before, inevitably, punning 'Bennie And The Nyets'.

The Harvey Goldsmith-promoted comeback tour was billed as 'Elton John – A Single Man In Concert with Ray Cooper'. After all these years, it was a chance for fans to get close to the action. On the tour poster, an effective design by David Costa recreating the black-clad Elton from the cover artwork of the *A Single Man* album, images of Elton were used, remembers Costa, 'Magritte-like [with] hundreds of them in the sky'. For Cooper, the fact that Elton was committed to touring again, in whatever form, would ultimately be a help to the rest of the band members.

'I was very happy and honoured to be a part of the structure and circumstances that helped to give Elton the confidence to return to the performing platform again,' is how Cooper puts it. 'I thought that everyone would benefit from the two-man show, because it meant that Elton would be reinvented and the back catalogue revisited and so there would be a reinvestment in Elton John.' 'We did 130 concerts in one year,' adds Cooper. 'I broke a rib when I tripped and fell onto his piano, just before the gig in the South of France. At one stage I also got pneumonia. I was wearing a three-piece suit and a tie on stage every performance, I must have been crazy. Despite the few mishaps after a hundred plus concerts I was the fittest I had ever been.'

The lengthy tour was to stretch Elton to the limit. 'What a massive change, to go from an eight-to-ten-piece band to just you,' marvels Gary Osborne. 'Elton was the cake, Ray was the icing and basically every note that Elton played and every note that he sang had to be perfect. There wasn't anything covered up by amplification or by other musicians or backing singers. I think he actually improved as a pianist and as a singer by doing all those solo concerts.'

The format involved Elton taking to the stage and playing what was basically a full solo set in the first half of the evening, while the second half would feature the drama that is Ray Cooper. 'The first half was just him, piano and voice, and over an hour,' says Cooper. 'That was probably enough. But then again, in his generosity, and wanting the audience to have more, there was a second half which began with the intro to "Funeral For A Friend". Then there was a puff of smoke and people were ready for something new. But the something new happened to be more theatrical and illusionist and had very little to do with rock and roll.' 'Ray likes to make the best possible entrance, standing there like something out of Madame Tussaud's chamber of

horrors,' said Elton. During the course of the tour, Cooper would vari-
ously be referred to in the press as 'the gravedigger', 'a bank clerk', 'a
deputy headmaster', 'a 46-year-old punk', 'Steptoe dressed up to go to
a disco' and 'a demented civil servant'.

In May 1979, Elton set off on his historic trip to Russia, taking
with him a small entourage of Cooper, Derf and Sheila, the promoter
Harvey Goldsmith, John Reid, Reid's legal man, Geoffrey Ellis, and the
soundman Clive Franks with his fiancée Carla, who also was in charge
of Elton's make-up. The party also included the famed sitcom writers
Dick Clement and Ian La Frenais, who were filming the trip with a view
to making a documentary, and two journalists – Robert Hilburn of the
Los Angeles Times, the man who had written the rave review of Elton's
Troubadour concert nearly a decade earlier, and David Wigg of the
Daily Express. The party flew from London to Moscow with Aeroflot
then were taken by train to Leningrad.

'The hotel in Leningrad was large and dreary,' recalls Geoffrey Ellis.
'The hotel restaurant, where we had all our meals, served meat, fish
or fowl, not otherwise described and which all tasted the same. Meals
were washed down with sweet champagne-style wine.' 'We were told to
be very careful about what we said when we were over there, because
although everybody acted like they only spoke Russian, they could
speak perfect English,' says Clive Franks. 'So we were told not to say
anything derogatory about the country or anything else.' There was
some time for sightseeing, although a hangover meant Elton missed
out on the trip to the Winter Palace. He did, however, make up the
numbers for a trip to the Hermitage Museum, where, said an amazed
Ellis, 'The authorities specially opened for us the Treasury, full of staggering gold artefacts and jewellery, not then open to the general public.'
There would be receptions and the usual after-shows. 'I was very lucky,
at the British Embassy to meet the great poet Yevgeny Yevtushenko',
remembers Ray Cooper.

Elton's audiences in Russia were drawn from 'approved families and
schools'. He played four consecutive nights at the Bolshoi Concert
Hall, Leningrad (now St Petersburg), where officials asked him not to

kick his piano stool away as he usually did during 'Bennie And The Jets' as this would be damaging Soviet property. They also raised concerns at the inclusion in the set list of the Beatles' 'Back In The USSR'.

Each show began with the first rows occupied by high-ranking officials. The audience sat respectfully, applauding dutifully at the end of each number. If anyone dared to stand, guards pushed them back into their seats. Yet as each show progressed and the officials were happy that nothing approaching a riot would ensue, the officials would leave and the genuine fans could move towards the front of the stage. 'Every performance is a test of one's musical and performing abilities but I think it's fair to say that both Elton and myself found ourselves on a performing platform in a way that was initially very different from anything that we had experienced before and it was fantastic. The Russian audiences wanted to listen to our music,' says Ray Cooper. 'The concerts in Russia, unlike those in the USA, would not start with the audience screaming and shouting. As I've already stated they wanted to see us, listen to us and experience the music. I had experienced this response in the theatre as an actor, but never at a rock 'n' roll concert. It was an exhilarating experience wherein Elton and myself had to work extremely hard and received the most positive response from the Russian audiences. It was like building a wonderful bridge between ourselves and the audience.'

The duo then played four nights at the Rossiya Concert Hall, just off Red Square in Moscow. The tour had been scheduled in order to avoid the end of the harsh Russian winter, but by the time they reached Moscow, they were surprised to find heatwave temperatures. The final concert, played on May 28, was broadcast live on BBC Radio 1 and was ahead of its time: it effectively began the *Unplugged* format of presenting live popular music, a decade before MTV 'invented' the format.

The entire Soviet Union trip proved to be groundbreaking. A year before the Moscow Olympics, it brought the Brezhnev regime some much-needed good publicity. For Elton himself it was also a moving experience. 'I can't get Leningrad out of my mind,' he was to admit. The people he met were warm-hearted, polite and inquisitive. He would sign his autograph and only get halfway though before the recipient would whisk the book away, thinking the name completed. 'We were there when Perestroika was just forming as an idea, and it was very exciting,' says Ray Cooper. 'You got the feeling that things were changing.'

Clive Franks recalls the journey home: 'We flew back on Aeroflot, and as we were hurtling down the runway, suddenly there was this scream from both Elton and Bob Halley who were sitting behind me. I turned round and all I could see were the soles of their feet sticking up in the air. Their seat wasn't bolted to the floor, so, with the thrust of the plan taking off, their whole seat tilted backwards. Luckily there was nobody behind them or they would probably have killed them. They were in fits of laughter. It was only when the plane levelled out that that could move upright.'

On their safe arrival back in Britain, Watford FC were making startling progress under the stewardship of Graham Taylor and his second-in-command, the former Arsenal manager Bertie Mee. Having won successive promotions, they were now in the Second Division. Off the pitch, Elton remained generous to a fault.

'He held a fabulous garden party for the club every year at Woodside,' remembers Gary Osborne. 'There were egg-and-spoon races for the children and a five-a-side game between the footballers' children and the directors and the chairman on Elton's own football pitch. Later on, he even had Sinclair C-5 races. It was a wonderful period. Luther Blissett and the young John Barnes were there. Graham Taylor was fantastic and a good friend to Elton. Later on in his career, of course, when he became England manager, he would have something in common with Elton: death by tabloid.'

Osborne remembers Woodside as a place of opulent good taste. 'It was beautiful, and always a work in progress. The inside was full of beautiful *objets d'art*, a lot of Art Deco stuff and Tiffany lamps. He built a swimming pool and then he built the house out so that it encompassed the pool. One time I was there it was an outdoor pool and then the next time I went it was indoors. He had greenhouses full of vegetables and grew huge marrows that could have won prizes. Fred, Elton's step-dad, was a builder and he used to do a lot of work at Woodside. There was also a disco and a cinema. Elton would get a movie, the new Bond film or something like that, and get all his mates in to watch it. There was also, of course, a room full of rows and rows of records, all correctly catalogued.'

By 1979, Elton John must have possessed one of the largest music libraries in the country. A sizeable portion of this collection had been purchased from BBC producer Bernie Andrews, the man who, along with Jeff Griffin, had been at the spearhead of bringing new music, and new talent such as John Peel, into what was then the Light Programme. 'Bernie Andrews and Elton were good friends,' remembers Bob Harris. 'Bernie had a house in Muswell Hill that was beginning to slip into its footings; literally sinking under the weight of this massive vinyl collection. Elton got to hear about all this and bought Bernie's record collection pretty much lock, stock and barrel.'

However, the 1970s would end on a sour note for Elton. Both 1978 and 1979 were the years of disco. Like other British artists of his generation, Elton liked what he heard. At the end of 1978, the other rock star with his own home football pitch, Rod Stewart, had hit the Number 1 spot in the UK with the rather excellent 'Do You Think I'm Sexy?', a song so self-regarding that it demanded full marks for cheek as well as, of course, for the excellent tune and the disco bass. Roxy Music were also in on the act: a remix of their track 'Angel Eyes' from the *Manifesto* album had made the Top 5 in the summer of 1979. Other sounds from 1979, ranging from M's 'Pop Music' to the Eurobeat of Abba's 'Gimme Gimme Gimme', were stamped through with the disco sound. Even established artists such as ELO began putting disco bass lines in their songs, while art-rockers David Bowie and Talking Heads also filtered disco grooves into their more abrasive music, albeit less overtly. However, the ones who really showed how it should be done were Blondie. In 1979, they took new wave attitude and a joyous disco groove and created the signature sound of the year, 'Heart of Glass'.

With disco all around, it was only natural that someone as observant of current trends as Elton John would have a go. Sadly, the result was a disaster. Recorded at Musicland, Munich, and Rusk Sound Studios, Hollywood, and released in October 1979, everything about the *Victim Of Love* album was misjudged. From the dreadful sleeve and promotional photos featuring Elton's less-than successful hair transplant to the overlong songs, which seldom got out of first gear, it was a well-intentioned project that stalled on the launch pad.

For the project, Elton had hooked up with Pete Bellotte, the British-born and Munich-based producer. Bellotte had worked with Giorgio Moroder on a number of Donna Summer singles, including the 1977 classic 'I Feel Love', a fusion of Kraftwerk and American soul. However, Elton stipulated that he didn't want to be involved in the actual songwriting this time around. This turned out to be the record's Achilles' heel for, try as Bellotte might, he could not bring together the sort of material that suited Elton's style and voice. The seven songs – six co-written by Bellotte, plus a cover of 'Johnny B. Goode' – simply made it sound as if Elton was a guest on someone else's record. The reviews were the worst of his career to date. Stephen Holden in *Rolling Stone* concluded that the album 'hadn't a breath of life'. *Melody Maker's* Colin Irwin wrote: 'This album can't even be blithely dismissed as a bore. There are moments when it's thoroughly objectionable.' Even the official sleeve notes for the CD 2003 reissue of the album refer to it as 'experimental' (code for: no one bought it) and admit that even Elton was 'capable of a miscalculation' (code for: What the hell did he think he was playing at?).

Victim Of Love peaked at Number 41 at home and Number 35 in the US. Just five years earlier, Elton's first *Greatest Hits* package had been Number 1 for nearly three months in Britain. The first signs of a commercial downturn had been there at the end of 1976 with the modest success of *Blue Moves* and then with Elton's *Greatest Hits Volume II*, which reached only Number 21 in the States and Number 11 in the UK. Yet now, even as a live act his star was waning. In November 1979, *Melody Maker* reported that the star's eight-night run at New York's

Palladium had not sold out, while the same newspaper's Steve Pond, reviewing Elton's show at the Universal Amphitheatre in Los Angeles, wrote 'Elton John seems curiously dated on stage, an odd little artefact from another era'. In truth, *A Single Man* had performed creditably, reaching Number 8 in Britain and Number 15 in the US, but *Victim Of Love* seemed to show that the days of multi-platinum sales and media hysteria had well and truly gone.

The big question was – would they ever return?

CHAPTER 11

NEW YORK SUNSET

'And I miss John Lennon's laugh.'

'Blues Never Fade Away'; lyrics: Bernie Taupin; music: Elton John

'You can always replace things; it's only people you can't replace.'

Elton John to his godson, Luke Osborne, Christmas Day, 1980

I t's encore time at the biggest gig of his career to date. Almost half a million people have gathered to watch Elton perform on September 13, 1980 at a free concert in New York's Central Park. The fashion designer Calvin Klein is sponsoring the show to raise awareness of the 'greening of Central Park' initiative. The crowd basks in the glorious late-summer sunshine. John McEnroe is spotted in their number. Backstage, Dudley Moore is canoodling with Susan Anton, a former Miss California. He is giving away eight-and-a-half inches in height – not to mention 15 years in age. Bernie is backstage too, along with Judie Tzuke. All attention, however, is on the main stage and the man himself.

Elton walks with a grin to the piano stool to perform 'Your Song'. The only problem is that he cannot get his legs under the keyboard properly. The reason? He is dressed as Donald Duck. It's a blue-and-white costume with a bib, massive yellow flipper feet and, frankly, a huge arse. Elton waddles comically around the stage before sitting as close to the keyboard as his massive costume will permit and then plays the plaintive piano opening. He begins to sing the song but simply cannot stop laughing. Then, after his fit of giggles finally subsides,

Elton decides to punctuate the lyrics with quack noises. So, Taupin's heartfelt line is rendered, with perhaps unintentional comic irony: 'Or a man who makes potions (Quack!) in a travelling show'.

The next song, probably mercifully, given the possibility of serious injury, is Elton's final contribution to the gig, the encore 'Bite Your Lip (Get Up And Dance)'. For this song, Elton, perhaps unwisely, decides to leave the piano and march around the stage in his very own, and rather literal, version of the duck-walk. Unsurprisingly, he almost trips over before making it to the area in front of Nigel Olsson's drum riser. Before the newly reinstated drummer, who sits smiling and wearing his trademark headphones and motorcycle gloves, Elton turns and wiggles his bum at the audience, his hand on his hip. Again, ambitiously, he then stands on one leg before walking with his oversized yellow feet to the second keyboard opposite his own, that of James Newton Howard, and playing a few bars of boogie.

As Elton might have said, it's completely quackers.

*   *   *

The whole day had been one of surreal scale. Elton had performed a long and enthusiastic set. Although commentators were saying that his record sales and career were in decline, on the evidence of this demonstration of public support, and the strong showing of his new single, 'Little Jeannie', this would appear not to be entirely the case – at least, not in the US. Halfway through the set, he threw in a cover version: 'We're going to do a song written by a friend of mine who I haven't seen for a long time,' announced Elton. 'He only lives just over the road.' Against the backdrop of the late-afternoon New York skyline, he began the simple, elegiac piano melody that opens John Lennon's 'Imagine'. In a few weeks, Lennon would himself be back in the singles charts with '(Just Like) Starting Over' and in the album charts with *Double Fantasy*, his collaboration with his wife, Yoko Ono. A few weeks after that, he would be dead.

Rocket act Judie Tzuke, fresh from the success of a big hit single with the ballad 'Stay With Me Till Dawn', opened for Elton that day. 'Me and Elton sat in the tour bus drinking whisky before I went on stage,' remembers Judie. 'I went on absolutely drunk out of my mind and hardly remember the gig. I think Elton carried on drinking, so I have no idea what state he was in when he went on. It was terrifying. I used to drink to calm my nerves but it never really worked. I remember all the songs going twice the speed they normally did and I think our set, which normally took 45 minutes, was over in about 25. So I'm sure it was pretty dreadful, but I'm so proud I was there and I can tell my kids I did it.

'I think there were some people who thought the duck outfit was a mistake, but I thought it was quite funny,' continues Judie. 'It just made me laugh,' explained Elton nearly three decades later about one of the few stage costumes he would never sell off. 'I didn't have a rehearsal in how to get in it, so I was backstage at Central Park trying to get in it and I would have my arm through the leghole and my leg through the armhole. I couldn't get in it for laughing... I cannot go onstage without dressing up. It's a British thing, I think, because we grew up with pantomime and we grew up with a theatrical way.'

The duck costume was amusing. In 1980, it was an indicator of Elton's stage silliness. Twenty-five years later, bizarrely, Courtney Love was to wear it. Courtney was a fan. Michael Stipe of R.E.M. once told Elton of the times when he would drive around LA with Courtney listening to *Goodbye Yellow Brick Road*. Having agreed to perform at an Elton John charity concert, the Hole singer asked if she could borrow the Donald Duck outfit to sing 'Don't Let The Sun Go Down On Me'.

Nevertheless, the business with the costumes was all beginning to get a bit gratuitous, a bit silly, maybe even a bit annoying. In the early 1970s, Elton's spectacular spectacles, feathers, glittery suits and all-round glam image had fitted the times. By the early 1980s, with glam long gone, dressing-up seemed out-of-kilter. Yet Elton's response, as the decade went on, was to make bigger, bolder, and ever sillier stage costumes. He needed the visuals to attract the audience's attention, when maybe he knew that his new songs couldn't. It was almost as if he had lost confidence in himself as a performer. As Elton John headed towards middle age and began putting on more weight, the

Elton sent up his celebrity in the Seventies with ever-dafter stage spectacles.

LEFT: Elton with Rocket signing Kiki Dee. Their 1976 duet, 'Don't Go Breaking My Heart', was Elton's first UK Number One single in 1976.

OPPOSITE: 'I Wanna Kiss The Bride'. Elton marries sound-technician Renate Blauel on 14 February, 1984, in Sydney, Australia.

BELOW: Elton's competitive nature was nowhere more evident than on the tennis court. Here he is in 1975 with Billie Jean King.

Elton looks on as Jeanne White places her hand on the body of her son, Ryan, who died of AIDS complications aged 18 (Indianapolis, April 1990).

Westminster Abbey, 6 September, 1997: Elton John performs a hastily rewritten version of 'Candle In The Wind' at the funeral of Diana, Princess Of Wales.

ABOVE: Watford FC chairman, Elton John, with team-manager Graham Taylor.

ABOVE: Elton with lyricist Gary Osborne, on holiday in Antigua, 1981.

ABOVE: Los Angeles, California, 27 March, 1995. Elton and lyricist Tim Rice win an Academy award for best song for 'Can You Feel The Love Tonight?' from *The Lion King* soundtrack.

ABOVE: 21 December, 2005: Sir Elton John and David Furnish celebrate their civil partnership outside Windsor Guildhall.

The newly knighted Elton John with partner David Furnish (left), mother Sheila, and stepfather Fred Farebrother, outside Buckingham Palace, 24 February, 1998.

stage costumes would, he thought, camouflage his expanding girth. Unfortunately, they had the opposite effect.

'The costumes used to hide a lot, you know,' Elton admitted in 1994. 'Because I was quite large. I used to think, well, I'll wear a big outfit and people won't notice how large I am. Of course, it accentuated the size and people looked at you more because you looked kind of outrageous.' His various stage guises included Tina Turner (in a wig and short skirt), Ronald McDonald, a punk with a Mohican haircut, a rocker with an outlandishly high quiff and Mozart in a periwig, blusher and beauty spot. At one function, Elton was photographed wearing a model of the Eiffel Tower on his head.

What none of these looks were, however, was fun. Instead, they came across as contrived and overblown. 'Some of the things I wore were horrendous… I took it way too far for too long,' Elton was to admit after the fact. It must have been difficult even for his fellow rock stars to take him seriously. 'The first time I met Sting I was dressed as Minnie Mouse and he's never let me forget it,' admits Elton.

The harsh reality was that for the next two decades, his music mostly failed to come anywhere near the peak moments of his classic 1970s records. It would be foolish to dismiss out of hand all of Elton John's records in this period. However, it is a fact that, whereas in the past, his albums were, if not always brilliant, then at the very least entirely listenable, his 1980s and 1990s records contained perhaps three or four strong songs, with the remaining tracks fillers. A couple of albums were out-and-out stinkers with not a single memorable moment. Elton had begun to chase the fashionable sounds of the day and, when artists do that, they tend to lose what it was that was so distinctive about them in the first place.

He was not alone in this, however. In the mid-1980s, even that most hitherto sure-footed of musical experimenters, David Bowie, made records he now virtually disowns. Rod Stewart, Bruce Springsteen, even Lou Reed released music which was heavy on style but light in content: the big drum sound, the cheesy synthesizer chord and the lousy guitar solo ruled. Along with the bad music went the bad hair, as personified by that mid-decade favourite, the mullet; short at the front, long at the back, as worn by Jon Bon Jovi and Michael Bolton. Even Elton would try his own version with what hair he had left.

Elton would still have numerous chart hits, sell copious quantities of albums and singles and remain a superstar. Yet, in terms of critical acceptance, the wounds inflicted on him in the punk era by the new breed of rock journalist were slow to heal. The result was that, not only would Elton's new music be dismissed out of hand: his legacy would be tarnished. Elton, like Liz Taylor in the film world, was in danger of becoming famous for being famous. He was undoubtedly a superstar, but it was as if nobody could quite remember what he was famous for. Nobody talked about his old records; nobody cared much for the newer ones. With his weirdly fascinating and astonishingly colourful private life, he was more famous for appearing on chat shows and in the inches of the gossip columns than as an artist to be taken seriously.

There were, by now, other much more credible artists around who possessed the mystique and the music: Michael Stipe, Michael Jackson, Madonna, Morrissey. As journalists hung on every word Michael Stipe famously mumbled, or identified great artistic intent in every quotidian Madonna video, the musical world of Elton John seemed an utter irrelevancy. His records were seen as shamelessly pandering to the mainstream, bought by non-rock fans who were into easy listening. He was simply another Cliff Richard or Chris De Burgh, admired as a non-threatening entertainer, as a purveyor of trite sentiment and pallid pop. It was a situation that Elton seemed unwilling or unable to do anything about for a very, very long time.

'We're into the fifth year of the Elton John crisis and frankly some of us here on the Elton watch are getting worried.' So wrote *Rolling Stone*'s Ken Tucker in his review of Elton's new record, *21 At 33*, released in May 1980. The title was a reference to the number of albums Elton had released in his career and to his current age, presumably to remind the public what a prodigious talent Elton had been. Since he had, by any reasonable calculation, released only 19 albums up to that point (including live and compilation albums), the numbers didn't seem to add up to anything more than an overselling of the artist.

Unlike *A Single Man*, the new album was written by committee. Gary Osborne had been retained and Bernie Taupin allowed back in, while Tom Robinson and Judie Tzuke were added. Unsurprisingly, the result lacked the sort of thematic unity of style and content that made the best Elton albums click. '*21 At 33* was written in France,' says Osborne. 'Elton was renting Danny La Rue's place, a lovely villa in Grasse on the Côte d'Azur. Most of the backing tracks were recorded in a place called Superbear Studios in the mountains in France just outside Nice. It was a lovely place to record.' Clive Franks, once again in charge of the production along with Elton, was less than impressed with the studios. 'There were a lot of technical problems. We decided that we would go over to LA to finish the record off and on the last night, as I was trying to complete some rough mixes to take to Elton, the console burst into flames!'

In football parlance, *21 At 33* was very much a game of two halves. The first side had some of the strongest material Elton had made for years. 'Little Jeannie', although obviously of the same musical DNA as 'Daniel', possessed a memorable tune and lyric and was the highlight of the entire record. A collaboration with Gary Osborne, it would eventually reach Number 3, residing in the Billboard charts for an impressive 21 weeks, his biggest hit since 'Don't Go Breaking My Heart' four years earlier. The title and the line 'I want you to be my acrobat' were Elton's own and offered to Osborne, who could elect to keep or reject them when writing his own lyric to Elton's melody. Of course, Osborne kept them in.

'"Little Jeannie" was the only time that he ever asked me to rewrite anything,' reveals Osborne. 'Everything else I ever wrote, he just took it straight into the studio and sang it. On this occasion, he said that he didn't like the line "You take it where it strikes and give it to the likes of me," which was a shame, because I did. I liked the internal rhyme for a start and it captured what I wanted to say about the character of the girl in the song, a girl who was beautiful but didn't realise her own worth, a woman who would sleep around because of her low self-esteem. It took me a week to write the song, and a month to rewrite that verse. Anyway, we were at Bear Studios and he said, "It's time to do 'Jeannie' now." I said, "I've got that new verse," and he said, "Oh, it's OK, I've got used to the old one now."'

With the backing tracks completed, the team flew to LA to finish the recording. It was at this stage that an old friend rejoined the fold. 'The feeling was that the drummer, Alvin Taylor, wasn't quite right for this track,' says Gary Osborne. 'So we took the original drum part off and put Nigel Olsson on. Nigel put some kicks in there and gave it a lovely feel.' In fact, before Clive Franks decided to look up Nigel Olsson, who at that time was living in LA, Elton had been intent on scrapping the track completely. 'Nigel did his part as a first take and he sounded amazing,' says Franks. 'I thought Elton would tear my head off when he found I had called up Nigel to play on the track, but he was fine about it. We brought Dee Murray, who was also living locally in LA, back into the studios too.'

'I'm awfully glad he didn't scrap "Jeannie", because it's still my biggest American hit, four weeks at Number 3, and it was Elton's biggest American hit for years too', says Gary Osborne. 'I got to sit in Elton's production seat while he was away, and helped Clive produce the over-dubs which mainly consisted of the backing vocals, the horn section and the fabulous sax solo by Jim Horn.'

After 'Little Jeannie', the other standout on *21 At 33* was 'Sartorial Eloquence', one of two collaborations with Tom Robinson. As leader of the Tom Robinson Band, Robinson had made his name with a series of intelligent pieces of power pop. '2-4-6-8 Motorway' was one of the finest singles of 1977 and 'Glad To Be Gay' one of the bravest of 1978. For 'Sartorial Eloquence', Elton provided one of his best melodies. Released as the second single off the album, it turned out, despite its high production values and big chorus, to be only a minor hit. 'Two Rooms At The End of The World', one of four songs written by Bernie Taupin, featured the catchiest of guitar riffs by Richie Zito and some really excellent drumming from Alvin Taylor.

The lyric was a direct comment on the state of the Elton-Bernie partnership, written in the third person as if describing two fictitious characters. The main theme of the song was that the distance that separated them was a physical, not an emotional one. Taupin took the chance to remind everyone that 'together the two of them were mining gold'.

The album's second side, however, failed to sparkle. Bernie was also misfiring. His 'White Lady, White Powder' was a mundane piece of self-analysis that was too blatant to work. The closing song, 'Give Me The Love', co-written with Judie Tzuke, was pleasant, though hardly classic Elton. 'He sent me the track and the title and asked me to write words to it,' recalls Tzuke. 'I wrote loads of words and sent them in with a note saying, "Use whatever you like." Actually, I thought he left out some of the better lyrics and used ones I didn't like, but I'm still very proud to have written a song with him.' 'I preferred *A Single Man* as an album,' admits Clive Franks. 'At one stage, *21 At 33* was going to be a double album but I didn't think the songs were strong enough. Elton was not as focused, maybe, as he could have been. A lot of the time, he just didn't turn up. He would leave a lot of the decision-making up to me.'

The upside of *21 At 33*, however, was that, as Gary Osborne puts it, Elton 'felt liberated. He found that he could work with people other than Bernie'. Despite all the tabloid speculation, the split with Bernie had never been intended to be permanent. 'I wasn't at all surprised when Elton starting working with Bernie again,' says Osborne. 'It looked to the outside world that I was a replacement for Bernie, but I was never that. I was an *addition* to Bernie. I always got on very well with Bernie. I was always very respectful towards him and he was always very gentlemanly towards me. His *people*, however, were not. I remember a party at which his manager, Michael Lippman, told me: "You know, you're really quite a nice feller, but we'd prefer it if you didn't exist." I was bit shocked by this. He'd said "We'd prefer it," as if he was using the royal "we". Maybe his tongue was somewhere near his cheek, but it came over rather cold.'

The autumn 1980 tour had seen Elton reunited with Dee Murray and Nigel Olsson. Yet Ray Cooper, absent from the album sessions, was not part of the touring band. 'He's actually just been doing a film, the Robert Altman film of *Popeye*, that's why he's not on the *21 At 33* album, if any of the fans want to know,' Elton told the BBC. 'But I'm sure we'll work together again. I adore the man. He has taught me such a lot; not musically, he's been educating me a lot. He is an educated man. I love him very dearly. He's brought me through a lot of crises.'

On a personal level, Elton was swinging from one short-term relationship to the next. 'Drugs, sex and doomed liaisons were my form of destruction,' he was to later say, looking back on an unhappy time in his personal life.

Among Elton's lovers would be Charles, a colourful character nicknamed Chloe, then the young and apparently very sweet Vance, the addressee of the big hit 'Blue Eyes', and then Gary Clarke, who sold the story of his relationship with Elton in the form of a biography.

Clive Franks remembers Chloe: 'I got on well with him, and so did my wife, Carla. He was very upper crust English and he looked very smart and wore nice clothes. But he was a bit of a bounder. He ended up marrying a girl I had a little fling with called Bianca, who was an air stewardess on one of the Starship planes we had in the Seventies. I never thought he was gay actually.'

Elton's various addictions did not help in his search for a lasting relationship. On cocaine, Elton has admitted that he was impossible to be with: illogical, outrageously moody, yet feeling liberated to play out his sexual fantasies.

In his private life, it seemed that Elton would often make a fool of himself. Friends would try to warn him, but although their warnings might have a short-term impact, in the long term, Elton's addictive personality always won through. Graham Taylor was one of the people who tried to get through to Elton. 'I was very unhappy, and drinking a lot of brandy,' said Elton. 'The team were playing Luton Town on

Boxing Day and I turned up in a coat that had cost £300 but looked like a dressing gown. The next morning, Graham called round to my house. He put a bottle of brandy on the table and said, "Here you are, are you going to drink that? What the hell's wrong with you?" He brought me to my senses.'

Someone else who tried to make Elton see sense was the forthright George Harrison. 'He actually administered quite a few telling-offs to me about my drug problem,' Elton told *Rolling Stone* in 2002. 'There was this one night in Los Angeles when he said, "Listen, for God's sake, go easy on the marching powder, because it's not going to do you any good." That was the evening I tried to change Bob Dylan's wardrobe. I was saying, "You can't keep going round in clothes like that; you've got to come upstairs, I'll give you a few clothes." And the abject look of horror on Bob Dylan's face was unbelievable. Can you imagine? I was like, "Oh, yeah, I've got a couple of Versace numbers upstairs that'll really suit you, Bob." And George was present for this. So he administered a little talk to me.'

For many major rock stars, the early 1980s proved were the most hedonistic of times. Elton was a gleeful visitor to celebrity parties and happening events. Studio 54 in New York was a particular favourite. This now legendary disco, opened in April 1977 in Manhattan, had became infamous for refusing admission to Nile Rodgers and Bernard Edwards of Chic, who would write a song with the hook 'Aaah, fuck off!' in direct response to their bad treatment by the doorman. The song, 'Le Freak', with the line changed to 'Aaah, freak out!' became Atlantic Records' biggest-selling single ever. Studio 54's logo depicted a half-crescent man in the moon smiling down on a silver spoon of cocaine. It was a place where drugs, dancing and casual sex ruled.

'Until people started dying in great numbers from various excesses, nobody cared what anybody did,' says Paul Gambaccini. 'It didn't occur to them to be judgmental. There was a woman who was a critic for a posh publication who, at a party given by top publicist Tony Brainsby, had sexual intercourse with a dog on the billiard table. Now, OK, people thought this was weird, but they didn't condemn the woman, because everyone was experimenting and pushing the boundaries and almost nothing was considered too gross. And then more people started dying of drug overdoses and, of course, when HIV came in this whole idea of widespread sexual license was just over.'

'As Elton did more and more coke, I got more blame,' says Gary Osborne. 'As far as his friends and family knew I was spending more time with Elton than anybody and so was a prime suspect. The irony was I never could keep up with Elton. A gram of cocaine would normally last a couple of people an evening, maybe. For four or five people, a couple of grams would do. But you've got to double all those figures when you're talking about Elton.' Sheila was so distressed by her son's behaviour that, for a time, she went to live in Spain with Derf just so that she didn't have to be exposed any longer to Elton's lifestyle.

Where Bernie Taupin was quiet and reserved, Gary Osborne was a much more extrovert character. 'Gary and I were friends,' says Bob Harris, who had just finished his long stint as presenter of *Old Grey Whistle Test*. 'Gary had a house at Regent's Park with Jenny. It was very easy for everybody to stop off there on the way home and everybody did. Gary had a basement that he had transformed into a pretend beach, with loads of sand on the floor. There was a little cocktail bar and you sat on deckchairs. The ceiling and walls were blue and there was a mural on the wall, which made it feel as if you were looking out to sea. Elton and Kiki in particular, I remember, would often be there. But it was all getting a bit druggy. A lot of people wanted to push the boundaries and experiment with things, but then they began to take over your life.'

One of the lowest points for Elton was Christmas Day 1980. He had planned to spend the holiday period with his boyfriend Charles, or Chloe as Elton called him. Chloe was meant to be flying in from the States to rendezvous with Elton, who himself was due to arrive home on Christmas Eve having completed a tour of Australia. On Christmas morning, the phone rang just as Gary Osborne, his wife Jenny, and their son Luke were opening their presents and preparing for a family

Christmas with Gary's mum. 'It was Elton, in tears,' remembers Gary Osborne. '"Chloe hasn't arrived. I have no idea where he is, what he's doing, why he's not here," he sobbed. "Well, who's there?"' I asked him. "Just me," he replied. "I've given everyone the week off." I said, "We'll be right down." So we cancelled our own plans and went down to Woodside to try to keep him from falling apart. We stayed the week.

'When Jenny, Luke and I got there, we walked into the kitchen and there was this huge turkey with one slice out of it and a massive cake, again with one slice out of it. And there was Elton, pacing round the room in tears.'

After Elton had calmed down a little, some sort of normality returned, at least for a while. 'Elton collected Tiffany lamps,' recalls Osborne. 'There was one in particular that he told us had cost £10,000. An hour later, my kid was running through the room, tripped on the wire and smashed this lamp to smithereens. My wife and I were in absolute shock. Elton didn't bat an eyelid. He picked Luke up and cuddled him, and said: "Don't worry darling, it's only a thing. You can always replace things; it's only people you can't replace." That tells you more about Elton than all his songs put together.'

There would be further moments of despair and depression. Osborne recalls a period not long afterwards when Elton was obviously not well. 'We were in a fantastic flat overlooking the Seine in Paris and Elton refused to come out for a month. These were supposed to be the sessions for some of the songs that ended up on *The Fox* and *Jump Up!* We had the studio at £1,000 a day and the band, producer, engineer, road crew and management were all there in hotels. Everyone except me was on wages and *per diems*, and Elton wouldn't come out to play. He wouldn't go to the studio; he wouldn't even get dressed. So, I was there in the flat with Elton, his PA Bob Halley and Vance, and we had this sweet girl called Faith cooking for us.

'We just played poker and we took drugs for a month. And John Reid was banging on the door shouting "Let me in!" And without thinking I went to the door. "Don't answer that," said Elton. "Gary, you let me in," screamed JR but Elton screamed back: "You dare let him!"'

Musically, Elton was still capable of penning an excellent pop single, but the years of invulnerability, when the Elton John team produced hit album after hit album, looked as if they would never return. The popularity of MTV, which launched in 1981, meant that all major artists had to present glossy visuals to go along with the music. Of the established stars of the 1970s, very few made the successful transition and those who did were artists like David Bowie and Michael Jackson who had always been as visually alluring as they were musically inviting. For Elton – tubby, thinning on top, and lacking in Bowie's arty gravitas or Michael Jackson's fleet-of-foot dance moves – the new age of the visual put him at a disadvantage. However, this did not stop him from making a feature-length video for his upcoming album, *The Fox*, on which each song was accompanied by a promotional film of middling quality.

For *The Fox*, Clive Franks again handled the original production work. Franks thought he had completed the album, but on his return from honeymoon to finish the mix, was told by John Reid's assistant in a phone call that Chris Thomas had been appointed producer. Thomas would go on to work with Elton on six of the nine tracks included on the album. The news that he had been dropped 'made me physically sick, actually,' says Franks. 'Elton wouldn't speak to me about it and neither would John Reid You would think that if you worked for someone that long that they could tell you in a nice way rather than have some bloody office assistant ring you up. I had nothing against Chris Thomas at all, I had known him way back, and Elton had mentioned before I started work on *The Fox* that he might be bringing him in to work *with* me. After I had been dropped, we wound up the Frank N. Stein company that Elton and I had set up for our production work, although I have continued to work on Elton's live sound to this day. Elton says he wouldn't have it any other way.'

'*The Fox* was a bit of a dog's dinner,' admits Gary Osborne. 'It was done all over the place, and we used bits and pieces left over from *21 At 33*.' *The Fox*, like *21 At 33*, was half a good album, containing as it did several pretty unmemorable moments intermingled with four or five classic pieces of Elton pop. It garnered generally positive reviews.

Rolling Stone's Stephen Holden, the man who had penned what read like Elton's musical obituary just two-and-a half years earlier with his demolition of *A Single Man*, wrote: 'These 11 songs make up John's most consistently listenable collection in years.'

With its sing-along chorus and buoyant verses, how the implausibly catchy 'Just Like Belgium' failed to chart is one of the mysteries of Elton's career. It was certainly Bernie's best pop song for half a dozen years. On the bluesy 'Heart In The Right Place', Osborne took on the subject of the British press and Elton's unfair treatment therein: 'I'll ask you some questions, I'll tell you some lies/ You'll open your heart like a friend/ I'll make up some answers you won't recognise/ The you I create with my pen.'

On the ambitious 'Carla/Etude-Fanfare-Chloe', Elton attempted the sort of dynamic marriage of instrumental music and song he had so successfully pulled off on such earlier classics as 'Funeral For A Friend/ Love Lies Bleeding' from *Goodbye Yellow Brick Road* and 'Tonight' from *Blue Moves*. The romantic sweep on the instrumental section, featuring the London Symphony Orchestra, was named 'Carla' after Clive Franks' wife. James Newton Howard co-wrote the synth part that gave way to the confessional 'Chloe', a plea to Elton's then partner, Charles: 'Chloe, what you gonna do about me?' The penultimate number, 'Elton's Song', with lyrics by Tom Robinson, described a homoerotic teenage crush but was set against a wholly unmemorable tune. The paucity of killer melodies on the album was an obvious weakness, as it would prove to be on almost all of Elton's records of the period.

'Nobody Wins' must rank as one of Elton's most musically innovative songs yet – significantly – it was not an original Elton melody. In France in the summer of 1980, Elton had heard a song, 'J'Veux d'la Tendresse' by Janic Prévost and had fallen in love with it. In Gary Osborne, a man who as a teenager had made a living out of translating foreign language songs into English, he had the ideal partner to translate the French lyric written by Jean-Paul Dreau. Osborne didn't disappoint. He took the spirit of the original, but gave it a very personal twist and in doing so produced unarguably one of the finest sets of lyrics for any

Elton John song: 'And it's the innocent who pay/ When broken dreams get in the way/ The game begins/ The game nobody wins.' Osborne had turned the song into an emotionally supercharged description of the psychological damage inflicted on the young Elton by his parents' disintegrating marriage.

'Of all the songs we worked on together, I like "Nobody Wins" best,' says Osborne. 'I thought I knew a bit about Elton's mum and dad and their relationship. I wondered about what it must have been like for Elton, listening to his parents fighting, believing that his father didn't love him.'

Elton was so troubled throughout 1981 that he simply could not summon the enthusiasm or willpower to fight for a single that failed to zoom into the Top 40 on its first week of release. It was if he had taken umbrage at the fact that his singles were no longer instant chart smashes, as if it was beneath him to actually get out and promote it. This was in stark contrast to the man who had spent the first ten years of his career promoting his music with gusto on every record station and in every town he could get to.

'This was around the time when Elton had something like a nervous breakdown,' reflects Osborne. 'The single came out and started slowly, but that wasn't a disaster because, in those days, many big hits took a few weeks to get into the Top 40. In those days, one of the things that was guaranteed to get a record into and up the charts was a *Top Of The Pops* appearance. Elton said, "I won't do it unless it goes into the Top 40." It went to 43. Now, if he'd appeared on *Top Of The Pops* that week, the single would at the very least have got to the mid-30s the next week and the record stations that were playing it would have kept playing it. But he refused to do it.

'I ended up going round and playing poker with him on the night when he should have been doing *Top Of The Pops*. At one point in the evening, he had a very good hand and I had a fucking fantastic hand. He said, "I'll bet you that car." I said, "Well, what can I put up against a car?" "You told me you had a new fridge? I'll bet you this car against your fridge." We used to do this quite often. One night I won five Bentleys off him, but I bet five Bentleys against his driver so I could have the driver *and* the Bentleys, and then I lost them all back, and that was how we would play. He would win my fridge or my telly and then he would lose it back to me.

'So I won the car but I thought no more of it, because I thought he would win it back. Anyway, I was just leaving, about four in the morning, and he stuck a cheque in my hand for about two-and-a-half grand. I said, "What's this for?" and he said, "The car." I said, "Oh come on, I'll lose it back to you." And he said, "No, no, fair do's, here's the cheque for the car." I said, "Do you know what? I'm going to take it, because you shouldn't have been playing cards with me tonight, you should have been promoting the single, and then I would have made a lot more than two-and-a-half grand." The car is still in my garage.'

Although Elton had decided to take 1981 off touring, he made an exception for a gig that was unarguably one of the most nerve-racking of his career. 'It was for Prince Andrew's 21st birthday at Windsor Castle,' recalls Clive Franks. 'I've never seen him more scared in his whole career, because he was playing for the entire Royal Family and their guests.'

The concert took place that June, just a matter of weeks before the wedding of Prince Charles and Lady Diana Spencer. 'I had to go to Moss Bros to rent a bloody penguin outfit,' says Clive Franks who, once again, was responsible for Elton's live sound. 'Halfway through the show, I felt someone standing next to me and it was Princess Margaret in her tiara and jewels. She said, "You don't mind if I stand here, do you? I'm dying for a fag!" After Elton's performance, there was a party. 'I will never forget it,' marvels Franks. 'There was the Queen, in the disco, dressed in a peach-coloured dress with a glittering tiara, and covered in diamonds. She had this little handbag on her arm which was swinging around as she danced with this 90-year-old count.' Reportedly, Elton would go on to dance with Princess Anne to 'Hound Dog' and with the Queen to 'Rock Around The Clock'.

By now, Elton had signed to Geffen Records in the US, a label founded in 1980 by the entrepreneur and philanthropist David Geffen. Elton was, along with John Lennon, one the label's first signings. John

Reid had attempted to get Elton re-signed to MCA, only to storm out of a meeting with the MCA board when his demand for $25 million for five albums for North America alone was rejected. According to Philip Norman, Reid flew into a rage when negotiations stalled, called the board 'assholes' and attempted to rip one of Elton's gold discs off the wall, shouting: 'I made this fucking company, they can stick their fucking records.'

One of Geffen's early successes, albeit in tragic circumstances, was the John and Yoko *Double Fantasy* album. New York, the very city in which Lennon had felt so comfortable, the city that treated rock stars with respect and largely left them in peace, was still very much an American city and part of a culture that allowed anyone, regardless of his mental state, to roam the streets with firearms. The murder of John Lennon on December 8, 1980 sent shockwaves round the world. Within the entertainment business, nothing would ever be the same again for high-profile rock stars. What had happened to Lennon could also happen to Bowie, Elton, McCartney or any of the other major rock stars with a super-fanatical following.

Bernie and Elton had been quite close to Lennon in the mid-1970s. Having signed to Geffen, Elton had even voiced his ambition to record with his new stable-mate. This never came to fruition, and Lennon's death hit both Elton and Bernie hard. In the public imagination, Taupin is perhaps best known for his tribute to Marilyn Monroe, 'Candle In The Wind', yet his tribute to Lennon, 'Empty Garden (Hey Hey Johnny)' is vastly superior. Taupin wrote it the day after the tragic news broke: 'What happened here?' the song opened. 'As the New York sunset disappeared/ I found an empty garden among the flagstones there'. He depicted Lennon as the caring, nurturing gardener who 'grew a good crop' but now nothing grows, his music and talent having been razed to the ground. 'It's funny how one insect can damage so much grain', wrote Taupin, in an obvious reference to Mark Chapman. 'A gardener like that one no one can replace'. In the heartrending chorus, the demise of Lennon was equated with the loss of childhood friendship. His friends were calling for him but, suddenly, there was no one there to answer the door: 'Oh, and I've been calling, oh hey, hey Johnny/ Can't you come out to play?' Taken together with Elton's beautiful music, the song must surely rank amongst the partnership's best-ever work. It is without doubt one of the best tribute songs ever penned.

'Empty Garden' was to be the first US single from the 1982 album *Jump Up!* In the UK, that honour went to 'Blue Eyes', another Gary Osborne collaboration and a song with a complicated birth. On first inspection, the melody given to Gary seemed to lack promise. 'Blue Eyes' was one of five tunes Elton had written in just one morning's work at home in Woodside. He then flew to Montserrat to cut the backing tracks, leaving Gary in the UK to finish the lyrics, which he would then telex over to Elton. Thinking that 'Blue Eyes' was the runt of the litter, Gary attended to some of the more promising songs first, only to receive in the post a cassette with the backing track for the song completed and urgent instructions to complete the lyric. 'It was the quickest lyric I ever wrote. I did it that afternoon; it's only two verses,' he recalls. An exceptionally slowly paced song, its simple, warm melody needed some suitably romantic words, and Osborne, again in an attempt to see the world through Elton's eyes, wrote a love song to Elton's new partner.

'Elton was seeing a lovely guy called Vance, who tragically later died of AIDS,' he explains. 'He was a humungous fan of Bowie, which was always a big bone of contention between them! Vance had blue eyes. Elton had five goes at recording [the song]. The first time he sounded like Dean Martin and I didn't like it because I thought it sounded corny. Then he did a version that sounded like Sinatra. Then he did a version that sounded like Elvis. Then he did a version that sounded like Elton John and finally he did a version that sounded like a combination of all of those singers, and that's the version we've got.' The single would be the biggest hit off the album, reaching Number 8 in the UK and Number 12 in the US, the first single to be Top 20 hit on both sides of the Atlantic since 'Sorry Seems To Be The Hardest Word' six years earlier.

Jump Up! was the first Elton John album to be recorded at Air Studios in Montserrat. 'The reason we ended up doing that album in Montserrat,' says Gary Osborne, 'was that when Elton was having that breakdown, when he wouldn't come out the flat, I said, "Well, I'm going on holiday." He said, "Can I come with you?" I took him to Antigua and he fell in love with the place, and with the Caribbean in general. George Martin's studio was on the next island, so he went and had a look at it and decided to record there.'

Jump Up! included 'Ball And Chain', which featured Pete Townshend playing 12-string guitar, and the topical 'Princess'. 'Elton was very enamoured of Princess Di,' says Osborne. 'It was around the time of the royal wedding, so I wrote this light-hearted love song which was supposed to be Charles singing to Di.' Another strong cut was 'Legal Boys', Elton's first collaboration with one of the world's most successful lyricists, Tim Rice. 'It was originally written for something I was going to do with Andrew [Lloyd Webber] for *Tell Me On A Sunday*,' says Sir Tim, 'but then Andrew decided to do it with the lyricist Don Black and the singer Marti Webb. I was left with this lyric and I knew that Elton liked lyrics first, so I sent it to him. To my amazement, he did it.' The song was a sad story of a divorce, with legal language inserted into a salutary tale of what happens when love lost turns into financial gain for the legal profession: 'It says something for the legal boys/ But nothing much for us/ That all we had together/ Is so quickly ended thus.'

The album received some favourable reviews. *Creem* said, 'If you ever listened to him and stopped, *Jump Up!* gives you the reason to start all over again. Maybe the fact that he's not everywhere on the air any more is what makes *Jump Up!* such a great surprise. Then again, it may be that ol' Four Eyes has here put together the best pop *album* of his career.' Elton even supported the album with a major world tour, his first in two years, ending with a 16-night pre-Christmas residency at London's Hammersmith Odeon. For the first time since 1977, Davey Johnstone was back playing in the live band. Yet Elton himself cut a faintly ridiculous figure on stage. His new costume, described by the singer as his 'Ruritanian general's outfit', consisted of breeches, a tunic with epaulettes, a sash and a silly military hat.

On the opening Hammersmith night, Elton was informed only

minutes before he was due to go onstage that Nigel Olsson had been taken ill with flu. His black mood darkened still further during the course of the show, when he kicked his piano stool away with such force during 'Bennie And The Jets' that the low-flying object hit a 24-year-old fan, Seana Connolly, causing some bruising on her cheek and right arm. Elton was fulsome in his apologies, meeting Ms Connolly backstage and presenting her with a bottle of champagne and a leather jacket. He also offered to pay for a new dress.

John Hall of Rocket Records told Philip Norman how the PR initiative didn't exactly go according to plan: 'Someone from the office took this girl out and she bought the world's most expensive dress. That night, we were having a big end-of-tour party at Xenon and I had also invited her along to that. We sent a limo for her, and, of course, she turned up in the dress Elton had bought her. It had a cutaway at the top of the arm, which highlighted the bruise the piano stool had given her. After all the trouble we had gone to, to keep the thing quiet, there she was parading round Xenon showing her bruise off to everyone.'

The final, Christmas Eve, show would go out live as part of the *Old Grey Whistle Test*'s annual festive concert. The contrast between the Elton of 1982 – sweaty, overweight, in a ridiculous stage outfit and seemingly going through the motions – and the Elton who had wowed the same venue eight years earlier when he was at the peak of his career was all too obvious. Lurching from one doomed relationship to the next, offstage Elton seemed to be in an emotional freefall. What he needed was stability. He was to find it where he and those around him least expected it – in a relationship with a woman.

273

CHAPTER 12

I WANNA KISS THE BRIDE

'Don't you know I'm still standing better than I ever did
Looking like a true survivor, feeling like a little kid.'

'I'm Still Standing'; lyrics: Bernie Taupin; music: Elton John

'You may still be standing but we're all on the fucking floor!'

A 'congratulatory' telegram from Rod Stewart's manager, Billy Gaff, on
the occasion of Elton's marriage to Renate Blauel, February 14, 1984

Elton is not sober but he is just about still standing. It has been a
very long day. He's been up since 4am working on a video for his
new single. 'I'm Still Standing', with its career-encapsulating title
and lyric and bouncy sing-along chorus, has well and truly announced
The Elton John Comeback. Uncharacteristically, the video, produced
by the Australian Russell Mulcahy, has required Elton to perform a first:
to dance, convincingly, in a tightly choreographed routine along with a
suitably grandiose collection of beauties, both male and female.

Filmed mainly on the promenade outside the Carlton Hotel in
Cannes, Elton has strutted his stuff in two complementary outfits
– one blue-grey, the other a more James Bond-like all-white affair with
black dicky-bow – both topped off with a boater, hat and cane. One
shot shows Elton touching the bum of one of the female dancers, while
elsewhere he is surrounded by his whirl of courtier dancers. Elton's
Chaplin-esque poses reinforce the mood of slightly forced jollity. In
another sequence, a child actor plays the rock star, sitting in Elton's own

12-cylinder Jaguar, later sold at auction for $90,000. But it will all look good. This will be Elton's first 'proper' video.

Toward the end of a very long day, Elton decides he needs a pick-me-up. Joining some of the members of Duran Duran, he drinks eight vodka martinis in about half an hour. He doesn't remember much else.

*   *   *

The video-maker Marcello Anciano, who often worked with Russell Mulcahy, remembers the day of devastation. 'When we got there, Simon [le Bon] went off with Elton for a chat and got him absolutely pissed. This was when Elton was a complete fiend. The next time I saw Russell, he asked, "What the fuck did you do to Elton?" Apparently, Elton had come back from the bar and then proceeded to do these elaborate stripteases in front of the camera, rolling around on the floor naked then running off, changing into the most outlandish costumes, coming back and doing another extraordinary striptease. All the time he was demanding that the camera continued to run – and it was all Simon's fault.'

'I can't really remember the rest of the video,' admitted Elton, reflecting on his session with Simon Le Bon, during which he recalls downing six martinis, not the eight found in other accounts of the carnage. 'I woke up the next morning and I had all these cuts and bruises all over me. I had destroyed one of the rooms and completely blacked out. Thank you, Duran Duran.' At one stage a fight broke out between Elton and John Reid which resulted in Elton sitting on top of his manager and former partner, punching him and breaking his nose. Was this new making videos lark really such a good idea?

Elton was never the best of companions once he had been drinking. His sunshine-and-showers temperament invariably made him an unpredictable work colleague. Back in 1976, when rehearsing for a tour, he had apparently flown into such a rage that he physically lifted his piano and tried to overturn it. The man was no shrinking violet. The fact that

John Reid stayed with Elton, despite having an impromptu free nose job, says a lot for his commitment to the cause.

In terms of pop videos, Elton came late to the party and left early. Other established acts had begun making lavish promos well before him and, his enthusiasm for video never that great, he soon grew to loathe them and, when he appeared in them at all, only do so grudgingly. Elton's videos tended to be workmanlike rather than inspired, with 'I'm Still Standing' probably the best of the dozens he went on to make.

Mulcahy was a safe choice to work with in the early 1980s, having already filled up his CV with several groundbreaking promos. In fact, the first video aired on MTV was the Mulcahy-produced UK Number 1 by Buggles, 'Video Killed The Radio Star'. By 1983, he had worked on a trio of videos for Duran Duran for their *Rio* album, as well as the similarly grandiose 'Vienna' for Ultravox. He would also give Elton a contemporary look on video. It was all part of the re-branding of Elton John and his music.

'I'm Still Standing' had the potential to be a career-defining song for Elton. It appeared to declare war on the critics who wrote him off but it was, perhaps more accurately, a warning shot across the bows to Geffen Records. 'At that point, I was struggling with my American record company, and it was kind of defiant,' he has reflected. Plus, of course, Elton hadn't really been away. In the past five years, he had scored several big hit singles in the States and, although his record sales had been nowhere near as strong as in his mid-1970s prime, they were hardly the disaster that many have since thought.

The 1983 album *Too Low For Zero* was a strong and consistent collection of songs and arrived at a time when the public and media seemed more excited than they had been for several years by an Elton release. Yet the biggest improvement seemed to come from Elton himself. For the first time in years, he sounded committed as both vocalist and performer and the album contained at least five great self-penned melodies that could bear comparison to his very best work.

The album had obviously benefited by having a settled team. In all essentials save the producer, it was a reconstruction of the much-loved Elton line-up of the 1970s. Davey Johnstone was back on lead guitar after a strained period in his relationship with Elton, who had also retained the old rhythm section of Dee Murray and Nigel Olsson from the recent tour. James Newton Howard, Kiki Dee and Ray Cooper featured, as did the harpist Skaila Kanga, absent since the early 1970s. As a result, the album was a restatement of the classic Elton sound, with a few contemporary production flourishes thrown in by Chris Thomas. However, the biggest news was that Bernie Taupin was back as the sole lyricist.

Gary Osborne remembers the full restoration of Elton's former sole writing partner very vividly: 'What happened was that *The Fox* had been disappointing sales-wise and, although *Jump Up!* did quite well, Geffen Records wanted the old team back. At the time, Elton had something against Davey and I was in an awkward position because I kept on at Elton telling him he should get Davey back. What I didn't realise was that the minute that Davey was asked back, suddenly it was the old band, and Geffen said, "Well, let's go all the way and have Bernie, and it will be like the old team."

'Remember, we were just coming off a worldwide hit in "Blue Eyes" and I was not expecting to be dumped. I learnt from reading it in the papers. Elton did an interview with Robert Hilburn in the *LA Times* and somebody in LA sent it to me. I was pretty gutted. Later Elton said to me, "I just fancied it doing the other way again, Bernie writing the lyrics and me then doing the tunes. I'm getting a lot of pressure from Geffen and from John to just go back to the old team," Elton told me. I said, "I quite understand. It's all been a bonus for me but it's your prerogative. Of course, I'm hurt but I'm a big boy and I've done quite nicely!" There was no doubt that by this time, it was more convenient for John Reid not to have me to deal with too. I was the man who had got Elton back in the recording studio after his retirement, so, for a while, I was a hero and a blue-eyed boy to him, because of course then Elton had to start touring again, so the money was coming back in. But by 1983, I had outgrown my usefulness.'

For Bernie Taupin, the decision was a logical one. 'I told Elton, "We've got to collaborate totally, or it's never going to be any good,"' he told Philip Norman. 'To me, our songs had always worked in total, with a feeling of continuity between them. I didn't want to keep on doing odd or obscure tracks on albums of other people's work. We had to try to get back to that complete closeness and understanding we had when we started out.' 'It was a healthy time apart,' Elton has said. 'If we hadn't had that break, we might never have survived.'

Osborne, however, would be kept hanging around by Elton, semi-detached from the star, still signed to his publishing company, but with little prospect of working with him on a regular basis again. Elton then tried to cushion the blow of departure for Osborne, but it only served to make things worse, says the lyricist: 'Elton said, "Give me some lyrics and I'll see if I can do them that way [rather than writing the music first]. I just don't want to write tunes at the moment. I want to do it the other way." I don't do it that way very well. It's not my thing. I knew that Elton was just being kind, but it was incredibly unkind, because I then spent six months writing lyrics that I knew weren't going to be used. Remember, I was signed to his publishing company and still getting advances. I wrote a sheaf of lyrics and I gave them to Bob Halley, his PA. Some years later, I asked Bob if Elton had ever looked at them. He said, "No." Still, if that is the worst thing Elton John ever did to me – and it probably is – it's not bad, is it? I am standing in a house bought by 'Blue Eyes' and I'm looking at the sea. I'm a lucky fucker.'

The year of 1983 was to see a comeback of sorts for Elton John. That same year saw other major 1970s stars re-establish themselves in the public imagination. Rod Stewart scored a Number 1 with 'Baby Jane', his first in the UK for five years. David Bowie's *Let's Dance* album and Michael Jackson's *Thriller* became their biggest-selling albums ever. By the end of the year, even Slade were fighting for the Christmas UK Number 1 with their single 'My Oh My'. And Elton joined the party with an album that reminded his core support just enough of former glories and contained just enough classy songs to satisfy expectations.

Along with 'I'm Still Standing', the other major single on *Too Low For Zero* was 'I Guess That's Why They Call It The Blues', a transatlantic Top 5 single featuring a harmonica solo by Stevie Wonder. Elton did his piece, apparently, in a single take. He has always heaped praise upon the song, pointing out its versatility. Live, it can be played in different tempos and styles and it's a number he never tires of singing. 'Kiss The Bride', however, was more likely to appeal to those hankering after a taste of the classic *Goodbye Yellow Brick Road* era. 'Crystal', however, was named after the nickname of Elton's then partner, Gary Clarke. Elton and Gary were together before he married Renate. He was generally considered to be much too young for Elton. According to his biography, they met in December 1980. He was a 'nondescript kid who had dropped out of high school' at the time and worked as a clerk in the State Law Department in Melbourne.

The album sent out a confused message that reflected the mid-1980s Elton's real life. On the title track, with its intriguingly spartan arrangement and effective use of electronics, he appeared to be branching out into a much more leftfield style (sadly, a line of musical inquiry he would soon drop). Yet the strongest song was the simplest, 'Cold As Christmas (In the Middle Of The Year)', with a lovely piano melody from Elton and Bernie's sad tale of the end of a relationship and 'a love burned out by silence/In a marriage minus heart'. Bernie's lyrics were now discussing adult themes: love, relationships, divorce, death. Gone were the spectacular flights of fantasy of his early work. Now aged 33 years and married again, to Toni Lynn Russo, Bernie seemed self-consciously to want to deal with affairs of the heart.

Flushed with success, Elton adopted the old 'if it's not broken' adage and began work on the follow-up record using almost exactly the same personnel. Recording, which began at the end of 1983, was done, as with *Too Low For Zero*, at Air Studios in Montserrat. During the recording, it became obvious that Elton had struck up a friendship with the album's engineer, Renate Blauel.

Renate, in her late twenties and hailing from a suburb of Munich, had worked with Elton as a tape operator when he was finishing off some vocal overdubs for *Too Low For Zero* at Air Studios in London. For his next project, Elton insisted that Renate was part of the team from the beginning. Her usual uniform for studio work was T-shirt and jeans, and she was good at her job and popular. With a good command of English, she was a friendly but reserved young woman. A brunette with a cheeky dimpled smile, she was a sympathetic character and Elton soon fell for her.

Nobody, however, could quite comprehend what happened next. On tour in Australia one night, in the early hours of the morning, Clive Franks was woken up by a phone call. It was Elton: 'Sid!' went the over-excited voice on the other end. 'It's Sid! We are having a party downstairs in the hotel bar! Sid, I'm getting married!' 'I just went, "Yeah, right, OK, very funny,"' remembers Clive Franks. 'And Elton said, "No, honestly, I'm getting married!" I said, "Who are you getting married to?" He replied, "'Renate." And I said, "Yeah, right, I'll come down to the bar, and you'll all laugh and I'll have made a fool of myself. I don't believe a word of it." I stayed in bed, fell asleep and totally forgot about it. The next morning under my door was the daily newspaper and on the front page the headline was "Elton John To Wed". I thought, Jesus Christ! That was for real last night! I couldn't believe it because Elton… is gay.'

Elton and Renate were married on Valentine's Day 1984 at St Mark's Church in Darling Point, Sydney. His former lover John Reid was the best man. The £100,000 reception was held at the Sebel Town House Hotel, where the touring party was based. The response from Elton's friends and colleagues was a mixture of incredulity and affection. Elton, in grey morning suit and top hat, smiled to the camera, just a hint of the knowing fraud in the glint of his eyes and a you're-as-surprised-as-me semi-smile playing around his lips. One onlooker was heard to call out, 'Good on you, sport, you old poof! You finally made it!' 'It just goes to show how wrong you all were,' came Elton's retort. 'All credit to Chris Thomas, who was my producer at the time,'

Elton was to acknowledge two years later. 'He was very encouraging and helpful. I am glad I got married in Australia because it meant that the British press couldn't get over there. And I have a love affair with Australia, anyway.'

Elton seemed to have had two very powerful reasons to get married. The first was that he genuinely loved Renate and Renate loved him. The second was that he wanted children and, in Renate, he obviously thought he had found a loving, caring partner and future mum. He was not, of course, the first major rock star to 'in' himself. Tom Robinson, his former collaborator, would make the same move. David Bowie, in 1983, had even gone as far as telling *Rolling Stone* that his admission of bisexuality all those years earlier had been the biggest mistake he had ever made. Cultural commentators have posited that the move from gay to straight was merely a reflection of the times. With Aids becoming an issue and a new Puritanism sweeping through the baby-boomers of the Reagan and Thatcher era, it was no surprise that some major figures, eager to retain their popularity, were appearing in the media to correct their more unorthodox pasts.

'Renate was a sweetheart,' says Charlie Morgan, Elton's drummer. 'But I think what was happening was that Elton was losing popularity, particularly in the Deep South. I think he persuaded himself that he wasn't gay and that he was bi, and therefore he could have a hetero-sexual marriage. I also think they had a genuine friendship.'

Renate Blauel was, Elton thought, the companion who would fill the colossal emotional black hole in his life. 'I got married because I didn't confront the real problem in my life, that I was a drug addict,' he was to admit years later. 'I thought getting married would change all the unhappiness the drug addiction brought me. I got married to a wonderful woman who loved me very much. I loved her but not, obvi-ously, in the physical sense. I thought it would change. I thought, "This will change it. I'll now become happy." But the problem was that when I got married I still stuck cocaine up my nose and I still drank a bottle of Scotch a day. Nothing changed.'

A psychologically damaged drug addict and alcoholic, Elton John was arguably unable to feel much at all. He craved love and he craved acceptance, but was unable to respond to either when offered them. 'It was easy for me to get recognition in front of 20,000 people. I loved it,' he admitted ten years later. 'But then I used to come home and I was left with me again and that wasn't enough.'

It seemed heterosexuality was catching. John Reid would also get engaged in the mid-1980s. His betrothed was Sarah Forbes, the daughter of Bryan Forbes and Nanette Newman. He was 35; she was 18. 'It wouldn't have been fair [to marry her],' Reid admitted to a journalist in 2001. 'I knew I was gay, she knew I was gay, she thought I could change, I knew I couldn't. She's still my best friend.'

If *Too Low For Zero* rekindled interest in Elton John, its follow-up *Breaking Hearts* was flat. Although a sizeable seller at the time, it was a grave disappointment. With its chugging rockers, unmemorable ballads and modish production, it now sounds terribly dated in a way that Elton's 1970s records don't. Cliché and pastiche ruled, not just in the music, but in the lyrics too. The man who had brought us the tender yet clever sentiment of ballads such as 'Your Song', now sounded world-weary and out of new ideas. 'I was always in the thick of things/ I always had the heart of every woman on a string', he moaned in the flaccid title track.

There was little here that was clever or unexpected in Bernie's messages, little that hundreds of other lyricists weren't writing at the same time. His view of the opposite sex on 'Slow Down Georgie (She's Poison)' – 'She's just another divorcée/ An undercover lover of a hundred/ Other little fish in the sea' – was just another addition to the ever-growing canon of pop songs of the 'She done me wrong' variety. Interestingly, in what was perhaps an unintentional, but no less significant switch given Elton's re-branding in the mid 1980s as a married man, there was a high proportion of boy-girl scenarios on *Breaking Hearts*.

Perhaps the most puzzling song was 'Passengers', a sizeable UK hit. The lyrics appeared to express some admirable sentiments concerning the need for racial equality and an ending to apartheid. However, this sentiment did not rest so easily with the fact that, in defiance of a UN-sanctioned cultural boycott of South Africa, Elton had played four gigs with Rod Stewart at the Sun City Super Bowl in July 1983.

The biggest event in Elton's social calendar for 1984 came on May 19 when his beloved Watford FC reached the FA Cup Final. Under Graham Taylor, the team had made an astonishing ascent through the divisions. In the 1982/83 season, they found themselves in the top flight, the old First Division, finishing runners-up to the champions, Liverpool, that season. This high placing meant qualification for the UEFA Cup. A season on from that, they were at Wembley to face a resurgent Everton team under Howard Kendall. Watford were the out-and-out underdogs and, unsurprisingly, succumbed to goals by Graeme Sharp and Andy Gray, one either side of half time. Elton shed a tear at the final whistle and referred to it as 'the biggest day of my life'. In 1986, he revealed that he had invested £2.5 million of his own money in the club.

Elton returned to Wembley Stadium a year later, not as a spectator but as a performer in the Live Aid charity concert on July 13, 1985. Such an array of talent been never before been assembled on one bill. Along with Elton were other undisputed greats including the Who, David Bowie, U2 and Paul McCartney. Queen stole the media headlines with their populist pandering, but the real emotional core of Live Aid was a film of dying children in Africa, introduced by Bowie and set against the soundtrack of the Cars' recent hit, 'Drive'. The images, relayed on huge screens to an emotional crowd at Wembley and around the world into millions of homes, were a graphic a reminder of what the world had come to.

The 1985 Live Aid concert was supposed to be a wake-up call for society. Despite the sentiment, the emotion, and the significance of the day, very few made good on the promise of that day as clearly as Elton. Of course, as a multi-millionaire superstar, he was in a position to give huge sums of money to various charitable causes. But, in his humanitarianism both before and after Live Aid, he was one rock superstar who didn't need reminding of his responsibilities.

'There was a wonderful feeling of good will that day,' says Mike Appleton, who for so long had been the producer of *Old Grey Whistle Test* and who was in charge of the production of Live Aid. 'It was an amazing thing to do. Nobody had mobile phones, nobody had faxes; everything was done by telex and on the phone. Everybody performed well on the day, apart from Bob Dylan, who was a shambles. Queen made a huge impact. The doctors had told Freddie Mercury not to go on stage because he was ill and had a throat problem, but he went against his doctor's orders and performed.'

Elton took the stage at dusk, opening his 20-minute set with 'Bennie And The Jets'. As he sang 'The spotlight's hitting something/ That's been known to change the weather', he pointed to the skies. The day had been warm and sunny and the thousands of people pressed at the front of the crowd near the stage had been regularly hosed down throughout the day. As he uttered these lines, there was a short downpour. Kiki Dee duetted with him on 'Don't Go Breaking My Heart'. His other guests were George Michael and Andrew Ridgeley from Wham! In a moment of unintentional humour, Elton introduced Michael but initially forgot to introduce Ridgeley, who had marched onstage alongside him.

'I remember I wasn't the slightest bit nervous until the moment when Billy Connolly, who came on to introduce Elton, said, "I have just heard that 75 per cent of the world's TV sets are tuned in to us this moment,"' recalls the drummer Charlie Morgan. 'My heart leapt into my mouth and I couldn't find any saliva. I walked to the stage thinking, "Oh shit!" Then my onstage monitors didn't work so I couldn't hear Elton and he couldn't hear me. All I could do for the first two songs was to watch him and follow the tapping of his foot in time to the beat.'

Live Aid was indisputably a brilliant day despite various technical hitches. Everyone remembers the performance towards the end of the event when Paul McCartney sang 'Let It Be', the first two-thirds of which was inaudible. A despairing Clive Franks was the man behind the console desperately trying to fix the situation. 'I was asked to mix Paul

McCartney because Paul was playing Elton's piano,' said Clive. 'His people were really nervous about it and kept calling me before the day, but I assured them that everything would be OK. But unknown to us a technician backstage had unplugged two of the three piano mics and the vocal mic – a total disaster!'

By the time of Live Aid, Elton had performed yet another of his regular musical spring cleanings. For his new album, to be titled *Ice On Fire*, he had hired an array of top session musicians. Recording began in the spring of 1985. Olsson and Murray were out again. 'Elton abandoned his old rhythm section and I think there was a lot of politics going on,' is how Charlie Morgan puts it. 'I heard that Nigel suddenly decided that he wanted equal treatment to Elton, so he got the elbow. I think he kind of got a little bit above his station as a musician.' 'We were called by someone,' Olsson said in 1999. 'I wish Elton had made the call himself. It would have been much easier. The reason why he let us go, as far as I read in the press, was that he wanted to change musical direction. And I don't think he's quite got that together yet. Still the records sound like me and Dee playing in the background.'

Tragically, having contracted skin cancer, Dee Murray would die of a stroke in January 1992, aged just 45. 'We were very close and living in Nashville,' said Nigel Olsson. 'A few weeks before Dee died, I visited him. One of the last things he said to me was, "Nige, I wish we'd been told what the hell we did to be fired. We never got the right story." That really saddens me and there's really not a day that goes by I don't think about Dee.'

David Paton, by the mid-1980s a top session bassist but formerly the voice of the 1970s pop group Pilot, who enjoyed hits with 'Magic' and 'January', joined some of the sessions for the new record. Recording again took place at Gus Dudgeon's Sol Studios at the Mill in Cookham, with Dudgeon back as producer after a gap of nine years. On the first day of the sessions, Paton and drummer Dave Mattacks recorded 'Nikita', a song that also featured Nik Kershaw on guitar.

'Gus Dudgeon was very friendly and very good at putting you at ease,' says Paton. 'He wasn't a musician as such, but he had a fantastic ear. I can see him now looking at me as I'm playing, full of smiles and encouragement. Elton was a workaholic. Sessions would normally start at 10am. Elton was there when I arrived and he would still be there at the piano when I left. He had more enthusiasm for his work than a man half his age.'

'I played on "This Town" and the duet with George Michael, "Wrap Her Up",' says Charlie Morgan. 'Elton introduced himself in his usual manner, shaking your hand and at the same time looking away. He has always been very shy. It's funny that he should be so flamboyant and yet so acutely shy when he meets people for the first time. There's this fleeting eye contact and then he looks at the ground and shuffles his feet!' 'I was invited to the playback of *Ice On Fire* and there were a lot of people around, including Queen, because Roger Taylor and John Deacon had played on the album too,' recalls David Paton. 'After "Nikita" came on, Elton jumped up and said, "I think the bass part on that is absolutely superb. A big hand for David Paton."'

'Nikita', released at the end of 1985, was a massive hit for Elton, his biggest in the UK since his heyday in the mid 1970s. The video again depicted a boy-girl scenario, this time Elton's love-that-can-never-be with a beautiful Russian guard, the addressee of the song. Elton played the free Westerner reaching out to the still-shackled eastern European in a toe-curling piece of trite sentimentality. The video's sexual politics were equally baffling, given that, in Russian, 'Nikita' is, of course, a man's name.

At the end of 1985, Elton could also be found lending vocals and piano to another chart hit, 'That's What Friends Are For', a charity single for the issue which dominated the mid-to-late 1980s – Aids and HIV. Featuring Dionne Warwick, Elton, Gladys Knight and Stevie Wonder and a quite ghastly melody, the record would barely make the UK Top 20, but would reach Number 1 on the Billboard charts. Like the year's earlier charity biggie, 'We Are The World', the execrable content of the record obviously proved something of a bar to the British public, despite the charitable intentions.

While 'Nikita' and the success of *Ice On Fire* continued Elton's mid-1980s commercial comeback, 1986 was to prove a disappointing year. It seemed as if Bernie was still stuck in an MOR rut and his lyrics didn't fire Elton's imagination sufficiently to tease out memorable melodies. Bizarrely, Bernie wasn't having this problem with his other, non-Elton songs. 'These Dreams' by Heart and 'We Built This City' by Starship, both co-written with Martin Page, were massive singles in the US.

Elton's 1986 album *Leather Jackets* was half of a twin musical disaster, the other being *Victim Of Love*. Both works totally lacked brio. 'Gus was going for broke and working 18 hours a day, seven days a week. That was a bit painful, and I didn't particularly like the album either,' says Stuart Epps. 'The idea was to record 25 tracks then select the best 10. There probably weren't ten great tracks, but then suddenly [people thought] every track was amazing.' In fact, not a single track was amazing, and a couple were utterly dire. In an album of multiple nadirs, 'Don't Trust That Woman' was the pits. A co-write between Cher and Elton, writing under the pseudonym of Lady Choc Ice, it possessed such charming lines as 'She's a real ball-buster, don't trust her' and 'You can rear-end her/ Oh it'll send her'.

Any creativity that might have existed in the lacklustre set of songs was sucked out by Dudgeon's over-fastidious production, a classic exercise in over-polishing a turd. *Leather Jackets* would be the last time Elton ever worked with Gus in the studio. The final track, 'I Fall Apart', just about summed it up. What all of Elton's albums of that period lacked was Elton himself. No longer such a distinctive or versatile singer, he also did nowhere near as much actual piano playing on the new records, something he admitted at the time. 'Sting said to me this morning,' Elton revealed to *Q* in 1986, 'that I should do more pieces with just piano.'

Leather Jackets was mainly recorded at Wisseloord Studios in Hilversum, Holland. Renate, although thanked in the sleeve notes, was not present at the sessions. 'Thanks to Lady Choc Ice for being such a source of inspiration,' wrote Lord Choc Ice. Yet by 1986, Elton and

Renate had become semi-detached. One of the many problems was that the marriage contained not two, but three partners: Renate, Elton and an ever-present line of cocaine.

'I always tried to do a good vocal through it all, but there are some records where I was not together at all,' Elton frankly admitted in 1997. '*Leather Jackets* comes to mind, with its biker cover. [It was] very butch but a total disaster. I was not a well budgie: I was married and it was just one bag of coke after another.' Gary Osborne, whose song 'Memory Of Love' would be their last collaboration, also remembers it as a difficult time. 'I had given up cocaine and Elton was still doing copious quantities. It's very difficult when you're trying not to do it, but it's there if you want it, a big bag of something which for the last five years you'd have been thrilled to see.'

'Gus Dudgeon dared to say to Elton that a couple of tracks were substandard,' recalls Charlie Morgan. 'It was right in the middle of his worst drug days. I remember we started work in the studios in Holland at 11am and worked through to 3am, and then the next day we'd do another ridiculous stint, from say noon until 4am. During a two-week period we actually lost a day somewhere. We were in a microcosm where nothing else seemed to exist. We got a lot done in a short period, but the majority of the material was not good. Elton's mood was up and down so much. On one occasion he walked out of the studio, got into his car and drove off to the hotel, then turned round and came back, all smiles and apologies.'

Unsurprisingly, *Leather Jackets* stiffed, reaching Number 24 in the UK and a humiliating Number 91 in the States. 'Heartache All Over The World', the first single, failed to reach the Top 40 on either side of the Atlantic, while the follow-up 'Slow Rivers', a mawkish ballad with Cliff Richard, didn't even make the American Top 100. In an interview with *Q* magazine, Elton finally admitted that the interview he had done a decade earlier with *Rolling Stone*, in which he came out as bisexual, was still causing him problems: 'It did me a lot of damage, and I'm still fighting to get that radio [play] back.' Perhaps the most worrying thing, in terms of the future of Elton John, was his vocal performance on the album. His voice sounded strained and coarse, his range diminished. Little did he know he had a serious problem.

Furthermore, 1986 was also the year when his former mentor, Dick James, died of a heart attack, a matter of weeks after one of the most painful events in Elton's life. Elton's people had decided to take James to court. In a writ that had taken John Reid a staggering nine years to compile, Elton's whole relationship with DJM was itemised and criticised. The days were long gone when Elton would claim, as he did back in 1971: 'Dick is a straight, right-down-the-middle Jewish publisher. To me, he has been like a father. If there's any problem, Dick will sort it out for me. If there is anything I need, Dick will sort it out. Dick's very, very aware of money but I'd rather have him on my side than anyone else, because Dick is honest.' Now the claim was that James had taken unfair financial advantage of Elton. In the court case at the High Court in London, Elton's defence council portrayed the star as an innocent, duped out of millions.

'I really didn't want to go to court,' Elton later told Q. 'It was unfortunate. It means a soured relationship between the James family and me, which I didn't have before. Before we went to court, I tried to have lunch with Dick. I tried to say, "Let's settle this." He wouldn't. I stood in that box and I didn't hate him at all. I didn't enjoy the experience very much and we got a very big financial settlement. It was a shame, because I did have a good relationship with Dick James and it spoiled it.'

The writ was served on DJM, This Record Company and Dick James personally, the latter a fact that deeply offended the mogul. Both Elton and Bernie seemed baffled by most of the proceedings, and it emerged that both had taken only the most cursory of interests in their finances over the years. On being presented with a spreadsheet containing his, Bernie's and DJM's earnings over the years, Elton replied, 'I can't comment on them, I'm not a chartered accountant.' Justice Nicholls' final verdict ordered the payment by DJM of substantial backdated royalties, but rejected allegations of fraud by James and his organisation. It also refused to order the return of copyright to Elton as the claim was too late.

Yet the verdict painted Dick James in a bad light: 'To have tied two young men at the beginning of their careers to a publishing agreement for six years on the terms in question represented an unacceptably hard bargain,' said Justice Nicholls. 'It was clear, on the facts, that the first defendant had assumed a dominating role over the plaintiffs and the 1967 publishing agreement was thus unfair. However, given the significant increase in the plaintiff's experience and commercial aware-ness at the time of conclusion of the 1970 agreement and the improved escalating royalty rates contained in it, that agreement was not an unfair transaction.'

According to Geoffrey Ellis, one of the trial witnesses, the outcome was a compromise. The fact that DJM were able to retain the copyright of Elton and Bernie's songs was the most significant aspect of Justice Nicholls' decision. 'A few years later, Stephen James was able to sell the company, complete with Elton John and Bernie Taupin copyrights [to PolyGram], for a sum vastly in excess of what it would have been worth without them,' notes Ellis.

In the mid-1980s, Elton John was almost ever-present on the live circuit. He warmed up for a late 1986 tour with a couple of high-profile celebrity guest slots in June of that year. In the first, the Prince's Trust's tenth anniversary birthday party at Wembley Arena, Elton joined Paul McCartney for three numbers, finishing with 'I Saw Her Standing There', the song he had played with John Lennon at Madison Square Garden all those years before. Later, in June, Elton appeared on stage at Wham!'s final gig at Wembley Stadium dressed, horrifically, as Ronald McDonald. Elton, along with Charlie Morgan, can also be found on Wham!'s final single, 'The Edge Of Heaven'. 'George [Michael] was a nice person but preoccupied and tense,' says Charlie Morgan. 'Elton used to say, "I wish he'd come out of the closet." We all knew he was gay and Elton was very concerned about him. "He's too scared of losing his fan base," Elton would say.'

Despite the booze, the drugs, and confused nature of his marriage to Renate, Elton was, on his day, still riotously good company, and generous to a fault. 'I remember once on tour in 1986, there was a knock on my hotel door and there was Elton,' says David Paton. 'Under his arm were several CD Walkmans, the very latest technology at the time. He said, "This one's for you," and threw one over to me.' Clive Franks also recalls being at the receiving end of an astonishing act of largesse earlier in his career: 'We were doing a UK tour in 1976 and I was watching TV with Davey Johnstone in his hotel room in Bristol. Elton stopped by and after a while he asked me if I could have any car in the world, what would it be? I said a Mercedes 350 SL and then he asked me what colour. I said silver, and with that he left the room. A few weeks later when the tour was over Elton called me at home and told me to come to his house in a taxi. When I arrived he took me out to his row of garages, opened up one of them and there was a brand-new silver 350 SL, which he said was a present for me. I was totally stunned! I sat in it shaking for about half an hour before I dared reverse it out of the garage and drive it home.'

The 'look' for the 1986 Elton tour derived from the album cover design concept for *Leather Jackets*. Rather obviously, the recording team was photographed in leather jackets. 'My God, we had fun doing this and yes, of course it was obvious and camp beyond belief, but again driven very much by EJ, who participated (as did all the band) with unsolicited enthusiasm,' says David Costa, again in charge of the album artwork. 'They all took to the clothes and the posturing with absolutely no direction from either [photographer] Gered Mankowitz or myself; they all just all fell into that bad-boy Brando thing.

'Then there was the day when the whole band, Gus Dudgeon, the associated sound crews and all the stylists and hangers-on were having lunch in the dining room at the studio. Elton was next door, playing at a grand piano while we all ate and laughed. I suddenly became aware of the hundreds of people – staff, technicians, secretaries, accountants, record company people, all of us – all sitting around and earning a living from this one funny, brilliant person sitting at a grand piano, doing what he naturally did, at the apex of a huge money-making pyramid.'

The *Tour de Force* tour (or 'Tour Divorce' as it became known, such was the high incidence of marital break-ups in the camp at the time) played the States that autumn, followed by a series of Australian dates leading up to Christmas. 'Billy Connolly saw us at the Universal Amphitheatre in LA,' remembers Charlie Morgan. 'He walked into the dressing room and said, "Christ, you look like the Beverley Hills chapter of the Hells Angels."' Billy, under the same management team as Elton, would be a regular visitor on tour. 'He never stopped doing his routine,' is how Charlie Morgan puts it. 'He was a super-nice guy and was so enthusiastic about life, this spiky-haired wild-eyed being.' 'If you had dinner with Billy Connolly, you couldn't eat for laughing,' confirms David Paton.

It was during the American leg of the tour that Elton began to have serious problems with his voice. After several dates were cancelled, early press reports claimed the singer simply had bad laryngitis. He was told to rest his voice wherever possible, and, although he regained it sufficiently to perform, during the day he had to play dumb. 'We were on tour in New York and I got a phone call from Renate saying, "Go up to Elton's apartment and bring your video camera," says David Paton. 'And there was Elton, dressed as Harpo Marx, with a blond wig, a long mac and one of those air hooters. He also had an Etch-a-Sketch pad and wrote on it, "I've lost my voice. I have to cancel three days at Madison Square Garden!" Then he wrote, "Follow me, keep your camera on." He was knocking on people's doors that were on the tour and pressing his horn. A lot of people didn't even recognise him. Later, he invited me up to his suite at the top of the hotel and Elton was there on the couch cuddling with Renate. I looked out the window and said, "Elton, you've got a fantastic view." He wrote "Follow me" and led me into an elevator that went straight from his rooms up on to the roof. We were looking out on the New York skyline and he was writing on his Etch-a-Sketch: "Chrysler Tower, Empire State Building, Twin Towers". It was just magical.'

After America, the Elton John band went on to Australia. If Elton's behaviour was unpredictable, John Reid also seemed also under incredible strain. 'I remember we landed at one airport and there was a lot of press on the tarmac waiting for Elton to get off the plane,' says Paton. 'John walked off the plane with a rolled-up newspaper and started hitting them all, telling them to get out of the way. Also, one day on the Australian tour, John had parked his car and gone into a shop and had come out to find a truck double-parked and blocking him in. He flew off the handle with the truck driver but he picked the wrong man because the driver followed him and thumped him. John ended up in hospital.'

The *Leather Jackets* tour was Elton's aesthetic meltdown. Having rehired his old costume designer, Bob Mackie, he was now at liberty to indulge in silly visual fantasies, the daftest of which must have been his Ali Baba outfit complete with turban. There was also a Tina Turner number and a crimson costume complete with an astonishing four-foot-high peacock-like display, all of which confirmed that Elton simply didn't care what anyone thought. The effect of the pantomime 'he's behind you' school of rock performance was to trivialise his music. It seemed that Elton had finally descended into complete and utter kitsch.

'He's got an entertainer mentality,' says writer Phil Sutcliffe. 'And he's set up a problem for himself on stage. If you're loaded with sequins and feather boas and you sit down to play "Candle In The Wind", there's a strange contradiction between the performer and the persona. I guess his audience, like Queen's audience, would appear to embrace that. But it seems to place emotion in the zone of kitsch and then treat the emotion seriously and that's a strange conundrum.'

Nowhere would this strange conundrum be more evident than when Elton performed with the Melbourne Symphony Orchestra. James Newton Howard, soon to become one of the most in-demand composers for films such as *The Fugitive*, *The Sixth Sense* and *Pirates*

Of The Caribbean, was given the task of adapting Paul Buckmaster's and his own arrangements for the 88-piece orchestra. The first half of the show would feature a conventional Elton rock performance while the second would revisit songs such as 'The Greatest Discovery' and 'Sixty Years On' backed by the full orchestra. Musically, it was a first for Elton and he was thrilled to be working with such a prestigious orchestra. A live album was planned and Gus Dudgeon was on hand to mix the orchestra for the live set and for an Australian Broadcasting Corporation (ABC) broadcast of the final night's concert.

Elton began his eight-night residency on December 1 but his voice kept disappearing. He would sing as hard as he could but, on occasions, it was if somebody had turned the volume control down. On December 9, he collapsed on stage in the middle of introducing the orchestra. Clearly something was badly wrong and Elton was persuaded to seek out specialist help. The diagnosis was not good. 'We were all at the bar at the Sebel Town House when he came back,' Dudgeon told Philip Norman. 'He said, "They think it might be throat cancer." It was a terrible moment. Elton just stood there in the crowded bar and burst into tears. John Reid shut the place down there and then. He went around turfing everyone out and saying, "I'm sorry, the bar's closed," like a little Scots bouncer.'

Elton's specialist recommended that he immediately cancel all the remaining shows but Elton soldiered on, despite a wobble on the afternoon before the planned live broadcast, where he threatened to pull the show. ABC filmed the final night, December 14, and Rocket Records released the second half of the show as a live album, *Live In Australia*. Back in wig and costume, Elton performed as a latter-day Mozart in front of 12,000 contented fans. Indeed, his version of 'Candle In The Wind' would become a major hit single, despite the raspy vocal. Looking ridiculous, he sang with earnestness and delivered the message with complete authority, yet the fact remained that this was closer to pantomime than it was to rock theatre.

If 1986 had been an artistic low, however, then 1987 was to prove

Elton John's personal *annus horribilis*. The star was now on a downward spiral of depression and addiction. It would take three more years of abuse before he could finally see a way out.

PART 3

FINDING ELTON JOHN
1987–2006

CHAPTER 13

MY FAREWELL LETTER TO COCAINE

'I didn't want to die angry and bitter and sad, and that's what I had become, physically ugly, spiritually ugly, a slob, a pig.'

Elton John, 1992

*'And every one of us has to face that day
Do you cross the bridge or do you fade away?'*

'The Bridge'; lyrics: Bernie Taupin; music: Elton John

It's early morning. Looking out of the window of his lavish suite at London's Inn On The Park, Elton John picks up the phone to complain. He is about to make the most ridiculous rock-star demand in the history of twentieth-century rock-star foibles. Elton wants to know if someone on reception can do something about the wind in nearby Hyde Park. So cosseted and cocooned has he become, so unreal his reality, that this request is made in all seriousness.

Elton has always been fussy. Over the years, his homes have borne witness to a fastidiousness bordering on obsessive tidiness. Each record bought has been filed and catalogued in alphabetical order. Elton would habitually breeze through a house, plumping a cushion here, rearranging a vase of flowers there. The fact that the wind was too loud that day was just one of those many minor irritations that, to Elton, assumed cosmic proportions. Since that fateful day, he has told the 'wind outside my window' anecdote many times, sometimes switching the location from London to LA, from where he apparently called his London office, some 6,000 miles away, to see if they could do something about the wind.

'It's funny to look back on, but I was coming down off cocaine,' he told Tony Parsons in 1995. 'I woke up in the morning and the wind was blowing – I blamed the hotel. On drugs, I was divine, lovely and fabulous. Coming down off drugs, I was a nightmare. I used to fly over anger and land in rage. My personality couldn't handle the cocaine comedown. But I still get those rages. When you finally stop taking drugs you are stuck with the personality you were when you started out.'

By the late 1980s, the star was consumed by self-loathing. 'I'm a compulsive/impulsive person,' he admitted. 'I can't have one drink and I can't have one drug and I can't have one pair of glasses or one car. That's my make-up.' Indeed, Elton was a man with multiple addictions. The cocaine was still ever-present. Possessing what he calls 'the constitution of an ox,' he would stay awake night after night, coked out, and then do a rehearsal for a tour. 'Towards the end of it [his cocaine use], I would do it on my own, behind closed doors,' he has said. 'I'd stay in for two weeks and I'd be doing a line every four minutes. By that time, it was closing me down. It was no longer fun; it was just the opposite. For the last four years I did it, I didn't enjoy it at all. It was pure habit.' 'Sometimes, when I fly over the Alps, I think, that's like all the cocaine I sniffed,' the sober Elton would acknowledge, many years later.

In among all the pain, there were some tragicomic moments. 'Dope just made me very silly,' Elton has reflected. 'I remember going to Barry Gibb's house and he went off to play tennis and someone handed a joint around. It was fucking lethal. On the wall there was a photo of the Bee Gees and one of the O'Jays. I was so stoned I couldn't tell the difference. Barry came back and I said to him, "That's fucking clever, that. Two groups in one. The Bee Gees and the O'Jays are the same group." I had to ring up the next day and apologise. That happened quite a lot.'

Along with the drugging went the drinking. Elton was not a pleasant drunk. 'Quite often Bernie would ring me up and say, "You were so disgusting last night. I'm ashamed to know you." And I wouldn't remember a fucking thing.' Around this time, he also became bulimic. He admitted to existing on a diet of rubbish: a tub of Häagen-Dazs vanilla ice-cream, three bacon sandwiches, and four pots of Sainsbury's cockles, which he would then throw up.

Part of the problem, as Elton recently pointed out, was that his massive drug and drink intake never made it onto the front pages of the scandal sheets. Not once, from 1975 to 1990, was it discussed in the media. Even his first major biographer, Philip Norman, was unaware of the extent of Elton's self-abuse, writing in the first edition of his biography, *Elton*: 'He was the first rock star to adopt a clean and wholesome as opposed to a frowsty and depraved, lifestyle, and to spend his leisure hours not lying comatose in unlit rooms but engaged in energetic outdoor sports.' The reality, however, was that Elton, as he himself would say, was 'not a well budgie'.

It would be in this parlous physical and mental state that Elton endured 1987. The year began, however, with some good news. The singer underwent surgery in Australia on his throat. Had the growths on his vocal chords been cancerous then Elton was facing the prospect of his larynx being removed and further treatment. Fortunately, the nodules were non-malignant and were cauterised using a laser technique. The British tabloids made much of the fact that his wife Renate was not by his bedside, but 8,000 miles away in the UK.

Then, just six weeks after the surgery, the convalescing Elton found himself the central figure in an exposé in the *Sun*. The editor Kelvin McKenzie was of the opinion that the *Sun* catered for the 'real' British working class and their attitudes. As a rock star living a bohemian lifestyle, Elton was seen as fair game. Of the typical *Sun* reader, McKenzie was reported as saying: 'He's the bloke you see in the pub, a right old fascist, wants to send the wogs back, buy his poxy council house, he's afraid of the unions, afraid of the Russians, hates the queers and the weirdoes and drug dealers.' In 1982, McKenzie had been responsible for the 'Gotcha!' headline the day after the sinking of the Argentine warship, the *General Belgrano*, during the Falklands War. He also gave us 'Freddie Starr Ate My Hamster' in 1986. In Elton John, he thought he'd found a decadent man with a lurid private life who could keep his paper ahead of the *Daily Mirror* in the ratings war.

The *Sun* falsely claimed that Stephen Hardy, a rent boy, had attended gay parties at the home of Rod Stewart's manager, Billy Gaff, and that Elton had been present at these parties. 'Elton In Vice Boys Scandal' ran the front page of February 25, 1987. Under the alias of Graham X, Hardy claimed to be the pimp who provided youngsters for the pleasure of Elton and Gaff. Elton was depicted as a cocaine-snorting pervert into bondage and kinky sex. As Philip Norman pointed out, the allegations were presented 'not as an exultant soft-porn feast but as a solemn moral duty, with Graham X, in the bosom of the *Sun*, reformed and penitent: 'I am ashamed of what I did… I am speaking out to show how widespread this sort of thing is and to warn other gullible young kids to steer clear of people like these.'

Over the next six months there followed a series of ever more lurid 'revelations'. In a historically significant move and against the advice of Mick Jagger, who warned him that he could be unleashing a damaging media circus, Elton decided to sue. 'You can call me a fat, balding, talentless old queen who can't sing, but you can't tell lies about me,' he said, summing up his honourable intent. Yet the attacks kept on coming and would do so, sporadically, for almost a year. On April 15 1987, the *Sun* ran the headline 'Elton Porn Photo Shame', backing it up unconvincingly with three photos, none of them incriminating and all of them obviously dating from a much earlier period in Elton's life. But the *Sun* tripped up when it pinned one of the nights of gay sex to an actual date – April 30, 1986 – and a venue – Billy Gaff's house. Elton was able to prove that he was, in fact, in New York at the time.

By autumn 1987, Elton had lodged no fewer than 17 libel suits. The *Sun*'s allegations had become increasingly bizarre, including the claim that Elton had silenced the barks of the pack of 'vicious Rottweiler dogs' that shared his country estate near old Windsor by means of an 'horrific operation' which involved removing their voice boxes. The fact that there were no such dogs on the estate did not deter the newspaper from making the claims.

Throughout 1987, Elton also watched his marriage crumble in the full glare of tabloid media exposure. The British tabloids had been hinting for a couple of years that his relationship with Renate was a sham. Renate was conspicuous by her absence from Elton's 40th birthday party, held at Lockwood House near Rickmansworth in Hertfordshire, and the day after the party, a statement from John Reid's office confirmed that the two had decided to 'continue living apart'. 'We're really good friends,' Elton told the chat show host Michael Parkinson in April 1987. 'The marriage isn't over *per se*. We've just separated for a little while.'

In the mid-1980s, Renate had been trying to keep her own career in the music business ticking over. Apart from her regular studio work, she had worked on demos at Elton's home studio at Woodside. 'Renate was quiet, but a very kind person and easy to get on with,' says David Paton, who recorded at Woodside with Renate as his engineer. 'She was very feminine, with her long red nail polish and perfume. She was very attractive.' In the spring of 1987, when the news broke that Elton and Renate had decided to separate, it became clear that the tabloids were also keen on trying to link Renate with the idea of a gay affair.

The move to attack Elton backfired on the *Sun*. Far from uniting the nation against him, it seemed to have the opposite effect. 'I think the *Sun* realised it had misjudged the public mood with regard to Elton,' says the journalist and friend Chris Charlesworth, 'and that regardless of whether or not it was true, its readers did not want to know that lovable Elton had been mixed up with rent boys. So, along with pinning one of the orgies to an actual date where Elton was out of the country, it was a double own goal for them. Served them right for their own stupid prurient hypocrisy.'

The other main rival in the tabloid circulation war, Robert Maxwell's *Daily Mirror*, got hold of Stephen Hardy and got the truth. On November 6, 1987, the paper ran 'My Sex Lies Over Elton', in which Hardy admitted the story was a complete fabrication: 'I made it all up. I only did it for the money and the *Sun* was easy to con. I've never even met Elton John.'

It took another year for the dispute to be resolved. At the end of 1988, Elton settled out of court for £1 million, plus costs, which he donated to charity. A front-page apology, 'Sorry, Elton', followed. Elton, for reasons known only to himself, dignified the paper with an exclusive interview and some let's-make-up-and-be-friendly free publicity: 'Life is too short to bear grudges and I don't bear the *Sun* any malice,' Elton was quoted as saying. The *Sun* replied with the shameless strap line, 'When The Stars Make Friends, They Make Friends With The *Sun*'.

For Elton, taking on the tabloid and winning, was a key moment in his life. 'There are things I've done in my life that I'm proud of and I'm proud of the way I fought the *Sun*,' he told Tony Parsons in 1995. 'It was a year-and-a-half of sheer misery but I was prepared to spend every penny I had. There were some days when I would get up and look at the front page of the *Sun* and just cry my eyes out. It was a constant battle. At the time that was going on I wasn't a particularly well budgie so you can imagine the trauma it caused me.' His legal action against the paper was the first step towards reclaiming a sense of purpose and direction in his life. Despite his personal problems, Elton had shown that, deep down, he was not going to give up.

Giving an interview on his 60th birthday in 2006, an unrepentant Kelvin McKenzie said: 'Bloody Elton John. I think the *Sun* should have its million quid back. It hasn't damaged him at all, has it? Libel can only have a value if there has been some kind of damage, right? Where is the damage? Where? There's nothing wrong with him. So no, I don't feel bad about him, not at all.' On being probed about the patent lies most people would argue the *Sun* had printed over the years he replied: 'When I published those stories, they were not lies. But I don't really think of it all in the way you suggest. They were great stories that later turned out to be untrue – and that is different. What am I supposed to feel ashamed about?'

During the public humiliation of 1987, Elton kept a relatively low musical profile. A duet with Jennifer Rush on 'Flames Of Paradise' and a guest slot on George Harrison's *Cloud Nine* album aside, there would be no new Elton John product other than *Live In Australia*. However, by the beginning of 1988, he was ready to release a new album, the defiantly titled *Reg Strikes Back*.

The difference between *Leather Jackets* and the new album was the difference between night and day. Whereas on the former, Elton had sounded dead, on the new album, he had come alive again with a set of catchy, uptempo tunes and a confident vocal performance. Surgery seemed to have left him with a deeper, more sonorous voice. This wasn't Elton, or Bernie for that matter, at his best, but it was a statement of intent at least, and nowhere more so than on the middle finger to the modern world that was 'Goodbye Marlon Brando': 'Say goodbye to the tabloids, say goodbye to diet soda/ Say goodbye to new-age music from the Capa to the Coda/ Say goodbye to gridlock, goodbye to Dolly's chest/ Goodbye to the ozone layer if there's any of it left'. On this strident slab of rock angst, Taupin played the grumpy old man to great effect: the planet was an ecological disaster waiting to happen, the media was a massive intrusion, culture had dumbed down, modern music was rubbish and the fixation with celebrity was facile. 'I need to put some distance between overkill and me,' concluded Taupin in words that could equally be applied to the Elton John of 1988.

In 'I Don't Wanna Go On With You Like That', the new album also contained a classic Elton single. Although it performed moderately at home, staying in the charts for two months but only reaching Number 30, in the US it was a biggie, finally peaking at Number 2 on the Billboard charts. The distinctive drum sound came courtesy of an unlikely source. 'There was a finger click to the track piping out of the speakers near my kit as I played,' says Charlie Morgan. 'What we did was to replace the snare drum with the sound of me hitting the top of an empty tin of assorted biscuits with my drum stick and sampling that.'

Elton was still following his long-established way of working in the studio. 'I remember one day he put one of Bernie's lyrics up on the piano. He could knock a song off in minutes,' says David Paton. 'He called me over and he said, "What do you think of this?" and he played me this fantastic song, "Heavy Traffic". "The only problem is that I need another verse," Elton said. So he got on the phone to Bernie and the next minute he shouted out, "Pen, pen, pen!" and Bernie dictated another verse for the song to him over the phone, off the top of his head. And that was it. The song was written and recorded on the same day.'

Gus Dudgeon having been dropped due to the poor sales of *Leather Jackets* (a slightly unfair move, perhaps, given the quality of the music he had to work with), Chris Thomas was brought back to produce *Reg Strikes Back*. Unlike the exuberant and vocal Dudgeon, Thomas went about his business in a very different manner. 'Gus never had a hard time telling you when you'd done something good,' says Morgan. 'Chris was much more introverted. When we were doing *Reg Strikes Back* at Air Studios, I remember David Paton turning to me at one point and saying, "Are we all right? Do you know? Can you tell?" And I would say, "No, I can't tell." Gus was musical about the way he listened to things and Chris was technical. Chris would go through how we could record a particular song, while Gus would be more emotive. Gus would produce from the heart and Chris produced from the brain. That said, I thought *Reg Strikes Back* was an emotionally charged album and I don't think it ever got the credit it deserved.'

Elton could be something of an unpredictable presence in the recording studio. It was obvious that he was still under great emotional strain. 'There was one notorious day when we were recording "Town Of Plenty",' says Morgan. 'We played the backing track to that and then we started another song, but Elton was having problems. He burst into tears because he couldn't get it. He just shuffled out of the piano booth, walked straight out of the studio and on to Oxford Street, hailed a cab and went home. I think Chris Thomas gave chase in another cab. That was the whole of that day wiped out.'

Reg Strikes Back was released in June 1988. The days when Elton and Bernie were at the vanguard of popular music were, of course, long gone. In the year of rap, acid house and indie-dance, Elton's music had a contemporary AOR sheen, but it was hardly challenging.

Nevertheless, in the history of Elton John, this album was a significant one. It stopped the musical rot.

Elton was in the process of de-cluttering both his music and his life. After years of acquisitiveness, he embarked on a massive clear-out and the cover of *Reg Strikes Back* announced this to the world. Dozens of his costumes were posed for the camera, a black-and-white photograph of the five-year-old Reg Dwight inserted unobtrusively in among the avalanche of hats, glasses and stage outfits that Elton had decided to sell off at an auction to be held later that summer.

'Everything was being prepared for the huge Sotheby's auction of everything Elton possessed, or so it seemed,' says the art director David Costa. 'I wanted to do a kind of *Sgt Pepper* of all of his clothes, all his personae, all on mannequins, and as they were rolled out of the truck and stacked up in a studio designed for car photography in Portobello Road, the random scattering of them just seemed to take on a life of its own. Gered [Mankowitz, photographer] and I decided to keep it looser than we had previously planned. But more and more clothes kept coming and none of us could resist trying them on, which is why there's a mad Minnie Mouse chasing Donald Duck across the inner liners. Steve Brown, recently back with John Reid, was in the management role again, and we decided between us, having described what we were planning to EJ, just to get on with it and hope he liked it.

'Once we had the shots I stripped together a visual and flew to LA, met EJ at the Four Seasons an hour after landing, heart in mouth, visuals in hand, and he loved the whole thing. "Let's go show Bernie!" he said, and off we went to show him, stopping first to shop at Maxfields – which seemed significant, because I thought the whole point of the exercise was precisely because he'd stopped shopping and was getting rid of all of that über-dressing – and with EJ driving, which was a new and unnerving experience.'

The Sotheby's auction in September revealed the extent of what might be regarded as another of Elton's addictions: shopping. Jon Wilde in the UK magazine *Uncut* pointed out that Elton's penchant for retail therapy on a massive scale had already manifested itself in the early days of his career: 'On one early visit to America, he returned with 67 cases and 42 trunks of new acquisitions.' Sotheby's divided the huge collection into four sections: 'Stage costumes and memorabilia', 'Jewellery', 'Art Nouveau and Art Deco' and, finally, 'Diverse Collections,' the latter including Andy Warhol's *Marilyn* and a replica of Tutankhamen's state throne. The 2,000 lots made a staggering £15 million. Elton's Dodger Stadium suit, expected to reach £1,600, went for £6,200, and high prices were also paid for the massive Doc Martens he wore for the 'Pinball Wizard' scene in *Tommy* and the more recent Eiffel Tower boater worn in concert in Paris. Also sold were two items of historical importance to the rock fan: a tour programme autographed by Elvis and a set of lithographs by John Lennon.

Elton's marriage to Renate was now at an end and the two divorced in November 1988. It's a period of his life about which Elton obviously continues to feel a great sense of remorse. 'The biggest regret I have about getting married is that I hurt someone who was a special person, one of the funniest, nicest, most attractive and fabulous people that I've ever met,' he admitted in 1995. 'She knew what she was getting into by marrying me but she genuinely loved me. I knew I was being dishonest but I couldn't admit it, because I didn't want to be seen to be wrong. I went through with it because I was too frightened to go back on it. It would have been much easier for me to call it off and save her all that pain, although we did have a lot of good times together.'

Reports at the time suggested that Renate received £5 million in her divorce settlement. Since the divorce, she has acted with great dignity, neither selling her story to the papers nor dishing the dirt in high-profile television interviews. There has been one recent attempt by a UK tabloid to track her down. In 2000, the *Sunday Mirror* ran an 'exclusive' on the 'Sad, Lonely Life Of The Woman Who Loved And Lost Elton', which revealed that 46-year-old Renate was living 'as a virtual recluse in a small cottage'. 'Evergreen trees shield her home from prying eyes and she goes out only to walk her spaniel – her constant companion – or pick up groceries from the village shop,' the paper reported. One of Renate's neighbours was quoted as saying: 'We don't mention Elton's name because we know it still upsets her.' The article ended with a single quote from Renate: 'From behind a half-open door all she would say was: "I live very quietly here and people are very protective towards me."'

By September 1988, Elton was back on the road to promote *Reg Strikes Back*, performing five sell-out New York shows at Madison Square Garden. This was the first time that he used an electric keyboard instead of a piano. String parts were played by the synthesiser too, and so the Elton John sound changed quite markedly. He included such less well-known early songs as 'Burn Down The Mission', 'Have Mercy On The Criminal' and 'The Ballad of Danny Bailey' in the set, as well the usual classics. In November 1989, he played a guest slot at the Tokyo Dome with Eric Clapton and Mark Knopfler. The first six months of 1989 were likewise filled up with touring commitments in Europe and the UK.

For 1989, Elton sported a new look, his hair dyed platinum blond and topped with a Nehru cap. It aged him and, with his now fast-expanding girth, made him look older than 42. Throughout his years of addiction, he had managed to keep up an astonishing work rate. With the exception of 1987, there had been a new Elton studio album for every year of the 1980s. The 1989 offering was to be called *Sleeping With The Past*.

The new album, again produced by Chris Thomas, had a more contemporary sound, with some occasional references to the more laid-back dance grooves populating the charts of the day. Although by no means vintage Elton, there were some standouts. 'Whispers' was as melodic a ballad as Elton had penned for a long time and the reggae styling of 'Durban Deep' provided a surprising opener. Yet it was the second track, 'Healing Hands', which proved Elton still had it. In this rousing piece of gospel-tinged pop with its beautiful middle piano section from Elton, Bernie's words of hope – 'There's a light, where the darkness ends/Touch me now and let me see again' – seemed to have a prophetic air.

Elton was, once again, in confident mood, going as far as to say that the album was 'the strongest record we've ever made. We went back to our roots and tried to do something special… Bernie and I came up with the idea of making an album that paid tribute to all the great old soul songs we'd grown up with and I feel that also gives it a real sense of continuity.'

Obviously overjoyed at the renewed productivity of the Elton-Bernie muse, Elton dedicated the album to his songwriting partner: 'This album's for you, Bernie…' 'He [Bernie] was living in England when he was writing these songs,' he reasoned later. 'We spent a lot of time together, not writing but we spent a lot of time together. And I realised how valuable our relationship was and how much I really admired and respected him, and how much I really needed him as a part of my life.'

The big hit off the album would eventually turn out to be the ballad 'Sacrifice'. Originally released as the second single, it flopped in the UK, reaching a lowly Number 55, getting to a more respectable Number 18 in the US. However, reissued in the summer of 1990 as a double-A side with the first single off the album, 'Healing Hands', it would become, incredibly, Elton's first solo UK Number 1 single. It stayed there for five weeks, ultimately selling over 600,000 copies. Elton decided to donate the proceeds, the princely sum of £328,000, to four Aids organisations of his choice. He then declared that the proceeds from all his single sales in the UK would henceforth be donated to charity. On the back of the single's success, *Sleeping With The Past* climbed up the charts to become Elton's fifth UK Number 1 album.

For Bernie, 'Sacrifice' was a very personal song, and one that he regarded as the companion piece to 'Your Song'. While the latter had been written by a youthful ingénue, 'Sacrifice' was the product of a world-wearied man of experience. 'When I hear it I'm always surprised I wrote it,' said Bernie. The song has some illustrious admirers, including Sir Tim Rice, who says it is his favourite Elton number. However, by the time it reached Number 1, in the late summer of 1990, Elton John had to all intents and purposes said goodbye to the rock world altogether.

After years of alcoholism, drug dependency and eating disorders, by spring 1990 Elton had hit his own rock bottom, reaching a stage in life where he felt so ashamed, full of self-loathing and low that there was no alternative for him but to change. He finally summoned up the will to drag himself out of the oubliette of self-loathing of his early forties and to pull free into the daylight of sobriety.

At 43, Elton was three years older than his idol John Lennon had been when he was murdered and two years older than Elvis Presley on his death. The manner of the latter's demise had had a lasting impression on Elton. The image he had of Presley towards the end of his life was one that haunted him. 'I remember seeing Elvis in concert the year before he died,' he reminisced. 'My mom was there and we met him backstage. I knew he would be dead in a short time. He was so tragic. Yet within the tragic persona – he came onstage and was like a zombie – there were flashes of incredible brilliance. But it was suffocated by all the shit going on inside his body, the shit that he was doing to himself.'

In truth, there were shocking similarities between the Elton John of 1990 and the Elvis Presley of the mid-1970s. In the same way that Presley's performances had lurched into self-parody as he messed up his lines as well as his body, the British singer's band members recall how Elton too came to lower his hitherto impeccable standards on stage. His playing was simply not up to his usual high standards as his mind and body started to collapse under the weight of 15 years of self-abuse. That May, Elton played three concerts at the opening of a casino complex at the Trump Taj Mahal in Atlantic City.

'I think we could see that the writing was on the wall,' says Charlie Morgan. 'We could see he was off the rails. He was all over the place emotionally and his playing wasn't up to his usual standard. He was still putting on a good show, but it was almost as if it was by rote. There were a lot of concerned people in the Elton John organisation.'

'It really was Elvis Presley time again,' Elton admitted in 1992. 'You get cut off from people, isolated. It's easy to lose your values and self-respect. I got to where I didn't know how to speak to someone unless I had a nose full of cocaine. Nothing could satisfy me. I used to complain about everything down to the colour of the private jet.'

311

But the event that really shook Elton was the death, in April 1990, of an 18-year-old boy by the name of Ryan White. At the age of 13, Ryan had become infected with HIV from the blood product, Factor 8, which was used to treat his haemophilia. He was expelled from school (such was the widespread ignorance of HIV and Aids at the time) and he and his family were hounded out of their home in Kokomo, Indiana, and forced to relocate to the neighbouring town of Cicero. Michael Jackson bought their new house for them. In the later years of his life, Ryan became a national celebrity, appearing on network television in an attempt to inform the unenlightened about the true nature of the disease. In the 1980s, Aids was still regarded by a section of the public as 'the gay plague', a punishment from God, not something 'normal' people could contract.

'Aids has really changed my life,' Elton said in 1995. 'I've known a lot of people with Aids, especially in the 1980s, but at that time, I was such a drug addict. In fact, I think the Aids epidemic is probably why my drug habit increased. I just wanted to block out things that weren't good.'

Elton visited the dying young man. 'It made me realise what an insane, fantasy lifestyle I was living,' he later told Tony Parsons. 'I saw Ryan and his mother forgive all those people who had been so vile to them, when they came to say they were sorry. Seeing how brave that kid was – I just knew then that my life was completely out of whack.' After Ryan's inevitable death, Elton helped to organise his funeral and was one of the coffin bearers. 'When Ryan died, I went to Indianapolis with Hugh [Williams], who I lived with then, to perform at Ryan's funeral. But if you look at the footage of me at the funeral you see how dead I was. My hair was white. I was maybe 230 pounds, my eyes were dead, I was like a piano-playing Elvis Presley. I was so messed up.

'But the thing that happened to me as a result of seeing all that was that I started to see what really mattered, because of the experience of being with the Whites. When you see all of that happening, it touches you so deeply. And it has the power to change you. That's when I knew I had to change. I was either going to die or change. I thought, what have I come to? I'm either going to carry on like I am and die of a heart attack or an OD, or I'm going to get my life together.'

Shortly after the funeral, Elton's partner, Hugh Williams, decided to check himself into rehab. Taking the 'rehab is for quitters' approach, Elton's first reaction was one of incomprehension. 'At first, I was so angry about it: How dare you go into rehab? How dare you try and get better and do something about your life?' However, it was on a visit to see Hugh in Arizona that Elton uttered the words that would enable him to take the first step on the long road to recovery: 'I need help.'

'Hugh was in a halfway house in Prescott,' Elton has explained, 'and he said, "If you come and see me, there are some things I want to say to you. I'll have a counsellor and you'll have a counsellor and we'll sit and we'll talk." I said, "OK." I got there and was told to write down three things that annoyed me about Hugh and he was told to write down what he didn't like about me, what he thought I should change. I knew what was going to happen. I wrote these things down – I think they were "He doesn't put his CDs back in the case" and "He's untidy". I couldn't think of anything more. We sat knee to knee, touching, and I read mine out first.

'Then he read his out and it must have been a page long. He was terrified. Knowing my temper, he thought I would just say, "Fuck off! How dare you talk to me like that!" But I just sat there and I was shaking, and I said to myself, "You've got to stay here. You've got to stay and you've got to hear this. You've got to hear the truth." He said, "You're a drug addict, you're bulimic." Everything he said about me was true. After he finished, I said, "Yeah, you're right." It was an incredibly brave thing for him to do. I sat there and cried and I said, "I need help." And as soon as I said those three words, my soul came back, I could feel again and I knew, from that point on, I was going to get better.'

Despite his status and unlimited spending power, Elton had difficulty finding a clinic that would take him. They tended to be reluctant to take on people who had multiple addictions (in Elton's case, alcoholism, drug-addiction and bulimia). In the end, however, he was able to check in to the Parkside Lutheran Hospital in Chicago. The date was July 29, 1990.

This was not to prove an easy time for Elton. He was willing to be cured, but after years of telling people what to do, he was suddenly no longer the actor but the acted upon. The authoritarian approach did not rest well with the naturally free-spirited star. 'I tried to run away twice because of authority figures telling me what to do,' Elton later admitted. 'I didn't like that, but it was one of the things I had to learn. I packed my suitcase on the first two Saturdays and I sat on the sidewalk and cried. I asked myself where I was going to run: "Do you want to go back and take more drugs and kill yourself, or do you go to another centre because you don't quite like the way somebody spoke to you here?" In the end, I knew there was really no choice. I realised this was my last chance.'

The rehabilitation programme required Elton to write a farewell latter to cocaine. In 1995, he revealed part of the text of that letter to Tony Parsons. In it he addresses the drug, personified as his lover, for the last time:

'I don't want you and I to share the same grave. I'm fed up with you. I don't want to die like that. You have been my whore. I've flown you in on planes. I've sent cars for you. I've even sent trains for you. I've spent lovely nights with you. I have always come back to you when I've left you. And this time it's got to be goodbye.'

CHAPTER 14

KING OF THE JUNGLE

'I believe in love, it's all we got
Love has no boundaries, no borders to cross.'

'Believe'; lyrics: Bernie Taupin; music: Elton John

'Fucking videos! … I don't make records to do videos! … I don't like my
photograph being taken!'

Elton John reveals self-esteem issues on *Tantrums And Tiaras*

Elton John, hot and sweaty, has a face like a storm cloud. He is with his partner, David Furnish, in a lift taking them back up to their apartment. David is talking to him gently, trying to calm him down and attempting to ascertain what has brought on the latest episode of kangaroo-loose-in-the-top-paddock Elton bad-temperedness. It's textbook anger-management counselling. Anyone witnessing this scene might easily think that something quite serious has happened. And, in Elton's world, it has.

David: 'What happened?'

Elton (his face a picture of petulance): 'Nothing… I don't want to talk about it. It's supposed to be a fucking holiday!'

David: 'What's wrong?'

Elton: (silence; looks down, breathes heavily).

The only thing that distinguishes this run-of-the-mill episode of Elton losing it from other similar situations is that, this time, the display of childish moodiness is a very public one. David is pointing

315

a video camera in his face. This is reality television before it had been invented – except that, this time, there is actually something worth eavesdropping on.

Elton's rage is not to be cooled – not yet in any case. A short time later, he is filmed in his hotel room, a picture of grumpiness, firing off a list of instructions to his office in a curt, clipped, upper-middle-class tone. He wants to leave France tomorrow. This is the end of the holiday. A 6pm flight is booked to take him and his vast entourage of shoes and suits plus two tiaras (one for formal occasions, one for not quite so formal events) to Farnborough, so he can go home to Woodside.

What has occasioned the brutal truncation of his holiday? Elton's tennis has been interfered with. In a strop that would have put John McEnroe to shame, he has thrown his racquet to the ground and stormed off court. 'I just lost my temper at this woman at the other end of the court waving at me and going, "Yoo-hoo!"' he admits a few days later, still enjoying/enduring his holiday with David in France. 'I'm always having people waving to me going "Yoo-hoo!" I take my tennis very seriously, and I couldn't handle it.'

* * *

In 1995, Elton's partner of two years, the Canadian filmmaker David Furnish, decided to make what would turn out to be one of the best and most revealing rock documentaries of all time. *Tantrums And Tiaras*, an hour-long exposé of a year in the life of Elton John, was told with real affection and candour. It was painfully revealing about Elton as an individual, as well as showing the nature of rock superstardom in all its ridiculousness.

We saw Elton copying out his chart positions, dashing his tennis racquet to the ground when spotted by a fan and exploding like a human hand grenade when his outfit for a video shoot was late. We saw Elton the loving man giving his Nan a kiss for what turned out to be the last time; beaming when presented with his new puppy (whom he named, with eccentric glee, not Rex, Spot or Lucky but Graham);

expressing genuine sadness about his failed relationship with Renate and engaging in good-natured banter with his manager John Reid ('the fabulous Beryl') and his PA Bob Halley. We saw Elton, the consummate professional, collecting an Oscar, performing onstage and enduring the backstage waiting, hotels and constant travel that constitute life on the road. We saw the private Elton at his homes in Woodside and Atlanta and we saw him 'enduring' his holiday in France.

It was this section of the film that was, perhaps, the most revealing. Elton sat, half-bored, in the shade on his balcony, in the middle of the steaming heat of high summer on the French Riviera. It was obvious that this is a man who doesn't know how to relax. David tried to tempt Elton to the beach or to sit by the pool, but Elton simply refused to do anything. Even a romantic stroll down a secluded route couldn't tempt him out of his shell.

The picture of Elton that emerged from *Tantrums And Tiaras* was one of a man whose work is his life. He exists to create and perform, and he wants to be around like-minded people. In the documentary, Elton expressed incredulity bordering on annoyance at any suggestion from David that he was overworking and was in need of some downtime. What would he do during downtime? He seemed utterly incapable of being anything other than Elton John. Any last semblance of the kind of normality that his father had wished for him – the normality of a nine-to-five job, a family, holidays – had been expunged from his life with complete success.

'I told him a few years ago that he should take a break and come off the road for a while,' says Clive Franks. 'It's incredible the amount of work he does. At least when he comes off the road, we all get a break. It's almost like he doesn't want to be at home; he doesn't want to sit down and relax. In fact, he can't relax; he's just hyped up all the time. He's got to be doing this, he's got to be going there. I don't think he knows how to sit down and chat and relax.'

Elton the workaholic was just one aspect of the man revealed by the documentary. His love of music also came through loud and clear. His endless enthusiasm for new music was revealed as he was seen in his vast music library choosing some new titles for his CD player with all the thrill of his teenage years. Then it was the Beatles and the Beach Boys; now, it's Massive Attack.

However, it was a frank discussion between David Furnish and Elton's therapist, Beechy Colclough, that proved the most controversial part of the film. David confronted Elton with a videotaped extract from an interview he had recorded with Colclough when Elton had been away in the States. In this short sequence, David played the tape back to Elton. The public evisceration of Elton's character flaws made for uncomfortable television for the viewer, let alone for Elton.

The discussion centred on Elton's friends and colleagues. 'I think he buys them with his personality. I think he buys a lot of them with gifts,' began Colclough. 'I think a lot of people just feed off that. He's surrounded by some good, close people. Thank Lord God for it.' 'I always think it's like a medieval court,' confirmed Furnish. The problem, they both agreed, went back to Elton's self-loathing. 'He's happy when he's playing for moments, but then he doesn't believe the audience's reactions,' said Colclough of Elton's low self-esteem. He continued with a theatrical assessment of Elton's character: 'I think he is a born addict. He's a totally compulsive obsessive person. If it hadn't been the alcohol, it would have been the drugs. If it hadn't been the drugs, it would have been the food. If it hadn't been the food, it would have been relationships. If it hadn't been relationships, it would have been shopping. And do you know what?' Colclough held up his hand for further dramatic effect. 'I think he's got all five. I really do.' 'Listening to you, it was like a couple of vultures picking over a carcass,' was Elton's accurate assessment.

'The film was a bold move for Furnish,' says Charlie Morgan. 'We watched the rushes of *Tantrums And Tiaras* at his house and Elton was hooting with laughter at his behaviour. He doesn't see [his behaviour] when it's going on, but afterwards he obviously does. You're paying these people in your management, so you may as well give them a hard time. He never used to do it to musicians; it was very much aimed at the management. John Reid and Elton used to row all the time, but

John was the only one who was telling him if he was making a poor decision.'

Furnish's film showed Elton – or, more accurately, one side of Elton – as he really is. It is one of the funniest and most candid pieces of film that has ever been made about a major star. Elton has his failings, and he is willing to admit to them. Many admired his honesty. While so many of Elton's contemporaries have revealed very little of their actual selves, Elton appeared to want to reveal everything.

'The hissy fits? Oh, they're wonderful,' says his old chum Billy Connolly. 'I love seeing people throw tantrums, mainly because I never could throw one myself. What prompts them in Elton? Well, it isn't usually people, but circumstances. Something isn't there that should be, or is there that shouldn't be. It's all been painted the wrong colour, or isn't what he ordered.'

There was one problem, however, with *Tantrums And Tiaras*. It fixed Elton, in the public imagination, as a man more famous for his lifestyle than for his music. For those already poorly disposed towards him, it reinforced the image they had of him as a spoilt, petty, even greedy man. In the 1990s, Elton had become better known as a celebrity than as a musician. One of his most vocal champions in the print media over the last ten years, the journalist and *GQ* editor Dylan Jones, argues: '*Tantrum And Tiaras* was a great thing, but it was also a bad thing in a way. It was funny and it was accurate, but it showed one particular side to Elton. I think lazy journalists take that as a blueprint for what he is as a character and I think he's far more complicated than that and he's a lot nicer than that. If you've been famous for the last 40 years, then you expect a certain level of service from the people who work for you and from people who work for other people.'

Of course, had the documentary been made a decade earlier, in the midst of Elton's drug-fuelled promiscuity, it would have been less a matter of 'tantrums and tiaras' and more of 'septums and rectums'. In fact, it probably would never have been made. It was only because Elton had cleaned up his act and because he was now with a partner he trusted, that he was able to open up so effectively. Post-therapy, Elton the media figure appeared to find it impossible to lie. His interviews gave the impression of being media therapy sessions. Having always had forthright opinions, he now no longer felt the need, or even the willingness, to keep them to himself. So began a new phase in the life of Elton John – a phase of brutal honesty about himself, and about others too.

That new age dawned in the autumn of 1990. Without the prop of hard drugs, Elton was finally beginning to re-establish a meaningful connection with those around him. He slowly began to detox. He had started taking Prozac for depression just before he went into rehab. 'It really evened me out; no real highs or lows,' he said in 1995. 'I've been off it now for two or three years, but it stabilised me for a while.' In the early 1990s, he also managed to wean himself off another prescription drug, Dialantin, a muscle relaxant he took to combat the cocaine-induced seizures that were a feature of the days of his heaviest use. Sheila and Derf returned from their self-imposed exile in Menorca. Elton rented a property in London in Holland Park and, for the first year after his rehab, lived a low-key existence. He began attending Alcoholics Anonymous meetings and committed himself wholeheartedly to a new life. 'I got a dog from Battersea Dog's Home, Thomas, and we used to get up and go to a meeting every morning and concentrated on my recovery,' he reflected later. 'The only thing that really frightened me was that I didn't know how to work the washing machine. I was really ashamed of that. I'd always had everything done for me.'

The process of recovery was an ongoing one. When Elton attended receptions, he would look on with his alcohol-free lager as his guests got merry on champagne. Elton would attend AA meetings for three years until they outgrew their usefulness: 'I found that all I could talk about was how I didn't drink or take drugs. I would arrive at a party and see people going, "Oh, fucking hell, here he is." I just thought, well, I didn't stop all this nonsense just to constantly talk about the fact that I don't do it anymore. So I stopped going to AA meetings.'

The impact of the years of drug addiction stayed with Elton. He would admit that quitting alcohol had been relatively easy, although he still on occasion missed the odd beer or glass of wine. The allure of cocaine was something he found very much harder to resist, but resist it he did. In 1997, Elton told *Mojo*: 'I still wake up, seven years since I last had any, having had cocaine dreams where my mother is in the next room about to walk in and I'm there with powder all over my face. I can still taste it too, running down the back of my throat. You have to fight it because it invades your psyche like you wouldn't believe. I feel mature now, but in a way I'm glad I went through it.'

Elton had been lucky. Despite his promiscuity, an Aids test had come back negative. In the early 1990s, Elton was in a stable relationship with John Scott and, after they split up, they remained on good terms. 'John went on to manage the Elton John Aids Foundation until last year, when he became a full-time professional photographer,' says Charlie Morgan in 2006. 'He's very solid and down-to-earth. He and David [Furnish] are very similar personalities.'

With Elton's new sobriety came a fresh responsibility. Throughout his career, he had always been generous to a fault with his time and money. Now that he was emotionally more stable, he decided to channel his energies in a more co-ordinated fashion into humanitarian causes. As the 1990s progressed, he became one of the most altruistic figures in the entertainment business:

'I'd been given a second chance in life, which not many people get,' he said. 'And I thought, now maybe I've got a chance to do something about these horrible things that happen to everybody. By that time, of course, I'd lost so many more friends with Aids and I knew so many more people with HIV. I did a couple of benefits for people, but what I really wanted to do was to start my own foundation so that I could run things my way, make sure that I had something else in my life other than being Elton John, which is so self-absorbing and time-consuming.'

In 1992, Elton set up the Elton John Aids Foundation (EJAF) in Atlanta, Georgia. It's mission statement was 'to provide funding for programs that provide services to people living with HIV/Aids and educational programmes targeted at HIV/Aids prevention and/or the elimination of prejudice and discrimination against HIV/Aids-affected individuals.' Elton soon established himself as one of the world's leading figures in the fight against the spread of HIV. 'When this epidemic is wiped from the face of the planet, we'll all look back and have our heroes,' said Bernie Taupin. 'Elton is mine.' Speaking at a gala event for the EJAF in America in 1995, the singer said, 'This is where I came out, in this country. I've slept with half of it and I came out of it HIV-negative. I'm a lucky, lucky person. It's now my job to repay the debt.'

However, another defining icon of the 1970s and 1980s, Freddie Mercury, would not be so lucky. For five years, the world watched as the singer's frame and countenance changed beyond all recognition. By 1989, he was thin and gaunt; the last photographs of him in 1991 showed a skeletal man. He finally announced that he had Aids just one day before he succumbed to the disease on November 24, 1991. Elton, a good friend, visited the dying singer and also attended his funeral.

A month later, Elton's father, Stanley Dwight, passed away at his home in Hoylake, aged 66. Stanley had endured ill health for several years and in January 1983 had undergone a quadruple heart-bypass operation. At the time of his death, the two were still estranged. The last time Elton had seen his dad was at a football match, when Liverpool played Watford at Anfield in 1982. His father gave an interview with the *Sunday People*, which ran under the headline 'Dying Dad's Love For Elton: Heartbreak Message For Star Through The *People*'. On reading the headline, Elton reportedly called off a planned trip to see his ailing dad. Nor did he attend his father's funeral. His father or, more accurately, the role of his father in his upbringing would also be a favourite topic of conversation for the newly liberated Elton. 'I blame my father for a lot of things and I've said so in public, and it's caused a lot of furore with his widow,' he said in 2001. 'But I'm completely at peace now. He tried the best he could. He was a good man. But it shaped the way I am. And I'm grateful for that, because otherwise I wouldn't have been so ambitious.'

Musically, 1990 and 1991 were quiet years for Elton. At the end of 1990, a compilation, appropriately entitled *To Be Continued*, marked his silver jubilee as a recording artist. A fitting tribute, the CD included tracks from the 1960s such as 'Lady Samantha', most of his huge 1970s hits and a wise selection from the rather more fallow 1980s. For the art director David Costa, it would be his favourite package to date.

'The UK version had photos by Juergen Teller,' he says. 'The cover photo on the box – EJ smiling and slightly out of focus – is my all-time favourite photo of him. We just caught a moment. After all the set-pieces and fancy shoots with make-up artists and stylists and concepts and hordes of assistants, Juergen and I just took EJ to an empty ware-house with overhead daylight; no assistants, no lights, nothing; just Juergen with an old 35mm Leica, walking around with Elton, chatting quietly together. EJ loved it. He was out of rehab, clean, confident, rested, quiet.'

At the same time as the release of the box set, another compilation hit the stores in time for Christmas. *The Very Best of Elton John* would go on to become Elton's biggest-selling album ever in the UK. In 2006, a survey conducted by the Official UK Charts Company revealed that it was the 54th biggest-selling album of all time in the UK, with total sales of 2.13 million copies.

In March 1991, Elton made his live comeback at Wembley Arena, where he performed a duet with George Michael on his 1974 classic 'Don't Let The Sun Go Down On Me'. Released as a single that November, it became his third UK Number 1 single, as well as reaching Number 1 on the Billboard Top 100. The proceeds went to ten different charities. This level of success had not been foreseen by Elton, who had his doubts as to whether a live single, coming during a relatively fallow period for George Michael in the States, would be a hit.

On April 1, 1991, he played an April Fool's joke on his old spar-ring partner, Rod Stewart, at the latter's concert at Wembley Arena. During a more reflective moment in the set, Rod would sit himself on a stool to sing some of his softer ballads such as 'You're In My Heart'. However, on this occasion, he got a little more than he bargained for, including, probably, a dead leg. 'Elton came on in drag and sat on his knee,' remembers Gary Farrow. 'It took Rod about a minute-and-a-half to recognise him. He was expecting his wife.'

The end of 1991 saw the release of *Two Rooms*, a CD/video tribute to Elton and Bernie. The project was named after the 1980 song 'Two Rooms At The End of The World', a title which seemed to most accurately sum up the Elton/Bernie modus operandi, the (as journalist Robert Sandall said) 'I'll wash, you dry' way of working. Bernie and Elton did some press for the project and Bernie's almost total Americanisation was striking. His look, his world view, even his speaking voice (three quarters American drawl, one quarter Lincolnshire burr) indicated a man who was now living the dream: 'I'm much more Americanised in my ideology and outlook than Elton,' he admitted to *Q*. 'I have lived there for years. I'm an American citizen and I've always had an almost religious experience of travelling round the States.' Bernie also revealed himself to be the opposite of Elton in another crucial way: he was musically hidebound. At 41, he simply didn't really like modern pop music. 'I don't listen to anything modern at all now,' he confessed. 'Whenever I get into his [Elton's] car, he's playing stuff by these groups with initials for names. And they all use electronic percussion.'

The *Two Rooms* CD/video set collected together musical tributes in the form of cover versions, in celebration of one of the most successful songwriting partnerships in modern popular music history. Kate Bush's version of the 1972 classic 'Rocket Man' was a brave redefinition of the original and went on to reach Number 12 in the UK charts. Phil Collins made a good choice with 'Burn Down The Mission', a song that suited his own voice and the dynamics of his band.

Elsewhere, though, the interpretations were polite tributes from a predictable roster of mainstream acts. Eric Clapton had a go at 'Border Song' while Sting chose the less well-known 'Come Down In Time' and did it well enough. Jon Bon Jovi turned 'Levon' into stadium rock. Tina Turner performed the song she had long had in her live set, 'The Bitch Is Back', and the Who did 'Saturday Night's Alright For Fighting' with Roger Daltrey on lead (although Pete Townshend sang a short snatch of 'Take Me To The Pilot' in the middle). On 'Your Song', Rod Stewart replaced Elton's piano with a lightly strummed acoustic guitar, plus organ, violin and some muted lead guitar to produce an understated performance. The project was nice but never spectacular, and proved how difficult it is for anyone else to cover Elton and Bernie's songs. Unlike Dylan's versions of his own originals, Elton's versions are so definitive that finding a new way in was to prove impossible for most of the talents on display here.

The book to accompany the release, which collected the thoughts of Bernie and Elton and some archive photography, was likewise the very definition of 'polite'. 'The unthrilling "revelations" of the song-writing duo,' said Tom Hibbert in his two-star *Q* review, 'become quite exhausting quite soon and the reader is left longing for some faint squeak of dissent – for Elton to say, perhaps out of the blue, "Well, actually, I always reckoned that Bernie was a complete tosser." If only...'

The Elton John we all know and love today, of course, is an Elton with hair. The famously balding singer first introduced his hairweave to the public in April 1992, at a Wembley Stadium tribute concert for Freddie Mercury, *A Concert For Life*, where he sang 'Bohemian Rhapsody' with LA rocker Axl Rose. Some commentators raised a quiz-zical eyebrow at the pairing, particularly since the Guns N'Roses song 'One In A Million' contains the couplet 'Immigrants and faggots/they make no sense to me': evidence, it was said, of Rose's homophobia. Rose denied the charge, claiming he was singing the song in character, and Elton himself would later pour cold water on notions that the rocker was anti-gay. But as for the hair? Well, it certainly made a difference to his look. As the years passed, however, it seemed, in a strange way, merely to emphasise his baldness. It drew attention to it because we all knew that, instead of the undeniably vigorous growth, there should have been a shiny bald pate.

In 1992, Elton John the studio artist returned after an uncharacter-istic three-year hiatus. *The One*, recorded in Paris, was again produced by Chris Thomas. For Elton, it was the first album he would record without the props of drink and drugs. Perhaps unsurprisingly, he approached the first day of recording with trepidation. 'We went into the studio on the first day and he lasted about 20 minutes,' revealed John Reid. 'He said he couldn't do it. He just wasn't ready but we went back the next day and eventually it was fine. The album just flowed.'

Ultimately, *The One* is best remembered for the title track ballad plus 'Simple Life', a very strong opener with an evocative harmonica refrain and funky dance beat. There was also 'The Last Song', an emotional final track in which Bernie Taupin's lyrics depicted a reconciliation between young man dying of Aids and his father (the CD itself would be dedicated to Elton's former lover Vance Buck, who had succumbed to the disease). The first word of the song was 'Yesterday', sung, in an obvious homage, to exactly the same melody as the Beatles' famous ballad.

Elsewhere, however, the album was Elton-by-numbers. There was more piano-playing than on some of his recent product and certainly more reliance on programmed drum sounds, but little that was musically startling. 'Buying an Elton John album these days is like investing in a mutual fund,' wrote Jim Farber in *Rolling Stone*. 'You won't get a huge pay-off but you probably won't get burned either.'

The album wasn't helped by the fiddly, neo-classical kitsch of the cover artwork. The credits named Elton's close friend, the fashion designer Gianni Versace, as the creator of the cover. According to David Costa, however, 'We had lunch with Versace at his sumptuous apartment in Milan to discuss his design of *The One* and agree on how we would work together. A great man and a great moment, but all we ever received from him for the album was a silk scarf. Sadly, not even that, in truth, but just a transparency of a silk scarf. A truly inspired and beautiful man, though, in anybody's language. Elton used to say that Gianni would describe anything beautiful as "triple heaven", the word "triple" to rhyme with "trifle" and "heaven" as "'eaven". Such style...'

Elton also asked Versace to work on his upcoming world tour. 'I met him on the 1992 tour because he was doing the stage set and the design,' remembers Charlie Morgan. 'He looked at me and said, "You very nice." And then he looked at Guy Babylon, who was wearing too much black, and he said, "You – more gold! I want you wear more gold!" He and Elton fell out a couple of times. At one point, Versace thought his stage-design duties included deciding what songs to play. He said, "Elton, you're playing too many boom-boom songs. I want you to play those soft ballads." And I think the next night Elton said, "Here's another fucking boom-boom song for Gianni.'"

With the first single, 'The One', peaking at Number 9 on the Billboard charts and Number 10 in the UK, Elton John toured Europe in the early summer of 1992, before crossing the Atlantic to America, where, on August 30, he revisited the scene of his huge 1975 triumph, Dodger Stadium. Eric Clapton played a two-hour set before Elton took the stage looking trimmer and healthier than he had done for many years, although it was hard to get used to his rather unusual new hairstyle, leather trousers and Versace tops. In the 1980s he had tended to look ludicrous and the attempt to make him look fashionable in Versace's image made him arguably even less appealing. With the predominance of long-haired, leather-trousered musicians sharing the stage with him, he was not alone in looking a tad cheesy.

With Davey Johnstone as musical director, Charlie Morgan on drums was a versatile foil for Elton, funky when he needed to be, and dependably steady for the rock and ballad numbers. However, the replacement of the more natural timbre of an actual piano by the synthetic sound of Elton's Roland electric keyboard continued to grate. His 1992/93 touring schedule was reminiscent of his 1970s programmes in its sheer relentlessness. After the European and North American dates, the band toured Australia before returning for yet more shows in the US and Europe, this time resurrecting Elton's old partnership with the percussionist Ray Cooper.

As the end of the tour drew near, Elton was getting a completely new and different project ready for release. One of the main themes of his work in the 1990s and beyond has been collaboration with other artistes. In the autumn of 1993, he released his *Duets* album, which would threaten the upper echelons of the charts – in the UK, at least. It featured an Elton/Kiki Dee team-up on 'True Love', the Cole Porter song originally sung by Bing Crosby and Grace Kelly in *High Society* in 1956. Kiki's previous collaboration with Elton, 'Don't Go Breaking My Heart', was unfortunately reinvented as a contemporary dance track and all but murdered by Elton in tandem with the American drag artist RuPaul. There seemed to be little rhyme or reason in a project that included talents as dissimilar as P.M. Dawn and Leonard Cohen on one CD and lacked big names like Rod Stewart, Mick Jagger or Paul McCartney. The result was that Elton dwarfed those he performed with, including his 1950s idol Little Richard, then several decades past his prime. *Q* gave the album a two-star review, citing the collaboration with P.M. Dawn as 'the pick of an otherwise tepid bunch'.

The next year kicked off with another honour. On January 19, 1994, Axl Rose inducted Elton into the Rock And Roll Hall Of Fame. 'When I first heard "Bennie And The Jets", I knew I had to be a performer,' Axl claimed. Elton remained on tour almost continually throughout the year. The percussionist Ray Cooper also produced the show. 'It was more refined than our previous tour together in 1979,' says Cooper. 'We filmed it at the Greek Theatre in Los Angeles. Elton did so reluctantly, as he hates cameras and videos.' The year also saw Elton toured with Billy Joel. Their combined pulling power was astonishing. Joel was one of the very few performers on the planet whose commercial stock in the US was comparable to Elton's own.

Joel proved a friendly, down-to-earth man, generous with his time and money, as Charlie Morgan reveals: 'Elton is very gregarious but he is selectively so. He would hang out with us lot a bit before the gig, but he'd stay in one place and fly in and out of the gigs in a private jet. If we were one-and-a-half hour's flight from his home in Atlanta, Elton would prefer to fly in and out. Billy would stay at the same hotel as us, at the actual venue. On occasions, he would be at the bar, take over the piano and start singing Beatles songs. We would still be singing at 2am.

'On the opening night of the tour, Liberty Devitto, Billy Joel's drummer, had an allergic reaction to shellfish. We were at the Veterans Stadium in Philadelphia, which holds 50,000 people and, at very short notice, I filled in for him. Next day, Billy presented me with a card, which showed a girl, from behind, looking over her shoulder, wearing nothing but chaps, and her butt was sticking out. Inside it, he wrote, "Thanks Charlie, you saved our asses!" and taped a $1,000 dollar bill. The EJ Band got to eat out a few times that week courtesy of Billy Joel.'

Even more importantly, 1994 was a major year for Elton in that it saw him break into an entirely new field of musical endeavour: film. A phone call from Tim Rice had presented him with the opportunity to get involved in a completely different sort of project. 'I remember discussing with Elton's manager, John Reid, way, way back the possibility of doing something in the theatre with Elton,' Sir Tim says now. 'When I was signed up to the lyrics for the movie which would eventually be called *The Lion King*, Disney asked me who they wanted to do the music. I think my biggest favour to the Disney organisation was in suggesting Elton John, because it made sure that *The Lion King* would have a musical soundtrack unlike that of any previous Disney animated film, veering from Broadway influenced to rock. Elton said, "What's this all about? It sounds quite intriguing." I said, "It's an animated film and it's not even got a title yet. I am doing four or five songs and it's going to be fun. I thought you might enjoy it as a different string to your bow." He said, "Well, I would, but the deal is terrible, so I'm afraid I can't do it." Then, about two days later, John Reid rang up and said, "When do we start?" I thought, well, Elton must have got a pretty good deal after all.'

Elton was writing the music for *The Lion King* during his 1992–93 tour. 'Two of the songs, "Hakuna Matata" and "Circle Of Life", he wrote while I was there, but 90 per cent of the time I would send him the lyric,' says Rice. 'Most of my work was getting the lyrics to fit the plot. I was able to write whatever lyric was needed for the scene and would get that more or less approved by Disney before sending it to Elton, who would record it. We would then see how it fitted into the overall context of the movie, which it usually did.'

The film, known as *King Of The Jungle* in the early phases of production, would reach the movie screens as *The Lion King* in June 1994. It would go on to become a massive box office hit, the third-highest-grossing animated feature film ever released in the States. The soundtrack CD was also a huge hit, reaching Number 1 on the Billboard charts. 'The album was a mega success, even by Elton's standards,' says Rice. '"Hakuna Matata" has become a children's favourite, but I like them all. I think "Circle Of Life" is probably slightly more original in what it says

329

lyrically, but both that and "Can You Feel The Love Tonight?" have such strong tunes that I couldn't choose between them.'

Some, of course, greeted the film and the songs with less than unconditional enthusiasm. Writing in the *Sunday Times*, the ever-reasonable Julie Burchill complained: 'That Rice-John score is *every bit as bad* as we dreamed it would be! Just five – count 'em – lousy songs by the pair and each one weaker than the last. We're not just talking Eurovision standard here; we're talking *bottom third of Eurovision*.'

Despite this, *The Lion King* would be the most important single development in the career of Elton John for two decades. Almost over-night, he had a completely new audience. 'When you've been around for a long time, like Elton or the Stones, it's very hard to sell albums, however brilliant they are,' says Rice. 'There is always a core that will go out and buy them, but you won't get eight million sales automatically any more, simply because the people who grew up with you don't buy records as often. They will go and buy a greatest hits package occasion-ally and they will go and see the shows with enormous enthusiasm, but they just don't get round to buying the new stuff.

'What *The Lion King* did was to introduce a new audience to Elton. It was a huge seller because it hit every market: the children, their parents and also the existing Elton John fans. It sold about ten million in America alone, at least initially, and it's still selling. Worldwide it's probably as big as any of his albums.' 'Nowadays, I get mobbed at airports by six year olds!' Elton confessed in 1995.

The success of 'Can You Feel The Love Tonight' meant that Elton had had a Top 40 hit on the Billboard chart for each of the last 25 years – an achievement he would call the proudest of his career to date. The song was actually going to be dropped from the film until Elton insisted that a Disney film without a love song or some love interest would not be a Disney film. The next year, it won an Academy Award. For Tim Rice, the recipient of an Oscar for co-writing 'A Whole New World' with Alan Menken for *Aladdin* two years earlier, it was not a new experience.

'Award ceremonies are pretty ghastly,' Rice says. 'As far as awards are concerned, the Oscars are the only one that really matter, because people have heard of it. But you shouldn't get carried away. In the end you get an award for being around a long time and, if you're quite good at what you do, you'll eventually pick up a couple of awards. But the actual Oscars ceremony is hysterical, because you get some horrendously bad speeches, political nutters trying to change the world and Hollywood people thinking they're very important because they've made a couple of films. And then there's the over-the-top emotion. It's fascinating.' For Elton himself, it was recognition from a whole new area of the entertainment industry. In his acceptance speech he dedicated the award to his grandmother, Ivy, who had died the week before. Tim Rice dedicated his award to Denis Compton.

The same year, 1995, saw the release of *Made In England*. 'Greg Penny produced the record and he tried to keep it as organic as possible,' says Charlie Morgan, who was once again on drums. 'He was a really nice guy, probably too nice to crack the whip with Elton. Elton was in a good song-writing period and had got back into his songwriting craft without the use of drugs. "Believe" was a really good, torch-song ballad. I also think the lyrics were very strong at the time because Bernie's father was dying and he had to leave Elton with a lyrics book to go back to his father's bedside. I think Elton was really motivated by the lyrics to write good songs.'

Indeed, 'Believe', which Elton has referred to as a protest song against bigotry and intolerance, was one of his strongest of the 1990s. A slow-paced piece of orchestral pop, it was arranged by Paul Buckmaster, back after a gap of almost 20 years. Reflections that are personal to Bernie – 'Cancer sleeps/curled up in my father' – are set against a universal plea, in a world of hatred, war and intolerance, for love to conquer all: 'Love has no boundaries, no borders to cross'. On the jaunty, Beatles-like title track, Bernie's words were a defiant response to Elton's recent flagellation at the hands of the tabloids: 'You had a scent for scandal/Well, here's my middle finger'.

The Elton of the *Made In England* cover looked for all the world like a middle-aged re-creation of a gauche, teenage Reginald Dwight. With modest, round-framed spectacles and a full head of hair, he looked out rather blandly like a forty-something Piggy from *Lord Of The Flies*. The album performed creditably enough, reaching Number 4 in the UK and Number 13 in the US, but none of the four singles – 'Believe', 'Made In England', 'Blessed' and 'Please' – reached the Top 10 on either side of the Atlantic.

Nevertheless, Elton committed to a gruelling touring schedule to promote the album. When the bassist Bob Birch was knocked over in a road accident and seriously injured, David Paton was reinstated in the band. However, for Paton, the atmosphere had changed. 'It was totally different from the tour of 1985/86, which was a lot of fun and where Elton was in a very happy mood. Maybe he was indulging in certain things he shouldn't have, but he was very sociable and after most gigs there would be a party in his apartment. When I went back to do the 1995 tour, nobody wanted to go anywhere and there was no socialising. It was dull. I enjoyed playing the music, but the only one who was having fun was Davey Johnstone. We are both from Edinburgh and we see things in the same light. He would have a bottle of champagne in a bucket and a packet of roll-ups.'

The days of debauchery were long gone. Elton would still, however, perform the odd bit of mischief, just to keep him entertained. One favourite was checking into hotels with ever more ludicrous *noms de plume*. One favourite was Binky Poodle Clip, while he has also admitted checking in at least once as Sir Horace Pussy. 'My mother had to say that she was Mrs Pussy,' he divulged. But to Charlie Morgan, the Elton he now faced was totally different man from the one he had met over a decade earlier. 'He was a lot more insecure about who or what he was. In the 1980s, drugs and drink masked his insecurities and he was often full of bravado. But in the 1990s, to a large extent, I met the real Elton.'

Part of the new touring party would be John Jorgenson. Able to play just about every instrument in the band, John was brought in as second guitarist for the tour. 'On the first night of the tour there were a few songs I'd never even heard, let alone rehearsed!' says Jorgensen. 'One was "Pinball Wizard", which I knew, of course, so that was OK. One of the most memorable concerts was at the Waldbühne in Berlin, where Hitler used to address his troops. It was infested with mosquitoes when we were there, and the legend is that it was because Eva Braun didn't like the sound of frogs croaking, so Hitler had them all killed.'

For one member of the touring band, Ray Cooper, the mid-1990s was to mark the end of his professional relationship with Elton. For many Elton fans, the inclusion of Ray in the line-up was almost a guarantee of a good night's entertainment. Towards the end of every gig, Ray would perform a five-minute percussion solo and then lead the crowd in a call-and-response audience participation sing-a-long known to some Elton fans as the 'Way-O'. 'The solo became part of the end of the show and then Elton would come back in and finish the set,' says Cooper. 'By then we had gone through the emotional gamut of the main show, and what I was doing now as the performer was thanking the audience: "This is us and you, let's do this together." It was like, "Hey, the show is over now, this is the drum solo and you can join in. You're dying to, anyway!"'

'I loved Ray and respected him,' Charlie Morgan reflects now. 'But I did feel there was a bit of a rift between him and the band. He wanted to stay in the same hotel as Elton and have first-class travel.' 'One of the things that I heard had been said about me, which hurts me, although I don't understand it, is that I wasn't a team player,' counters Cooper. 'Sure, offstage, I am a little different. I have different interests and maybe I always did have. But that's my personal life. Onstage, I've always done everything I can to support every musician there.' In addition, the years of battering the conga drums were taking their toll on Cooper. 'I had a very bad circulatory problem, which was diagnosed as Raynaud's Syndrome, which affects the hands and feet,' he says. 'The first attack was in South America. Elton was based in Rio and flying everywhere. He likes things really cold, whether it be aeroplanes or cars and he always has the air conditioning on. However, I was obviously a bit run-down and when I got off the plane to go to the gig, my hand would not warm up. It was completely white. So I taped my fingers, but during the performance one finger turned black and I almost passed out. Under the nail I actually had little spots of gangrene.'

By the mid-1990s, Elton John's life was on a sound footing, both personally and professionally. His working relationship with Bernie Taupin was good and, while it had failed to produce consistently, it was still capable of coming up with at least two or three strong songs per album. Elton's collaboration with Tim Rice had shown that his 'extra-curricular' work could also flourish. He was still a massive live draw and, although his new work was seldom a hit with critics, the public continued to back Elton via their wallets.

'I've been very lucky in my professional relationships', he said in 1995. 'Bernie for 28 years; my manager, John Reid, for 25; Howard Rose, my agent, for 25, Connie Hillman [tour producer] has been around for 25 years; Sarah McMullen [publicist] has been around me for over a decade; Bob Halley [personal assistant] has been around me for 18 years; Bob Stacey, my wardrobe manager, and Clive Franks, my soundstage engineer, have been around me for 28 or 29 years.'

However, it was Bob Halley who was closest to Elton on a daily basis. 'If it hadn't have been for Bob, I would have been dead by now,' is Elton's stark but simple assessment. 'Elton and Bob are inseparable,' confirms Clive Franks. 'He's a very calm person and puts up with all the bullshit. He started as Elton's housekeeper, with his then wife Pearl, and then he was Elton's chauffeur. Later he became his personal assistant. There have been 30 or more years of tantrums for him to endure. Any normal human being would have run off years ago. There have been times when Bob has had enough and has quit, or Elton has fired him, and then in a few hours they've realised that they need one another and they've come back together.'

However, the most important person in Elton's life was, of course, the Canadian-born David Furnish. When they met at a dinner party at Woodside in October 1993, Furnish was working as an advertising executive at Ogilvy & Mather. According to *Punch* magazine, also present were Princess Diana, Sylvester Stallone and Richard Gere, the latter two squaring up after a row over Cindy Crawford. Furnish, then just 31, was 15 years Elton's junior.

Furnish was cute, dark-haired and somewhat reserved, but what impressed Elton about him was the fact that, unlike so many of Elton's other lovers, Furnish had an independent income and career. At their first meeting, David was shy, but let slip that *Caribou* was the first album he had ever bought. He gave Elton his number. Elton knew David was off to a Halloween Party and so waited until respectable time, 11am, and took the plunge and called him. The two met that evening in London for dinner. It was the start of a very special relationship.

By the time of the making of *Tantrums And Tiaras* in 1995, the two had settled at Woodside. David's office was based in a tram Elton had bought on a whim while on tour in Australia and had had shipped back to the UK, at not inconsiderable cost. 'We have been together for quite a while now and David gives me a lot of love, which I find very difficult. And yet it's what I always wanted,' Elton reflected in the mid-1990s, once again revealing the complex psychology that prevents him from accepting what he craves the most. Woodside itself was de-cluttered and reorganised. The days of drinking and drugging were long gone. For the first time in maybe 20 years, Elton seemed to be on an even keel, both professionally and emotionally.

John Jorgenson and his wife spent a week at the Woodside estate in 1996, finding their superstar host relaxed and generous. Jorgenson could not fail to be impressed by Woodside, which seemed to be the very height of elegant good taste. 'I thought it might be cold, but it's not at all, it's very homey,' he reflects. 'Everyone was sitting round the kitchen table in their bathrobes.' 'Before it was full of stuffed bears,' said Elton recalling the days when Woodside was the home of a decadent rock star. 'Now it's full of love and peace.'

'David is very friendly – he's got a little bit of that Canadian self-effacement,' says Jorgenson. That said, Elton had to have everything just so: 'There are flowers everywhere and ceramic figures. Everything is tidy and placed just perfectly. As Elton was showing my wife and me around the house, if a cushion was askew or a figurine was out of place, then he would adjust it as he went around.

'There were also lots of dogs: two very large dogs, Irish wolfhounds if memory serves me, some pedigree dogs and a stray, which was equally loved. Elton also had nine or ten border terriers. They are uncommon in the USA and their personality is so great that we fell in love with them. Elton said, "I'll send you one." A couple of months later he called me in my house in LA and said, "OK, we've got your puppy. We've got to name him. I think you should call him Kevin, or William." I said, "I can't picture myself calling my dog Kevin! Why don't you send me a picture of him and I'll see what he looks like?" Literally, the next day, a Fed-Ex of Elton holding the puppy arrived. So I looked at the puppy and said, "Oh, this is a Benny." And that dog has been the greatest gift anyone has ever given me.'

Jorgenson was also given a guided tour of the Woodside grounds. There was a tennis court and an indoor swimming pool. At the time we visited he was having an Italian-style garden done. There also an amazingly beautiful organic vegetable garden with some absolutely huge fruit and vegetables being picked. And there was, of course, the train car which David used as his office.'

After a week at Woodside, John and his wife planned to drive around England and do some sightseeing. Elton told them to come back if the weather was bad. Yet what struck Jorgenson was the matter-of-fact way that Elton dropped into the conversation who his next guests would be. 'I remember him saying that Gianni Versace and Princess Diana were coming round for lunch. It wasn't unusual for him to have such celebrity guests. They were his friends.' Within a year of this lunch date, however, both of Elton John's VIP friends would be dead.

CHAPTER 15

CELEBRICIDE

'Rightfully, people say, "Fucking 'Candle In The Wind'!" Even I wouldn't sing it for two years. It was too painful.'

Elton John, 2004

'I could find a shop in the Sahara Desert.'

Elton

I t is Saturday September 6, 1997. Elton John has just played the final chords of 'Candle In The Wind', a song he has sung hundreds of time before in public. But today the moment is very special and the audience very different. This is the funeral of Diana, Princess of Wales, and the venue is Westminster Abbey. Inside are rows of mourners. Outside, thousands are gathered. And watching on their TV sets is a total global audience of well over two billion people.

Up until the moment that Elton sits down at his piano, the programme has been formal and conventional: classical music by Mendelssohn, Vaughan Williams, Bach and Elgar is played before the congregation rises for the National Anthem. The Dean of Westminster has spoken. Hymns have been sung. There have then been readings by the Princess's sisters, Lady Sarah McCorquodale and Lady Jane Fellowes, then another hymn and a reading from Corinthians by the Prime Minister, Tony Blair. Elton John is there to represent popular culture and popular song and his contribution is significant because, uniquely, it represents an area of artistic endeavour traditionally deemed inappropriate for such sombre and formal occasions.

To celebrate the life and commemorate the death of a woman who was not only a world-wide icon but also a personal friend, Elton sings the rewritten lyrics powerfully, drawing on a career's worth of performance experience, his nerves are revealed only by the apparently independent and uncontrollable movement of his right eyebrow, which seems to have a life of its own as it rises at the enunciation of each new earnest phrase.

That day, Elton John is a conduit for the astonishing wave of grief that is apparently sweeping across the nation. As he sings, people in the Abbey cry (including, so it is reported, Diana's sons, William and Harry). And as the TV coverage of Elton's performance is intercut with images of the mourners outside, it seemed that his song has united a nation in tears.

*　*　*

For many, of course, the outward display of mass grieving merely confirmed the power of the media to manipulate the emotions and sentiments of a particular section of society. 'There can be no doubting the deep grief felt by some people,' reported one academic study. 'But it was the feeling of a highly vocal minority, not a countrywide reaction. Most people felt that, while Diana's death was a very tragic event, especially for her two boys, they couldn't feel grief for someone they didn't know. And they couldn't understand how others could feel deep grief for a woman who was ultimately a stranger, not a friend.' The study added, 'Most of the country was not in deep grief after Diana's death and couldn't identify with how they thought others were reacting. But the intolerance towards alternative views meant that it was only after September 1997 that people felt able to say so.'

Yet if the sense of loss for Diana was not as universal or as a profound as the media made out, the *manner* of her death has remained very much a topic of debate. The driver of the car, Henri Paul, was drunk and Diana was not wearing a safety belt. Furthermore, it has also been revealed that, as she lay trapped and semi-conscious in the wreckage of her car, the paparazzi, who had been following in a high-speed chase, crowded round her and took photographs. It was this aspect that was emphasised by Diana's brother, Earl Spencer, in his funeral speech, in which he claimed that his sister was 'the most hunted person of the modern age'.

In this respect, the original lyrics for 'Candle In The Wind' were actually more apt than the specially rewritten version. In the new version, Taupin used the language of romance: 'You called out to our country/And you whispered to those in pain/Now you belong to heaven/And the stars spell out your name'. In contrast, the 1973 version contained couplets that were much more appropriate to both the life and death of Diana. 'Never knowing who to cling to/When the rain set in' could have referred to Diana's quest for love, while 'They set you on the treadmill/And they made you change your name' could have been applied to her transition from private to public figure. 'Loneliness was tough/The toughest role you ever played' was an apt description of the emotionally troubled woman, while 'Even when you died/Oh, the press still hounded you' sounded like her epitaph. It seemed almost an act of protocol to re-write the song in order to make it less controversial.

'There were a couple of very good lines in that piece, there was a line which I thought was coming close to Blake in there,' was how broadcaster and writer Spencer Leigh summed up the tribute. 'I didn't think it was as bad as some people said it was. I actually think it must have been pretty difficult for Elton John, when he had sung one lyric all his life, to suddenly have to sing another one in those circumstances. It must have been horrendously difficult, worse than singing a new song, because there's a danger you'd go into the wrong verse.'

Amazingly, Bernie's new version of 'Candle In The Wind' had come about entirely by accident. After he had been asked by Buckingham Palace to sing at the funeral, Elton had rung Bernie to tell him that the radio stations had been playing 'Candle In The Wind' in tribute to Diana. 'I thought he said, "Let's rewrite the lyrics, or at least some of the lyrics, to 'Candle In The Wind'," confessed Bernie. 'What he actually meant, I later learned, was, "Could we write something new that was similar to

Candle in The Wind?" I totally misunderstood him on that initial phone call.' Taupin felt under extreme pressure to come up with the goods: 'My reaction was like somebody putting a hand around my heart and squeezing it, because I felt an immediate sense of intense pressure.'

After the funeral, Elton went on to record the new version with the legendary Sir George Martin as producer. Released as 'Candle In The Wind 1997', the single was a double A-side with 'Something About The Way You Look Tonight', a ballad from his new album, *The Big Picture*. It was a maudlin and somewhat trite combination, yet, wittingly or unwittingly, the caring public waived any claim to good taste and bought it in their millions. Keith Richards of the Rolling Stones made a barbed comment about Elton making a name for himself writing 'songs for dead blondes', which led Elton to retaliate: 'He's so pathetic, poor thing. It's like a monkey with arthritis, trying to go onstage and look young.'

One journalist in a quality newspaper rewrote the lyric as follows: 'Now it seems to me, you lived your life/ Singing songs best in the bin/ Your talent burned out long before/ Your legend ever did.' Emma Forrest in the *Guardian* called it 'drive-thru grief': '"Her footsteps on England's greenest hills…" in Versace stilettos? Diana was always in London. She hated the countryside. What are you talking about, Elton?'

The problem for Elton was, of course, to avoid accusations of cashing in. With a new album long scheduled for a September release, he was, as John Pareles of the *New York Times* said, 'in the odd position of trying not to capitalise on his best media exposure in at least a decade'. There was another source of irritation for Elton in the formidable figure of the entrepreneur Richard Branson. Branson was not only one of the few people in the world who, like Elton, could count his small change in millions, but he was also a close friend of the Princess and had played a leading role in mobilising the music industry to support his own idea of a tribute CD. According to biographer Judy Parkinson, Branson accused Elton of donating the song to the album initially, and then changing his mind. Elton counter-claimed that the two projects might happily co-exist and sell in the squillions in the name of Diana, adding that it would be unfair to expect the public to pay for 'Candle In The Wind 1997' twice, once on a single, once as a track on a CD. Just to reinforce his honourable intentions, Elton refused to allow any footage of his own performance to be used in the video that accompanied the release of the single.

In the end, all was well. By January 1998, *The Diana Princess Of Wales Tribute* CD had raised a reported £40 million. At the end of 1997, Elton handed over a cheque for £20 million to the memorial fund set up to commemorate the princess. And 'Candle In The Wind 1997 eventually became the biggest-selling single of all time. On the very first morning of its release it sold 250,000 copies in the UK alone. In Canada, it was Number 1 for 45 weeks and spent three years in the Top 20. By the end of 1997, it had sold 33 million copies worldwide.

Even the Government was playing ball. In 1984, the then Prime Minister Margaret Thatcher had initially refused to waive VAT on sales of the Band Aid charity single 'Do They Know it's Christmas?' before bowing to public pressure. In 1997, the Labour Chancellor Gordon Brown agreed to waive VAT on the Diana tribute record, resulting in a reported loss to the Treasury of £2.5 million from the first wave of sales alone. In February 1998, Bernie's handwritten lyrics fetched nearly £280,000 at a charity auction at Christie's. It was the highest price ever paid for a pop lyric manuscript.

By the end of 1998, it was estimated that the single had sold 4.8 million copies in the UK, eclipsing the 3.5 million sales of the previous biggest-selling UK single, 'Do They Know It's Christmas'. Back in third place, on a distant 2.5 million, were Queen and 'Bohemian Rhapsody'. 'Yes, it's even sold more than "The Macarena",' Elton joked to his band on hearing the news that the single had become the biggest seller of all time. In the end, even Elton grew tired of the song, realising that it had suffered from over-exposure: 'It's the sort of song that, I dunno, people might say if I never heard that song again, I'd be very, very happy.' 'The only way I'll ever sing it again is if the children [Princes William and Harry] ask me,' he added. 'Otherwise, it would be totally inappropriate.'

Yet Diana and Elton had been genuinely close for many years. Although her favourite band was Duran Duran, Diana obviously had a soft spot for him. 'Your Song' was one of her favourite Elton songs and Elton would say that the line 'Yours are the sweetest eyes' always reminded him of her. 'I think her greatest physical attribute were those eyes. They flirted with you; they were sorrowful and they were laughing. She had those beautiful eyes. I got to know her quite well and, of course, we had some things in common. We were both bulimic for a start and we both had marriages that failed and we were both extremely interested in Aids. You could talk about those and other issues with her in a way that you probably couldn't with any other member of the Royal Family. That's why she was such a special person.'

Diana had, of course, also met the Elton John band. Charlie Morgan remembers one particular exchange. 'I was wearing ear monitors,' he recalls. 'They had a pink fleshy colour and they were built for my ear. I had them in my hand, and Diana looked at them and said, "Good grief, what are those? I won't tell you what they look like." She meant, of course, that they looked like foetuses.'

Elton, being Elton, was usually in an almost perpetual state of break-up and make-up with his friends. For a short period, the relationship between him and Diana had also been frosty. 'We had a kind of falling-out just before, well, about a year before she died, just over something, you know. We were both pretty stubborn. It was one of her charity things that I had organised and she pulled out of it. I wasn't too happy and I let her know that. And she wrote me a very terse letter.'

Diana and Elton had, in fact, made up in July 1997. It had taken the death of one of Elton's closest friends to occasion the rapprochement. At the memorial service to Gianni Versace, who had been shot dead outside his house on July 15 that year, the world saw a grief-stricken Elton being comforted by Diana. 'He shone so bright with a lust for life/ Like the Sun King that he was' Elton was to sing almost a decade later in 'Blues Never Fade Away'. 'It was only when Gianni Versace was murdered that Diana and I got on the phone to each other and said, this is stupid,' revealed Elton. 'We hadn't talked, you know. It's one of those things that friends sometime do. You know, they're too proud to pick up the phone.'

Versace and Elton had also been very close friends. They would speak to each other twice, maybe three times a week, and jokingly greet each other as 'bitch'. 'He was like a soul mate really, someone more or less the same age as me,' Elton was to reflect. 'Completely obsessive, slightly mad, always wanting to change things, learn things. He taught me so much about art [and] architecture. If we were in Venice, he would take me to every church. You would never have a dull moment with him.' Yet their relationship was not sexual. Versace had a long-term companion in Antonio D'Amico. 'He was like a brother, really,' said Elton. 'We were both very much the same. We were both very impulsive. We both loved life. We both loved shopping.'

The year that was to culminate in a summer of tragedy had begun in frivolous style. Elton kicked off 1997 with a bit of modelling. In a series of quite bizarre and, some would say, mildly disturbing photos, he pouted and preened in a Versace dress, heavily made-up with a Shirley MacLaine-like hairdo. The headline in the *Sunday Times* read 'Ciao, Chubby. Revealed: Versace's New Supermodel'.

But it was in March that Elton would grab the headlines with the most over-the-top outfit of his career. For his fiftieth birthday party, he decided to go eighteenth century. With its three-feet-high silver wig and 15-foot feather train, his astonishing costume would have put even the Sun King himself to shame. The problem was that the dress was simply *too* ambitious, as John Jorgenson reveals: 'His fiftieth birthday was a fancy dress party. Brian May dressed as Dame Edna, Davey Johnstone went as a pirate and Elton's mum, Sheila, came as the Queen. There was a giant entrance and a red carpet and the venue itself was very classy. Elton had a huge wig, on top of which was a Spanish galleon that shot smoke out of the cannons.

'It got to the point where he was supposed to make a grand entrance and he wasn't there. I remember asking his PA, Bob Halley, where he was, and he had this look of, "Don't even ask, it's really bad" on his face. Because the wig was so big, Elton couldn't fit into a normal vehicle, so they had had to get a lorry. They decorated it as a throne room and they had two thrones, one for Elton and one for David, but it didn't have any windows or anything. The truck got stuck for 45 minutes or an hour in traffic and Elton had this 50lb wig on. There was nothing he could do. So, by the time he got to the party, he was really hot and sweaty and in a bad mood. He quickly made his entrance and then took the wig off and put on a smaller wig for the rest of the party.'

According to reports, Elton spent £120,000 on catering for the evening, including £6,000 on the cake alone. He later donated his costume to charity. In return, of course, he got some suitably unusual gifts from his celebrity friends. Elton had bought Rod Stewart a Zimmer frame for his fiftieth birthday 18 months earlier and Rod retaliated in suitable style. 'He sent me one of those old-fashioned ladies' hairdryers you sit underneath with the message: "The only thing I forgot to buy was the hair to go with it." It's like a Joan Crawford/Bette Davis relationship. Rod's never lost his vicious British humour and that's why I adore him.'

The fans also queued up to pay tribute to Elton. A week after his fiftieth birthday, Elton met Stephan Heimbecher, the founder in May 1988 of Rocket Fan, an Elton John fan club that, under the name of Hercules, subsequently became the biggest in the world. 'We named a star after him and Bernie,' says Heimbecher. 'It was one of the last stars visible with the naked eye from Earth which had yet to be named. It's now called "Elton Hercules John and Bernie Taupin". I also presented him with a leather ledger full of messages, drawings, photos and kisses from 300 fans from around the world. He seemed genuinely touched to be remembered by the fans.'

Elton cut another studio album in 1997, *The Big Picture*, a record that saw him reunited with Chris Thomas after a gap of five years. The album was not one much loved by its co-creator, Bernie Taupin: 'The production is abysmally cold and technical,' was his assessment. 'It's a dark album, introspective and ballad-oriented,' says Charlie Morgan, who also worked on the record. 'But the chord progressions are innovative on some of the tracks. "The River Can Bend" was an inspirational gospel tune, while "Love's Got A Lot To Answer For" was really sarcastic.

'"Live Like Horses", the duet with Pavarotti, was originally a cut from *Made In England*. That song had a great Bernie lyric about the death of his father and him being released from the shackles of life. Bernie really had something meaty to get his teeth into and the death of his father during *Made In England* was a real catalyst. The problem was that there were far too many slow tracks selected for the final running order of the record, and the lead-off single, "Something About The Way You Look Tonight", was just Elton by rote.'

'I remember whenever Elton was writing songs there would be this place in the song where there would be this chord change that sounded so classic Elton John,' says John Jorgenson. 'He would try every other chord he could think of to get away from that sound. But at the end of the day he would always go back to whatever the first one was. It was just interesting to see him go through the process; he wouldn't just take what came along. He was going to try out everything.'

'Elton would write a lot of the songs to a drum loop,' says Jorgenson. 'He would ask Charlie to give him a loop at a certain tempo and work from that. Davey and I did a lot of our guitar parts together actually because Chris was a hard taskmaster and we felt more confident doing it together. He could be intimidating.'

Thomas also saw fit to challenge Elton. 'I remember Chris Thomas daring to say something was substandard, which resulted in Elton storming out of the studio,' says Morgan. 'Chrissie Hynde was in the next studio and Elton barged past her and almost pinned her to the wall, shouting, "Not only is he a fucking bastard, he's a deaf one too." And Chrissie looked at me as if to say, "Oh, well, nothing's changed then," and walked back into the studio.'

Like so many of Elton's albums of the 1980s and 1990s, *The Big Picture* garnered mixed reviews, selling acceptably for an artist of Elton's stature. It was released the same month as Bob Dylan's *Time Out of Mind*. While Dylan's' record was hailed as a massive return to form and given ample column space, Elton's latest offering was seen as underwhelming, *just another* Elton John album. There was simply little new on display. Typically, in his two-star review in *Q*, Robert Yates wrote: 'The album offers as others before it and others after it, ballads with an anthemic undertow… If the album occasionally seems too neat, the songs' lyrics a touch trite or sentimental, well, that's part of the package too and plenty, doubtless, will approve.'

Elton embarked on a major world tour to promote the new record. If the record itself failed to yield any classic Elton cuts, his fans nevertheless supported the new tour with renewed fervour. 'The concerts after the death of Diana went up to a whole new level in terms of audience reaction,' says Jorgenson. 'It had made audiences realise what a treasure Elton was and not take him for granted. I remember saying to Davey, "These audiences are just ballistic. Was it more intense in the 1970s?" Davey said, "No, it was about like this." During the show, Elton covered "Sand And Water" by Beth Nielsen Chapman, because it said all he wanted to say to Gianni and Di.'

If the audiences loved it as ever, some of the critics didn't. Barbara Ellen, in the *Observer*, for example: 'Either when God was giving out attention spans he mistook me for a flea, or Elton John's 25-song show at Glasgow Scottish Exhibition Centre was far too long. Halfway through, I started wishing that I had brought some knitting, or a large jigsaw. Near the end, as yet another of Elton's epochal piano solos chewed another great chunk out of my allotted life span, I had actually to make a conscious effort not to clamber on to my seat and wave a white flag. Sure, Elton John is a big talent, with a big back catalogue to get through, but that doesn't mean his sets have to last longer than Hanson's combined puberty. I thought this tour was mean to be for Christmas, not for life.'

At the end of 1997 it was announced in the New Year's honours list that Elton was to receive a knighthood. This new honour came just two years after he had been awarded the CBE. Officially, his knighthood was 'for services to music and charitable services', although Elton's detractors couldn't help but point out the proximity of the award to his leading role in the tributes to Diana, Princess of Wales a few months earlier. According to David Bourke, a specialist in Elton-related anagrams, one anagram of Reginald Kenneth Dwight is the incredibly apt 'The weird England knight.'[1] 'Occasionally we send each other emails – "Dear Sir Elt... love, Sir Tim",' says Sir Tim Rice. 'It always strikes me as being rather strange that some people will quite happily accept a showbiz award yet don't want to get one from their country. Both are equally valid, in my view, or equally invalid. "I turned it down" sounds more arrogant than accepting it in the first place. In fact, I don't think you should be allowed to turn it down. You should get it and if you choose not to use it, that's your business.'

The huge success of *The Lion King* meant that Elton had become one of the very few rock performers to make the transition to writing for screen and stage. Later in the 1990s, Elton would collaborate with Tim Rice on the stage presentation of *Aida* and on another Disney film, *The Road To Eldorado*. 'I think the Disney films presented Elton with a lot of challenges that were new to him,' says the writer and broadcaster Spencer Leigh. 'Elton and Tim had to write a song before the animation was completed and they had to get it just right for the storyboard. And later, the way they did *The Lion King* on stage was just brilliant.'

Aida won a Tony Award for best score, running for four years on Broadway and playing almost everywhere around the world except the UK. 'The show did well,' confirms Rice. 'It wasn't a huge *Phantom Of The Opera* or *Evita*-type smash but it was a substantial hit and Elton wrote a lovely score. It has one or two of my favourite Elton songs. I think, "Elaborate Lives" is as good as "Can You Feel The Love Tonight". There is also a song called "Not Me" which I think is terrific.'

---

1 Two other Elton anagrams by Bourke are 'Anus-mad artist rant' (*Tantrums and Tiaras*), and the astonishing 'Shag it, and hurry! – Shirt-lifting faggot' for 'Saturday Night's All Right For Fighting.'

Sir Tim was less satisfied, however, with a 1999 CD, *Elton John And Tim Rice's Aida*, which saw a collection of talents ranging from Sting to the Spice Girls reinterpret the songs. 'I didn't think that particular album was successful. It was a bit of a mess. It was quite prestigious, but it didn't do that well. The cast album was much better and that also picked up a gold record. The problem with the first album was that none of the performers had a clue what the whole project was about. They all did it as a favour to Elton and one or two of them got words wrong. In the Tina Turner track, there are a couple of lines of absolute gibberish. I thought, "Why can't you get the words right?"'

For the next three years, Elton experienced a period in which his musical career seemed to be at its least energised. He would be a constant fixture, as ever, on the road, but the media talked about everything but his music. For example, in July 1998, the *Tatler* ran a survey that concluded that, in a league table of fantasy invitees, Sir Elton John was Britain's top party guest of choice. 'He comes highest because he touches so many different worlds – football, pop, fashion, films, shopping,' they concluded.

Elton's performances were never less than professional. In January and February 1998, *The Big Picture* tour played in the US and this was followed in March and April with another set of concerts with Billy Joel in Australia, New Zealand and Japan. Elton would sing a version of 'Uptown Girl' while Joel performed 'Your Song'. *The Big Picture* tour went back to the USA in April and May, before illness led to Joel pulling out of dates in the summer. In August and October, there was a further American leg. At the end of 1998, it emerged that *The Big Picture* had become Elton's 21st platinum album of his career. He had now sold a total of 60.6 million albums in the US, just ahead of Billy Joel's 60 million but still behind the country star Garth Brooks, the biggest-selling artist of all time in the US with 81 million albums.

Meanwhile, Elton kept up his involvement with Watford FC. He had bought the club for a second time, appointing Graham Taylor as director of football in 1996 (after Taylor's disappointing spell as England manager) and making him manager again a year later. Successive promotions from the Second Division to the Premiership meant the club was back in the big time for the 1999–2000 season. However, despite an early morale-boosting result when they defeated Liverpool at Anfield, the season turned out to be one of under-achievement and they were relegated, finishing bottom of the league. After reaching just ninth in the Championship the following season, Taylor announced his retirement. His successor, the former Italian international and Chelsea manager Gianluca Vialli, was a high-profile appointment who also failed to win promotion back to the Premiership.

If Elton's relationship with Graham Taylor remains close, his relationship with his long-standing business associate (and, of course, former lover) John Reid, has not stood the test of time. In fact, the two would split in the full glare of the media. The man who brought John Reid down was Benjamin Pell. Dubbed 'Benjy the binman' by *Private Eye*, Pell was given to rummaging through the bins of the rich, famous and powerful, unearthing documents of a private and sensitive nature and then selling them to the press. He was an OCD-afflicted man who for a short time became a highly successful operator and whose behaviour, it has been said, was the result of his unexpected failure in his law degree final exams, a rejection he was never able to come to terms with. His mission seemed to be to cause the maximum disruption to the rich and famous. 'I ruined his life,' Pell would later say of John Reid.

Pell's unofficial biographer, Mark Watts, calls him a 'bizarre, surreal man': 'Pell does see himself as wronged by the world and any victory over people, who by being successful, famous or powerful personify the world, he views as justice for himself. Reid had done nothing to Pell, but to Pell he represented a means to make money and inveigle himself into the lives of celebrities. Thus he was legitimate and fair game and, in Pell's Talmudic (il)logic, ruining Reid was vindication of his unrecognised genius and compensation for the way the world had wronged him.'

Pell had in his possession a letter from Elton's accountants, Price Waterhouse, of January 7, 1998. The letter, published by the *Mirror* on January 26, was a source of quite some embarrassment for Elton, as it stated that the 'available headroom' in his cash flow was due to run out in April. It seemed that, despite his huge wealth and massive annual income, Elton's personal expenditure was on such a luxurious scale that it was in danger of wiping it out. Reid was in America when the *Mirror* published the story: '£527,859 In One Day' ran the headline, as the full extent of Elton's expenditure became a matter of public knowledge.

Elton moved swiftly. He called Reid and angrily demanded to know who had sold the story to the *Mirror*. Reid began an investigation but immediately realised the seriousness of Elton's mood. He called his therapist, Beechy Colclough, from his home in Manhattan and said, 'This could cost me Elton'. When the culprit was found, John Reid served a writ on Pell and took legal action against the *Mirror* and the publicist Max Clifford, who had sold Pell's story to the paper. An audit of Elton's business empire began in order to find out where the money was going. The audit, conducted by KPMG, revealed a £20 million shortfall.

Elton also reacted angrily to a claim made in the papers that he was forced into borrowing some £25 million. He responded that he needed the loan to finance the buyback of the copyright of his and Bernie's songs from 1969–1973 from PolyGram, pointing out that financiers do not part with such huge sums to people who are bankrupt. He seemed to find the very thought that the public might think he was in financial trouble an affront.

For John Reid, it was the professional and personal low point of his long career. In February, his mother had died. His close friend from Rocket days, David Croker, died of a heart attack at the age of 48. And then, on May 11, 1998, Elton John sacked him. He had to lay off 20 members of the 26-strong staff of John Reid Enterprises. 'It was the unhappiest day of my life,' he admitted. 'I never though this could happen to me, but it has.'

'I always got on well with John Reid,' Charlie Morgan says. 'I would say that probably counted against me, because soon after he got sacked, I was told I wouldn't be required any more and that the reason for my departure was that my performances had dropped off, which wasn't true. John Reid had put Andrew Haydon in charge of John Reid

Enterprises. I never trusted him; he was constantly trying to cut my wages. Reid, to his credit, basically said, "Yes, I made a very poor decision putting Andrew Haydon at the reins, I can see that, but I really want to sort this out." Elton said, "Too late, you're sacked."

'Reid was very, very low at that point. I made it public that I felt that Elton really hadn't given enough chances to the man who had kept his career alive for nearly three decades, including resurrecting it in the early 1990s by getting him *The Lion King* score. I love John. I think he was also struggling with drugs at certain times and he had a very hard time with Elton. Obviously, he's a quick-tempered man but I really feel he was very much made the whipping boy in all of this.

'I think in the 1990s he was very much trying to come to terms with himself and he was becoming a better person and although he'd had a chequered past, I really felt as if he was trying to make amends. For that to happen to him in the late 1990s was really a big blow. Besides, Elton really didn't want to know about his finances. He wanted to walk around, playing gigs and spending money, and for someone else to sort it all out for him. The problem was he really didn't want any say in his fiscal affairs other than the spending of it.'

Reid settled with Elton out-of-court for $5 million but Elton went ahead with his action against Haydon and Price Waterhouse for the alleged missing £20 million. He made additional accusations of alleged breach of trust, breach of contract and negligence. The crux of the dispute was whether the costs charged to Elton's companies named in the action – Happenstance Limited, William A Bong Limited and J Bondi Limited – should instead have been borne by John Reid Enterprises. Elton claimed that, in effect, he was being double-charged and that tour expenses should not have been charged to Elton's companies. Haydon countered that this was standard practice in the entertainment business.

An informal agreement had been reached in 1984 between Elton and John Reid, whereby Reid's commission would be increased in return for him taking a tighter control over all aspects of Elton's finances. Elton claimed that he clearly remembered (even though no written or taped record of their discussion existed) that Reid had agreed to bear the cost of all overseas tour expenses. When he discovered that all foreign tour expenses had been charged to his own companies, he saw this as sharp practice, although Reid denies that he would ever have entered into a verbal agreement with Elton to the effect that he would bear the cost of touring out of his own company. At one stage in the hearing, Elton lost his cool, claiming, 'Why would someone with a criminal record be incapable of doing something like that?' He immediately apologised and withdrew this smear on Reid's character.

There was more embarrassment to come for Elton. As the trial went on, the sheer ridiculousness of his spending became increasingly evident and was reported by a gleeful, if disbelieving press. It emerged that between 1996 and 1997 he had spent £40 million, including £293,000 on flowers alone and £250,000 on just one visit to a Versace store.

Elton lost the court case. The judgement of April 11, 2001 found against him and the singer was burdened, according to reports, with legal fees of around £8 million. A leave to appeal was also rejected. Had it all been worth it? After all, £20 million was just small change for Elton. In his eyes, there had been a betrayal of trust and Elton wanted a public proof of wrongdoing. He didn't get it.

Reid appeared totally traumatised by the experience. His role as manager of Michael Flatley, the star of *Riverdance* and *Lord Of The Dance*, was also to end in a high-profile court case in 1998. Of Elton, Reid said, 'He chose just to cut me off – I'd seen him do it to other people in the past.'

'I am still good friends with John Reid and he has been fantastic to me,' says singer Judie Tzuke, who for many years recorded on Rocket Records. 'I know he can be difficult, but so can everyone. Elton and John's relationship lasted much longer than that of most managers and artists. I think it's a real shame that they're not friends any more.' For his part, Reid was adamant that he had left rock management for good: 'I wouldn't manage again if Elvis and Jesus came back.'

By the early 1990s, Elton might have beaten cocaine addiction, alcoholism and bulimia, but shopping remained the one of his 'addictions' he has never been able – or, arguably, tried – to combat. 'For Elton, when the going gets tough, the tough go shopping,' a close friend has said. 'I'm addicted to buying a piece of property, doing it up, and then buying another piece,' admitted Elton in 1998. 'My mum always wanted me to put my money in bricks and mortar instead of up my nose.'

When one has almost limitless wealth, money stops being legal tender and simply becomes Monopoly cash to play with as one pleases. The good side is that Elton John has always given huge chunks of it away. Less laudably, his accumulation of consumer goods, from CDs to shoes, from artwork to suits, gives the impression at least of someone a little out of control. In the same way that Elton used to gorge himself on ice cream and cockles, he developed over the years what we might call 'Retail Bulimia'.

A feature of Elton's private life has been the accumulation of wealth in the form of commodity goods then the purging of this wealth, as huge chunks of his belongings are sold, auctioned off or given away. Duly purged, he then feels able to build up yet another million-dollar collection of something else, which he will then most likely give away or sell at a future date.

'Elton is an all-or-nothing person,' says Charlie Morgan. 'I feel that there's an element of Elton not having addressed the reason for his addictions. It seems to me that he's moved his addiction from drink and drugs to shopping. It's the act of buying that gives him the pleasure. I've been in Versace in Milan and he has just cleared the racks and thrown down his platinum credit card – it's something to see. And he buys everything, in every size, so he can give it to his friends. He's really generous. Shop assistants would be following him around, clearing the rails. If we were in a particular city where there was a major artist, the artist would bring in their paintings to show him and Elton would sit in his dressing room and say, "Yeah, I'll take that one, that one, that one and that one," point to three or four things on the wall, and then the artist would hand Elton the bill, pack them up and send them to him.'

Gary Farrow, who for many years has worked with Elton as his publicist, remembers how spending sprees at Tower Records would go. 'They would usually open about 9.30am and Elton would get there about 9am and have the whole shop to himself. They would probably do more business in that half-hour than in the rest of the day. Elton would get a trolley and buy two of everything. He just loves music. I remember once he bought 100 copies of an album by Craig Armstrong [composer for films such as *Moulin Rouge, Romeo and Juliet* and *Love Actually*] purely because he loved it so much. He sent it to all his friends. That's what he does – he loves helping and nurturing talent. He's so unsung for that.'

Of course, so much of what Elton spends is for others and at least the public benefit from his ritual purges. In November 1997, he opened up his own second-hand shop, Out of the Closet, with all proceeds going to his Aids charity. Out of the Closet was only open for a few days, but it was the shop's third appearance, with a previous opening in London and one in Atlanta. On this occasion he sold off 10,000 items of clothing and shoes at just 10 per cent of their original price. His Versace shirts sold for £25. 'People [companies] always give you stuff,' he explained. 'It always amazes me that, when you are struggling, you have to buy stuff and when you have made it and can afford to buy it, people give you tons of stuff. It's nice that people will get the benefit of me being a shopaholic and [I can] raise money.'

Elton was showing few signs of wanting to slow down. In July 1999, however, he had a little warning that he wasn't immortal after all. Playing tennis at home in Nice he'd felt dizzy and the original diagnosis was a viral infection that had affected his ear. He was due to fly to Dublin and travel to Luttrellstown Castle to sing at the wedding of David Beckham and Victoria Adams, or, as the world knows her, Posh Spice. Elton was taken ill aboard the plane and tests revealed that he had an irregular heartbeat and needed to be fitted with a pacemaker.

The operation, which took place at Wellington Hospital in north London on July 9, was a routine one and a complete success. Elton was not given a general anaesthetic but a local anaesthetic and a Valium-type tranquilliser that kept him asleep for most of the operation. 'I was unconscious for an hour-and-a-half and woke up for the end of the operation,' he said. 'Thank God for the British medical system because I went through every test known to man to find out what was wrong. I thought I had sunstroke.' Elton returned to work at the end of August, when he played for a private party in Orlando, Disney World. 'I know what it's like to be 50,' he joked there. 'After last month, I know what it feels like to be 70.'

In November, Elton incurred the unlikely wrath of the Scout Association after a controversial performance at London's Royal Albert Hall as part of a concert to commemorate the gay rights association Stonewall's tenth anniversary. He sang Dusty Springfield's 'In Private' and the Pet Shop Boys' 'It's A Sin'. 'Never one to err on the side of caution or good taste, Elton, 52, squeezes into a tight red suit (Versace probably) and is followed on to the stage by a troupe of dangerously young-looking dancers in scout uniform,' reported Paul Clements. 'The overtones are obvious and discomforting but we go with it. It's a joke, right? On command, the boys loosen their woggles, bare their chests and, well, writhe.' Stonewall stonewalled: 'We apologise to the Scout Association if it has caused them any offence, but I'm sure no offence was intended.'

In 2000, Elton kept up the incredible pace in terms of live perfor-mances and played a series of intimate solo shows – just him and a piano. The year's big event, however, would be the recording of an all-star bash at Madison Square Garden in October. Entitled *One Night Only*, it was in fact culled from two performances. 'I remember a lot of the guests had trouble getting to Madison Square Garden because of traffic,' says John Jorgenson. 'We were on our feet all day rehearsing and so we were tired before show time. And I don't think any of us did our best on the first night. On the second night, the energy was better. Ronan Keating seemed very nervous to me. And it seemed odd to include him as he wasn't really that well known in America. Anastasia was good, but Mary J Blige wasn't particularly friendly. Billy Joel was there, as was Kiki Dee, one of the greatest voices of her time.'

Yet there remained a feeling that Elton needed to refocus, to turn his career around. Yes, he was super-famous. Yes, he was still a live draw. But he was now more famous for his riches than for his records. Elton, in his mid-fifties and with a 35-year career behind him, was about to enter another, more musical, more creative phase of his career. For Elton John, it was time to go back to basics.

CHAPTER 16

MUSICAL REHAB

'Who'll walk me down to church when I'm 60 years of age?
When the ragged dog they gave me has been ten years in the grave?'

'Sixty Years On'; lyrics: Bernie Taupin; music: Elton John

'Music has always been like an addiction for me, but it's the only one of
my addictions that never caused me too many problems. I've always been
completely devoted to music.'

Elton John, 2001

The song starts with a Lennon-esque piano melody, the sort of slightly echoey production to be found on the *Plastic Ono Band* album and, of course, on the signature ballad of the 1970s, 'Imagine'. But then the voice kicks in and it's unmistakably Elton. It's a different, older, pared-down version of the man on display here. For the first time in years, there is nothing extraneous in the production, no distractingly cheesy synth fills, just a voice, a piano, and then a big fat drum sound and what sounds like a long-lost George Harrison lead guitar part. Primal, eloquent, and beautiful, 'I Want Love' is the best Elton single for a quarter of a century. And Taupin's words, in their sincerity, openness and simplicity, are a perfect match for the classic chord changes: 'I want love/But it's impossible/A man like me/So irresponsible.'

It's a lyric by Bernie Taupin and it's the story of both his life and Elton's. By the time the song is released as a single in the early autumn of 2001, Bernie and Elton have been making music together for 35 years, with just one short break. It has been the most successful and longest-lasting songwriting partnership in popular music history. And now, with both men in their fifties, their songs, perhaps understandably, tend to look back, to assess, to evaluate. 'I Want Love' has been written by a man who has been married three times for a man who seems to have spent the whole of his life searching for the elusive love of his life. 'Despite all the success,' Elton has said, 'I think I just wanted to be loved. I wanted someone to love me.'

Soon the song is being lauded as a genuine comeback. But when it appears on music TV, there is no sign of Elton. Paradoxically, just as he appears more alive and eminent within his own music, he chooses to disappear from view in the promo. His place is taken by actor Robert Downey Jr, a perfect choice. The excellent video shows Downey lip-synching to Elton's words as he moves around a deserted mansion. Again, in its simplicity it reminds us of John and Yoko's film for 'Imagine', with Lennon sitting at the piano of their home in Ascot while Yoko moves slowly round the domestic setting, opening the curtains, letting in the light.

Downey has recently served a custodial sentence for breaking parole after a succession of drug and drink charges, and his life has very publicly been appraised and his personality dissected. He is going through a period of rehabilitation, much the same as Elton had undergone a decade earlier and Taupin himself in the late 1970s. The song's message, about wanting to re-establish some sort of emotional contact after a dark period of self-abuse and turmoil, sounds utterly convincing.

The director is the artist Sam Taylor-Wood: 'It took 16 takes to do that video and we used the last one. Robert Downey Jr was so incredible to work with. It was quite a marketing point for him, because it was the first thing he did when he came out of rehab and back on the straight and narrow. It's proper acting he's doing, not pop video acting; when he first did it, it was like the disco version, arms and legs going everywhere. I had to gaffer-tape his hands into his pockets for him to learn to keep them down.'

Elton has grown to dislike making videos. With so many hang-ups about his weight, his size, his looks and his hair, it is perhaps inevitable that he would remove himself from his promos altogether. With the emphasis at the beginning of the tiresome *Pop Idol* era placed very firmly placed on youthful good looks, a middle-aged man with middle-aged spread presents a mildly ridiculous picture on MTV. The lithely T-shirted Downey, in his late thirties, shows enough grey hairs to make the song of experience believable, but his photogenic good looks conveyed the kind of sexiness Elton knows he himself does not have. With the notable exception of the visibly elderly and failing Johnny Cash, who turned the video for his remarkable reading of Nine Inch Nails' 'Hurt' into a visual last will and testament, rock stars of a certain vintage, like Elton, have begun phasing themselves out of their own promotional videos.

This does not, however, mean that Elton has followed his contemporaries in all but abandoning the idea of having hit singles. Far from it. Such is his astonishing competitiveness that he simply refuses to submit to the notion that a man in his mid-fifties cannot remain a fixture in the pop charts. In the new decade, Elton has come out fighting. 'I've had a few relegation seasons but with this new album, I feel I'm back in the Premiership,' he tells the *Mirror* in August 2001. 'I'll never be Manchester United but I'll settle for being a pop version of Watford: serious contenders playing attractive, sexy football.'

*   *   *

It was time to face facts. The brutal truth was that he had not recorded a classic Elton John record for many, many years, arguably not since *Blue Moves* back in 1976. There had been good, and sometimes great, moments on albums since 1976 and the idea that he somehow went missing in the late 1970s and early 1980s does not bear close scrutiny. The truth was that, on the 15 studio albums released since *Blue Moves*, almost every one had been pretty good in parts. But none had been good across the board. This was something Elton and Bernie now intended to rectify.

In 2000, they held a 'summit meeting' at Elton's house in Nice. Elton had already spoken 'very frankly' to Bernie Taupin: 'And I said to him, and he totally agreed with me, that when I do things now, people think of Elton John as someone who's very rich, who lives an extravagant life-style, spends a lot on flowers, has had a hair transplant and now a hair weave, is homosexual, has an Aids foundation, is chairman of a football club, has written *The Lion King* – and then they'll think, "He also makes records". And I thought: this has got to change. I *am* a larger-than-life persona. But the thing that got me here was the records. So… I've gone back to basics.' 'We took it all more seriously; we weren't so flippant as we were before,' confirmed Bernie. 'We were very aware that we went through a period of time when we weren't making our best material.'

'Bernie had already written a load of lyrics and he brought some of them to Nice. I think the main decision was that we had to be really harsh on ourselves,' Elton explained to a journalist. 'We had to draw a line in the sand and say, "By the time this album comes out, I'm going to be 54. I want to make a really strong, perfect album! The best album I can do at the time." And I think with this album, we've already achieved that.'

With the new album, *Songs From The West Coast*, Elton stripped back his sound to its essential elements. The songs should be recorded simply, with a minimum of production fairy-dust. They should be well constructed and memorable, with a live band sound. Elton's voice and piano playing should be at the fore. One influence on the new record would be Ryan Adams and his *Heartbreaker* album. Elton was impressed by its simplicity. He wanted his own new music also to stand or fall on its simple charms.

Elton was wont to compare this new, more primal style of music to his work of the early 1970s. It was certainly true that his new songs contained much of the musical DNA of his classic records of the first half of the 1970s. But there were, of course, some major differences too. Elton's voice had changed. In 1971, it was the voice of a young man; in 2001, it was deep, sonorous and much more manly.

Likewise, the new Elton John records were now about mature reflection. There were songs about relationships, politics, love and death. Three decades earlier, the songs had been youthful narratives about the Wild West, or pipedreams about movie stars. Likewise, the frenetic pace of a 'Saturday Night's Alright For Fighting' and the unabashed pop of 'Daniel' were now nowhere in evidence. Elton's new music was seldom either rocky or poppy. But perhaps nowhere was the new Elton so unlike the old than in the production. The detail of Gus Dudgeon's production, the intricacy of strings, acoustic elements, electronic instruments and rock guitar, had created a weave of sound that could never be repeated. In its place was a not unbecoming simplicity.

Songs From The West Coast was a massive return to form, an album good all the way through, in places as good as Elton had ever been, on a par with his greatest moments from the 1970s. 'I really admire Elton for taking that step and saying, actually, the records of the last 20 years haven't been great. Let's address this and do something about it,' says the writer Patrick Humphries. 'He obviously analysed what made a good Elton John record and for Elton John to do that is really admirable. One wishes some of his peers and contemporaries would take a leaf out of his book.' 'All the songs were written in Los Angeles and performed and recorded there, except for the vocals, which I did in England,' said Elton. 'I called it *Songs From The West Coast* because that seemed appropriate. I had never really made a full album in Los Angeles before. Everybody who worked on the album lived there. My band lived there.'

The tone was set in the first ten seconds of the album. 'The Emperor's New Clothes' began with a classic Elton piano melody with a touch of greatness about it. There then followed a succession of truly memorable Elton songs. The funky 'Dark Diamond' featured Stevie Wonder on clavinet and harmonica, while 'Look Ma, No Hands' had a wonderful melody. But it was track four, 'American Triangle', featuring Rufus Wainwright on vocals, that catapulted the album from very good to brilliant. Bernie's lyric dealt with the death of a 21-year-old American student, Matthew Shepard, murdered in a sexually motivated attack. Shepard had been picked up, driven to a remote locale and then robbed, beaten, tied to a fence and left to die. When he was found, barely alive, 18 hours later, it was said that his entire face was red with blood, except for two startling white streaks left by his tears: 'I've seen a scarecrow wrapped in wire/Left to die on a high ridge fence'.

'Original Sin' was another wonderful song and would soon become a live favourite. 'Ballad Of The Boy In The Red Shoes' was Bernie's story of a ballet dancer who, dying of Aids, reflects on his youth. 'I wanted to make as harsh a condemnation as I could of the Reagan White House for initially ignoring the existence of this disease and refusing to fund research,' said Bernie. The album's tearjerker of a final track, 'This Train Don't Stop There Anymore', was arguably the best ending of any of Elton's albums.

The album was a well-deserved success, reaching Number 2 in the UK, although surprisingly only Number 15 in the States. The first single, 'I Want Love', reached Number 9 in the UK but flopped completely in America.

For the next two single releases, Elton hired David LaChapelle to make the videos. They were superb. For 'This Train Don't Stop There Anymore', the 1970s Elton was played with total believability by Justin Timberlake. The camera followed Timberlake as he walks through a backstage area just before a gig, turning on the charm for the camera, greeting fans and promoters, receiving a gold disc with a Bernie look-a-like. It was a vivid re-creation of the depersonalisation of the star, the sadness behind the smile.

For the third single, 'Original Sin', Elton and Elizabeth Taylor played the concerned parents of an Elton-obsessed daughter, played by Mandy Moore. In a homage to *The Wizard of Oz*, her dream came true when she was whisked back in time by the Good Witch of the North along the yellow brick road to a 1976 Elton John concert. As Elton was about to come on stage, she took her seat in an audience comprising very accurate look-alikes, among others, Bette Midler, Sonny and Cher, Barbra Streisand and Liza Minnelli. At the end, the girl was transported back to her own world: as in the film, it was, of course, only a dream. As the two parents comforted their daughter, Elton the concerned dad was heard to say, 'Who is this Elton John anyway? Not some goddamn fudge-packer, I hope!' Priceless.

The album's cover was also one of Elton's best. Elton sits at a table in an LA bar, a white dove to his left. He seems unaware of the police car parked outside, visible through open Venetian blinds. The police are searching a middle-aged man with goatee and sunglasses, played by Elton's personal assistant, Bob Halley. The distinguished, grey-haired man peering through the window is Mike Hewiston, Elton's valet. The younger man in a cowboy hat the bar is none other than David Furnish himself. The album was dedicated to Matthew Shepard and to Oliver Johnstone, Davey Johnstone's nine-year-old son who had tragically died in the family's swimming pool.

In 2002, the Elton John world lost another favourite in tragic circumstances. On July 20 that year, Gus Dudgeon and his wife Sheila were killed in a car accident on the M4. Gus was 59. 'Just before Gus died he was telling me that Elton had asked him to engineer the orchestra for a concert with the Royal Opera House,' says Stuart Epps. Dudgeon was Elton's best producer, of that there is no question. At the memorial service at St Andrew's Church, Cobham, Surrey, Elton called him 'the greatest producer of a generation. He was a loving and inspiring man, and between 1970 and 1975 we made 17 albums together. I can't remember a happier time,' Elton said, and performed 'High Flying Bird' as a tribute.

Songs From The West Coast was well reviewed and Elton's career had a new lease of life. Finally, after years of being famous for being famous, he was now once again famous for being a brilliant songwriter. Not that this stopped him, of course, from attending to his extra-musical activities, central to which was his tireless charity work.

In July 1999, Elton had initiated the White Tie and Tiara Ball, a charity event at his home in Woodside held in support of the Elton John Aids Foundation. This fund-raising event has been an annual fixture ever since and an important part of the summer social season for the rich and famous. Each year has a different theme and Woodside is decorated lavishly in appropriate trappings.

In 2003, for example, the theme was Imperial Russia, and the event was compèred by Dame Judi Dench. 'Under a vast marquee decorated with real gold to resemble the onion domes of traditional Russian churches, a six-course banquet was served to celebrity guests who had jetted in from around the world,' gushed *Hello* magazine. Among those quaffing the vintage champagne were the Duchess of York, Naomi Campbell, Jemima Khan, David and Victoria Beckham and Kylie Minogue. A total of 500 guests partied the night away in a Russian winter wonderland – complete with ice rinks and performing figure skaters – created in the grounds of the singer's Windsor mansion. The musical entertainment was provided by Barry Manilow, Donna Summer and Elton, who formed a power-ballad super-group for a version of 'Could It Be Magic'.

In 2005, an African-themed event raised £3.9 million. Chic and Patti Labelle provided the music while the 600 guests enjoyed smoked tilapia with banana-and-pineapple relish on plantain crisps and pepperberry-marinated beef entrecote served with sour cherry jus. Elton threw in some live giraffes for good measure. In 2006 the theme was fifteenth century Mogul India and the guests included Kylie, Sharon Osbourne, Rod Stewart and Jake Shears of the Scissor Sisters, who sat down to dinner in a marquee decorated to look like a mini Taj Mahal. A charity auction raised £4.6 million. According to the *Daily Telegraph*, 'a mystery woman bid a cool £500,000 for the chance to have Sir Elton John and Sir Tim Rice record a unique, made-to-order CD in her honour.' The re-formed Take That provided the main musical entertainment.

It was a world away from the life of Elton's half-brother, Geoff Dwight. Geoff lives in a small terraced house in Ruthin, Wales, where he makes Celtic harps in his shed and is a devotee of Eastern religions. According to *Blender* magazine, 'He's only met Elton – 20 years his senior – three times, but claims he lost what respect he had for him when John failed to attend their father Stanley's funeral.

*

For the newly energised Elton, 2002 and 2003 would be two of his best years in the UK charts. In the summer of 2002 he was back in the Top 5 of the British singles charts with a version of 'Your Song' with Alessandro Safina. Another of his oldies, 'Sorry Seems To Be The Hardest Word', reached Number 1 in December 2002, this time covered by the boy band Blue in collaboration with Elton. Also that Christmas, another Elton compilation, *Greatest Hits 1970–2002*, reached Number 3 and would spend a year in the UK charts. In September 2003, 'Are You Ready For Love?', recorded in 1977 but not released until 1979, found new exposure when Sky TV in the UK used it as the backing music for their sports channel. By way of confirmation that Elton had entered a new phase of hit making, the single, re-released by Norman Cook, aka Fatboy Slim, on his Southern Fried label, would reach Number 1.

Unlike so many of his contemporaries, Elton had never given up on the pop charts. Although aware that the days of him dominating the charts were over, he knew he was still able to sell in sufficient quantities to be played on mainstream radio. He didn't want to become a niche act, speaking to an ever-dwindling hard core of supporters. Elton still cared about connecting with his natural constituency, which was nothing if not the mainstream.

In the autumn of 2004, Elton released *Peachtree Road*, the second album to follow his musical rehab session with Bernie. 'I called it *Peachtree Road* because it's the one road that goes through the whole of Atlanta,' Elton told BBC DJ Steve Wright. 'I have an apartment on Peachtree Road, but the studio is 15 miles away, and that's still on Peachtree Road. There is "peach tree" everything in Atlanta. It's my American base and I've been there 13 or 14 years. I'd never written or recorded an album in Atlanta, but I really wanted to because I love the city so much so it was kind of an homage to my American home.' 'Elton's new album is a songwriter at the top of his game,' said one of his most vocal supporters, Elvis Costello. 'There are a couple of melodies which are up there with his best, particularly "My Elusive Drug".'

In interviews to promote *Peachtree Road*, the significance of Elton's decision in 1990 to enter rehab was still very much apparent. It was something that he still couldn't stop talking about. 'I'm most grateful for just having my life back after I wasted 16 years of it doing drugs,' he said. 'One thing the 12-step program teaches you is gratitude and I've been blessed a million times over. My life is the best it's ever been and it seems to get better. I've done a lot of work on myself. Like the song "Weight Of The World" says, "I'm happy to see a sunset/Instead of a line." That's exactly where my life's at today.'

The songwriting on the new album was not as distinctive as it had been on *Songs From The West Coast*. There was a slight air of retread about the rootsiness of it all. 'The whole album is a bit of a throwback to those days, because we went into the studio and played it live and we were writing the songs in the studio. It's very Southern, country, blues, gospel-y,' said Elton. 'It's a little bit introspective. "Weight Of The World" is written by Bernie about how I am now, and 'My Elusive Drug' is about me and how I have now found the drug I was looking for, which is my partner David. 'There is a lot of hope on the album. "Too Many Tears" is a hopeful song, as is "Answer In The Sky" and "All That I'm Allowed". They give messages of hope.'

Yet, despite Elton's dogged determination to tour the album for over a year and his decision to re-release it with additional tracks, it failed to take off, reaching only Number 17 in the US and Number 21 in the UK. 'It is probably one of my lowest-selling albums of all time,' he told the *Telegraph*. 'It was disappointing everywhere in the world, so I have to hold my hands up and accept that the songs just didn't connect. I'm proud of *Peachtree Road*, but if I think about it logically, people may have 10 or 12 Elton John albums in their collection already. Do they need another one?'

If *Peachtree Road* had failed to ignite, there were other areas of the pop arts in which Elton enjoyed huge success. He continued to write for the stage, achieving a huge hit with *Billy Elliot*, based on the 2000 film of the same name. Whereas the film had classic pop from the likes of T Rex, the Jam and the Clash, for the stage show Elton wrote a completely new score. Set in the UK in the mid-1980s, at the time of the miners' strike, it told the story of a working-class lad from County Durham with a talent for ballet.

By 2005, Elton had become the most successful composer working for the stage, with productions of *The Lion King*, *Aida*, and *Billy Elliot* all running. And all this by being what Michael Riedel in the *New York Post* called 'Broadway's first virtual composer'. 'Because he might be performing anywhere in the world at any given moment, John writes his musicals by fax, e-mail, or even cell phone,' marvelled Riedel. 'During the three-month tryout of *Billy Elliot*, the director Stephen Daldry would sometimes hold up his cell phone in the wings so John could hear the dialogue that set up the song he was writing.' A single from the show, 'Electricity', reached Number 4 in the UK charts at the end of July. With endearing candour, Elton told an interviewer: 'Just between you, me and the gatepost, I'm not really a lover of musicals.'

A little earlier that same month, Elton found himself again on top of the UK singles charts. A sample of his 1971 song 'Indian Sunset' was used by Eminem in his version of the 2-Pac song 'Ghetto Gospel' and became a posthumous Number 1 for 2-Pac. Some found Elton's admiration for Eminem puzzling. 'I've always admired Eminem's thinking,' said Elton. 'That's the reason I wanted to appear on the Grammys with him [duetting on a version of 'Stan'] when I was asked, despite all the nonsense talked about his being homophobic.' Boy George, however, was far from impressed: 'It's like me singing with Pol Pot. People call you a fag or whatever occasionally, but it's so much more prevalent now and he [Eminem] has to take some responsibility. He was an arsehole and I think every gay person with a brain cell found it hideously offensive to see Elton performing with him.'

Elton also began a residency in Las Vegas with his *Red Piano* show, which debuted in 2004. Back in the day, the Who had cried, 'I hope I die before I get old'. But, as we know, all rock stars are fibbers and sell out in the end. In 1976, Elton had told *Sounds*, 'That's the side I hate. I can't bear showbiz people. I hate Vegas. People say to me, "Oh, you'll probably be doing Vegas, won't you?" I say, "You must be joking, I've got more pride!"' Three decades on, Elton had changed his tune. The show's visuals were designed by David LaChapelle with the extensive use of video technology and a huge LED display panel. The film 'The Bitch Is Back' showed Pamela Anderson pole-dancing. For 'I'm Still Standing', LaChappelle created a career-spanning pop-art montage of Elton through the ages.

But the most important thing was that, perhaps against the odds, Elton John had re-established himself as a credible artist. By 2004, he was facing up to the extraordinary fact that he was in danger of becoming cool. There were echoes of Elton's music in many of the new acts. Ben Folds in America was one such example with his piano-led pop. In Britain, Robbie Williams had arguably based his entire post-Take That career on the sort of populist agenda laid down by Elton. Williams' song 'Angels', a massive European hit, was the sort of power-rock ballad Elton had patented in the 1970s. But the group most obviously minted in Elton's image was the Scissor Sisters. Their self-titled debut album pastiched the glam-era Elton of 'Benny And The Jets' on the rollicking piano pop of 'Laura' and 'Take Your Mama Out'. They sounded more like Elton than Elton did. Elton himself does not fully agree with those who say the band are Elton clones. 'I heard bits of David Bowie, I heard bits of Pink Floyd, bits of the Bee Gees,' he said of the first album.

He could not, of course, help but be a fan. 'You are a shining example of people who want to write great songs that come from the heart,' said Elton, interviewing Scissor Sisters in 2006 for *Interview* magazine. 'That's very rare these days – to have a mixture of melody, fun, rhythm, homage to the past, but with your own stamp on it. I mean, people said to me, "Oh, it sounds a lot like you," and I thought, yeah, maybe on one or two tracks, but it also has your own stamp on it.' The band's massive-selling 2006 UK single, 'I Don't Feel Like Dancing', was actually co-written by Elton.

Another aspect to Elton's new coolness is his candour. He is no longer dismissed as an MOR horror act with an endless repertoire of dodgy ballads. Rather, he is now championed for his outspokenness. A national treasure, Elton John is now virtually untouchable. He can say almost anything, safe in the knowledge that his huge stature commands such respect that he is unimpeachable. In the space of just a few weeks in the autumn of 2004, for example, Elton reportedly announced at the *Q* Awards that Madonna 'should be shot' for allegedly lip-synching on tour, called a posse of pushy Taiwanese photographers at Taipei Airport 'rude, vile pigs' and even managed to upset the suits at Radio One by swearing live on air at 9am during the Chris Moyles breakfast show. Thinking the programme was being pre-recorded and having already used the word 'fucking', Elton went on to ask if 'wank', 'tits', 'bugger' and 'bollocks' were also on the banned list. 'I apologise to the young boys and girls,' said Moyles on air, 'but it *is* Elton John.'

In fact, Elton didn't actually say that Madonna should be shot, but rather that people who charge exorbitant prices for tickets and then lip-synch should be shot. Although he undoubtedly did say, 'Madonna best fuckin' live act? Fuck off. Since when has lip-synching been live?' 'The Madonna thing was said... and you would have to have been there ... at one of those irreverent lunches,' said Elton. '[Compere] Jonathan Ross was very irreverent to all of us; it was very funny. Some of the jokes that were going on could never have been repeated on any radio station in the world, I would think. And I just got up and said what I felt, that if Madonna had been nominated for best show, I would have had no qualms about it, but it's an open secret that those kind of shows use music on tape and I didn't think it was fair to people in that category who go out and play night after night. Having said that, she is one of my favourite artists on record, *Music* is one of my favourite records of the last five years and she is the least culpable of those people. Do I regret saying it, in the heat of the moment? Obviously I do, because I do like her. I didn't say anything that nobody had thought. I just thought, no big deal.' Two Christmas cards to Madonna that year were apparently returned unopened.

It seemed as if Elton was enjoying the fun. Seldom a month went by without him having a spot of verbals with someone or other in the music business. In 2006, Oasis's Noel Gallagher was quoted as saying,

'Life is a great thing, why shut yourself away from it? I can't understand people like Elton John…' The expletive-riddled retort from Elton was: 'After what fucking Noel Gallagher said about me, I couldn't give a shit about Oasis. I go into shops all the time myself. He's just such a tosser and he looks like Parker from *Thunderbirds*.' This was followed by a slightly surreal intervention by Serge from Kasabian: 'Elton's just a fat man in a tracksuit, whereas anything that comes out of Noel's mouth is absolute genius. Noel is the last man you want to start with. He's so quick he can destroy anyone. Elton John needs to watch out.'

Yet above all, it was the paparazzi that were guaranteed to make Elton's blood boil. As a young man, he had been happy to be snapped and accommodating to photographers. As he grew into middle age, however, he began to hate the intrusion. At the Cannes film festival in 2006, Elton and Liz Hurley were joint hosts of honour for the Chopard Trophy ceremony and Elton was asked to present an award to Kevin Zegers. Having started his speech, he took exception to the noisy phalanx of photographers who continued to hold their private conversations. 'I'm talking, you fuckwits,' Elton told the assembled lensmen, adding, 'Fucking photographers, you should all be shot.' 'What?' came a lone voice from the chuckling cameramen. 'You should all be shot,' repeated Elton. 'Thank you. Kevin, take this and get it out of my hands because they're a nightmare.' 'Being unreasonably emotional makes me feel like I've had a line of coke or something,' Elton would later admit when challenged about his short fuse. 'The venom comes out. It's a bit like *The Exorcist*.'

Elton continues to be an enthusiastic fan of contemporary popular music. 'If you had two people you could have as your "phone a friend" on *Who Wants To Be A Millionaire* on the music theme, you'd want him or Paul Gambaccini, because he knows everything,' says Gary Farrow. Unlike so many established rock stars, for whom it almost seems to be a badge of honour not to have listened to any new music since 1986, Elton seeks it out and, as he has been throughout his life, is open-minded about any style of music. Just because the music he makes might be close to the mainstream does not mean that his listening tastes have to be along similar lines.

Nothing could be further from the truth in the musical world of Elton John. In 2005, he spoke glowingly of Björk's courageous *Medúlla* album. He also praised the theatricality of the Killers, hardly standard fare for the average fifty-something. Yet he does seem severely unimpressed by some of the pop acts of the day. He called Hear'Say 'the ugliest band in pop', claiming Danny Foster was 'a dead ringer for Shrek'.

'There is no charisma any more,' Elton has lamented. 'We know everything about everyone. If I see one more photo of Britney or J-Lo or Ben Affleck, I'm going to spit. I want mystery! That's why Morrissey has had some success again; he's a bit of an enigma.' Elton was also no admirer of the trend towards manufactured pop success. 'I think shows like *Pop Idol* and *The X Factor* have had their day and are hopefully coming to an end. I feel really sorry for Michelle McManus. I think they picked her because of her size and because she's different,' he opined. 'She's a good enough singer, but she's not a pop star. Her situation is cruel and I feel sorry for her.'

Whether consciously or not, Elton has become something of a godfather to the British music business. As such, he seems to feel his role includes offering wise counsel or putting a consoling arm round the shoulder of any his showbiz friends who he thought might need it. Very close to David and Victoria Beckham, he was also not shy in voicing concerns about an erratic George Michael in 2004, claiming that he was a 'in a strange place' and that there was 'a deep-rooted unhappiness in his life'. The pair subsequently made up over a dinner cooked at Michael's north London home by the celebrity chef Gordon Ramsay.

Elton also stated the opinion that the tabloid revelation of the model Kate Moss's cocaine use was a generally good thing and that, had he been exposed by the press as a drug user, it would have done him a big favour and saved him a decade of trauma. 'Elvis Presley would not have died at 42 if he'd lived in England,' he declared. 'They don't breed that reverence. I love America very much but I'd rather be treated with less reverence than get treated as royalty like they do in America.'

The most bizarre example of Elton's policy of direct action towards his fellow celebrities is described in Chris Heath's official biography of Robbie Williams, *Feel*. Heath even describes Elton's attempt to get Williams into rehab as 'kidnapping', although it seems rather an exaggeration to describe what looked to be a well-intentioned, if rather direct, response by Elton as such. Needing help, Williams had called Elton at his home in Atlanta. Elton told Williams to spend some time at Woodside. 'Elton's really, really generous, really wanting me to be well, and I really, really thank him for that,' said the former Take That star.

Several months later, when Williams was finishing off his *Life Thru A Lens* album, he was meant to call in on Elton at his home in London to play him some new tracks. When he arrived, he was in such a bad way that Elton drove him straight to Woodside. The next morning he was driven to the Churchill detox centre. On arrival, he was asked to write down a list of the substances to which he was addicted. According to Williams, 'there was no love or care' at the centre, and he discharged himself almost immediately. Later, Williams checked himself into a detox centre of his own choosing, Clouds in Wiltshire. 'Elton sort of tried to do what he thought was best and obviously came from a very loving place,' reflected Williams. 'But the whole thing for me is tarnished with a lack of professionalism.' So began a frosty relationship between the two stars. In December 2006, while both were on tour in Australia and, by chance, were staying at the same hotel, Robbie revealed to thousands of fans at a gig the hotel room number Elton was staying in. Elton reportedly retaliated by slipping a note under Robbie's door, reminding him of the renewed success of the band he left behind: 'Dear Robbie, Take That… Number 1 single and album. Great result. Love Elton.'

Perhaps the closest Elton has come to a walking rock 'n' roll disaster zone was on July 2, 2005 at the Live 8 concert at Hyde Park. Elton's 'duet' with Babyshambles singer and tabloid bad boy Pete Doherty on T Rex's 'Children of The Revolution' saw Doherty in what looked like a semi-conscious state, slurring his way through the song and tottering round the stage. That the singer is an icon to many is one of the most mystifying features of modern rock culture. 'I spoke to Davey Johnstone just before that show,' says Gary Osborne. 'He told me he got stoned from just standing next to Doherty!'

The event itself, coming as it did 20 years after Live Aid, was a vast disappointment, save for a pristine performance by a reunited Pink Floyd. 'I thought it was a bit of an anti-climax, to be honest', Elton told the *Daily Telegraph*. 'The thought behind it was fantastic, but Hyde Park is a charisma-free zone. There was no sense of occasion and from a musical point, I didn't think there were too many highlights.'

Meanwhile, December 22, 2005 would go down in history as the day on which, under the Civil Partnership Act, same-sex unions became legally allowed in England and Wales. Elton John and David Furnish were one of 678 gay couples in England and Wales to enter into a civil partnership on that day. After a low-key ceremony at Windsor Guildhall, the happy couple were snapped waving and blowing kisses, soberly attired in dark suits. Two fans from New Zealand presented the happy couple with an apple ice-cream cake named 'Applely Ever After'. The media lent the event the air of a Royal wedding, aided and abetted perhaps by the fact that, in his ostentation, grandness and sheer stature, Elton had become more regal than the royals. *The Sun* ran the headline 'Elton Takes David Up The Aisle'.

David and Elton had been together for 12 years. Furnish was giving away several stone in weight and 16 years in age to his very famous partner. In a sense, their kind of relationship was common in celebrity circles: the older superstar, with money and power, and the younger cohort. It was the same scenario as played out in heterosexual circles by Jagger, Bowie, Rod Stewart *et al.*

'It could only happen for Elton,' remarked Lulu on the two-mile traffic jam of celebrities leading up to the reception at Woodside. Trapped and snapped in their cars, the rich and famous included Terry Wogan, the Beckhams, the Osbournes, Ringo Starr, Boris Becker, Trinny and Susanna, Graham Norton, Liz Hurley, Cilla Black, Claudia Schiffer, Michael Vaughan, Matt Lucas, Greg Rusedski, Lulu, Michael Caine, Donatella Versace and Hugh Grant. There were some high-profile absentees, among them Rod Stewart, David Bowie and Iman and Robbie Williams, who was reported to have stayed away because he didn't want to socialise with his old band mate, Gary Barlow, who would be singing at the reception. Janet Street-Porter was 'best man'. A huge marquee had been erected in the grounds at Woodside. Following the reception, the happy couple departed for a holiday in Venice.

Elton and David's wedding was historically significant because it was the first high-profile same-sex civil union in the world. By his own admission, Elton John is 'the most famous poof in the world. And I love it. I wouldn't have it any other way.' He has been an inspiration to a whole generation of gay people, many of whom were living an unhappy life of frustration. Elton has encouraged them to be open: 'Living a lie is just not worth it.' He speaks his mind and is not averse to revealing quite intimate details. He has sex 'maybe twice a week, which is fine by me'. He also admits he is still attracted to other men. 'I still fancy other people, even though I'm with David. We'll walk down the street and I'll say: "Cor, I wouldn't mind shagging him." I tend to go for younger people. David tends to go for more mature types. But casual sex is not an option for either of us.'

Elton and David's only current regret is that they do not have any children. 'The only time we started talking about the difference in our ages was when we talked about adopting a child,' admitted Elton in one joint interview. 'I said, "Listen, David, I am just too old for this." I didn't want to be 70 years old with a teenage child and all the worry that entails. I'm too selfish. I'm too set in my ways. But it's a shame, because David would have been a fantastic dad.' 'Oh, I think you would have been too,' replied Furnish. 'And frankly,' concluded Elton, with a flourish, 'I refuse to breast feed.'

Elton John uses his celebrity well. He speaks in what sound like natural sound bites and, as someone who loves words and jokes, he is able to encapsulate a lot in a few words. 'Up yours!' was his 2006 verbal two-fingered salute to John Howard, Prime Minister of Australia, for opposing same-sex marriages. The Catholic Church also comes in for a hard time. 'There are so many things going on in the world that are horrible, but the Aids epidemic is not going away,' he said in 2006. 'We have the information to educate people in our hands, but to not to be able to educate a new generation is terrible. The Catholic Church has been responsible for so many people dying – it's unbelievable. It's genocide. I'm sorry, but it's true.' Elton then went a step further: 'I think religion promotes hatred and spite against gays. But there are so many people I know who are gay and love their religion. From my point of view, I would ban religion completely. Organised religion doesn't seem to work. It turns people into really hateful lemmings and it's not compassionate. The world is near escalating to World War III and where are the leaders of each religion? Why aren't they having a conclave? Why aren't they coming together?'

On the music front, 2006 got off to a somewhat indifferent start. Elton went from his honeymoon straight into recording a new studio album. He and Bernie had also written the score for *Lestat*, a musical adaptation of the Anne Rice novel *Interview With The Vampire*. *Lestat* had a strong score, yet flopped badly at the box office and was summarily murdered by theatre critics, who thought the plot impenetrable and the show substandard. The run was so short-lived that the cast album of the show, though recorded, was never released.

In September 2006, Elton released *The Captain And The Kid*. And if ever proof were needed of Elton's continued relevance in the pop world of today, here was that proof. The idea for the album had come not from Elton, or from Bernie, but from Elton's then manager, Merck Mercuriadis. Elton was always commenting on how Bernie had become the Brown Dirt Cowboy, living on a ranch in California and raising cutting horses, and about how he had lived the dream and become Captain Fantastic. Why not write an album about the transformation?

It was an ambitious project. The *Captain Fantastic* album had told the story of the struggling songwriting team in the late 1960s. It was a seamless marriage of lyric and melody and was extremely focused. There was nothing extraneous to any of the melodies Elton wrote, while Bernie's lyrics were a brilliant critique of the dying days of

London's Tin Pan Alley and a vivid re-connection with their former selves. If *Captain Fantastic* was about the creation of the two characters then, as Bernie said, the sequel, *The Captain And The Kid*, covered the disruption of those characters. 'The first album is a joyous album about failure,' he said, 'and the second is a dark album about success.' His task was to somehow encapsulate not three years but 36 years on one CD's worth of songs. Written in chronological order, Elton recorded the songs in sequence too, just as he had done for the original *Captain Fantastic* album.

The fact that he came close to pulling off an album which was as good as the original is testimony to his continued class as a lyricist. 'I wanted the album to be stripped down and honest,' said Bernie. 'I said to Elton, "Whatever you do, you've got to do this just with you and the piano." I read one review which said that it almost sounds like a demo record. I took great pride in that.'

Some of the songs ranked alongside acknowledged greats such as 'Tiny Dancer' and 'Rocket Man'. The opening piano sequence of the first track, 'Postcard From Richard Nixon', for example, was classic Elton. 'Tinderbox' was one of his greatest melodies and Bernie's lyrics captured their relationship in the mid-1970s, when angst and anxiety had replaced hope and aspiration. 'My life was to be on the road and to be part of the band. We were joined at the hip,' said Bernie. 'It was incredibly stressful. Where do you go from there? You can't get any bigger.'

Another memorable track was 'And The House Fell Down,' the tale of two lives destroyed by excess. 'Cocaine is all about being jacked up and jarred and jittery,' said Bernie. 'You're a jacked-up puppet on a string, manic, up for three days in a row.' His lyric was dark and expressed the mood of addiction in sombre terms, begging a suitably 'heavy' and portentous musical treatment. Elton, however, had other plans. 'Elton put this music hall music to it, which I thought was just a stroke of genius,' said an admiring Bernie.

The Captain And The Kid dealt, with almost uncomfortable intensity, with loss. 'Blues Never Fades Away' was a song about losing someone close to you. It mentioned three friends of Elton and Bernie's who had died: a restaurant owner they knew who died of Aids, a young woman who died of a brain haemorrhage on the pavement of a shopping mall and Gianni Versace, gunned down a decade earlier. The arbitrary nature of death was perfectly encapsulated in the couplet: 'And how did we get so lucky/ Targets on the rifle range/ Who makes the call and who gets to choose/ Who gets to win and who gets to lose'.

Unfortunately, and unfairly, the album was not a major success. 'Elton put so much love into that album,' Rod Stewart revealed to *Rolling Stone*. 'He told me, "This is the one." And I feel so sorry for him… But not too sorry for him, of course.' The absence of a big ht single was an obvious handicap and, unlike the albums in Elton's classic period, the music certainly didn't carry the necessary depth in the production to make the songs really sonically come alive.

However, as a piece of rock autobiography, it's a fine work. 'It's better than writing a book in a way because I've never really wanted to write a biography or autobiography. You have to be blatantly honest in those things and you could hurt a lot of people's feelings. By writing songs you don't have to do that,' was Elton's opinion in 2006. 'You are just writing about yourself and what you have experienced and how you went off the rails and how you became successful. It's all there in the record.'

*   *   *

The Elton John of today is musically and personally in fine fettle. 'His performance consistency on stage is amazing,' is John Jorgenson's forthright assessment. 'He plays and sings well, no matter what. Every once in a while he might be in a bad mood and the patter with the audience might not be as comfortable, but the performance standard never drops.'

Perhaps unsurprisingly, the only occupational hazard is that the decades of playing stupidly loud music have inevitably taken their toll and according to Clive Franks, Elton has lost some of his hearing. 'His monitors on stage are the loudest in the business,' says Franks. 'I've worked with the Who and he's louder than them onstage. His monitors are at 118 decibels.' Bernie Taupin too confessed as long ago as 1992 that he was '30 per cent deaf in one ear [from] standing in the wings of all Elton's shows in the early 1970s'.

Elton can surely now not have too many hang-ups about his appearance. Poised to turn 60, he looks remarkably well-preserved. On stage, whether through the influence of his partner, David, or from listening to wise counsel from the backroom staff, he dresses flamboyantly yet elegantly. Brits have grown very fond of him and his loud-mouthed opinions. He's not just liked, but loved.

Because Elton's success has never really been dependent on notions of youthful perfection, as he got older and entered middle age, he found the transition far easier to make than other rock stars who have had to go to often outrageous lengths to maintain the illusion of youthful rude health. In fact, by his fifties, Elton arguably looked younger than the pristine specimens he did battle with in the 1970s, an irony which must surely have brought him a little frisson of pleasure.

Up until quite recently, however, Elton would have been dismissed by all but his most loyal fans as someone who made some good records centuries ago in musical terms, but who has since become an ageing pop star who has run out of ideas, a peddler of trite sentimentality and ever more painful and predictable tunes. This is no longer the case.

His music is back on form and it is now time to start seeing Elton John for what he is. For a start, he's an excellent and underrated pianist. He's also a very gifted composer, as well as being technically still a fine singer. That time from 1970 to 1975, when everything he touched turned to musical gold, will never return. But there is no denying that a new Elton John album is still never less than a treat, and, on occasion, it can form part of the soundtrack of one's life.

'I'm not everybody's cup of tea,' Elton has said. 'But sometimes criticism can be hurtful. Be respectful – I'm a good piano player, I can sing well, I write good songs. If you don't like it, fair enough. But give me a break. I know I'm dismissed sometimes as "Elton the MOR rocker", but it's hard to be anything else on the piano. It's not an instrument you can throw into an amp or into the audience.'

'I've played on a Lennon record. I've played on a Ringo record. I've played on a Dylan record. And I've played on a George Harrison record. I'm very, very happy to have had the privilege,' he reflected in 2002, looking back on an astonishing career.

The problem for Elton, as for all artists of a certain vintage, is simply that their audiences are there not so much to listen to their new music, but to relive their youth through the old songs. Rock audiences mistrust change. Nevertheless, there is still a future for Elton John as a recording artist. 'Apart from a brief foray into disco, most of his records sound the same,' says writer and friend Dylan Jones. 'That is not meant as a criticism. It's just that he's remained pretty constant. He's a singer/song-writer and the instrumentation of his records is used to show that off.'

One thing Elton might be expected to do in the next few years is to cut back on a touring schedule that would exhaust a performer half his age. Fans are by now accustomed to the almost annual appearance of the legendary Elton John onstage retirement speech. Elton managed to get through his summer concerts in 2006 with only one threat to retire. It was in Dublin. 'We had rehearsed "Goodbye Yellow Brick Road" and he was in a foul mood,' says Clive Franks. 'When he was on stage, he said, "Well, I'm supposed to be doing 'Yellow Brick Road' now, but I hate the damn song and I hate the album it came from and I'll never do it again." Then he retired onstage and said he'd never tour Europe again. It was the opening night of the tour. Everyone was having a good time. When something like that happens it really deflates people. In fact, I've got a dozen, maybe two dozen retirement speeches at home in the cupboard which I actually played to him a couple of years ago. We had a good laugh together – they were hilarious.'

Elton is not overly enamoured of the rock festival either. 'Oh, welcome to Paradise,' he said sarcastically at one rain-sodden event. 'Thank you for coming out and standing in the rain, but I'm not going to play any of these fucking festivals again.' He has even vowed never to record again. As recently as 2001, he told an audience at the Verizon Wireless Arena in Manchester, New Hampshire: 'I'm fed up with it. I love you guys but I hate all the record industry. This is the last record I'll ever make. I've made 40 albums and it's about time for me to get out.'

During a concert in 2006, Elton went as far as to attack his record label for what he perceived as its failure adequately to promote *The Captain And The Kid*. Yet he must know by now that all the publicity, all the management, all the planning in the world cannot create a hit. Pop artists are notoriously bad at taking responsibility for failure.

Elton John can count on some of the most loyal fans in the pop world. In turn, Elton fans can count themselves as perhaps the luckiest of any of the followers of the long-established stars. Their icon is almost constantly on the road playing gigs and, while the touring schedule isn't as heavy as it once was, he is still out there performing.

Elton also records new music on a consistent basis. When new material is out there, he promotes it on radio and TV. He is also seldom out of the news. Hardly a month goes by without a scurrilous remark here, a controversial swipe there. And finally, Elton fans are well treated when it comes to his back catalogue. Reissues are carefully produced and designed, with as many extras as can be dug out of the vault as possible. DVD releases are excellently produced. For example, in 2004, a four-DVD box set called *Dream Ticket* contained three recent concerts plus a fourth CD retrospective of some of his best songs, with exclusive interviews with Elton and collaborators.

On the internet, eltonjohn.com arrived relatively late on the scene. Unlike some of his contemporaries like David Bowie, Elton is definitely not an internet person, which is surprising given his addictive mentality. 'Elton doesn't even have a mobile,' reveals Gary Farrow. However, his website offers excellent content, exclusive packages and regular updates. And, unlike the sites of other established stars, since Elton is constantly doing something, the news pages are actually very busy. The overall picture is one of a superstar who genuinely cares about his fan base.

In March 2007, Elton John will celebrate his sixtieth birthday at New York's Madison Square Garden, a venue which, by coincidence, he will be playing for the sixtieth time. He also promises a new album for 2007, rumoured to be a collaboration with dance and hip hop artists. And, of course, his tireless work for charity goes on. In 2006, the legendary music producer Bob Ezrin called Elton 'the humanitarian of the century'. He added: 'All the things Elton has done for the community, from the commitment to Aids awareness and for making Aids an acceptable subject of discussion in our industry, and getting so much money to fight Aids and HIV, it's staggering. We can only hope to be like him some day.'

'The great thing about rock and roll is that someone like me can be a star,' Elton once said, looking back on a time when prettier and hipper stars were winning the plaudits, while he sat behind the piano and bashed out the songs. In the end, despite his astonishing life to date, Elton John might just be the most normal pop superstar who ever lived.

BIBLIOGRAPHY

Below is a list of the most important books consulted during the research of this book. Special mention to Philip Norman's detailed Elton biography and to Paul Gambaccini's short but informative published interview with Elton and Bernie from 1974.

BOOKS

Bernardin, Claude and Tom Stanton. 1996. *Rocket Man: Elton John From A–Z*, Praeger.

Bright, Spencer. 1998. *Essential Elton*, Chameleon.

Bowie, David and Mick Rock. 2005. *Moonage Daydream: The Life and Times of Ziggy Stardust*, Cassell Illustrated.

Cass, Caroline. 1998. *Elton John's Flower Fantasies: an Intimate Tour of his Houses and Gardens*, Phoenix.

Charlesworth, Chris. 1986. *Elton John*, Bobcat Books.

Chippindale, Peter and Chris Horrie. 1992. *Stick It Up Your Punter!: The Rise And Fall Of The Sun*, Mandarin.

Clarke, Gary. 1995. *Elton, My Elton,* Smith Gryphon Limited.

Ellis, Geoffrey. 2004. *I Should Have Known Better: A Life In Pop Management – The Beatles, Brian Epstein and Elton John*, Thorogood.

Ewbank, Tim and Stafford Hildred. 2003. *Rod Stewart: The New Biography*, Portrait.

Forbes, Bryan. 1993. *A Divided Life*, Mandarin.

Gambaccini, Paul. Ed. 1974. *Elton John And Bernie Taupin*, Star Books.

Giles, David. 2000. *Illusions of Immortality: A Psychology of Fame And Celebrity*, MacMillan.

Harris, Bob. 2001. *The Whispering Years*, BBC.

Heath, Chris. 2004. *Feel: Robbie Williams*, Ebury Press

Heatley, Michael. 1998. *Elton John: The Life Of A Legendary Performer*, Colour Library Direct.

Herman, Gary. 2002. *Rock 'n' Roll Babylon*, Plexus.

Howe, Peter. 2005. *Paparazzi*, Artisan Books.

Humphries, Patrick. 1998. *A Little Bit Funny: The Elton John Story*, Aurum.

John, Sir Elton. 2005. Foreword to *4 Inches*, Co & Bear Productions.

John, Elton and Bernie Taupin. 1991. *Two Rooms: Elton John And Bernie Taupin In Their Own Words*, Boxtree.

Jones, Dylan. 2005 *iPod, Therefore I Am: A Personal Journey Through Music*, Weidenfeld & Nicolson.

Jones, Lesley-Ann. 1997. *Freddie Mercury: The Definitive Biography*. Hodder & Stoughton.

Leigh, Spencer. 2000. *Brother Can You Spare A Rhyme? 100 Years Of Hit Songwriting*, Spencer Leigh Limited.

Lim, Gerrie. 2005. *Idol To Idol*, Cyan Books.

Malins, Steve. 2005. *Duran Duran: Notorious – The Unauthorised Biography*, André Deutsch.

Morgan, Piers. 2005. *The Insider: The Private Diaries Of A Scandalous Decade*, Ebury Press

Napier-Bell, Simon. 2002. *Black Vinyl, White Powder*. Ebury Press.

Norman, Philip. 2000. *Sir Elton: The Definitive Biography Of Elton John*, Pan.

O'Neill, Terry and A.A. Gill. 2003. *Celebrity: The Photographs of Terry O'Neill*, Little, Brown.

Parkinson, Judy. 2003. *Elton: Made in England*, Michael O'Mara Books.

Paytress, Mark. 2002. *Bolan: The Rise And Fall Of A Twentieth Century Superstar*, Omnibus Press.

Peebles, Andy. 1981. *The Lennon Tapes*, BBC Publications.

Peebles, Andy. 1981. *The Elton John Tapes – Elton John In Conversation With Andy Peebles*, '21 At 33.'

Quaye, Caleb with Dale A. Berryhill. 2006. *A Voice Louder Than Rock & Roll*, Vision Publishing.

Rojek, Chris. 2001. *Celebrity*, Reaktion Books.

Rosenthal, Elizabeth J. 2001. *His Song: The Musical Journey Of Elton John*, Billboard Books.

Stephenson, Pamela. 2001. *Billy*, Harper Collins.

Taupin, Bernie. 1976. *The One Who Writes The Words For Elton John – Complete Lyrics From 1968 to Goodbye, Yellow Brick Road*, Aldridge, Alan & Mike Dempsey eds. Jonathan Cape.

—1988. *A Cradle Of Haloes: Sketches Of A Childhood*, Aurum.

Venables, Terry and Neil Hanson. 1995. V*enables: The Autobiography*, Penguin.

Watts, Mark. 2005. *The Fleet Street Sewer Rat*, Artnik.

Windsor, Barbara and Robin McGibbon. 2001. *All Of Me: My Extraordinary Life*, Headline.

ARTICLES

Aizlewood, John. 2001. 'Sir Elton John: Cash For Questions', *Q*, 172, January.

Anon. 1971. 'Rasen's Top Of The Pops Wedding', Market Rasen Nostalgia website, http://www.featurestoday.co.uk

Anon. 1971. 'The Rock Family Affair – Elton John', *Life*, 24 September.

Anon. 1994. *Barbara Walters Special* [Elton John interview] transcribed by Bev Vincent, http://www.vex.net/~paulmac/elton/articles/19940321_bw.html

Anon. 1997. 'Ciao, Chubby. Revealed: Versace's New Supermodel', *The Sunday Times Magazine*, 5 January.

Anon. 'Fired By The Rocket Man', *Punch*.

Anon. 2000. 'Kiss... And Break up', [Interview with John Reid], *Scotland's Daily Record-Mail.co.uk*.

Bangs, Lester. 1972. 'Bernie Taupin', *Phonograph Record*, March.

Bernardin, Claude. 2005. 'A Single Man', Internet essay. http://www.vex.net/~paulmac/elton/articles/ASingleMan.html

Berryhill, Dale. 2000. 'Interview With Nigel Olsson', *Elton Expo 2000*, 2 September, http://www.angelfire.com/ca/nigelfanclub/berryhill.html

Black, Johnny. 1995. 'Eyewitness [account of Elton's gig at Shoreditch College, 1977], *Q* 101, February.

Bronson, Harold. 1973. 'What Do Bowie, Elton, And Mantovani Have In Common?', *Music World*, 1 June.

Buckley, David. 2006. 'A Life Less Ordinary – The Continued Comeback of The Queen Mum Of Pop' [Captain And The Kid review], *Mojo*, October.

Burchill, Julie. 1994. 'I'm The King Of The Bungle', *The Sunday Times*, 9 October.

Cardiff University. 2002. 'Research Reveals Myth Of A Nation United In Grief After Diana's Death', www.scienceblog.com/community/older/2002/G/20021855.html

Carr, Roy. 1978. 'A Single Man', *NME*, 28 October.

Charlesworth, Chris. 1973. 'Elton's Finest Hour!', *Melody Maker*, 15 September.

Christgau, Robert. 1976. 'Elton John', from *The Rolling Stone History Of Rock & Roll*.

Chittenen, Maurice. 2005. 'Secrets Of A Fleet Street Rubbish Man', *The Sunday Times*, 13 March.

Clarke, Rick. 2002. 'Gus Dudgeon, 1942–2002', *Mix*, 1 October.

Clements, Paul. 1999. 'Stonewall Equality Show', [live review] http://www.Music365.co.uk 2 December.

Coleman, John. 1970. 'Elton John: The Radio One Hype', *Friends*, 2 October.

Coon, Caroline. 1975. 'Elton John: I Want To Chug, Not Race', *Melody Maker*, 21 June.

Cooper, Mark. 1991. 'Trembling' [Review of *Two Rooms*], *Q* 62, November.

Couzens, Gerard. 2000. 'Sad, Lonely Life Of The Woman Who Loved And Lost Elton', *Sunday Mirror*, 4 June.

Cowton, Mike. 1973. 'Don't Shoot Me I'm Only The Lyricist', *NME*, 10 March.

Cromelin, Richard. 1973. 'The Elton John Career', *Phonograph Record*, November.

Cromer, Ben. 1997. 'Producer Dudgeon's Flair Felt Beyond His Elton Classics', *Billboard*, 26 April.

Dangerfield, Andy. 2006. 'Kelvin MacKenzie: Old Mac Opens Up', *Press Gazette*, 11 October.

Deevoy, Adrian. 1995. 'Nobody's Perfect' [Elton John Interview], *Q*, 103. April.

Dodd, Vikram. 1999. 'Elton John Has Pacemaker Fitted', *The Guardian*, 10 July.

Doyle, Tom. 2006. 'Fantastic Voyage', *Mojo* 155, October.

Duncan, Andrew. 2000. Elton John Interview, *Radio Times*, 20–26 May.

Edmonds, Ben. 1975. 'Elton John: Rock Of The Westies (MCA)', Phonograph Record, November 1975.

Ellen, Barbara, 1997. 'It's A Little Bit Funny – How People Love Elton', [Live review], *The Observer*, 14 December.

Falco, Sue. 2001. 'Elton John Guitarist Davey Johnstone Suffers Loss Of Son', Yahoo.com., 10 May.

Farber, Jim. 1992. 'Elton John: The One: Music Reviews', *Rolling Stone*, 638.

Farndale, Nigel. 1997. 'Honest John', *The Sunday Telegraph Magazine*, 14 September.

Felton, David. 1971 'Elton John', *Rolling Stone*, 10 June.

Flynn, Paul. 2005. 'Interview with Elton John and David Furnish, *The Sunday Times*, 27 November.

Fong-Torres, Ben. 1974. The Four-Eyed Bitch Is Back: Elton. *Rolling Stone*, 21 November.

Forrest, Emma. 1997. 'The Singer Not The Song', *The Guardian*, 10 September.

Fountain, Nigel. 1976. 'Elton John: A Matter Of Numbers', *Street Life*, 19 May–11 June.

Frith, Simon. 1975. 'Elton John: *Greatest Hits*; Randy Newman: *Good Old Boys*; Pete Atkin: *Secret Drinker*', *Let It Rock*, January.

—2001. 'Pop Music', in Simon Frith, Will Straw and John Street (eds.), *The Cambridge Companion To Pop And Rock*, Cambridge University Press.

Furnish, David. 1996. 'My Life With Elton', *Radio Times*, 6–12 July.

Gambaccini, Paul. 2005. 'Captain Fantastic And The Brown Dirt Cowboy', sleeve notes.

Garrett, Susanne. 1976. 'Bernie Taupin In Words And Pix', *Melody Maker*, 17 April.

Gilbert, Jerry. 1973. 'Starship Trouper', *Sounds*, 15 September.

Gittins, Ian. 2004. 'He's Still Standing', *The Guardian*, 13 November.

Goldman, Albert. 1993. 'Rock Goes Hol-ly-wooood!', from Albert Goldman, *Sound Bites* (Abacus, 1993) [originally published in *Travel And Leisure*, 1974]

Goldman, Vivien. 1976. 'Elton John: Ol' Four Eyes Is back', *Sounds*, 8 May.

Greenfield, Robert. 1970. 'Elton John Steams 'Em Up', *Rolling Stone*, 12 November.

Grove, Valerie. 2001. 'Elton Chose To Just Cut Me Off. I Had Seen Him Do It In The Past' [Interview with John Reid], *The Times*, 21 April.

Headley, Caroline. 2005. 'Exclusive: Go To Elt', *The Mirror*, 23 December.

Hibbert, Tom. 1992. 'Two Rooms [book review],' *Q* 65, February.

Hilburn, Robert. 1992. 'Elton John On His Days Of Drugs And Despair', *Chicago Sun-Times*, 30 August.

—1997. 'Relighting "Candle" For Di', *LA Times*, 14 September.

—1997. 'Amid All Of His Sorrows, He's Still Standing', *LA Times*, 26 September.

Holden, Stephen. 1979. 'Elton John: No Future? Apathy In The U.K.' [*A Single Man* review], *Rolling Stone*, 25 January.

—1981. *The Fox* album review, *Rolling Stone*, 6 August.

Hope, Adrian. 1975. 'Honky Château', *Studio Sound*, May.

Irwin, Colin. 1979. 'Elton: No-Go Disco', *Melody Maker*.

Jackson, Alan. 2004. 'Tantrums And Tributes' [Interview with Elton John and Billy Connolly], *Radio Times*, 27 November–3 December.

Jahr, Cliff. 1976. 'Elton John: It's Lonely At The Top', *Rolling Stone*, 7 October.

Jenkins, David. 2001. 'His Songs', *Sunday Telegraph Magazine*, 9 September.

John, Elton. 2006. Elton John interviews Scissor Sisters, *Interview*.

Jones, Cliff. 1997. 'Sound Your Funky Horn: Elton John,' *Mojo* 47, October.

Jones, Sam. 2004. 'Elton's Radio 1 Outburst', the *Guardian*, 9 November.

Joseph, Tim. 1994. 'Reg Dwight's Piano Goes Pop' Liner Notes, October.

Kane, Peter. 1994. 'Mangled' [review of *Duets*], *Q*, January.

Kelso, Paul. 2000. 'Elton John Tells of His Epic Spending Sprees', *The Guardian*, 16 November.

King, Larry, 2004. Interview With Elton John, CNN. Transcript: http://www.hyenaproductions.com/whois+may2004.htm

Leve, Ariel. 2004. 'Honest John', *The Sunday Times*, 31 October.

Maconie, Stuart. 1993. 'Little Miss Can't Be Wrong' [Kate Bush Interview], *Q*, 87, December.

Matlock, George. 1999. 'Healing Hands' [interview with Nigel Olsson], *Hercules,* November.

Mendelssohn, John. 1970. 'Elton John: *Elton John*', *Rolling Stone*, 12 November.

McCormick, Neil. 2005. 'Elton The Indiscreet', *Daily Telegraph*, 4 August.

McGibbon, Rob. 2006. 'Press Conference With... Kelvin Mackenzie', www.robmcgibbon.com, 11 October.

McGrath, Rick and Mike Quigley. 1971. 'This Is Your Song: The Elton John Interview', *The Georgia Straight*, 11 April.

Murray, Charles Shaar. 1972. 'Step Right Up And Feel The Man's Muscles: *Honky Chateau*', *Creem*, June.

—1974. 'Elton John', *NME*, 26 January.

Nauman, Zoe, 2005. 'I Was Nearly Mrs Elton John', *Sunday Mirror*, 18 December.

Newton, Victoria. 2006. 'Elton John: My Lost Friends', *Sun*, 15 September.

O'Sullivan, Kevin. 2005. 'Elton: I'm Glad Kate Was Caught', *The Mirror*.

Parales, Jon. 1997. 'Critic's Notebook', *New York Times*, 15 September.

Parsons, Tony. 1995. 'Elton John', Daily Telegraph, 8 April.

Pond, Steve. 1979. 'Elton John's Subdued Return', *Rolling Stone*, 15 November.

Prentice, Thomas. 1978. 'Can TV's Mr Jingle Rock Elton John Back To The Top Of The Hit Parade?', *Daily Mail*, 5 September.

Raphael, Amy. 2004. 'A Star Is Reborn', *The Observer*, 19 September.

Rensin, David. 1973. 'Performance: Elton at the Hollywood Bowl, 9/7/73', *Rolling Stone*, 10 November.

Reidel, Michael. 2005. 'The Musical King', *New York Post*, 27 July.

Robbins, Wayne. 1974. 'Elton John: Goodbye Yellow Brick Road', *Creem*, January.

Salewicz, Chris. 1986. 'The Fall And Rise Of Reginald Dwight', *Q*, December.

Sandall, Robert. 1992. 'Bernie Taupin: Him Indoors', *Q*, July.

Schwartz, Larry. 2005. 'Turing Raw Talent Into TV Stars' [interview with John Reid], 14 May, theage.com.au

Scoppa, Bud. 1976. 'Elton John: *Caribou*', *Phonograph Record*, August.

—'Elton John: Blue Moves', *Phonograph Record*, November.

Sculatti, Gene. 1982. 'Elton John: *Jump Up!*', *Creem*, August.

—1974. 'Elton John', *NME*, 26 January.

Shaw, Greg. 1975. 'Elton John: *Captain Fantastic And The Brown Dirt Cowboy*', *Phonograph Record*, June.

Simpson, Dave. 2002. Elton John Live Review, Kings Dock, Liverpool, *The Guardian*, 11 July.

Sischy, Ingrid. 1995. 'Elton John: 150 per cent Involved', *Interview Magazine*, April.

Snow, Mat. 1995. The *Q*100 Interview: Elton John, January.

Standish, David and Eugenie Ross-Leming. 1976. *Playboy* Interview, January.

Sutcliffe, Phil. 1976. 'The Real Elton John Stands Up – "Hoorah!"', *Sounds*, 18 December.

—1988. 'Elton John: You've Got To Laugh', *Q*, August.

—1992. 'Sober' [review of *The One*], *Q*, August.

Sutcliffe, Thomas. 2000. 'Elton John Spent Over £290,000 On Flowers. Why? Because He Can.' *The Independent*, 16 November.

Sweeney, John. 1989. 'The Sun And The Star', *The Independent*, 11 February. Reprinted in Dylan Jones, ed. *Meaty Beaty Big And Bouncy!: Classic Rock and Pop Writing from Elvis to Oasis*, Hodder & Stoughton, 1996.

Swenson, John. 1974. 'Elton John: A Few Moments Of Candor On The Yellow Brick Road', *Crawdaddy*, February.

Tannenbaum, Rob. 2003. 'Dear Superstar: Iggy Pop', *Blender*, September.

Tennant, Neil. 1998. Elton John Interview, *Interview*, January.

Thomas, Pat. 1985. 'The Story of Elton John: Still Standing', *Beat*, December 1985.

Tobler, John. 1973. 'The Elton John Story: Final Part', *ZigZag*, April.

—1975. Elton John: *Captain Fantastic And The Brown Dirt Cowboy*, *Zigzag*, November.

—1995. 'Don't Shoot Me I'm Only The Piano Player' (This Record Co.) sleeve notes.

—1998. 'Too Low For Zero', (Rocket Records) sleeve notes.

Trakin, Roy. 1981. 'Elton John: Concert in Central Park, September 1980,' *Musician*, January.

Turner, Steve. 1972. 'Bernie Taupin: The B-Side of Elton John', *Beat Instrumental*, February.

—1973 'Elton John', *Beat Instrumental*, January.

Udovitch, Mim and David Wild. 2002. 'Elton John Remembers George', *Rolling Stone*, 17 January.

Wainwright, Martin. 2001. 'Elton Tells Audience: Latest Album Is My Last', *The Guardian*, 3 December.

Welch, Chris. 1973. 'Elton John Steps Into Christmas', *Melody Maker*, 24 November.

White, Timothy. 1997. 'Elton John: The Billboard Interview', *Billboard*, 4 October 1997.

Wild, David. 2004. 'Sir Bitch Is Back', *Rolling Stone*, 3 November.

Wilde, Jon. 2001. 'Elton: The Magnificent Showman', *Uncut* 52, September.

Williams, Richard. 1970. 'Elton Storms The States', *Melody Maker*, 26 September.

Wishart, John. 1978. 'Elton Moves On', [*A Single Man* review], *Record Mirror*, 21 October.

Valentine, Penny. 1971 'Elton John: Tumbleweed Connection', *Sounds*.

—1971. 'Elton John: the Record Rise Of A Superstar Called Reg', *Disc and Music Echo*.

Yates, Robert. 1997. 'The Big Picture Review', *Q* 134, November.

Young, Robin. 2004. 'Was 1976 The Best Year Of Your Life', *The Times*, 17 March.

RADIO AND TV

Jones, Ben. 2005. Elton John Interview, Virgin Radio, 11 October.

Moyles, Chris. 2004. Elton John Interview, BBC Radio 1, 8 November.

Ross, Jonathan. 2001. Elton John Interview, BBC Radio 2. http://www.bbc.co.uk/radio2/shows/ross/interviews.shtml.

Walker, Johnnie. 2005. Interview With Elton John And Bernie Taupin, BBC Radio 2, October.

Wright, Steve. 2004. Elton John Interview, BBC Radio 2, 8 November.

INTERNET SOURCES

Of particular help when researching this book were Cornflakes & Classics, a detailed Elton timeline; the excellent Hercules Fan website, and Eltonography, an on-line Elton discography.

Baldry, Long John, Homepage http://www.johnbaldry.com/

BBC News http://news.bbc.co.uk/

Cole, B.J., official site http://www.bjcole.co.uk/Index.html

Cornflakes And Classics http://www.vex.net/~paulmac/elton/ej.html

Dee, Kiki. The Kiki Dee Information Bureau http://www.kikidee. info/

Eltonography – the illustrated Elton John website http://www.eltonography.com/

The Guardian http://www.guardian.co.uk/0,,,00.html

Google groups alt.fan.elton-john http://groups.google.co.uk/group/alt. fan.elton-john?lnk=lr&hl=en

Harris, Bob, official site http://www.bobharris.org/

Hentschel, David, official site http://www.thekeyboard.co.uk/index2. html

Hercules International Elton John Fan Club http://www.eltonfan.net/ index.shtml

John, Elton, Aids Foundation http://www.ejaf.org/

John, Elton, official site http://www.eltonjohn.com/flash_index.asp

John, Elton, World http://www.eltonjohnworld.com/

Jorgenson, John, Official Site http://www.johnjorgenson.com/

In Loving Memory Of Dee Murray http://members.tripod. com/~longdancer/dee.html

LaChapelle, David, http://www.davidlachapelle.com/home.html

Olsson, Nigel, official Site http://www.angelfire.com/ca/nigelfanclub/ index3.html

Paton, David, official site http://www.davidpaton.com/index.shtml

Quaye, Caleb, official site http;//www.calebquaye.com/

Rice, Sir Tim, official site http://www.timrice.co.uk/main.html

Roberts/Optique, Dennis Boutiquehttp://celebritysunglasses.com/ Index/elton_john_m.htm

Taupin, Bernie - A Fan Tribute http://www.bernie-taupin.com/home. htm

Judie, Tzuke, official site http://www.tzuke.com/

White, Ryan, official site http://www.ryanwhite.com/

Yorkshire Folk, Blues And Jazz Festival, Krumlin, 1970 http://www. ukrockfestivals.com/krumlin-mud.html

PODCASTS

BBC Podcast 2006 (John Wilson interview with Bernie Taupin), *Front Row*, BBC, 14 June.

The Times Podcast 2006. (Interview with Elton John and Bernie Taupin), September.

DISCOGRAPHY

COMPILED BY DAVID BODON

SINGLES

Year	Single	US releases	UK releases	US chart top	UK chart top	Weeks in Hot 100 US chart	Weeks in UK chart
1968	I've Been Loving You	–	Philips BF1643 (7")				
1969	Lady Samantha	DJM 7008 (7")	Philips BF1739 (7")				
1969	It's Me That You Need	–	DJM DJS205 (7")				
1970	Border Song	Congress C6022 (7")	DJM DJS217 (7")	92		5	
1970	Rock And Roll Madonna	–	DJM DJS222 (7")				
1970	Your Song	UNI 55265 (7")	DJM DJS233 (7")	8	7	14	12
1971	Friends	UNI 55227 (7")	DJM DJS244 (7")	34		9	
1971	Levon	UNI 55314 (7")	–	24		10	
1972	Tiny Dancer	UNI 55318 (7")	–	41		7	
1972	Rocket Man	UNI 55328 (7")	DJM DJX501 (7")	6	2	15	13
1972	Honky Cat	UNI 55343 (7")	DJM DJS269 (7")	8	31	10	6
1972	Crocodile Rock	MCA 40000 (7")	DJM DJS271 (7")	1	5	17	14
1973	Daniel	MCA 40046 (7")	DJM DJS275 (7")	2	4	15	10
1973	Saturday Night's Alright (For Fighting)	MCA 40105 (7")	DJM DJX502 (7")	12	7	12	9
1973	Step Into Christmas	MCA 65018 (7")	DJM DJS290 (7")		24		7
1973	Goodbye Yellow Brick Road	MCA 40148 (7")	DJM DJS285 (7")	2	6	17	16
1974	Candle In The Wind	–	DJM DJS297 (7")		11		9
1974	Bennie And The Jets	MCA 40198 (7")	–	1	37	18	5
1974	Don't Let The Sun Go Down On Me	MCA 40259 (7")	DJM DJS302 (7")	2	16	15	8
1974	The Bitch Is Back	MCA 40297 (7")	DJM DJS322 (7")	4	15	14	7
1974	Lucy In The Sky With Diamonds	MCA 40344 (7")	DJM DJS340 (7")	1	10	14	10

Year	Single	US releases	UK releases	US chart top	UK chart top	Weeks in Hot 100 US chart	Weeks in UK chart
1975	Philadelphia Freedom	MCA 40364 (7")	DJM DJS354 (7")	1	12	21	9
1975	Someone Saved My Life Tonight	MCA 40421 (7")	DJM DJS385 (7")	4	22	13	5
1975	Island Girl	MCA 40461 (7")	DJM DJS610 (7")	1	14	15	8
1976	Grow Some Funk Of Your Own	MCA 40505 (7")	DJM DJS629 (7")	14		11	
1976	Pinball Wizard	–	DJM DJS652 (7")		7		7
1976	Don't Go Breaking My Heart	MCA PIG40585 (7")	Rocket ROKN512 (7")	1	1	20	14
1976	Sorry Seems To Be The Hardest Word	MCA 40645 (7")	Rocket ROKN517 (7")	6	11	14	10
1977	Bite Your Lip	MCA 40677 (7")	Rocket ROKN5226 (7") Rocket RU1 (12")	28	28	6	4
1977	Crazy Water	–	Rocket ROKN521 (7")		27		6
1978	Ego	MCA 40892 (7")	Rocket ROKN538 (7")	34	34	8	6
1978	Part-Time Love	MCA 40973 (7")	Rocket XPRES1 (7")	22	15	10	13
1978	Song For Guy	MCA 40993 (7")	Rocket XPRES5 (7")	110	4		10
1978	Funeral For A Friend/ Love Lies Bleeding	–	DJM DJT15000 (12")				
1979	Mama Can't Buy You Love	MCA 41042 (7") MCA 13921 (12" EP)	Rocket XPRES20 (7")[1] Rocket XPRES1312 (12" EP)	9		18	
1979	Victim Of Love	MCA 41126 (7")	Rocket XPRES21 (7")	31		10	
1979	Johnny B. Goode	MCA 41159 (7")	Rocket XPRES24 (7") Rocket XPRES2412 (12")	–			
1980	Little Jeannie	MCA 41236 (7")	Rocket XPRES32 (7")	3	33	21	7
1980	Sartorial Eloquence[2]	MCA 41293 (7")	Rocket XPRES41 (7")	39	44	12	5
1980	Harmony	–	DJM DJS10961 (7")				
1980	Dear God	–	Rocket XPRES45 (7")[1]				
1981	I Saw Her Standing There	–	DJM DJS10965 (7")	–	40		4
1981	Nobody Wins	Geffen 49722 (7")	Rocket XPRES54 (7")	21	42	13	5
1981	Just Like Belgium	–	Rocket XPRES59 (7")				

1 Withdrawn from circulation
2 USA version title: "Don't You Wanna Play This Game No More"

Year	Single	US releases	UK releases	US chart top	UK chart top	Weeks in Hot 100 US chart	Weeks in UK chart
1981	Chloe	Geffen 49788 (7")	–	34		13	
1982	Empty Garden	Geffen 50049 (7")	Rocket XPRES77 (7")	13	51	17	4
1982	Blue Eyes	Geffen 29954 (7")	Rocket XPRES71 (7")	12	8	18	10
1982	Princess	–	Rocket XPRES85 (7")				
1982	Ball And Chain	Geffen 29846 (7")	–	–			
1982	All Quiet On The Western Front	–	Rocket XPRES88 (7")				
1983	I'm Still Standing	Geffen 29639 (7")	Rocket EJS1 (7") Rocket EJS112 (12")	12	4	16	11
1983	Kiss The Bride	Geffen 29568 (7")	Rocket EJS2 (7") Rocket EJS22 (7") Rocket EJS212 (12")	25	20	12	7
1983	I Guess That's Why They Call It The Blues	Geffen 29460 (7")	Rocket XPRES91 (7")	4	5	23	15
1983	Cold As Christmas (In The Middle Of The Year)	–	Rocket EJS3 (7") Rocket EJS33 (7") Rocket EJS312 (12")	–	33		6
1984	Sad Songs (Say So Much)	Geffen 29292 (7")	Rocket PH7 (7") Rocket PH712 (12")	5	7	19	12
1984	Passengers	–	Rocket EJS5 (7") Rocket EJS512 (12").	–	5		11
1984	Who Wears These Shoes	Geffen 29189 (7")	Rocket EJS6 (7") Rocket EJS612 (12")	16	50	14	3
1984	In Neon	Geffen 29111 (7")	–	38		13	
1984	Breaking Hearts (Ain't What It Used To Be)	–	Rocket EJS7 (7")	–	59		3
1985	Act Of War [with Millie Jackson]	Geffen 28956 (7") Geffen 203470 (12")	Rocket EJS8 (7") Rocket EJS812 (12") Rocket EJSR812 (12")	–	32		5
1985	Wrap Her Up	Geffen 28873 (7")	Rocket EJS10 (7") Rocket EJS1012 (12")	20	12	14	10
1985	That's What Friends Are For	Arista AS19422 (7")	Arista ARIST638 (7") Arista 12638 (12")	1	16	23	9
1986	Nikita	Geffen 28800 (7")	Rocket EJS9 (7") Rocket EJSD9 (7") Rocket EJS912 (12")	7	3	18	13

Year	Single	US releases	UK releases	US chart top	UK chart top	Weeks in Hot 100 US chart	Weeks in UK chart
1986	Cry To Heaven	–	Rocket EJS11 (7") Rocket EJSD11 (7") Rocket EJS1112 (12")	–	47		4
1986	Heartache All Over The World	Geffen 28578 (7") Geffen 205630 (12")	Rocket EJS12 (7") Rocket EJSD12 (7") Rocket EJS1212 (12")	55	45	8	4
1986	Slow Rivers	–	Rocket EJS13 (7") Rocket EJS1312 (12")	–	44		8
1987	Flames Of Paradise [with Jennifer Rush]	Epic 3407119 (7") Epic 4906829 (12")	CBS 6508657 (7") CBS 6508652 (12")	36	59	13	3
1987	Your Song [live]	–	Rocket EJS14 (7") Rocket EJS1412 (12")	–	85		
1987	Candle In The Wind [live]	MCA 53196 (7")	Rocket EJS15 (7") Rocket EJS1512 (12") Rocket EJSCD15 (CD)	6	5	21	11
1988	Take Me To The Pilot [live]	MCA 53260 (7")	–	–			
1988	I Don't Wanna Go On With You Like That	MCA 53345 (7") MCA 23870 (12")	Rocket EJS16 (7") Rocket EJS1612 (12") Rocket EJSCD16 (CD)	2	30	18	8
1988	Mona Lisas And Mad Hatters	MCA 23917 (12")	–	–			
1988	Town Of Plenty	–	Rocket EJS17 (7") Rocket EJS1712 (12") Rocket EJSCD17 (CD)	–	74		1
1988	A Word In Spanish	MCA 53408 (7")	Rocket EJS18 (7") Rocket EJS1812 (12") Rocket EJSCD18 (CD)	19	91	13	
1989	Through The Storm [with Aretha Franklin]	Arista AS19809 (7")	Arista 112185 (7") Arista 612185 (12") Arista 162185 (CD)	16	41	11	3
1989	Healing Hands	MCA 53692 (7")	Rocket EJS19 (7") Rocket EJS1912 (12") Rocket EJCD19 (CD)	13	45	15	5
1990	Sacrifice	MCA 53750 (7")	Rocket EJS20 (7") Rocket EJS2012 (12") Rocket EJSCD20 (CD) Rocket EJS22 (7") Rocket EJS2212 (12") Rocket EJSCD22 (CD)	18	1	17	15

Year	Single	US releases	UK releases	US chart top	UK chart top	Weeks in Hot 100 US chart	Weeks in UK chart
1990	Club At The End Of The Street	MCA 79026 (7")	Rocket EJS21 (7") Rocket EJS2112 (12") Rocket EJSCD21 (CD) Rocket EJS23 (7") Rocket EJS2312 (12") Rocket EJSCD23 (CD)	28	47	16	3
1990	You Gotta Love Someone	–	Rocket EJS24 (7") Rocket EJS2412 (12") Rocket EJSCD24 (CD)	43	33	13	4
1990	Easier To Walk Away	–	Rocket EJS25 (7") Rocket EJS2512 (12") Rocket EJSCD25 (CD)	–	63		2
1991	Don't Let The Sun Go Down On Me [with George Michael]	Columbia 3874086 (7") Columbia 44K74130 (CD)	Epic 6576467 (7") Epic 6576465 (12") Epic 6576462 (CD)	1	1	20	10
1992	The One	MCA 754423 (7") MCA 54435 (CD)	Rocket EJS28 (7") Rocket EJSCB28 (CD) Rocket EJSCR28 (CD)	9	10	22	8
1992	Runaway Train	MCA 754452 (7") MCA 54472 (CD)	Rocket EJS29 (7") Rocket EJSCD29 (CD) Rocket EJSCB29 (CD)	–	31		4
1992	The Last Song	–	Rocket EJS30 (7") Rocket EJSCD30 (CD) Rocket EJSCB30 (CD)	23	21	20	4
1993	Simple Life	MCA 754581 (7")	Rocket EJS31 (7") Rocket EJSCD31 (CD)	30	44	16	2
1993	True Love	MCA 754762 (7")	Rocket EJS32 (7") Rocket EJSCD32 (CD) Rocket EJSCX32 (CD)	56	2	12	10
1994	Don't Go Breaking My Heart [with RuPaul]	MCA 54796 (12") MCA 54831 (CD)	Rocket EJS33 (7") Rocket EJCD33 (CD) Rocket EJRMX33 (CD)	92	7	2	7
1994	Ain't Nothing Like The Real Thing [with Marcella Detroit]	–	London LON350 (7") London LONCD350 (CD) London LOCDP350 (CD)	–	24		4
1994	Can You Feel The Love Tonight	Hollywood HR645432 (CD)	Mercury EJS34 (7") Mercury EJCD34 (CD)	4	14	26	9
1994	Circle Of Life	Hollywood HR645182 (CD)	Mercury EJSCD35 (CD) Mercury EISCX35 (CD)	18	11	20	12
1995	Believe	Rocket 422856014 (7") Rocket 422856711 (CD) Rocket 422856713 (CD)	Rocket EJSCD36 (CD) Rocket EJSDD36 (CD)	13	15	20	7

Year	Single	US releases	UK releases	US chart top	UK chart top	Weeks in Hot 100 US chart	Weeks in UK chart
1995	Made In England	Rocket 422852172 (7") Rocket 422852093 (12") Rocket 422852093 (CD) Rocket 422852173 (CD)	Rocket EJSCD37 (CD) Rocket EJSDD37 (CD)	52	18	10	5
1995	Blessed	Rocket 422852394 (7") Rocket 422852394 (CD)	Rocket EJSCD38 (CD) Rocket EJSDD38 (CD)	34		20	
1996	Please	–	Rocket EJSCD40 (CD) Rocket EJSDD40 (CD)	–	33		3
1996	You Can Make History (Young Again)	–	–	70	70	17	
1996	Live Like Horses [with Luciano Pavarotti]	–	Rocket LLHCD1 (CD) Rocket LLHDD1 (CD)	–	9		6
1997	Something About The Way You Look Tonight/ Candle In The Wind 1997	Rocket 3145681087 (7") Rocket 3145681082 (CD)	Rocket PTCD1 (CD)	1	1	42	24
1998	Recover Your Soul	Rocket 3145687622 (CD)	Rocket EJSCD42 (CD) Rocket EJSCX42 (CD)	55	16	20	3
1998	If The River Can Bend	–	Rocket EJSCD43 (CD) Rocket EJSDD43 (CD)	–	32		2
1999	Written In The Stars [with Leann Rimes]	Rocket 3145669182 (CD)	Rocket EJSCD45 (CD) Rocket EJSDD45 (CD)	29	10	10	8
2000	Someday Out Of The Blue	Dreamworks 4459039 (CD)	–	49		15	
2001	I Want Love	–	Rocket 588706 (CD) Rocket 588707 (CD)	110	9		10
2002	This Train Don't Stop There Anymore	–	Rocket 588896 (CD) Rocket 588897 (CD)	–	24		4
2002	Original Sin	–	Rocket 588999 (CD) Rocket 582850 (CD)	–	39		2
2002	Your Song [with Alessandro Safina]	–	Mercury 0639972 (CD)	–	4		10
2003	Are You Ready For Love [Remix]	Ultra UL11776 (12") Ultra UL11772 (CD)	So. Fried ECB50 (12") So. Fried ECB50LOVE (12") So. Fried ECB50CDS (CD)	–	1		14
2004	All That I'm Allowed (I'm Thankful)	–	Rocket 9868689 (7") Rocket 9868257 (CD) Rocket 9858258 (CD)	–	20		5

Year	Single	US releases	UK releases	US chart top	UK chart top	Weeks in Hot 100 US chart	Weeks in UK chart
2004	Turn The Lights Out When You Leave	–	Rocket 9870664 (CD) Rocket 9870663 (CD)	–		32	2
2005	Electricity	–	Rocket 987234 (7") Rocket 9872183 (CD) Rocket 9872184 (CD)	–	4		

ALBUMS

Year	Album	US first issues	UK first issues	US chart top	UK chart top	Weeks in top 200 US chart	Weeks in UK chart
1969 (UK) 1975 (US)	Empty Sky	MCA 2130 (LP)	DJM DJLP403 (LP)	6		18	
1970	Elton John	UNI 73090 (LP)	DJM DJLPS406 (LP)	4	5	51	22
1970	Tumbleweed Connection	UNI 73096 (LP)	DJM DJLPS410 (LP)	5	2	37	20
1971	Friends Soundtrack	Paramount PAS6004 (LP)	Paramount SPFL269 (LP)	36		19	
1971	11-17-70	UNI 93105 (LP)	DJM DJLPS414 (LP)	11	20	23	2
1971	Madman Across The Water	UNI 93120 (LP)	DJM DJLPH420 (LP)	8	41	51	2
1972	Honky Château	UNI 93135 (LP)	DJM DJLPH423 (LP)	1	2	61	23
1973	Don't Shoot Me I'm Only The Piano Player	MCA 2100 (LP)	DJM DJLPH427 (LP)	1	1	89	42
1973	Goodbye Yellow Brick Road	MCA 210003 (LP)	DJM DJLPH10012 (LP)	1	1	103	88
1974	Caribou	MCA 2116 (LP)	DJM DJLPH439 (LP)	1	1	54	18
1974	Greatest Hits	MCA 2128 (LP)	DJM DJLPH442 (LP)	1	1	107	84
1975	Captain Fantastic And The Brown Dirt Cowboy	MCA 2142 (LP)	DJM DJLPX1 (LP)	1	2	43	24
1975	Rock Of The Westies	MCA 2163 (LP)	DJM DJLPH464 (LP)	1	5	26	12
1976	Here And There	MCA 2197 (LP)	DJM DJLPH473 (LP)	4	7	20	7
1976	Blue Moves	MCA/Rocket 211004 (LP)	Rocket ROSP1 (LP)	3	3	22	15
1977	Greatest Hits Volume 2	MCA 3027 (LP)	DJM DJLPH520 (LP)	21	6	20	24
1978	A Single Man	MCA 3065 (LP)	Rocket TRAIN1 (LP)	15	8	18	26

Year	Album	US first issues	UK first issues	US chart top	UK chart top	Weeks in top 200 US chart	Weeks in UK chart
1979	The Thom Bell Sessions	MCA 39115 (LP)	–	51		18	
1979	Victim Of Love	MCA 5104 (LP)	Rocket HSPD125 (LP)	35	41	10	3
1980	21 At 33	MCA 5121 (LP)	Rocket HSPD126 (LP)	13	12	21	13
1981	The Fox	Geffen GHS2002 (LP)	Rocket TRAIN16 (LP)	21	12	19	12
1982	Jump Up!	Geffen GHS2013 (LP)	Rocket HISPD127 (LP)	17	13	33	12
1983	Too Low For Zero	Geffen GHS4006 (LP) Geffen 40062 (CD)	Rocket HISPD24 (LP) Rocket 8110522 (CD)	25	7	54	73
1984	Breaking Hearts	Geffen GHS24031 (LP) Geffen 9240312 (CD)	Rocket HISPD25 (LP) Rocket 8220882 (CD)	20	2	34	23
1985	Ice On Fire	Geffen GHS24077 (LP) Geffen 924077 (CD)	Rocket HISPD26 (LP) Rocket 8262132 (CD)	48	3	28	23
1986	Leather Jackets	Geffen GHS24114 (LP) Geffen 9241142 (CD)	Rocket EJLP1 (LP) Rocket 8304872 (CD)	91	24	9	9
1986	Live In Australia	MCA 28022 (LP) MCA MCAD8022 (CD)	Rocket EJLP2 (LP) Rocket 8324702 (CD)	24		41	7
1988	Reg Strikes Back	MCA 6420 (LP) MCA MCAD6240 (CD)	Rocket EJLP3 (LP) Rocket 8347012 (CD)	16	18	29	6
1989	Sleeping With The Past	MCA 6321 (LP) MCA MCAD6321 (CD)	Rocket EJLP4 (LP) Rocket 8388392 (CD)	23	1	53	42
1990	To Be Continued…	MCA MCAD41011 (CD)	Rocket 8482362 (CD)	82		13	
1992	The One	MCA MCAD10614 (CD)	Rocket 5123601 (LP) Rocket 5123602 (CD)	8	2	53	18
1993	Duets	MCA MCAD10926 (CD)	Rocket 5184781 (LP) Rocket 5184782 (CD)	25	5	22	18
1994	The Lion King Soundtrack	Walt Disney 608587 (CD)	Walt Disney 5050466689726 (CD)	1		88	
1995	Made In England	Rocket 3145269151 (LP) Rocket 3145261852 (CD)	Rocket 5261851 (LP) Rocket 5261852 (CD)	13	3	46	14
1996	Love Songs	MCA MCAD11481 (CD)	Rocket 5287881 (LP) Rocket 5287882 (CD)	24	4	76	48
1997	The Big Picture	Rocket 3145362662 (CD)	Rocket 5362662 (CD)	9	3	23	23
1999	Elton John and Tim Rice's Aida	Rocket 3145246282 (CD)	Rocket 4246512 (CD)	41	29	7	2

Year	Album	US first issues	UK first issues	US chart top	UK chart top	Weeks in top 200 US chart	Weeks in UK chart
2000	The Road To El Dorado Soundtrack	Dreamworks 004450259 (CD)	Dreamworks 4502192 (CD)	63		8	
2000	One Night Only – The Greatest Hits	Mercury 4400130502 (CD)	Mercury 5483342 (CD)	65	7	18	13
2001	Songs From The West Coast	Rocket 3145863302 (CD)	Rocket 5863302 (CD)	15	2	24	34
2002	Greatest Hits 1970–2002	Rocket 4400634782 (CD)	Rocket 0634992 (CD)	12	3	67	54
2004	Peachtree Road	Rocket B000364702 (CD)	Rocket 9872301 (LP)	17	21	10	8
2006	The Captain And The Kid	Universal B000754502 (CD)	Universal 1705710 (CD) Universal 1705730 (LP)	18	6		

VIDEO RELEASES AND SIGNIFICANT TELEVISION APPEARANCES

Year	Video Title	Format	Comments
1971	Sounds for Saturday	BBC broadcast	8 songs performed from the Madman Across the Water album
1971	Andy Williams Show	broadcast	Elton performs on two songs
1972	Royal Festival Hall	BBC broadcast	Elton performs 10 songs with the Royal Philharmonic Orchestra
1974	Elton John and Bernie Taupin say Goodbye Norma Jean and Other Things	broadcast	Documentary covering the recording of Goodbye Yellow Brick Road album
1975	Tommy	film	Elton performs Pinball Wizard in this rock opera
1975	Russell Harty Documentary	broadcast	Documentary covering the legendary shows at Dodgers Stadium
1975	Rock Music Awards	broadcast	Elton co-hosts with Diana Ross
1975	Cher	broadcast	Elton performs on three songs in Cher's debut episode
1975	Soul Train	broadcast	Elton performs two songs
1976	Live in Edinburgh	BBC broadcast and video	Coverage of solo concert
1977	The Muppet Show	broadcast and video	Elton performs four songs
1977	The Michael Douglas Show	broadcast	Elton is interviewed in a two-part series

Year	Video Title	Format	Comments
1979	To Russia With Elton	broadcast and video	Documentary covering Elton's concert series in Moscow
1980	The Tonight Show	broadcast	Elton performs Sorry Seems To Be The Hardest Word
1980	Live in Central Park	broadcast and video	Coverage from Elton's outdoor concert in New York
1980	Paul Gambaccini Interview		BBC broadcast Interview with Elton in his England home
1981	Visions	video	Collection of music videos for the entire Fox album
1982	Saturday Night Live	broadcast	Elton is the musical guest, performing two songs
1984	Breaking Hearts Tour & The Nighttime Concert	video	2-part live concert from Wembley Stadium
1985	Live Aid	broadcast and video	Elton performs five songs, joined by Kiki Dee and George Michael
1986	Live in Australia	broadcast and video	Coverage from Elton's symphony concerts in Sydney
1990	Ryan White Funeral	broadcast	Elton pays tribute to Ryan by performing Skyline Pigeon
1990	Farm Aid IV	broadcast	Elton performs three songs
1990	MTV Unplugged	broadcast	Elton performs seven solo songs
1991	Two Rooms	broadcast and video	All-star documentary celebrating the songs of Elton John and Bernie Taupin
1991	The Very Best of Elton John	video	Collection of videos to complement the UK hits collection album
1992	The Last Song	video	Charity interview with video of The Last Song
1992	Live In Barcelona	video	Coverage from this live concert in Spain
1996	Love Songs	video	Collection of videos to complement the hits collection album
1997	Tantrums and Tiaras	broadcast and video	Elton's personal live is exposed in this behind-the-scenes biography
1997	Storytellers	broadcast	Elton performs live from the House of Blues in Louisiana
2000	One Night Only	broadcast and video	Coverage from Elton's concert at Madison Square Garden
2002	Classic Albums: Goodbye Yellow Brick Road	video	retrospective documentary with interview about the album
2004	Radio City Music Hall	broadcast	Coverage of Elton's symphony concerts in New York
2005	Larry King Live	broadcast	Elton is interviewed and performs three songs from his home
2005	Philadelphia Freedom Concert	broadcast	Elton headlines this free concert, and performs five songs
2005	Inside the Actors Studio	broadcast	Elton is interviewed and plays some songs by request

INDEX